# Does God Need the Church?
## Toward a Theology of the People of God

*Gerhard Lohfink*

Translated by

*Linda M. Maloney*

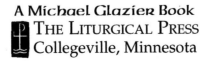
A Michael Glazier Book
THE LITURGICAL PRESS
Collegeville, Minnesota

A Michael Glazier Book published by Liturgical Press

This work was originally published in German under the title *Braucht Gott die Kirche?* (Herder: 1998 [ISBN 3-451-26544-3]).

Cover design by Greg Becker

ISBN 13: 978-0-8146-5928-1
ISBN 10: 0-8146-5928-4

7          8

**Library of Congress Cataloging-in-Publication Data**

Lohfink, Gerhard, 1934–
    [Braucht Gott die Kirche?   English]
    Does God need the church? : toward a theology of the people of God /
  Gerhard Lohfink ; translated by Linda M. Maloney.
       p.   cm.
    "A Michael Glazier book."
    Includes bibliographical references and index.
    ISBN 0-8146-5928-4 (alk. paper)
    1. Church—Biblical teaching.   2. People of God—Biblical teaching.
I. Title.
BS2545.C5L5813   1999
262—dc21                                                98-32331
                                                 CIP

*For Cardinal Joseph Ratzinger*

# Contents

Why I Am Writing This Book    vii

Part I: Why God Needs a Special People    1

    1. God is God, and Not World    1
    2. Evolution and History Belong to Creation    7
    3. God Risks a History Tainted by Sin    15
    4. God Wills the Salvation of the Whole World    21
    5. The Salvation of the World Demands a Concrete Place    26
    6. That Concrete Place Is Israel    31
    7. What Does It Mean to Say that God Is Almighty?    39

Part II: The Characteristic Signs of Israel    51

    1. Gathering as a People of God    51
    2. A People of Faith    60
    3. The Exodus Experience    67
    4. The Torah as Social Project    74
    5. A History of Resistance    88
    6. The Scarlet Thread of Salvation History    97
    7. The Quest for the Form of the People of God    106

Part III: Jesus and the Figure of the Twelve    121

    1. What Is "New" About the "New Testament"?    121
    2. The "Todayness" of the Reign of God    134
    3. Salvation Superabundant    139
    4. The Basic Sacramental Structure of Jesus' Actions    150
    5. The Manifold Character of Vocation: Apostles, Disciples, People    164

6. Table Manners in the Reign of God   173

7. The Death of Jesus: A Death for the People of God   184

Part IV: The Characteristic Signs of the Church   203

1. The Exodus Continues   208

2. The Church Gathers   218

3. The Church's Most Intensive Moment Is Remembering   236

4. The Church Is to Be the Body of Christ   253

5. Faith Must Be Learned   264

6. The Church and Wholeness   273

7. The Church's Deepest Wound Is Disunity   290

The Church and I   311

Church, What Do You Have to Say for Yourself? (Arnold Stötzel)   323

A Word of Thanks   325

Index   327

# Why I Am Writing This Book

In 1982 I published a book called *Wie hat Jesus Gemeinde gewollt?*[1] It went through many editions and was translated into numerous other languages. I received a great many invitations, especially from adult education institutes and parishes, to come and explain how parishes could be renewed according to the model of New Testament communities.

Apparently my book, and especially its title, suggested that one could derive a model from the New Testament on the basis of which *communities for today* could be newly created. At any rate there were many people who were seeking, on the basis of my book, to obtain concrete directions for the renewal of their parishes. I could not give them. It seemed as if the material itself refused to be made use of as a set of directions for pastoral practice.

At the same time, quite unexpectedly, something happened in my own life during those years that caused me to reflect more and more deeply. I encountered the Catholic Integrated Community,[2] and, without having sought

---

[1] Published in English as *Jesus and Community* (Philadelphia: Fortress, 1984). The German title translates more precisely as "What Kind of [Church] Community Did Jesus Want?"—Tr.

[2] The Katholische Integrierte Gemeinde was formed in Munich after World War II, arising out of the efforts of young people from the Catholic youth movement to find a new way toward a living Church in face of their horror that the Holocaust could occur in a Christian Europe. The word "integrated" expresses the idea that the saving power of faith and the sacraments effects a deep communal bond among the members and penetrates every facet of daily life. In 1978 and subsequent years the community was recognized by the Church as an apostolic community of laity and priests in the German dioceses of Paderborn, Munich-Freising, Rottenburg-Stuttgart, and Augsburg, and in Morogoro (Tanzania), Rome, and Vienna. The community has no desire to be associated with movements of "integralism."

Contact address: *Katholische Integrierte Gemeinde,* Schulgraben 2, D-83646 Bad Tölz, Germany (Tel. 49-8041-76119-0; Fax 49-8041-76119-53).

it, I entered into an increasingly close theological and personal dialogue with that community. In 1986 I resigned my professorship in Tübingen so that I could live and work entirely within the context of the community. For me it was a new and delightful experience of what Church is.

Since then it has become increasingly clear to me that I would not write that other book the same way again. The story of the gathering of the people of God from Abraham until today never took place according to a model. It was always the Spirit of God who brought about new initiatives in the Church, often quite surprisingly and contrary to every expectation. God's plans do not coincide with our human plans. Therefore following the plan of God means trusting in God's promises and remaining open to things that are humanly unforeseeable, in the knowledge and confidence of being sustained and led.

The Bible does not concern itself anywhere with pastoral plans and strategies. Instead, on almost every page it reveals that God does not act anywhere and everywhere, but in a concrete place. God does not act at any and every moment, but at a particular time. God does not act through anyone and everyone, but through people God chooses. If we do not come to recognize that again there will be no renewal of the Church in our time, for this principle of salvation history is true today as well.

Consider, for example, the scene in Bethlehem at the time of King Saul. The prophet Samuel, at God's command, is to anoint a new king for Israel. Therefore he asks Jesse to bring forward his sons. Seven are brought, and each is more magnificent than the next. No one has even thought of David, the youngest. No one has called him to come. After all, David was not yet as big as his brothers, and he was far away with the sheep. But it was precisely this one, David, whom God had chosen to be king.[3]

---

[3] 1 Samuel 16:1-13. Something may be said in general terms about the use of the Bible in this book: What is normative for theology and the Church is not a set of historical reconstructions, but what the Bible itself intends to say. To put it in literary-critical terms, the statement of the final text of the Bible is what is definitive. The Church is convinced that Sacred Scripture views reality as God sees it. Whoever accepts the Scriptures in faith cannot go behind this end point. No one may substitute for the Bible's point of view a different one influenced by another set of interests.

At the same time, it can be important for the correct understanding of the final text to reconstruct preliminary stages of the text or historical sequences, not in order to canonize a historical reconstruction, but in order better to understand what the final text says. Precisely in this matter of historical reconstruction modern biblical scholarship is extraordinarily helpful. Its conclusions and hypotheses will appear frequently in this book, but I hope that in my writing they always serve to enhance the understanding of the text itself.

The notes in this book will serve primarily to indicate sources and their location. Quite often these bibliographic notes also serve to point the reader to sources of further information. No exhaustive listing or discussion of the secondary literature is intended.

That is how things happen all through the Bible. God moves history forward differently from the way we think and plan it. The fact that someone came from Nazareth, one of the most insignificant villages in Israel, and began to call disciples; that one day he placed twelve of those disciples before the others and said, "this is the beginning of the eschatological Israel," is a completely improbable and, on the face of it, an "impossible" story. Most certainly many at that time gave their prognosis: "nothing will ever come of this." They were wrong. In the decades that followed, hundreds of Christian communities arose everywhere around the Mediterranean basin.

Nearly two thousand years have passed since then. The story that played itself out around Jesus has now become a "sacred history." It has long since been developed against a gilded background. We think we know it; we have gotten accustomed to it because we have heard it a thousand times—but we do not count on the possibility that God could act in God's people even today, that God is creating something new even now.

Because I have experienced—in a way I had not considered possible—that the old stories of the Bible have come alive again and take us by the hand to lead us on the way that God wants to go with the Church, I am now writing my old book in a new way. It is not that I now think the things I said then were wrong; but something crucial was lacking, and because of that the whole was dangerously off balance.

This book starts again from the beginning. It goes deeper, far back into the Old Testament, because we need to look back at the long history of the people of God in order to spell out again how God acts and why God chooses a people. This book goes back even beyond that, beginning with the questions of God, creation, evolution, and history, because otherwise the biblical concept of election, which has become a stumbling block for so many Christians today, cannot truly be understood.

That we thus find ourselves following a sequence that in many ways corresponds to the way Israel itself has seen and arranged its history is by no means a disadvantage. On the contrary: it would be theologically disastrous if we were to regard the world and history differently from the way the Bible sees them.[4]

---

[4] See the discussion in Gerhard von Rad, *Old Testament Theology*. Translated by D.M.G. Stalker. 2 vols. (New York and Evanston: Harper & Row, 1957) 1:115–128.

# I

# Why God Needs a Special People

If we begin by asking about God, and what creation is, and why there is such an elaborate process as evolution, and why God would permit a history marked by sin and the unimaginable suffering that results from it, all of this has a great deal to do with the people of God. There is a piece of territory that we must pass through first if we are to understand the unremittingly piercing and painful problem of talking about divine election: the choice of a single people among all the nations of the earth.

It cannot be a coincidence that the Old Testament does not begin with the call of Abraham. That is related only in the twelfth chapter of the book of Genesis. Before that the Bible tells of the creation of the world, the Fall, and the growth of the human race. It obviously knows quite well that there has to be an explanation of the reason why God needs a special people.

## 1. God Is God, and Not World

It is one of the great miracles of history that the people of Israel appeared in the world and that this people came to believe in the one true God, for tiny Israel was surrounded by great empires that pressured it without ceasing, and it lived under the cultural influence of powerful and mesmerizing religions in which many gods were worshiped. There were the fascination of Egypt, the constant temptations of Canaan, the power of Assyria and Babylon, the civilizing influence of Hellenism, and the imposing state religion of Rome. In all these cultures the world was full of gods. Israel, in contrast, entrusted itself to the leadership of a single god and confessed with increasing clarity in its statements of faith that there is only one God.

The real difference between the faith of Israel and the religions of the nations that lived around it or ruled over it was, however, not the number of gods—*one* god rather than ten or thirty. The difference lay deeper. The many gods of the nations were earthly forces and powers that represented ultimate realities for human beings; their perceptions did not extend beyond these elemental realities to which they had subjected themselves (cf. Gal 4:8-9). These were the powers of nature, unfathomable to human understanding: sun, moon, stars, storms, thunder, generativity; but they were also the powers human beings sensed within themselves: anger, hatred, erotic love, longing, and ultimately also the powers that shape history and society: knowledge, domination, violence, money, rivalry, war, life, death. All these powers bore divine names. People were fascinated by them. They experienced in them the profundity of the world and of existence itself. They surrendered to them. And yet there remained a nagging doubt. In Greece especially it showed itself at an early stage.

Israel's faith in a single god certainly did not mean that it had made one god out of the many, that it had concentrated the multifarious powers of the world into a single power. Such an integration of all things divine might, perhaps, have led to the world-*logos* of the Stoics, but not to the God of Israel. Instead, in a long process of enlightenment Israel learned that God stands in contrast to the nations and history—not as their own profound center, but over against them as the ruler of history. God is not a natural force or the expansion of the human soul. God is by no means a fragment of the world, not even the sum total of the world and its forces, nor is God the ultimate well from which the world flows; God is beyond the world as the Wholly Other who created it and therefore is not identical with it.

The great theologians of the people of God saw the difference between the gods of the world and the God of Israel with complete clarity. The author of the book of Wisdom, who wrote around the turn of the second to the first centuries before Christ, formulated the difference as follows:

> For all people who were ignorant of God were foolish by nature; and they were unable from the good things that are seen to know the one who exists, nor did they recognize the artisan while paying heed to his works; but they supposed that either fire or wind or swift air, or the circle of the stars, or turbulent water, or the luminaries of heaven were the gods that rule the world.

> If through delight in the beauty of these things people assumed them to be gods, let them know how much better than these is their Lord, for the author of beauty created them. And if people were amazed at their power and working, let them perceive from them how much more powerful is the one who formed them. For from the greatness and beauty of created things comes a corresponding perception of their Creator.

Yet these people are little to be blamed, for perhaps they go astray while seeking God and desiring to find him. For while they live among his works, they keep searching, and they trust in what they see, because the things that are seen are beautiful. Yet again, not even they are to be excused; for if they had the power to know so much that they could investigate the world, how did they fail to find sooner the Lord of these things? (Wis 13:1-9)

In this late text from the Old Testament every sentence reveals the author's Hellenistic education. It is the work of someone acquainted with Greek philosophy and able to make use of it for purposes of argumentation.[1] Probably this person was a resident of the great city of Alexandria, where there was an important Jewish community in which over a long period of time efforts were made to formulate the faith of Israel within the horizons of Greek thought and thus to make it available to the world.

This was a necessary and worthwhile attempt, for Greek was at that time not only the commercial language of the Mediterranean world but the most refined instrument for thinking about the world and comprehending reality. The Greek philosophers since the time of the Presocratics had developed a critique of the gods and religion that the author of the book of Wisdom puts into subtle application. Their theology had long since introduced the deduction from a work of art to the artist, and described God as "Being itself" and "the author of beauty." They had even begun to think of God as "the One." Plato, in the *Timaeus*, had already spoken of the demiurge, the one who made the world,[2] and Aristotle in his *Physics* wrote of the "first unmoved Mover," the ultimate cause of the entire universe.[3]

At first glance, then, our text appears to be unjust to the theology of the great Greek philosophers. Worse yet, it makes use of the apparatus of Greek philosophy but is silent about its highest achievements. And yet the author of the book of Wisdom is right!—for even the best Greek philosophers never passed beyond a certain point. Despite them polytheism remained a matter of course in popular religion and in the cult of the city states. It was so much a part of the order of daily life that even a man like Aristotle ordered in his will that "the image of his mother should be consecrated to Demeter and that there should be erected at Stagira, on account of a vow he had made to the gods, two marble statues, one to Zeus Soter, and the other of Athena Soteira."[4]

---

[1] Cf. Dieter Georgi, *Weisheit Salomos*. JSHRZ III.4 (Gütersloh: Gerd Mohn, 1980) 448–49.

[2] Plato also calls the demiurge "creator and father of the universe" (*Timaeus* 28). But this creator has to work with matter that has existed from eternity.

[3] Aristotle, *Physics* H 1; Q 5-6; *Metaphysics* L 6.

[4] Quoted from Etienne Gilson, *The Spirit of Medieval Philosophy* (New York: Charles Scribner's Sons, 1936) 45.

In addition Aristotle had no hesitation in accepting other "unmoved movers," namely the astral gods, alongside the "first unmoved Mover." After all, they were visible in the heavens and they were gods—divine beings with visible bodies. For Plato there was not only the highest idea of the Good and (identical with it or not—the experts are undecided) the demiurge, but also an eternal Matter. This Matter had always existed; the demiurge found it ready to hand.[5]

No matter how much the great Greek philosophers enriched Jewish-Christian thought about God with the insights provided by their scholarly inquiry, in one decisive point they never attained the unique aspect of Jewish belief in God: they could not reach the concept of genuine *creation*. However, it is just that concept that plays such a crucial role in Wisdom 13. It was inaccessible to the Greeks because they could neither free themselves from the numinous divinity of the world nor achieve a consistent idea of a God who is utterly Other, a God who stands over against the world and its history.[6] Plato, in the solemn formula of the concluding sentence of the *Timaeus*, calls the universe itself a god, wholly great and good, beautiful and perfect.

Even Neoplatonism, which took up Plato's philosophy anew in the third century C.E. and extended it, never attained to a genuine concept of creation. For Neoplatonism the world culminates in a final principle, the idea of the One and the Good that cannot be further derived, from which the world streams and cascades forth in endlessly varied reflections. Plotinus calls this outward procession "emanation."

What must be said of Greek philosophy is all the more true of the creation myths and creation hymns of the East. There, indeed, we encounter a great variety of statements about creation. Probably even the formula "creator of heaven and earth" (Gen 14:19) is borrowed from Canaanite mythology. But there the creating gods themselves are part of a more comprehensive reality. They arise from the primeval chaos and its divine forces. They rebel against their own ground of being, are successful in combating chaos, and form the world out of formlessness, but they do not stand over against the world as uncreated creator. Divinization (theogony) and the coming-to-be of the world (cosmogony) interpenetrate. Ultimately the Eastern gods are also "world," and the world is the self-development of the divine.

Whence did Israel acquire the power, in face of the thought of the best philosophers and against the religious ideas of the neighboring peoples, to distinguish between the world and God? How was it able to formulate the

[5] Cf. Plato, *Timaeus* 29-30.
[6] Cf. Etienne Gilson, *The Spirit of Medieval Philosophy* 42-83.

idea of genuine creation? How could it confess: "all the gods of the peoples are idols, but the LORD made the heavens" (Ps 96:5)? How was Jewish legend able to have the mother of the slaughtered Maccabean brothers say to her last son: "I beg you, my child, to look at the heaven and the earth and see everything that is in them, and recognize that God did not make them *out of things that existed*" (2 Macc 7:28)?

This ability to distinguish arose within the Old Testament people of God out of their long history: in Abraham it had been drawn out of Mesopotamia, and Jewish legend later interpreted this early exodus as a break with the gods of that land. But more than all else, it fled from Egypt under the leadership of Moses, from a theocracy in which every aspect of life was ruled by the gods. It had entrusted itself to a single God, with much grumbling and continually revived resistance, but nevertheless it had done so. The catastrophe of the exile it interpreted as the consequence of its turning away from the God who had led it, and as punishment for turning to the gods of the nations—and in that very moment of disaster and reflection on it Israel gained the power to recognize its God as the only god and the absolute creator of the world.

The sharp distinction between God and the world that Israel had discovered and from which all the history of enlightenment from then until now is derived was thus not a further development of Greek philosophy, nor was it a concentration or sublimation of the Eastern myths of the gods; it arose out of the experience of a God who constantly led it out of societies in which everything was static and divinized. In this very experience of constantly being led out Israel found that its God was revealed as the Wholly Other, absolutely distinct from a numinous, god-infused world.

These connections were clearly enunciated by the prophet Hosea. He was quite certain that the conviction of the people of God that it must worship YHWH alone and no other gods beside YHWH arose out of the experience that no other god had ever really helped them—and this experience rested on the fundamental event of the Exodus:

> . . . I have been YHWH your God
>> ever since the land of Egypt;
> you know no God but me,
>> and besides me there is no savior. (Hos 13:4)

Egypt had been a house of slavery. Its many gods had not helped, had not given freedom. Only the one God who led the people out of Egypt gave them freedom, and with it the ability to distinguish between a world that legitimated the rule of Pharaoh and was approved by the gods and a created world that released people into freedom. Israel's monotheistic faith would be formed out of this power of discernment, which in turn was won from its being led out: out of Egypt above all, but out of many other perilous situations as well.

The description of Jewish monotheism in the work of the Greek historian and geographer Strabo (written at about the time of the birth of Christ) is revealing. He supposes that the origins of the Jewish people lay with the Egyptian priest Moses; this Moses is said to have brought the world a new idea of God: "for, according to him, God is this one thing alone that encompasses land and sea—the thing which we call heaven, or universe, the nature of all that exists."[7] That is a wonderful description of the pantheism of the Stoa, but it has nothing whatever to do with the faith of Israel. However, the quotation again shows that outside the experience of the people of God it was apparently impossible for the people of the ancient world to make a clear distinction between God and the world.[8]

We thus arrive, for the first time in this book, at the distinction between religion and revelation. Since this will occupy a good deal of our attention—for the Bible demands it—we should perhaps offer some basic remarks in advance:

The religions of the nations and the ideas of the philosophers are not depreciated by this distinction. The world seeks its creator and reaches out unceasingly toward its source. There is not only the Word of God that gives meaning to the world, the self-revealing *logos,* but also the longing for God that is implanted in creation itself. It is the precondition for God's word being heard at all. The divine *logos* fills the world from the beginning.

The statement that everything is "divine" can be a first, but not yet distinguishing intimation of the creative power of God. That intimation is in the process of searching for the true *logos.* "Everything is divine" can, however, also be an absolutizing of the world and a subtle self-affirmation of the human being. In that case "natural" religion has already slipped into mere religiosity. When this book speaks of "religion" and "the religious," it is always this second, negative aspect that is intended: religion to the extent that it is in danger of equating God and the world and so of perverting the search for the true God.[9]

---

[7] Strabo, *The Geography of Strabo*, with an English translation by Horace L. Jones. 8 vols. London: Heinemann, and New York: G. P. Putnam's Sons, 1930. XVI.2, 35-39 (= 7:283).

[8] Cf. Yehoshua Amir, "Der jüdische Eingottglaube als Stein des Anstoßes in der hellenistisch-römischen Welt," *JBTh* 2 (1987) 58–75, especially 73–75.

[9] The twentieth century uses the word "religion" very differently in its sociological, philosophical, and theological expressions. At the moment a more positive use of the word is in the ascendant; it includes the Jewish-Christian revelation also within the concept of religion. Karl Barth, on the contrary, made negative use of the word. Readers will note that, in contrast to the current trend, I am inclined to move closer to Karl Barth. Nevertheless, I

Moreover, this deviation exists not only in religions. The faith that relies on revelation is also in constant danger of declining into something that is merely religious, focusing only on itself and using God purely as a legitimation for its own interests. To that extent the distinction between the religious and revelation is also a fundamental necessity here. The Bible fights constantly and on all fronts to maintain this distinction, and this is especially true of its texts regarding creation.

## 2. Evolution and History Belong to Creation

Obviously Wis 13:1-9 and 2 Macc 7:28 are not the only texts in the Bible that speak about creation. They are only the final expressions of a long reflection on creation. The most extensive, if not the oldest biblical text about the work of creation is Gen 1:1–2:4:

> In the beginning God created the heavens and the earth.
> The earth was waste and void.
> Darkness covered the face of the deep,
> and the Spirit of God swept over the waters.
> Then God said: "Let there be light!" and light was made. (Gen 1:1-3*)

At first glance this great creation text, only the beginning of which is quoted here, appears to be entirely immersed in the mythic language of Israel's environment. After all, it depicts the formation of the world from chaos. The first creative word God speaks does not bring forth matter from nothingness: not at all. The first creative word is "Let there be light!" Thus God's creative work begins with the bringing of light into formless chaos, a world that is waste and void. The forcing back of the chaos continues as God, working within the primeval flood (that still continues to threaten from above and below), sets the boundaries of a gigantic space within which *kosmos,* the formed world, can be.

There is no question today that the author of the Priestly writing, from which Gen 1:1–2:4a is taken, is here making use of a variety of mythical material available in his world, quoting it or echoing it or at least presuming its existence. But we should note the freedom and differentiating skill with which he shapes this material:

---

by no means wish to be identified with his position in the first volume of *Church Dogmatics* (cf. especially I/2 §17), hence the distinction I have made above! All religion is in search of God and bears within itself elements of genuine knowledge of God, yet all religion is also profoundly subject to the power of what Christian tradition calls "original sin." Faith in God's revelation cannot be a matter of condemning religion, but rather of purifying and redeeming it.

1. The sun and moon, which in the entire East were a god and goddess of the foremost significance, are deprived of their divinity; God simply hangs them up in the heavens as "lights," mere utensils (1:14-18). That is demythologization so radical that we can scarcely appreciate it nowadays.

2. There is no trace of the hideous struggle the Babylonian gods had to undergo in order to master the chaos. The God of the Priestly writing works in a sovereign and effortless manner. The primeval flood is (in contrast to Job 26:12 or Ps 74:13-14) no longer a mythical monster that must be conquered.

3. God works for six days and then rests on the seventh. Nowhere else in the Babylonian creation myths is there anything like this. The gods of Mesopotamia do not work. According to the Atrahasis epic there came a time when they had enough of the hard work that needed to be done in the universe. Therefore they found slaves to do the work for them. First they shoved the work off on a lower class of gods, but those soon revolted, so they created human beings. From then on it was humans who had to do the heavy work in the world. The Priestly writing sees it quite differently: here it is God who works. "God works and he rests; becomes engaged, then keeps his distance; gives of himself, then retires within himself. Moreover, God penetrates his creation with the unity-in-tension of work and leisure."[10]

This schema of seven days in which the Priestly writing depicts God's creative work is thus anything but naïve thinking. It is critical of the whole ancient world in which leisure was for the free and work was for the women and slaves; it already proposes the outlines of a new society in which creative work and divine rest alternate throughout the rhythm of the weeks, and the same is true for everyone.

4. At the end of the creation account, in Gen 2:4a, the author of the Priestly writing describes God's work of creation as "*toledot* of the heavens and the earth." Our translations often render *toledot* as "story of creation" (thus *NAB* 1970: "Such is the story of the heavens and the earth at their creation"). But literally *toledot* means "generations" or "births" (so *RSV, NRSV:* "These are the generations of the heavens and the earth when they were created"). How can the creation of the world be described as a series of "generations"?

There can be only one answer: behind this stands the idea, attested especially in Mesopotamia, that in primeval times the mythical divine pair

---

[10] Norbert Lohfink, *Great Themes from the Old Testament*. Translated by Ronald Walls (Chicago: Franciscan Herald Press, and Edinburgh: T & T Clark, 1982) 214–15. Cf. there the whole chapter, "The Work Week and the Sabbath in the Old Testament, and Especially in the Priestly Chronicle," 203–21.

"heaven" and "earth" coupled and begot all existing things. The author of the Priestly writing makes use of the concepts embodied in this idea and at the same time corrects them: The world as we know it was not mythically begotten, certainly not by a divine couple, but was created by the one God.[11]

At the same time the author does not go so far as completely to deny that life is brought forth from earth and heaven. If we think of this on the basis of our present knowledge of evolution it is by no means out of line to tell of the generative power of the earth. It speaks in favor of the wisdom of the author of the Priestly writing and his knowledge of what "nature" is—we could even say that it speaks for the "guidance" being given to his theology—that he incorporates at least partly in his presentation the cosmological notions of generation present in Israel's environment. He does this when he speaks of the origins of plants and animals. There God says:

> "Let the earth put forth vegetation: plants yielding seed, and fruit trees of every kind on earth that bear fruit with the seed in it." And it was so. The earth brought forth vegetation . . . . (Gen 1:11-12)

The same is true for the animals. God says:

> "Let the earth bring forth living creatures of every kind: cattle and creeping things and wild animals of the earth of every kind." And it was so. God made the wild animals of the earth of every kind, and the cattle of every kind, and everything that creeps upon the ground of every kind. (Gen 1:24-25)

Thus God does not create the plants and animals directly. The *earth* brings them forth. And yet God "made" the plants and animals. This is expressly stated in the case of the animals. But the passage also makes it clear that God gives the earth the command to bring forth plants and animals. The notion of primeval mythical generation is thus set aside, and yet what is correct in that notion is taken seriously: the special character and formative power of matter. Did the author of the Priestly writing somehow sense that the forms of life did not have to be created directly by God, but that God had placed within creation itself the power to develop and bring forth life?

However, there is another reason why the author speaks of the *toledot,* the history of the generations of the world. In his version of history, which follows immediately after the depiction of creation (cf. Gen 5:1-32) genealogies play an unusually significant role. They are the underlying

---

[11] Later the Christian creed would say of the *logos* that it is "begotten, not made." The concept of generation here expresses unity of being while the concept of creation represents differentiation of being.

structure of the Priestly text. They show how life is handed on from generation to generation, how humanity grows, and how history unfolds. These genealogies are also called *toledot:* generations, descendants. They are structured more or less according to a single scheme:

> These are the descendants *(toledot)* of Shem. When Shem was one hundred years old, he became the father of Arpachshad two years after the flood; and Shem lived after the birth of Arpachshad five hundred years, and had other sons and daughters. When Arpachshad had lived thirty-five years, he became the father of Shelah; and Arpachshad lived after the birth of Shelah four hundred three years, and had other sons and daughters. (Gen 11:10-12)

With the aid of such genealogies the author of the Priestly writing depicts an unbroken sequence of generations from the first human beings through Abraham to the sons of Jacob. But because he had already described the creation itself as "generations" and formally portrayed it with the brevity and sobriety of a genealogy he makes clear something that is anything but a matter of course: creation and history belong together. History is not added to creation as something alien to it; creation is from the beginning so designed by God that it will unfold itself as history.[12]

That this really is the opinion of the Priestly writer is evident from the motif of blessing that plays such a central role in his work: after creating human beings as male and female God speaks a solemn blessing over them, as previously over the animals, beginning with the words:

> "Be fruitful and multiply,
> and fill the earth . . . ." (Gen 1:28)

This blessing is given again to human beings and animals after the Flood, which had annulled the blessing, and which only Noah and his family had survived:

> "And you, be fruitful and multiply,
> abound on the earth and multiply in it." (Gen 9:7)

In somewhat different words, then, in the course of the patriarchal history the patriarchs Abraham and Jacob are blessed because the people of Israel will stem from them. The fulfillment of this entire blessing is then re-

---

[12] Norbert Lohfink shows in his investigation of the historical concept of the Priestly writing (cf. especially "The Priestly Narrative and History" in idem, *Theology of the Pentateuch. Themes of the Priestly Narrative and Deuteronomy.* Translated by Linda M. Maloney [Minneapolis: Fortress, 1994] 136–72) that the author of the Priestly narrative made the history available to him transparent to the present. In this connection he speaks of a "retranslation of history into myth." There need be no contradiction between this and what I am saying here. Every historical sequence can be understood and interpreted archetypally.

ported, finally, at the beginning of the book of Exodus. Israel in Egypt has grown into a great nation. The author of the Priestly narrative asserts:

> . . . the Israelites were fruitful and prolific;
> they multiplied and grew exceedingly strong,
> so that the land was filled with them. (Exod 1:7)

This notice is striking: its wording takes up the blessing of fruitfulness at creation and after the Flood. With it the Priestly narrative signals to its readers that the blessing given to humanity at the creation has been fulfilled in Israel's history. It thus becomes clear that all history, including the history of the people of God, is the unfolding of what God had placed within creation already in the course of the six days of God's creative work. Creation is of such a nature as to unfold itself in history. The blessing of creation brings forth the nations.

But it is not only in the Priestly narrative that creation and history are intimately connected. Deutero-Isaiah, the author of Isaiah 40–55, sees history as God's creation. God formed and created a people, and also the paradisiacal land that borders the people's pathway as it returns home. In leading Israel back to Zion God will create something utterly new and unheard of. It will be a new creation, powerful and glorious like God's previous works of creation.[13] Thus for Deutero-Isaiah creation is more than a one-time action of God at the beginning of the world. Creation continues. History—concretely the liberation of Israel from Babylon through the hand of Cyrus—becomes God's creation.

Creation becomes history, history becomes creation—the Old Testament presents some astonishing initiatives for sensing the dynamics of what creation is. However, today we again see the creation of the world with different eyes, since for us time has run on. For us there have opened unimaginable stretches of time in which the universe developed: a universe exploding for twelve (or more?) billion years and over three billion years of evolution from the first unicellular living things to human beings. Israel, despite Gen 1:24 ("let the earth bring forth living creatures of every kind"), had no inkling of all that. We simply know more about this, and for us the immense ages and the bewildering paths of evolution are not only fascinating, but also a piercing and unremitting question:

Why such an unimaginably long development until humanity finally appeared? Why the unfathomable expenditure of spiral nebulae so that on

---

[13] Formed and created: Isa 43:1, 15, 21; 44:21; paradisiacal land: Isa 41:17-20; utterly new and unheard of: Isa 43:19; new creation: Isa 48:6-7; like God's previous works of creation: Isa 41:2-4; 45:12-13; 48:13-15.

one planet, only a tiny grain of dust in the universe, human beings could emerge? Why the endless destruction of living substance on this very planet? At the end of the Permian era, about 245 million years ago, some 96 percent of all existing species vanished. Similar catastrophes occurred at the end of the Devonian period (365 million years ago) and at the end of the Triassic period (208 million years ago).[14] But we need not go back nearly that far. Within the last ten million years of the evolution of humanity there have again and again been new variations that have become dead branches of evolution. The Neanderthal, for example, despite their great cranial capacity (they had more brain mass than *homo sapiens*), fell by the wayside.

Again: why the incredible prodigality in creation, nature's constant experimentation with its own material, the many wrong turnings and dead ends in evolution that apparently led nowhere? Why should there be, in any case, this unremitting evolutionary change in our world, the exuberant dynamics of organisms, the unchecked inventiveness of life, the ever-new genetic tricks of viruses? Why, finally, the long-term costs of evolution: the devouring and being devoured?

Even if we do not regard the history of evolution through the eyes of Reinhold Schneider, who in his *Winter in Wien* shuddered, on visiting the Vienna Museum of Natural History, before the immeasurable world of forms, "this dreadful abundance of inventions,"[15] and certainly not with those of Franz Werfel, who was nauseated by the "obscene shapes" of the insects, the "ghastly hairiness of their limbs," their "lips grown into pincers" and their "faceted and goggling eyes"[16]—even if we contemplate the inexhaustible world of forms represented by the insects and molluscs soberly and without inappropriate feelings of disgust, the question remains: why these endless detours in evolution? Why this groping, not-finding, finally-finding by another route after millions of years?

The same question presents itself with regard to human history: why the long, long journey before the first city was built, the first book written, the first free constitution formulated? Like biological evolution, the development of human history has by no means followed a straight course. The so-called "primitive" societies were already highly differentiated and carefully balanced constructs with admirable achievements, and yet they

[14] See Niles Eldredge, *Fossils. The Evolution and Extinction of Species*. Photography by Murray Alcosser. Introduction by Stephen Jay Gould (New York: Harry N. Abrams, Inc., 1991) 127–28.

[15] Reinhold Schneider, *Winter in Wien. Aus meinen Notizbüchern 1957/58* (6th ed. Freiburg: Herder, 1958) 129.

[16] Franz Werfel, "Theologumena. Von dem Geheimnis der Inkarnation Nr. 33" in idem, *Leben heißt, sich mitteilen*. Fischer TB 9465 (Frankfurt: Fischer, 1992) 202–03.

were at some point overtaken by developments and became dead limbs of history. Why do we find here also this onerous groping for new forms of society, their discovery only through immense effort, and the constant danger that all will be lost again? The question of history is most intimately connected to that of evolution. Why is there history at all, why is there evolution?

Sometimes answers are easier to find if we first imagine the opposite possibility. The opposite in this case would be a universe without development, a world without evolution, people without a history. Everything would be already given in its final form. Nature would be complete and unchangeable. Human beings would be perfected and unchangeable. Society would be perfected and unchangeable.

One thing is certain in this scenario: in such a case there would be no freedom for human beings. For freedom to exist in time (perfected freedom in the presence of God is something quite different) it is indispensable that human beings be able to choose among different possibilities. Choice, however, presupposes that one can shift one's internal focus and thus change oneself; and the possibility of changing oneself presumes constant movement in human beings and in the world around them. We could also say that a person can only change if he or she can enter into new constellations of reality.

That Zaccheus could change his life presupposes that, driven by curiosity, he climbed up a sycamore tree, that Jesus was passing below that sycamore tree, looked up, and called to him: "Zaccheus, hurry and come down; for I must stay at your house today" (Luke 19:5). Zaccheus had entered a new constellation of reality. He encountered Jesus. This new constellation made it possible for him to see his life in a new way and to shift the focus of his life. However, the whole story presupposes that things and people are in motion.

What happened for Zaccheus on a small scale happens on the larger stage in what we call "history." History is nothing but a sequence of constantly new constellations of reality presented to human freedom—and that in turn presupposes a constant movement of things and people. Evolution was always moving, from the appearance of the first unicellular beings, toward this history of freedom. It makes it possible and sustains it. Evolution and history are therefore crucially bound up with human freedom.

God desires that creation should be much greater and freer than we imagine it. God truly set it "on its own feet," released it into its own independence and unique activity, without abandoning it or ceasing to care passionately about it. God made matter capable of developing into higher and higher forms, even if it took billions of years, enabling it to develop on its own. God allowed it all the time it needed to arrive, ultimately, at self-consciousness in humanity. Anyone who loves another gives that other time. Anyone who loves desires the development of the other, that the other may become conscious of herself or himself and be able to respond in freedom. In the human being, the pinnacle of evolution, creation should be able to reflect on who it is, whether it is itself everything, and thus divine, or whether beyond it there exists another who has desired it as a counterpart and left it free. We must look more closely at this infinite weight of freedom in the next chapter.

At this point we must first consider something else: the sumptuous multiplicity of forms that evolution has thus far produced—the total number of currently existing species of animals and plants is estimated at somewhere between thirty and eighty million—is apparently connected also with the wealth of the Creator. Psalm 104, Israel's great song of praise to the Creator, lists a multitude of creatures: light and darkness, mountains and plains, clouds and storm, animals and human beings. The abundance of the world of animals is depicted with special affection: from the storks that nest in the cypresses to the schooling fish of the seas: "living things both small and great" (Ps 104:25). In the conclusion of the psalm this abundance is then related to the glory of God and the divine joy in creation (Ps 104:31).

The creation text of Gen 1:1–2:4 points us in a similar direction. Its careful listing of the works of creation does not arise out of the Priestly writer's delight in classification, but is meant to illustrate the variety of creation. There are plants that bear visible seed, and trees whose seed is hidden in fruit (1:11). There are cattle and creeping things and the beasts of the field (1:24). God does not desire monotony and uniformity, but the surplus of created things.

The genealogies of the nations have a similar character. These the author of the Priestly narrative reconstructed (or rather constructed) as carefully as possible. For example, he mentions Madai, the ancestor of the Medes; Javan, the ancestor of the Ionians; Mizraim, the ancestor of the Egyptians; Canaan, the ancestor of the Canaanites (Genesis 10). All the many and varicolored people of the earth, who—according to the biblical conception—are descended from Shem, Ham, and Japheth, the sons of Noah, are creatures of God, for they were brought forth by God's creative blessing and their variety and difference was also willed by God.

Here again we find a fathomless difference between these ideas and Neoplatonism. For the latter multiplicity is radically opposed to The One. Only The One and whatever participates in it is good. Multiplicity and difference are characteristics of matter and therefore of atrophy, of nothingness, even of evil. For Israel, in contrast, the superabundance of created things is a sign of the overflowing goodness of God. "O LORD, how manifold are your works! . . . the earth is full of your creatures" (Ps 104:24). The blessing of all living things on the morning of creation not only gave it the power to reproduce and multiply itself, but also caused a sumptuous wealth of the most varied creatures to come into existence as a reflection of the glory of their Creator.

### 3. God Risks a History Tainted by Sin

Six times the Priestly creation account says: "And God saw that it was good." At the end, after the creation of human beings, and with a deliberate intensification of what is said of creation as a whole, the author writes: "God saw everything that he had made, and indeed, it was very good" (Gen 1:31).

This action of the Creator in finding creation to be good is often applied without much consideration to the world as we find it today: "The world is good." "The earth is beautiful." The Bible by no means thinks as naïvely as that. The author of the Priestly document knows that the world in which human beings find themselves is neither purely good nor simply beautiful. Consequently, a few chapters later, the author juxtaposes to God's judgment of creation a second divine assessment. While Gen 1:31 said that "God saw everything he had made, and indeed, it was very good," Gen 6:12 reads instead: "God saw that the earth was corrupt." There can be no doubt that these two statements are meant to refer to one another. When they are read together they tell us that human beings can only experience the glory of creation as something broken. The world is no longer what God saw at the creation. If people were to look at the earth as it really is, with the eyes of God and not through the veil of their own ideologies, they could only say with Gen 6:11-12: "Now the earth was corrupt in God's sight, and the earth was filled with violence. And God saw that the earth was corrupt; for all flesh had corrupted its ways upon the earth." The repetitions within the text reveal its heavy portent: all living things act violently, and reckless violence is the true sin of humanity. This is the sin that aims to destroy the other. It corrupts not only the life of human beings in community but even the earth that was God's good creation.

How did such evil break into the world? The Priestly document gives no answer to the question. It does not have a story about the Fall. It only states what humanity is, what the author sees: people are reckless, thoughtless, corrupting the earth, ripe for the Flood.

In this matter the Yahwist, the earlier narrator whose historical work is interwoven with the Priestly document in the five books of the Torah, goes a little farther. In Gen 2:4b–4:26 this author tells how sin came into the world and began to reproduce itself in various forms of violence. It is, of course, important that we do not misunderstand the Yahwist's narrative as a historical account of past events. The narrative of Paradise and the Fall, to which Cain's murder of his brother also belongs, is not about an original condition that human beings have lost, and certainly not about a golden age at the dawn of history; on the basis of Israel's experiences it develops some fundamental statements about the human situation. These experiences are expressed in images and symbols that are familiar throughout the world.

The text speaks of a garden with trees growing in it, a stream that waters it, sentinels who guard it, and a serpent in the midst of the garden who leads the human beings astray. These images and symbols are by no means primitive because the modern subconscious also brings forth all these symbols. Still less can one say that the images and symbols in Gen 2:4b–4:26 are naïve, for they describe the human condition with astonishing accuracy. They tell us what, in God's eyes, human beings could be and what they have in fact become.

They say: human beings could be very intimate with the *earth*. They could live in the world as in a garden. Of course the garden would not be a "land of Cockaigne" or lotus-land, a place of idleness. People would have to "till and keep" the garden of the world (2:15), but it would be a garden full of beauty and fruitfulness. People could also be on intimate terms with the *animals,* so intimate that they could give the right name to each one (2:19-20)—which means that they would understand the deepest nature of every animal.

Above all, people could be fully intimate with *each other,* so much so that the man could joyfully say of the woman: "This at last is bone of my bones and flesh of my flesh" (2:23). Finally, human beings could be fully intimate with *God,* so much so that they could boldly assert, with Gen 3:8, that God takes a walk in the garden in the cool of the evening.

Human beings could live in complete trust and confidence: trusting in the earth, the animals, other human beings, and God. They would live in the infinite gift of the freedom given them by God to build and shape the world. Everything would be open to them. They could eat from all the trees of the garden of the world (2:16). But that kind of human freedom would only be possible as long as that one tree, the tree from which no one may eat, stood untouchably in the midst of the garden (2:17). This tree represents God's commandment. It is meaningless to ask which particular commandment is meant by it. It is *the* commandment, pure and simple. It is the good and salvific will of God. Everything depends on this will of God's standing in the midst of the world and being obeyed.

Once again: what is depicted here in simple and vivid imagery is not a golden age of the world that existed at some time in the past, nor is it a mere dream of utopia conjured up as evening falls. Creation could have developed as the Paradise narrative describes, but that development existed as a real possibility in the salvific will of God. It was laid down in creation. That is how God willed the earth to be, and human beings as well.

However, the narrative of Paradise and the Fall not only tells us what human beings could be from God's point of view, but also what they really became. They constantly misuse the freedom God allows them. They can eat of all the trees of the world—they have unlimited possibilities—except for the one tree in the center from which they must not eat. That is: the commandment of God, the gracious will of the one who gave life to them, must be allowed to stand. This they must not touch. Here they have to trust.

And yet that is exactly what they do not do. They do not trust God. They are afraid of missing something. They suspect that something is being withheld from them. They want to be everything, in and of themselves. They want to be like God (3:5); that is, they want to be masters of themselves. And precisely that is sin. That is the enduring Fall that runs throughout human history.

The consequences are dreadful. The woman's and the man's eyes are opened indeed, but what they see is nothing but their own nakedness (3:7). Sin has opened no new possibilities to them; on the contrary, they have thrown away infinite opportunity. What God had placed within creation does not develop; it is perverted by human beings.

The earth that could be so beautiful is cursed because of humanity (3:17). The animals that could be so intimate with human beings remain strange or inimical to them (3:14-15). The work that could be cooperation with God in creation becomes miserable toil (3:17-19). The relationship between man and woman that could be so liberating is marked by domination and tyranny (3:16). God, who could be a sheltering presence to human beings, becomes a horror to them. They flee from God and hide themselves (3:8).

The narrative of the Fall clearly, soberly, and unerringly shows that sin does not create community. The man betrays the woman in the most pitiful fashion and shoves all the blame off on her; in fact, he even blames God:

> *"The woman whom you gave to be with me,*
> she gave me fruit from the tree,
> and I ate." (Gen 3:12)

The consequences of sin of course appear most fully in the story of Cain and Abel: it is only there that the story reaches its conclusion. Cain strikes down his brother. With this fraternal murder it is at last completely clear that sin not only undermines the relationship between the human being and God, but also destroys the relationship between human beings. Those who do not trust God can rely only on themselves, but those who rely only on themselves cannot really want to have their brothers and sisters with them. Life together becomes rivalry, and rivalry aims at removing the other from the world.

The narrative of the Fall is an "ancestor narrative"—that is, it embodies in the figure of the tribal ancestor everything that is true of the descendants of that ancestor. This insight into the genre of the text does not in any way imply a minimizing of the narrative's significance. On the contrary: such an insight makes the tale even more frightful, for it makes it clear that this is not a story of a single event, an individual case or a mere accident at the beginning of human history. This is what happens always and everywhere to all the descendants of Adam and Cain: a human being fails to trust God, rejects God and tries to be his or her own master, and that very thing leads him or her inevitably into misery.

The Bible tells the story of the Fall immediately after the creation of the world and humanity. This connection raises one of the most difficult questions of all: why did God create the world in the first place if human beings mistrusted God from the very beginning and corrupted the earth? Why is there a world that rolls on from one human catastrophe to another, piling up immeasurable suffering? Would it not be better if such a world did not exist at all? Since it does exist, must we not ask whether the God who is supposed to have created such a world exists? These are the questions that have been asked from ancient times until now, by believers and by atheists.

However, we must note that when the question is asked in this way it already participates in that basic mistrust of which we spoke above. There is no point from which one can start out, without personal involvement, to test whether God has made a success of the world. The most frequent form in which the Bible speaks of creation is divine praise, and that is not a coincidence. Those who stand on the ground of divine praise are already demonstrating trust and attributing meaning to creation by recognizing that God is not only infinitely greater and therefore can see more than the one who questions, but also that God is good. That of course does not mean that faith is not allowed to think. It can even doubt. But its critical questions will only receive an answer in the context of confident praise.

Why does God risk a history tainted by sin? One who begins to reflect on this question in faith will derive the beginnings of an answer from the Fall narrative itself. At the very point in the story where Cain notices that his brother Abel's sacrifice is accepted by God while his is not he is overcome by rage and casts his eyes on the ground. At that very moment the narrator has God speak to Cain in a most unusual way:

"Why are you angry, and why has your countenance fallen? If you do well, will you not be accepted? And if you do not do well, sin is lurking at the door; its desire is for you, but you must master it." (Gen 4:6-7)

This address by God promises Cain freedom. He can choose between doing right and doing wrong. He does not need to lower his head like a steer. He can raise his head and look his brother in the face. It is possible for him to master the violence that lurks at the door. In the same way Adam and Eve also had a choice between obedience and disobedience, between mistrust and trust in God. Apparently it is important to the Yahwist to emphasize human freedom.

Probably the risk that God takes with creation can only be understood in terms of freedom. God is entirely free, and when God shapes a creation that, in the person of the human being, can confront God as "thou," that creation must be given an enormous amount of freedom. The freedom of human beings is so indispensable that God must conceal himself, must become a *deus absconditus* in order not to overpower them. "[Mortals must] search for God and perhaps grope for him and find him," says Paul in his speech on the Areopagus (Acts 17:27).

The freedom and unique reality of creation was already in preparation in pre-human evolution, not yet as *personal* freedom, but as a kind of unbroken process of feeling the way forward, a play of ever-new possibilities, a constant testing and rejection. One may certainly not say that evolution was programmed by God toward a certain end, for then God would be a poor programmer. What drove creation ineluctably, despite countless failed experiments and side paths, toward humanity, at the same time independently correcting all its false attempts, was not a fixed program implanted in it by God, but the eternal creative Word of God that embraces the world while leaving it entirely free and yet calling it to itself.

It was an unimaginably long route that stretched over more than three billion years, from the first blue algae, the cyanobacteria, by way of the first amphibians that dared to move from the sea to the land, through the first mammals, to *homo sapiens*. At some time in the transition from the primates to the human being the first tools in the form of unshaped stones were employed. At some point, perhaps when the common hunt demanded more and more elaborate sequences of movement, brain structures changed, making possible more subtle neuronal calculations. At some time, perhaps because of a genetic "defect," the larynx moved downward and so expanded the speaking abilities of our still half-animal ancestors. At some time or other in the encounter with a more differentiated language came the first self-awareness, and with it, like a tender plant, the first freedom.

We do not know when for the first time a human being said "yes" or "no" in complete freedom, but it must have happened at some time, and at some point people must have begun to apply the unimaginable gift of their freedom and understanding in order to praise a higher being, however that higher being may have been conceived.

However, at some time human beings must also have begun for the first time to apply their reason and freedom with cold calculation to exploit others, to establish a reign of terror and to be more beastly than any beast. Human beings can misuse their freedom and they have done so until today, and without limit. But that in itself is what is required for human freedom to be possible. God desires a partner, a vis-à-vis, who can say "no," because God desires a partner who can say "yes."[17] Without freedom there would be only puppets and machines, but no human beings moved by trust and love.

There are a number of Jewish legends from the postbiblical period that all come to the same conclusion: that God hesitated before finally deciding to create. One version of the legend tells how God first debated with the Torah whether to create the world or not. The Torah was skeptical and reminded God that human beings would surely sin. The reply came that long ago, before creating anything at all, God had created repentance.[18]

Another legend tells how God, before beginning to create, saw the measureless suffering of the world, its sin and the misery that would result from sin. Then God said: "I cannot create the world." But then God saw the faith of Abraham and said, "See, I have found a rock on which I can build and found the world."[19]

A third legend says that God indeed created the world immediately, but left it in a preliminary state until the revelation of the Torah on Sinai. God said to the world: "If Israel accepts the Torah, you will continue and endure; otherwise, I shall turn everything back into chaos."[20]

All these legends take God's freedom seriously, but they take human freedom just as seriously; it is shown in repentance, in the faith of Abraham, and in Israel's acceptance of the Torah. Nevertheless, freedom is not the point of these three legends. Their real point is something else: not only is there the sin of the world, its history of guilt, human mistrust and wickedness, there is also a history of trust and of freedom that is not mis-

---

[17] Cf. Pierre Gisel, "Schöpfung und Vollendung," in Peter Eicher, ed., *Neue Summe Theologie 2: Die neue Schöpfung* (Freiburg: Herder, 1989) 19–125, at 41.

[18] Cf. Louis Ginzberg, *The Legends of the Jews* (11th ed. Philadelphia: Jewish Publication Society, 1961) 1:3–4.

[19] Jalq Nu § 766.

[20] Cf. Louis Ginzberg, *Legends* 1:52. The text Ginzberg cites is paraphrased from *b.Šabb.* 88a.

used. There is a history of salvation, represented by Abraham. Indeed, we must say still more: there is a history of salvation that arises out of repentance constantly renewed, and perhaps it is precisely the opportunity to repent and begin again like a child that keeps our world in balance.

At any rate, in its first book the Bible not only narrates the story of human sin, but also the beginning of the story of salvation with Abraham. Without looking at that history of salvation and trying to live within it no one can say whether God's creation is a success or not.

## 4. God Wills the Salvation of the Whole World

The Bible does not begin with the election of the people of God, but with the creation of the world. Its first figure is not Abraham, but the *ʾādām*, the human being, and in the first chapters of Genesis *ʾādām* refers not to a particular individual, but to humanity as a whole.[21] The Bible begins with humanity.

This observation, banal in itself, is of serious theological import, for it makes clear that everything the Bible goes on to describe is not only an action between God and God's people; it is aimed toward the nations, the world, the universe.[22] God's concern is not first of all for Israel, but for the whole world. Franz Rosenzweig says it this way: "God did not create religion, but the world."[23]

As universally as the Bible begins, so does it end. Its first image is the creation of the world out of chaos. Its last great image is God's *new* world, God's *new* creation in which all creation finds its goal and its perfection. This last image of the Bible is spread before us, in the Revelation of John, as a prophetic vision in Rev 21:1–22:5.

John deliberately connected his great closing vision to the opening chapters of the Bible. The book opens with "In the beginning . . . God created the heavens and the earth" (Gen 1:1) and now it closes with "Then I saw a new heaven and a new earth, for the first heaven and the first earth had passed away" (Rev 21:1). Whereas God, at the beginning of creation, placed the primeval sea, the embodiment of chaos, within its boundaries (Gen 1:1-10), so at the end the chaotic flood will be entirely destroyed so that it can no longer threaten the earth: "and the sea was no more" (Rev

---

[21] As a collective singular *ʾādām* is primarily the designation of a species. Cf. F. Maass, *ʾādām, TDOT* 1:75–87, at 75.

[22] This is formulated in light of Horst Dietrich Preuss, *Theologie des Alten Testaments* (Stuttgart: Kohlhammer, 1991) 1:271. English: *Old Testament Theology*. 2 vols. (Louisville: Westminster/John Knox, 1995–1996) 1:221–22.

[23] Franz Rosenzweig, *Der Mensch und sein Werk. Gesammelte Schriften* 3 (4th ed. Den Haag: Martinus Nijhoff, 1976) 153.

21:1). While after the Fall the fertile ground was cursed because of human beings, so that they must labor to till it until they return to the earth from which they were taken (Gen 3:17-19), now it is said: "Death will be no more; mourning and crying and pain will be no more" (Rev 21:4).

But above all: The primeval history contains the human attempt to build a city and within it a tower that would reach to heaven. The attempt failed. The city was not completed, and its people were scattered over the whole earth (Gen 11:1-9). Now, at the end of the Bible, the city is a success. It does not arise out of human arrogance but comes down from heaven as God's building plan to counter every previous city (Rev 21:2, 10), and this eschatological city does not scatter humanity, but gathers it (21:24).

John sees God's new creation, then, in the image of the *city*. Of course he thus reflects the prophetic traditions about the eschatological rebuilding of Jerusalem as found, for example, in Tob 13:10-18 and Isaiah 60, but what he has in mind is not only the tradition of Zion, but also the Hellenistic city. "It was the most progressive social structure in late antiquity, the object of deliberate planning and future-oriented projections."[24] "City," *polis,* in Greece represented all of what we today call "society." Aristotle, who was the first to specifically formulate the idea of "society," calls it *politikē koinōnia,* "association of the *polis.*"[25]

That the city in antiquity was an image of society must have played an important role in John's description of his final vision. God's eschatological new creation, of which he speaks with deliberate reference to the primeval history of the world and humanity, appears to him as a "city" and not as a "garden," although—as we shall see—the motif of Paradise is not absent from his image of the city. The new, redeemed creation is for him a "new society" in which there are "encounter, gathering, and full mutual communication."[26]

With its square plan (Rev 21:16) and principal street as an axis (21:21) the new city matches the major Hellenistic city plans,[27] and yet it explodes all conceptions of an ancient city, for its length and width are 12,000 stadia, or about 1,500 miles. The city is thus as large as the then-civilized world around the Mediterranean basin. The new Jerusalem is not only a

---

[24] Jürgen Roloff, "Neuschöpfung in der Offenbarung des Johannes," *JBTh* 5 (1990) 119–38, at 129.

[25] Aristotle, *Nicomachean Ethics* VIII 11 (1160a).

[26] Dieter Georgi, "Die Visionen vom himmlischen Jerusalem in Apk 21 und 22," in Dieter Lührmann and Georg Strecker, eds., *Kirche. Festschrift für Günther Bornkamm zum 75. Geburtstag.* Tübingen: Mohr, 1980, 351–72, at 365.

[27] This is persuasively demonstrated by Dieter Georgi, "Die Visionen vom himmlischen Jerusalem."

world city; this city is the world. This is also evident because its height, too, is 1,500 miles (Rev 21:16). John was certainly not thinking of the city as a cube. He simply wants to say that the new city is also the city on the hill. It has cosmic dimensions. It reaches to the heavens and so joins heaven and earth.

The wall of the city has three gates on each of its four sides, and it is explicitly said of these twelve gates that they are never closed (Rev 21:25). This diamond[28] city wall of course repels everything evil and impure (21:27), but at the same time it is meant to make clear the transparency and openness of the city to the entire world. For the image of the open gates is connected to another image that had an important place in the tradition of the post-exilic prophets: that of the pilgrimage of nations to Jerusalem at the end of time. In Isa 60:1-11 it appears in the following form:

> Arise, shine, for your light has come,
>   and the glory of the LORD has risen upon you.
> For darkness shall cover the earth,
>   and thick darkness the peoples;
> but the LORD will arise upon you,
>   and his glory will appear over you.
> Nations shall come to your light,
>   and kings to the brightness of your dawn. . . .
>   the abundance of the sea shall be brought to you,
>   the wealth of the nations shall come to you. . . .
> Your gates shall always be open;
>   day and night they shall not be shut,
> so that nations shall bring you their wealth . . . .

The motif-complex of the pilgrimage of nations includes the idea that the nations, drawn by the light that goes forth from Zion, will stream to Jerusalem in order to learn God's order for society and then to live it in their own countries (Mic 4:1-5). But it is also part of the schema of the pilgrimage of nations that the Gentiles will deposit their treasures as consecrated offerings in the Temple at Jerusalem. John incorporates these connected motifs in his description. In obvious reference to Isa 60:1-11 he says that the nations of the earth will live in the light of the new city, and that the kings of the world will bring their treasures into it (Rev 21:24-26).

---

[28] Cf. Rev 21:18. The Greek text does not have "diamond," but "jasper." But see Heinrich Kraft, *Die Offenbarung des Johannes*. HNT 16a (Tübingen: Mohr, 1974) 268: "Jasper in the Apocalypse is not the modest stone we call by that name, but one of the most precious stones, whose appearance and esteem approaches that of diamond. The comparison is all the more justified because diamond is not mentioned in the Apocalypse."

Hence it is clear that the new city is international; it is not a separate world or a closed society. It excludes nothing of the nations that is good, perfect, and beautiful, but instead constantly draws it in. It gathers within itself all the treasures of the earth. It is constructed of the materials of this world. It is in this very context that the description of the city reaches its most detailed climax. John cannot say enough in detailing the materials with which the city is adorned: pearls, gold, crystal, precious stones. Even these last are differentiated: diamond, sapphire, agate, emerald, onyx, carnelian, chrysolite, beryl, topaz, chrysoprase, jacinth, and amethyst (Rev 21:19-20). The city glitters and glows in all colors.

However, to the listing of the mere materials is added another image that develops the whole picture in a personal dimension: the bride. The new city is "prepared as a bride adorned for her husband" (21:2). This introduces the image of the wedding, and with it the wedding feast. The new society God desires is not needy and certainly not shabby. It has a high culture. It is in constant communication. It is pure feast. But it belongs to a feast to relativize the brass clock of time. At a real feast people forget the time and do not even ask about it. They live, at least for an hour, as if the feast would never end. This experience is also addressed in Rev 21:1–22:5: while in the Genesis creation account chaos was bound primarily by the creation of light and its separation from darkness, with sun and moon created to distinguish between day and night—that is, by the creation of time—in the new city there is neither sun nor moon, "for the glory of God is its light, and its lamp is the Lamb" (21:23). This means that the cosmic rhythms that create time no longer exist. The feast in the new city knows no time. Time has ceased.

The relationship between the city and nature is radically conceived as well. The city is not "in" nature; nature is integrated into the city. Only after the city has been described as a completely symmetrical structure conceived in considered beauty is anything at all said about nature (Rev 22:1-2). That means that the new society does not arise in an eschatologically renewed nature, but just the opposite: within the new city Paradise arises anew, and in an enhanced form compared to the beginning, for the tree of life that stood in the middle of the garden of Paradise (Gen 2:9) is replaced (with reference to Ezek 47:7, 12) by a long row of trees. They stand on either side of the river that flows through the city. The trees are watered by the stream and their fruitfulness is inexhaustible. Nature is thus brought within the redeemed society. Only because society has become whole is nature also whole and intact and able, in turn, to heal: "the leaves of the tree are for the healing of the nations" (Rev 22:2).

Finally, it is of the nature of the new city that there is no Temple in it. This is an unheard-of statement in comparison to all the older Zion traditions. Until now the Temple was always the center of the eschatological Jerusalem. The book of Ezekiel described the Temple of the end time from many sides and in the most minute detail: its gates and courts, its auxiliary buildings, the rooms for the priests, the cooking places for the sacrifices, the altar, the Holy of Holies, the Temple spring. Only a few lines at the end of the book were devoted to the holy city itself (Ezek 48:30-35).

It is quite different for John: he does not describe a Temple, but the city. It needs no Temple because God dwells in its midst: "its temple is the Lord God the Almighty and the Lamb" (Rev 21:22). While in Paradise all that was heard was God's steps and voice (Gen 3:8-10), now it is said:

> . . . they will see his face, and his name will be on their foreheads. And there will be no more night; they need no light of lamp or sun, for the Lord God will be their light, and they will reign forever and ever. (Rev 22:4-5)

With this the vision ends. It describes the perfection of creation and depicts it as a new society. The ultimate future of the world is not catastrophe, nor even the Paradise of the beginning, but a new society that is entirely the gift of God.[29]

The vision shows that God is not concerned for just one people, but for all nations. God's care is not only for every individual, but for society. God cares not only for the soul, but also for matter, for culture, for history, for the whole makeup of the world. Everything is included in the feast of the new creation.

It is true that the final vision in the Revelation of John says nothing about "universal reconciliation." The whole book is aware of the power of evil, of obdurate resistance to God's plan, of people and powers that put themselves in the place of God and thus thwart the possibilities in creation, and it is also aware of the necessity of separation and judgment. But it may be that the visions of judgment in Revelation, which cannot be ignored, show more clearly than all the visions of salvation that God is concerned for the redemption and healing of the whole world. God does not allow creation to be torn away; God struggles for it and desires to save it. The descriptions of judgment are meant to be a warning. They are intended to show what will surely bring ruin to the world.

God desires the salvation of the whole world. But how can that salvation succeed? We have thus far set aside a crucial mark of the new city: in

---

[29] Cf. the essay by Klaus Berger, "Tausendjähriges Reich und himmlisches Jerusalem. Vier Anmerkungen zur Apokalypse," *Frankfurter Allgemeine Magazin* 742 (20 May 1994) 18–22, at 18–19.

its description the number "twelve" plays an extraordinary role. The city wall has twelve foundation stones on which are the names of the twelve apostles (Rev 21:14), and it has twelve gates, with twelve angels on the gates. Names are written on the gates as well: "the names of the twelve tribes of the Israelites" (21:12). With this excessive use of the number twelve John makes it clear that the city is nothing other than the restored people of the twelve tribes, the people of God in its eschatological perfection. But then in turn it is clear that no matter how universal the eschatological city, God's new society, its arrival is not something that happens at just any time and everywhere; it is bound to a concrete place and time: to the people of the twelve tribes and its history. This connection is for many today a stumbling-block that can scarcely be overcome. The next two chapters are about this stumbling-block.

## 5. The Salvation of the World Demands a Concrete Place

God desires the salvation of the whole world. But how can that salvation be accomplished? A great many have already tried to change the world. Every revolution sought to free the masses, change circumstances, save people from their misery. Every revolution desires a new consciousness, a new society, a new economy, a new art, a new humanity.

However, all revolutionaries have one basic problem: they are short of time. Individual lifetimes are limited, and the masses are inert. If they want to see the new society of their dreams within their own lifetime revolutionaries have to change the old society in a relatively short time, and that they can only do by violent means. In fact the usual concept of revolution includes at least three elements: (1) that the masses are involved, (2) that the social overthrow happens relatively quickly, and (3) that it is brought about by open and direct violence.[30] The last paragraph of the Communist Manifesto reads:

> The Communists disdain to conceal their views and purposes. They openly declare that their ends can be attained only by the forcible overthrow of all existing social conditions. Let the ruling classes tremble at a Communist revolution. The proletarians have nothing to lose but their chains. They have a world to win. *Workingmen of all countries, unite!*[31]

---

[30] The overview by Dirk Käsler, *Revolution and Veralltäglichung. Eine Theorie postrevolutionärer Prozesse* (Munich: Beck, 1977) 11–32 is helpful.

[31] Karl Marx and Friedrich Engels, *Manifesto of the Communist Party.* Translated by Samuel Moore, edited by Friedrich Engels (Chicago, London, Toronto, and Geneva: Encyclopaedia Britannica, Inc., 1952).

In the middle of this decisive concluding paragraph of the Manifesto force is explicitly justified as an indispensable principle of world revolution. There is, in fact, no other possibility when one has no time and the whole world must be saved at one blow. The question is only: in that case where is freedom, and where does the revolution lead in the end? The Communist Manifesto of Karl Marx and Friedrich Engels was published in 1848. In its first fifty years it was almost completely forgotten.[32] Then, however, it became the basic text for one of the most terrible experiments in the history of the human race, one that lasted more than seventy years and brought casualties without number. Stalin's forced collectivization of the Russian peasant farmers (kulaks) alone, in the years 1928 to 1933, cost more than ten million people their lives.[33]

God's principle is different. God, like all revolutionaries, desires the overturning, the radical alteration of the whole society—for in this the revolutionaries are right: what is at stake is the whole world, and the change must be radical, for the misery of the world cries to heaven and it begins deep within the human heart. But how can anyone change the world and society at its roots without taking away freedom?

It can only be that God begins in a small way, at one single place in the world. There must be a place, visible, tangible, where the salvation of the world can begin: that is, where the world becomes what it is supposed to be according to God's plan. Beginning at that place, the new thing can spread abroad, but not through persuasion, not through indoctrination, not through violence. Everyone must have the opportunity to come and see. All must have the chance to behold and test this new thing. Then, if they want to, they can allow themselves to be drawn into the history of salvation that God is creating. Only in that way can their freedom be preserved. What drives them to the new thing cannot be force, not even moral pressure, but only the fascination of a world that is changed.

Clearly this change in the world must begin in human beings, but not at all by their seeking through heroic effort to make themselves the locus of the new, altered world; rather it begins when they listen to God, open themselves to God, and allow God to act.

This is precisely what the stories of the patriarchs in Genesis 12–50 are about. The first chapters of the Bible have told about the creation of the world, the unfolding of human history and—in a few sketchy lines—

[32] Cf. Richard Friedenthal, *Karl Marx. Sein Leben und seine Zeit.* dtv 10196 (Munich: R. Piper, 1981) 326, 335.

[33] Cf. Alan Bullock, *Hitler and Stalin. Parallel Lives* (London: HarperCollins, 1991; New York: Knopf, 1992) 259–77.

the growth of human civilization and culture,[34] but including also, from the very beginning, disobedience to God and with it the growth of rivalry and violence. Genesis 12 then makes a new beginning. It suddenly ceases to focus on humanity as a whole and commences the family history of an individual that will eventually lead to a world society that, at the end of the Bible, will be depicted in the image of the new city. God begins to change the world by starting anew at a particular point with a single individual:

> Now the LORD said to Abram, "Go from your country and your kindred and your father's house to the land that I will show you. I will make of you a great nation, and I will bless you, and make your name great, so that you will be a blessing. I will bless those who bless you, and the one who curses you I will curse; and by you all the families of the earth shall bless themselves." (Gen 12:1-3; variant reading in v. 3c)

The text shows at first glance that something new is beginning here. There is an exodus from the old society that will make possible a new society. God chooses an individual who is to leave country, tribe, and family and go into a land that is not even given a name. It is true that earlier, in the figure of Noah, there had been indications of something like an exodus. The letter to the Hebrews also rightly sees in the ancestors Abel, Enoch, and Noah the forerunners of Abraham (Heb 11:1-7). But here is something quite new in contrast to Noah. Abraham receives a promise that he will be the ancestor of a great nation. The new thing in the world begins as a *promise*—the promise of a land given by God, and the promise of a new people in the world.

Abraham believes in the promise: at the age of 75 he moves with Sarai his wife, who is also quite old, and his nephew Lot from Haran to Canaan (Gen 12:4-5). He will cross Canaan until he reaches the oracular oak at Shechem, and then move on to the hill country east of Bethel; there he will pitch his tent. He will travel south as far as the Negeb. He will leave the promised land and go into Egypt because there is a severe famine in the land (Gen 12:6-20).

It is by no means adequate to read such "journey narratives" only with the eyes of a geographer, a sociologist, a historian, or a literary critic. They must be read against the vast background of the first chapters of Genesis: the creation of the world, the expansion of humanity, the universal catastrophe of the Flood, people's attempt to build a city with a tower reaching to heaven. Only with these broad canvases as a background does the account of Abraham's journeyings in Genesis 12 achieve its theologi-

---

[34] For the development of civilization and culture cf. the remarks of the Yahwist in Gen 4:2, 17, 20, 21, 22; 9:20; 10:9, 11-12; 11:1-4.

cal profile: God begins with very small things, not by setting masses in motion. To change the whole world God has at first no one but Abraham.

However, the description of how Abraham moves from one encampment to another reveals something else: God is not in a hurry. In light of the problems of the world the movements of a wandering Aramean and his concerns for tent and flock seem positively laughable, and yet the reader senses that something crucial is happening here: the very fact that someone relies entirely on God's promise will change the world. God takes time, but it is not empty time. In *one* place in the world now faith is being practiced: not an otherworldly, world-ignorant faith, but faith that is at home in daily events and economic necessities and yet lives out of an endless promise.

The ongoing tale of the patriarchs should be read with this in mind. It is the very opposite of the temporal urgency of revolutionaries. How time stretches out when the biblical narrator describes the search for Isaac's bride (Genesis 24) or Jacob's service with Laban (Genesis 29–31)! How much space is allowed for the Joseph story (Genesis 37–50)! And so it goes on in the books that follow. God enjoys the luxury of leading Abraham's descendants back and forth through the wilderness for forty years before they can finally enter the promised land.

Should one conclude from this that God has nothing but time, that time is not urgent for God and neither is the trouble in the world? There are texts in the Bible that point in quite the opposite direction. Jesus will say: "There is no more time. Now is the crisis, the last hour!" For him time is so pressing that he does not even allow someone who wants to follow him to take leave of the family (Luke 9:61-62). The same had been true of the prophets. "Even now the ax is lying at the root of the trees," said the Baptizer (Luke 3:9), and Elisha, when Elijah called him from the plow, slaughtered his oxen in the field because he had no time for a farewell dinner at home (1 Kings 19:21).

All this makes it clear that from the point of view of terrible social affliction there is no time. From the standpoint of the world the hands of the clock are always close to twelve. And yet God continually provides humanity with more time, even opening gigantic periods before them, because God does not use force like a revolutionary in a blind rage. God favors a "silent revolution" that has time to see, to understand, to learn, and to repent.

At first Abraham moves from Shechem to Bethel and from Bethel to the Negeb as if he had all the time in the world. What he has is only the promise that one day he will be a great nation and a blessing for others. Of course that is an unimaginably great promise: "You will be a blessing."

That is: Abraham and the new thing that God is bringing into the world with him will be salvation for those who come into contact with him and share in this new thing. Still more: what is now beginning with Abraham is so precious in God's eyes that the way others treat Abraham will be decisive for the way God will treat them:[35] "I will bless those who bless you, and the one who curses you I will curse." This introduces a theme that runs through the entire Bible. In Matthew 25 Jesus gives it his own formulation: "just as you did it to one of the least of these who are members of my family, you did it to me" (Matt 25:40). In the last few decades this has become one of the most popular texts for preaching; "the least of these who are members of my family" are almost always equated with all the suffering people in the world. Jesus encounters us in every poor person, in every human sister and brother. The idea is beautiful, and it is true—but Matthew 25 is about something else.

In this passage in Matthew the least among Jesus' family are not the poor of the earth, but Jesus' persecuted disciples, and everyone who comes to their aid comes to the aid of Jesus' cause and belongs to those who are blessed by his Father. God has connected the changing of the world and its salvation to what began with Abraham and is continued by Jesus' distressed disciples. It is infinitely precious to God. Everyone who comes to the aid of this cause comes to God's aid. Those who do not come to help destroy their own lives. No matter how much God is on the side of all the poor, for God the most important cause in the world is the existence of God's people, because in the long run it is only through this people of God that the poor of the world can really be helped. The judgment scene in Matthew 25, with its contrasting of the blessed and the accursed, is in fact a concretization of what had been said to Abraham: "I will bless those who bless you, and the one who curses you I will curse."

Of course in Genesis 12 the statement about the evil that will befall the one who desires to bring this divine cause to ruin is immediately followed by a renewed promise of salvation: "in you all the families of the earth shall bless themselves."[36] With this concluding statement the "you will be a blessing" of Gen 12:2 is surpassed and expanded into a blessing encompassing all humanity. God's concern is for the whole breadth of the world of nations, for all the families of the earth.

---

[35] Claus Westermann, *Genesis: A Commentary.* Translated by John J. Scullion. 3 vols. (Minneapolis: Augsburg, 1984–1986) 2:150–51.

[36] The Hebrew text of this passage can be translated as passive (they will be blessed) or as reflexive (they will bless themselves *[NRSV]*). In principle both come to the same thing: when the families of the earth bless themselves in the name of Abraham "this of course presupposes that they also receive blessing." Thus Claus Westermann, *Genesis* 2:151–52.

Therefore no matter how small and unremarkable what begins in Genesis 12 with Abraham appears to be, the world-encompassing horizon has not for a moment disappeared from view. Here, as always, what is at stake is the world and God's world revolution, the universal reversal of everything toward salvation. But for the sake of human freedom there is no other possibility than that universal salvation should begin with *one* person and in *one* place.

## 6. That Concrete Place Is Israel

Why does God attach the salvation to be brought into the world to Israel? Why begin in Palestine, of all places? Why does God not have the silent revolution that is to touch all nations begin on the Nile or the Indus, among the Etruscans, the Greeks, or the Inca? It seems presumptuous to look for an answer to such questions. If God is really God we cannot expect to look over God's shoulder. On the other hand, in the story of the visit of the three heavenly beings to Abraham God says in a soliloquy:

> "Shall I hide from Abraham what I am about to do, seeing that Abraham shall become a great and mighty nation, and all the nations of the earth shall be blessed in him? No, for I have chosen him, that he may charge his children and his household after him to keep the way of the LORD by doing righteousness and justice; so that the LORD may bring about for Abraham what he has promised him." (Gen 18:17-19)

That is: God cannot complete what God has planned for the world without making Abraham a trusted companion, a participant in the divine plan and thus one who *understands*. The election of Abraham aims at a just society such as God has always desired for the world, and Abraham has to know this world-altering plan. We would by no means be doing justice to the whole of biblical theology if we spoke only of the incomprehensibility and darkness of God. We may look back, examine history, and seek understanding of the ways of God in light of the experiences of the people of God. We are even obligated to do so, for faith is only worthy of the human when it struggles for insight.[37]

Then why Israel? In our search for an answer we may find two concepts helpful: that of "confluence" and that of God's "choice" or "election." Of course these two concepts are not on the same level. "Election" sees the matter at issue from God's point of view, "confluence" from the point of view of the world and natural circumstances. "Confluence" is the

---

[37] Thus the well-known *credo ut intelligam* (I believe in order that I may understand) in Anselm of Canterbury's *Proslogion*, ch. 1, but also Augustine, *Sermo* 43.7.9 and *De doctrina Christiana* II.12.17. Both Augustine and Anselm refer to Isa 7:9 LXX.

coming-together into a single constellation of three things: the right place, the right time, and the right people. Election means that God alone makes the choice of where in the world to begin and where to pursue God's cause.

*The right place.* We have already seen that God starts small. This is not only true of Abraham. It applies also to the land that is promised to Abraham. It is a little land. "I am almost ashamed," Jerome wrote in 414 in a letter to Dardanus of Gaul,[38] "to give the breadth of the land of promise, for fear of evoking the pagans' ridicule. From Joppa to our spot at Bethlehem is only forty-six miles. Then immediately the wilderness begins."[39] Even Jerome, then, expresses what every visitor to Israel senses today: the smallness of the land. It can be crossed very quickly.

However, if one considers Israel as a place *in the world* the perspective changes. The little land is uniquely situated. Palestine, and Israel within it, lies between two seas: the Mediterranean, upon which there was an extensive trade at least by the thirteenth century B.C.E., and the Red Sea, which opens the marine road to Arabia, East Africa, and the Indian Ocean.[40] But most significantly of all, Palestine lies at the axis of three continents: Europe, Asia, and Africa. There is scarcely any other place on earth where the force fields of three continents, and with them totally different cultures, come together in such a way.

Especially as regards Asia and Africa this is fully obvious: Between the Mediterranean and the Arabian desert there is only a relatively narrow land bridge for settlement and traffic. It unites Africa and Asia. It ties together the ancient cultures on the Nile with Mesopotamia and beyond it with India. This land bridge is Palestine. Therefore in antiquity important international traffic routes passed through Palestine and made the region a transit zone for commerce and trade and a meeting point of the most diverse cultures.[41]

This very location between the high cultures had the potential to set creative forces in motion. In the Phoenician region the principle of alphabetic writing was invented: departing from signs for words and syllables, this system introduced signs for individual consonants. Our "western"

---

[38] Jerome, *Ep. ad Dardanum* 4. BKV ser. 2 vol. 18, 340.

[39] The distance from Joppa to Bethlehem as the crow flies is fifty-four kilometers, or about thirty-five miles.

[40] Apparently this route was also used by Israel: cf. 1 Kings 9:26-27 and Jer 6:20.

[41] For what follows, cf. Herbert Donner, *Geschichte des Volkes Israel und seiner Nachbarn in Grundzügen. I: Von den Anfängen bis zur Staatenbildungszeit.* ATD Ergänzungsreihe 4/1 (Göttingen: Vandenhoeck & Ruprecht, 1984) 29–52; Othmar Keel, Max Küchler, and Christoph Uehlinger, *Orte und Landschaften der Bibel. I: Geographisch-geschichtliche Landeskunde* (Zürich: Benziger, and Göttingen: Vandenhoeck & Ruprecht, c1982) 182–93; Sebastian Bock, *Kleine Geschichte des Volkes Israel: von den Anfängen bis in die Zeit des Neuen Testaments.* Herder Taschenbuch 1642 (Freiburg: Herder, 1989) 21–23.

systems of writing originated in the land bridge between the two great river-valley cultures.[42] And in the midst of Palestine was Jericho, one of the oldest cities in the world. Kathleen M. Kenyon's excavations in the years 1952–1958 have shown that the settlement of Jericho began about eight thousand years B.C.E.[43]

Palestine, however, is a land of transit not only in terms of traffic. Precisely because the commercial routes between Africa and Asia pass through it the great powers of all ages have waged bitter struggles for this land.[44] In the fourteenth century before Christ the Hittites, who dwelt in Asia Minor, expanded their borders to the northern frontiers of Palestine. Their expansive drive was halted by Egypt, which controlled Palestine from the west and regarded it as its own sphere of dominance. From the thirteenth century onward the Philistines steadily gained influence, though under a loose control from Egypt. They constituted part of the great migratory wave of "sea peoples." In the first millennium, then, Palestine fell successively under the domination of Assyria, Babylon, Persia, the Ptolemies, the Seleucids, and finally Rome. The fact that Palestine was constantly being overrun by the great powers brought endless suffering to its people. On the other hand Israel and its predecessors were constantly forced to deal with other nations and their cultures, social forms, and religion.

It should be noted that Israel was not only seated "in the center of the nations" (Ezek 5:5) but had the nations in its own midst. At first it was unable to conquer strongly fortified Canaanite cities like Megiddo, Beth-Shean, Beth-Shemesh, Gezer, and Jerusalem. Even later, in the New Testament period, purely Hellenistic cities like Tiberias, Sepphoris, Sebaste, Antipatris, and Scythopolis lay throughout the land. It is clear that the constant contact with other cultures and other religions must have sharpened their understanding and their powers of discernment.

Israel did, indeed, draw many of its ideas about the holy from the Canaanites, the Egyptians, the Assyrians, the Babylonians, the Persians, and the Greeks. It listened with great sensitivity to the cultures and religions of its environment. But the real miracle of its faith was that it did not surrender to the impressive religions that surrounded it. From the beginning, through its history with YHWH, it possessed the gift of discernment. It was indeed often in danger of falling under the sway of foreign cultures, but at the crucial moment it always found the strength to cling to its faith and even to deepen it in the midst of crises and catastrophes.

---

[42] Cf. Siegfried Herrmann, "Geschichte Israels," *TRE* 12:698–740, at 699.

[43] Ibid.

[44] Bock, *Kleine Geschichte* 21.

There is much in the Old Testament writings of which one can say: That is a Canaanite myth, that is Egyptian wisdom, that is Hellenistic philosophy. But it is always clarified, reworked, placed in a new context, and thereby altered to form biblical faith.

*The right time.* Pagan philosophers like Celsus and Porphyry charged Christianity that their Christ could not have been the Redeemer, for he came far too late. A God who had left all the nations of the past without redemption could only be regarded as perverse. The theologians of the early Church saw this accusation as one of the most dangerous arguments against Christianity, and repeatedly strove to combat it.[45] Why did Christ come so late?

A similar question could be asked about Abraham: why was God so late in beginning this new thing, this thing that Christian tradition calls revelation, salvation history, and redemption? Israel is a young nation, preceded by high cultures that were many centuries older. Egypt had a long flowering as early as the second millennium, when from the Egyptian point of view the place where Israel would later live was still inhabited by *mentshu* ("wild people") and *heriusha* ("sand dwellers").[46]

Israel itself always knew that it was a "late people." In contrast to the great, cultured nations of the ancient East who regarded themselves as eternal entities originating in the stories of the gods Israel spoke very soberly of its own late origins.[47] "A wandering Aramean was my ancestor" begins the salvation-historical credo of Israel in Deut 26:5-10, and yet it was precisely this late period that was Israel's true hour, its *kairos*, the condition for the possibility of the new. Only when cultures had arrived at their zenith, when there were balanced social systems and highly developed worlds of thought *(Sinnwelten)* could these be taken up, compared, and critiqued. Israel would always find its own unique character in contrast and in exodus, but exodus presumes fixed and developed societies. Only in departing from the ancient oriental social systems that used religion to fortify existing relationships of domination while at the same time concealing them is revelation possible: the revelation of a God who does not legitimate existing conditions but leads them into freedom and paves the way for a just society.

---

[45] Cf. Henri de Lubac, *Catholicism. A Study of Dogma in Relation to the Corporate Destiny of Mankind*. Translated by Lancelot C. Sheppard (London: Burns, Oates, and Washbourne, 1949) 126–43; Arnold Stötzel, "Warum Christus so spät erschien—die apologetische Argumentation des frühen Christentums," *ZKG* 31 (1981) 147–60.

[46] Cf. Othmar Keel, *Orte und Landschaften* 207–11.

[47] See Donner, *Geschichte des Volkes Israel* 1:23.

This kind of revelation is *enlightenment,* and the time for enlightenment always comes late. In Greece the time of *mythos* had to precede the time of *logos.* The European Enlightenment did not happen in the Middle Ages, but in the modern era. The faith of Israel, which broke through the world of religions, presupposes high cultures. Without the intensive experiences of the nations, without the gods of the pagans and the dry periods of disappointment that many had already endured Israel would not have been able to find its God at all.

*The right people.* The right place and the right time would, of course, have been of no avail if God had not found the right people who would open themselves to divine truth. The Bible does not speak of anonymous historical powers, but of concrete persons who listened to the word of God and thus made Israel possible: Abraham, Isaac, Jacob, Joseph, Moses. They constitute a series, and the series begins with Abraham.

It had to begin with *one person.* Why his name was not Socrates or Buddha or Confucius remains, ultimately, a mystery. Israel itself never ceased to reflect on this mystery, for the most part in the genre of legend, which is particularly well suited to this purpose. One of these legends tells how God first offered the Torah to all the nations:

> At first God went to the children of Esau. He asked them: Will you accept the Torah? They said right to His face: Master of the universe, what is written in it? He said: *Thou shalt not kill!* They replied: But this goes against our grain. Our father led us to rely only on the sword, because he was told: *By the sword shalt thou live* (Gen 27:40). We cannot accept the Torah.
>
> He then went to the children of Ammon and Moab, and asked them: Will you accept the Torah? They said right to His face: Master of the universe, what is written in it?" He said: *Thou shalt not commit adultery!* They replied: But our very origin is in adultery, for it is written *Thus were both the daughters of Lot with child by their father* (Gen 19:36). We cannot accept the Torah.
>
> Then He went to the children of Ishmael. He asked them: Will you accept the Torah? They said right to His face: Master of the universe, what is written in it? He said: *Thou shalt not steal!* They replied: It is our very nature to live only off that which is stolen, and that which is got by assault. Of our forbear Ishmael it is written *And he shall be a wild ass of a man: his hand shall be against every man, and every man's hand against him* (Gen 16:12). We cannot accept the Torah.
>
> At length He came to Israel. They said: *We will do and hearken.* (Exod 24:7)[48]

---

[48] Pesikta Rabbati Piska 21. From the English translation of W. G. Braude, *Pesikta Rabbati: Discourses for Feasts, Fasts, and Special Sabbaths.* 2 vols. Yale Judaica Series 18 (New Haven and London: Yale University Press, 1968) 1:417. Cf. also Günter Stemberger, *Das klassische Judentum. Kultur und Geschichte der rabbinischen Zeit* (Munich: Beck, 1979) 139–40.

This whole text is an interpretation of Deut 33:2: "The LORD came from Sinai, and dawned from Seir upon us." Israel's answer, drawn from Exod 24:7, promises action even before the content of the Torah is known. We could paraphrase it: "We will accept it now and ask about it later." Of course the whole is a relatively late legend, but it was often cited in Judaism and exists in many versions. It makes clear that God is concerned for *all* nations but can only begin the new social order—that is, the new society—where people are found who are ready to do God's will. The point of the legend is certainly not that Israel is morally better than the neighboring peoples but that it trusts its God: What God offers can only be good, because God is good.

The ingenious shape of the legend of course does not exclude the question of the content of the Torah even in the case of Israel; only the sequence is different: action comes first. This conclusion to the legend corresponds exactly to the way in which Abraham responds, in Gen 12:4, to God's command: "Go from your country." "So Abram went, as the LORD had told him." Abraham first of all does, silently, what God commands him.

Of course from a historical perspective this doing and hearing was an infinitely more differentiated process with initiatives and fragments in many nations. The theologians of the early Church would speak of the seeds of the "logos" among the nations.[49] But in Israel, beyond all preliminary stages, this process took a form that distinguished it fundamentally from all the Gentiles' hearing, and in the midst of Israel it ultimately found, in Jesus, its final goal.

The Jewish legend of the offering of the Torah to all nations also left its traces in Christian theology. It is probably in the background of a very comprehensive and at the same time very stringent saying of Maximus the Confessor: "It is not as if God chose Israel alone, but Israel alone chose to follow God."[50]

With this we arrive at the second concept, that of election. The "right constellation," after all, can by no means explain everything. That two people fall in love with each other of course presumes a certain combination of circumstances including, for example, that they meet at all (the right place, the right time). It includes also the predispositions existing in each of the two persons (for example, the image of the mother or the father). And yet in the end this constellation with all its pre-existing con-

---

[49] The first was Justin, *Apology 1*. 46; *Apology 2*. 8.3 and 13.3.

[50] Maximus the Confessor, *Coel. H.* 9. Quoted by Hans Urs von Balthasar, *Kosmische Liturgie: das Weltbild Maximus' des Bekenners* (Freiburg: Herder, 1941) 312 (2nd ed. Einsiedeln: Johannes, 1961) 306.

ditions cannot explain the decision of the two lovers, and it need not determine it. The element of "choice" enters, and is not derivable from anything else. In many cases it remains a mystery why someone falls in love with this particular person and not with some other. The mystery lies in the fact that in the ideal case two freedoms encounter one another.

Could it be any different with God and Israel? The election of Israel is like an anticipation of the mystery of the incarnation of the Son of God in this people. Such an election is, in its innermost being, not derivable any more than love is. This last fact is reflected repeatedly in the prophets:

> When Israel was a child, I loved him,
> and out of Egypt I called my son. (Hos 11:1)

> I give Egypt as your ransom,
> Ethiopia and Seba in exchange for you.
> Because you are precious in my sight, and honored, and I love you,
> I give people in return for you,
> nations in exchange for your life. (Isa 43:3-4)

The text from Isaiah must be read as the word of a lover; otherwise it can be misunderstood. Only the folly of love can say that it gives whole lands for the sake of the beloved. "Because you are precious in my sight, and honored" does not mean that Israel had special advantages over the other peoples. It receives its value solely through the eyes of the lover. In deuteronomic theology the groundlessness of God's love for God's people is sharply profiled. Israel has nothing special about it, nothing valuable, nothing that elevates it above the other nations—and yet God has chosen it:

> . . . the LORD your God has chosen you out of all the peoples on earth to be his people, his treasured possession. It was not because you were more numerous than any other people that the LORD set his heart on you and chose you—for you were the fewest of all peoples. It was because the LORD loved you and kept the oath that he swore to your ancestors, that the LORD has brought you out with a mighty hand, and redeemed you from the house of slavery, from the hand of Pharaoh king of Egypt. (Deut 7:6-8)

Finally, it is part of the biblical concept of election that it is always combined with a mandate. God's choice fell on Israel for the sake of the nations. God needs a witness in the world, a people in which God's salvation can be made visible. That is why the burden of election rests on the chosen people. Israel's being chosen is not a privilege or a preference *over others,* but existence *for others,* and hence the heaviest burden in history. Israel had to accept the consequences of being called out. It has been persecuted throughout the centuries, and the deepest reason for hatred of the Jews, beginning even in antiquity, continuing in the Church and finally leading to the Germans' million-fold factorylike murder of these people, was hatred of their election.

In fact the Church should for this reason reflect very deeply on the meaning of "divine election," of being "chosen." Today, however, the concept finds more despisers than lovers, despite its centrality and fundamental character in the Bible. Many simply repress it.[51] For others it is an insuperable offense. The very idea seems undemocratic, contrary to much-touted "open" and "global" thinking, and it is regarded as an indication of a dangerous fundamentalism. Election has become unappetizing.

However, in that case one ought to be consistent and relieve the whole Bible of its unappetizing character, for what is summarized in the concept of "election" is in fact central to it.[52] The concept crystallizes Israel's knowledge that God desires to liberate and change the entire world but for that purpose needs a beginning in the midst of the world, a visible place and living witnesses. This has not the slightest thing to do with preference, advantage, elitism, or being better-than, but it has a great deal to do with God's respect for human dignity and freedom. The first letter of Peter begins its circular to the Christian communities in Asia Minor with these words:

> Peter, an apostle of Jesus Christ, to the exiles of the Dispersion in Pontus, Galatia, Cappadocia, Asia, and Bithynia, who have been chosen and destined by God the Father and sanctified by the Spirit to be obedient to Jesus Christ . . . . (1 Pet 1:1-2)

We can see by the way this letter begins how central the concept of election is even in the New Testament. The author of 1 Peter does not hesitate to apply the great words of Israel's election to these Christian communities:

> . . . you are a chosen race, a royal priesthood, a holy nation, God's own people, in order that you may proclaim the mighty acts of him who called you out of darkness into his marvelous light. (1 Pet 2:9; cf. Exod 19:5-6)

In both texts the very sentence structure makes clear that election is not something for its own sake and that it does not serve the self-realization of those who are chosen. Instead, these are chosen *in order that* they may be obedient to Jesus Christ and *in order that* they may proclaim the mighty deeds of God.

---

[51] To take one rather comic example: some years ago, before there was any electronic word processing, a typesetter consistently changed every place in one of my manuscripts where the word "Erwählung" (election) appeared to read "Erwähnung" (mention). Sigmund Freud would have laughed.

[52] H. D. Preuß calls the entire first part of his *Theologie des Alten Testaments* "YHWH elects and obligates."

That God called people from Mesopotamia and Egypt, from Pontus, Galatia, and Cappadocia, is thus connected to the great divine plan for the whole world. But will God succeed? Will this plan come to fruition? Or will those to whom the plan has been entrusted misuse their mission, and will those for whom the plan was formed reject it? If so, God would be powerless. But if God's plan succeeds, why does that happen? Where can divine power lie, if for the sake of human freedom God rejects the violence of the revolutionaries and those who would improve the world?

## 7. What Does It Mean to Say that God Is Almighty?

The old catechisms asked, in their section on God's attributes, "Why do we say that God is almighty?" and answered: " We say that God is almighty because he can do everything he wills."[53] The answer was certainly correct, and yet it does not adequately express what the Apostles' Creed means to say, against the biblical background, when it asserts: "I believe in God, the Father Almighty (*pantokratora*)." When Scripture calls God the Pantocrator it is not in the first instance making an abstract statement about God's essence, but is speaking of God's concrete action in history: God is the one who governs all things.[54] God's creation does not go for naught. God's omnipotence consists precisely in the fact that God's plan for the world will succeed.[55]

The true significance of this statement of faith emerges, of course, only when one considers it in connection with human freedom. That a mechanically constructed creation should develop exactly according to the will of the constructor is easy to imagine and presents no problem. But God's creation is not a gigantic machine. Creation is "nature," something that grows out of itself, is called by God into an independent status and therefore moves, forms, and unfolds itself—and creation of this kind is a good deal more difficult to imagine in light of the omnipotence of God, that is, God's will that guides all things. Still, the independent status (*Eigenstand*) of nature is only the prelude to the freedom of the creature that is achieved in humanity. Human beings are the first creatures who are able to be entirely free. Therefore they can oppose God's plan. They can refuse to be a people of God. They can say: "I reject all of it."

[53] Bischöfliches Ordinariat Limburg a. d. Lahn, ed., *Katholischer Katechismus für das Bistum Limburg* (1936) 7; *Katholischer Katechismus der Bistümer Deutschlands* (Frankfurt a. M., 1955) 24.

[54] Cf. J.N.D. Kelly, *Early Christian Creeds* (3rd ed. New York: D. McKay, 1972) 136–39.

[55] *The Catechism of the Catholic Church* (Collegeville: The Liturgical Press, 1994) formulates accurately: "He is the master of history, governing hearts and events in keeping with his will" (# 269) 71.

The situation of God's omnipotence in the world is, in fact, even more problematic. It is not only that an individual human being can reject God and that in the course of history many individuals have done so. Sin does not remain confined within the individual: each is tied to the world outside by a thousand threads, and therefore every "no" to God incarnates itself in society, joins itself to the refusals of other individuals, and creates a potential for evil that already exists for those who come after, touches them in the depths of their being, and deprives them of opportunities for freedom and trust in God. Every refusal creates a particle of the history of evil in the world and narrows the possibility that a people of God can come to be. Christian tradition calls this pre-personal, social reality of evil into which individuals are born and whose models and structures of evil shape them even in their innermost being "original sin."[56]

Only against this background can we measure the weight of the statement that God is all-powerful. Acknowledging God's omnipotence then means not only believing in theory that God can do everything that lies within God's will, but much more concretely it means relying on the fact that God, despite all human refusals and in the face of all the history of evil that flows from it, will reach the goal in the end: a people that turns to God in confidence, and with that confidence and trust transforms the entire world.[57]

Jesus speaks, in fact, of this success of God's plan when he compares the reign of God with a mustard seed that grows into a great shrub:

> "With what can we compare the kingdom of God, or what parable will we use for it? It is like a mustard seed, which, when sown upon the ground, is the smallest of all the seeds on earth; yet when it is sown it grows up and becomes the greatest of all shrubs, and puts forth large branches, so that the birds of the air can make nests in its shade." (Mark 4:30-32)

The text immediately recalls the principle we encountered at the call of Abraham: God begins in the world in a small way. The parable of the mustard seed pushes this "smallness" to the limit: the seed of black mustard (*brassica nigra*) of which Jesus speaks here is in fact unusually small. One seed weighs approximately one milligram and has a diameter of 0.9 to 1.6 millimeters. It is certainly not to be expected that anything large can come from this tiny mustard seed, and yet the seed, the size of a pinhead, grows

---

[56] For more detail see Norbert Lohfink, "Das vorpersonale Böse," in idem, *Das Jüdische am Christentum. Die verlorene Dimension* (Freiburg: Herder, 1987) 167–99.

[57] Cf. the document of the diocesan synod of Augsburg 1990 (Donauwörth, 1991) 31: "God's omnipotence is shown most profoundly in that God has given us the freedom to say 'yes' or 'no' and nevertheless in the history of humanity achieves the goal of the divine plan through Jesus."

very rapidly into an annual bush with branches like those of a tree. The average height of a mustard bush is about five feet, and on the Sea of Gennesaret it can grow to a height of nine or ten feet.

A correct interpretation of the parable demands that we understand that the reign of God is not simply compared with the mustard seed but with the *whole process* in which the great bush emerges from the tiny seed. The reign of God is not like the mustard seed or the developed bush, but the whole process from seed to shrub. Thus the parable does not speak of the reign of God in static terms; it speaks of the way in which it comes. It tells how God accomplishes the divine plan, rule, and salvation in the world. God begins very small, but at the end something unexpectedly great comes from the tiny beginning.

When Mark speaks of the branches of the mustard bush and the shadow it throws, and of the birds that dwell in its shade, there are echoes of the mythic motif of the world tree. In the versions by Matthew and Luke[58] the motif emerges even more clearly. There the mustard bush is expressly called a "tree" in whose branches (not in its shade) the birds of the sky build their nests (Matt 13:32; Luke 13:19). Of course the world tree in the Old Testament and in the ancient Orient as a whole was the archetype of the king and the society that lives from the king's power. Therefore the symbol of the world tree always includes the birds and beasts that live in its shade:

> . . . a cedar of Lebanon,
> with fair branches and forest shade,
>    and of great height,
>    its top among the clouds.
> The waters nourished it,
>    the deep made it grow tall,
> making its rivers flow
>    around the place it was planted . . .
> its boughs grew large
>    and its branches long . . . .
> All the birds of the air
>    made their nests in its boughs;
> under its branches all the animals of the field
>    gave birth to their young;
> and in its shade
>    all great nations lived.

[58] For the question of the oldest version of the parable cf. Gerhard Lohfink, "Senfkorn und Weltenbaum (Mk 4,30-32 Parr). Zum Verhältnis von Natur und Gesellschaft bei Jesus," in Harald Schweizer, ed., ". . . *Bäume braucht man doch!" Das Symbol des Baumes zwischen Hoffnung und Zerstörung* (Sigmaringen: Thorbecke, 1986) 109–26, at 113–16.

It was beautiful in its greatness,
  in the length of its branches;
for its roots went down
  to abundant water.
The cedars in the garden of God
  could not rival it,
  nor the fir trees equal its boughs;
the plane trees were as nothing
  compared with its branches;
no tree in the garden of God
  was like it in beauty. (Ezek 31:3-8)

Against the background of this text from Ezekiel (cf. also Dan 4:10-12) we can clearly see that the parable of the mustard seed does not speak of the coming of the reign of God in the abstract. Rather the parable describes how a great people grows from the tiny beginning set by God, a world society in whose protecting shade the nations of the earth dwell. Still, independent of the symbol of the world tree it is a fact that whenever the Bible speaks of the royal reign of God, God's people, God's realm within the world is also in the picture. A sovereign without a people would be no sovereign at all.

The parable of the mustard seed is not isolated in Jesus' proclamation. It is part of a whole group of similitudes about the growth of God's reign in the world. Another example is the parable of the leaven:

> And again he said, "To what should I compare the kingdom of God? It is like yeast that a woman took and mixed in with three measures of flour until all of it was leavened." (Luke 13:20-21)

Again the tiny, insignificant thing is at the beginning: a bowl full of sourdough that will be kneaded into the flour to make bread. And again at the end there is something great, something extraordinary: the woman has mixed the sourdough with three measures of flour (almost ninety pounds of flour, enough for a meal for more than one hundred fifty people, or about one hundred ten pounds of bread).[59] The sourdough has leavened what for a normal household would be a gigantic amount of dough.

In contrast to the parable of the mustard seed, that of the leaven sets a new accent. The focus is no longer solely on the growth of something insignificant into something great, but also on "transformation": the sourdough leavens the whole mass of the flour, changes it, expands it and gives it taste. In the same way the reign of God, beginning in the world in such

---

[59] Ulrich Luz, *Das Evangelium nach Matthäus 2*. EKK 1/2 (Zürich: Benziger, and Neukirchen-Vluyn: Neukirchener Verlag, 1990) 333.

a small and hidden way, will at the end have changed and transformed everything. Jesus is absolutely sure of it.

Can we trust such certainty? Does it see the world as it really is, with its suffering, its guilt, its perversity, its darkness? Or is such certainty not really naïve and otherworldly? A third parable of growth shows that we cannot accuse Jesus of such naïveté:

> "A sower went out to sow. And as he sowed, some seed fell on the path, and the birds came and ate it up. Other seed fell on rocky ground, where it did not have much soil, and it sprang up quickly, since it had no depth of soil. And when the sun rose, it was scorched; and since it had no root, it withered away. Other seed fell among thorns, and the thorns grew up and choked it, and it yielded no grain. Other seed fell into good soil and brought forth grain, growing up and increasing and yielding thirty and sixty and a hundredfold." (Mark 4:3-8)

Differently from the parables of the mustard seed and the leaven, here we do not find an immediate story of success. On the contrary! Three-fourths of the parable describes opponents who threaten the growth of the grain and destroy some of the seed. Only the last quarter of the parable tells of success.

Of course we would miss the point of the parable if we were to see in it a set of statistics, a final accounting of God's success in the world, concluding that three quarters of God's efforts go for nothing and God has success in one one-fourth of all cases. The parable of the sower does not give an evenly balanced report about "different kinds of soil,"[60] but tells a story, one that aims at an end and clearly moves toward its climax.

We can more easily recognize this dynamic in the parable if we notice what the enemies of the seed do in each case: first we read of birds that eat part of the scattered seed. In this case the seeds do not even reach the point of sprouting. They are picked up immediately. Another part of the seed has a better chance: it sprouts and grows, but then it dries up because the layer of soil on the chalky stones is too thin. The part of the seed that falls among the thorns comes even closer to success: it sprouts, grows, and reaches a certain height, but it cannot produce its grain because it is smothered by the weeds that grow up with it. Thus the length of the seed's life increases and success comes closer and closer, but by the same token the destruction of the seed is more and more impressive. Only at the moment when the negative history of the seed has reached its climax, and

---

[60] A list of authors who understand the parable in this sense can be found in Gerhard Lohfink, "Das Gleichnis vom Sämann (Mk 4,3-9)," *BZ* 30 (1986) 36–69, at 48–49, reprinted in idem, *Studien zum Neuen Testament*. SBAB 5 NT (Stuttgart: Katholisches Bibelwerk, 1989) 91–130, at 105–106.

according to the law of popular narrative (three plus one) something new and conclusive is to be expected, does the narrative take a turn and describe an overwhelming success: part of the seed falls on good ground. The scattered seeds "increase," that is, they branch out at the lowest knob of the stock into numerous shoots and thus bear thirtyfold, sixtyfold, or a hundredfold.[61]

It is clear that here again we have a narrative about the work of God in the world. The whole parable describes how the reign of God comes into the world. Again we would miss the thread of the narrative if we said that only the rich yield at the end of the stalk is the reign of God. The parable describes the coming of the reign of God from the first words onward. That coming includes the sowing, the opponents that cause severe damage, and finally the abundant harvest that is brought forth in spite of all opposition.

However, another kind of reductionism must be avoided in interpreting the parable of the sower.[62] It is often said that the seed is the word of the gospel, and therefore the reign of God is present in the world only through the word. Not until the end of time will the reign of God break through the dimension of the word and appear in its full reality. That is a reductionist interpretation of the parable.

Mark 4:13-20, the oldest commentary we have on the parable of the sower, does interpret the seed as the word of God, but the same commentary (and this is often overlooked) also interprets the seed as the people who are sown: there are people who are sown on rocky ground, others sown among thorns, and finally people who are sown on good ground. The primitive Church's commentary on the parable in Mark 4:13-20 oscillates between the sowing of the word and the sowing of people.

For hearers at that time there was no contradiction in this, because on the one hand those living in the sphere of Greek culture were familiar with the idea that a teacher can drop words like seeds into the hearts of the hearers.[63] On the other hand there was a common idea in the East that a whole people could be sown like seed. In Jer 31:27 we read: "The days are surely coming, says the LORD, when I will sow the house of Israel and the house of Judah with the seed of humans and the seed of animals." The reference is to the growth of the people of God after the exile. God sows

---

[61] For more detail on the phenomenon of increase in Mark 4:3-9 see Gerhard Lohfink, "Das Gleichnis vom Sämann" 53–57 = idem, *Studien* 111–16.

[62] For what follows see Gerhard Lohfink, "Die Metaphorik der Aussaat im Gleichnis vom Sämann (Mk 4,3-9)," in *A cause de l'Evangile. Etudes sur les Synoptiques et les Actes. Mélanges offert à Dom Jacques Dupont.* LeDiv 123 (Paris: Cerf, 1985) 211–28; reprinted in Lohfink, *Studien* 131–47.

[63] For more detail see Gerhard Lohfink, "Metaphorik" 223–25 = idem, *Studien* 142–44.

people and cattle anew on the dried-up soil of Israel. Hosea 2:1-3, 23-25 formulates even more clearly: God will have mercy on Israel and will sow it anew. Then the people of God will spring up everywhere in the land like grain, and the old promise of the immeasurable growth of the seed of Abraham will be fulfilled.

In interpreting the parable of the sower one must take both of these interpretative possibilities seriously: the sowing of words and the sowing of people. Jesus wants to say that the seed of the gospel has been sown and the gospel now, as a newly creative word, begets the eschatological Israel. The people of God of the end time is already ripening, no matter how great the destructive power of its opponents.

This is certainly not naïveté or blind faith in progress. Jesus is very aware of the "impossibility" of the cause of God in the world. In his seed parables he depicts not only the unstoppable growth of the reign of God, but also the frightening smallness and hiddenness of its beginning; still more, he describes the superior power of the opponents who threaten the work of God from beginning to end.[64]

In doing so he does not take the path blazed by Jewish apocalyptic. That strain of thought was also deeply touched by the miserable condition of the people of God and the power of God's enemies in history, but the apocalypticists drew a different conclusion than Jesus did. For them it was no longer imaginable that God could still succeed in a world so damaged and depraved. In "this world," in "this eon," they said, the promises of God could no longer be fulfilled.[65] God must intervene violently in history, destroy the old world with fire and create a new world, the "new eon." Only in it could God's promises come true.

Jesus was no apocalypticist. He could certainly make use of apocalyptic imagery, but he did not teach an apocalyptic system. Above all, he never fell into the dualism of apocalyptic. This is evident from the material used in his parables of growth, all of it drawn from daily life. Jesus does not simply talk about the world tree, but begins with a banal mustard bush. He draws his imagery from the vegetable patch. And he speaks of something that a housewife in Israel did every day: grind flour, knead leaven into it, and bake bread. He speaks also of the poor fields belonging to the small farmers in the Palestinian hill country where the layer of soil is thin, where there are no fixed and fenced paths, and where thorns and thistles can scarcely be rooted out.

---

[64] Cf. also the parable of the weeds in the wheat in Matt 13:24-30.

[65] Cf. especially 2 Esdr 4:26-27: ". . . for the age [= this world] is hurrying swiftly to its end. It will not be able to bear the things that have been promised to the righteous in their appointed times *(non enim capiet portare quae in temporibus iustis repromissa sunt)*, because this age is full of sadness and infirmities."

With the aid of a world that was daily before the eyes of his audience he depicts the coming of the reign of God and thus makes clear that God's reign comes about in our ordinary, well-known, everyday surroundings. It does not come in apocalyptic thunderstorms, not in a grand action of God that no one can resist, but just as a mustard seed grows. The reign of God grows in secret, in the tiny, the insignificant, because God desires that the old world be transformed in freedom toward the reign of God. Jesus in his seed parables depicts a silent revolution, and the best symbol for it is growth. It happens in silence. A thing growing makes no noise.

Of course in this respect he has nothing in common with the theologians of the nineteenth and twentieth centuries who reduced the reign of God to a general moral development of humanity.[66] For Jesus the coming of the reign of God is indissolubly bound to the gathering of Israel, and the gathering of Israel is synonymous with following Jesus. "Whoever does not gather with me scatters" (Matt 12:30). For him the divine plan is not something vague, everywhere and nowhere, but is focused on a concrete people with clear contours, one that makes discernment possible.

Jesus says, with ultimate assurance, that the plan of God with this people will succeed, and will do so in this creation and this history, not just in the great beyond of the apocalypticists. Jesus says that God is not powerless, but in spite of all opponents will have success and—this is what is crucial—*not* by the use of violence, but precisely by means of human freedom, which God honors. What is the basis of this confidence?

Here again a parable can give us the answer. It is not one of the parables of growth, but is drawn from another group. Nevertheless it focuses precisely on our problem: how can the power of God and the freedom of human beings be reconciled? How can God be victorious in history without interfering in apocalyptic fashion in the world's course?

> "The kingdom of heaven [i.e., the kingdom of God] is like treasure hidden in a field, which someone found and hid; then in his joy he goes and sells all that he has and buys that field. Again, the kingdom of heaven is like a merchant in search of fine pearls; on finding one pearl of great value, he went and sold all that he had and bought it." (Matt 13:44-46)

Again we should note that the reign of God is not simply compared to the treasure and the pearl, but to the whole process by which a poor day-laborer finds a treasure and a rich merchant discovers a pearl. Thus here again Jesus is speaking of the way in which the reign of God comes; more precisely, he speaks of how it is possible for it to find lovers in the world.

---

[66] Characteristic representatives of this position in the nineteenth century were Richard Rothe and Albrecht Ritschl. Cf. the articles on eschatology and cultural Protestantism in *TRE* 10:325–29 and 20:230–43.

According to Matt 13:44-46 the starting points can be very different. There are people who stumble over the reign of God purely by chance. They were preoccupied with something completely different, but then, one day, they are confronted with the treasure. Others, like the rich merchant, have sought and looked everywhere, and finally they find what they have long dreamed of. As in all the double parables, then, the starting points are different, and therefore the thing that unites the two speaks all the more loudly: both these finders do not waste a minute. They are overcome by the sparkle of the treasure and the shimmer of the pearl. "When that great joy, surpassing all measure, seizes a man, it carries him away, penetrates his inmost being, subjugates his mind. All else seems valueless compared with that surpassing worth."[67] They sell what they have in order to acquire the thing found. The emphasis of the parable does not lie on the fact that they first must give all that they have.[68] What is crucial is the fascination exerted by their find, and the exuberant joy out of which they act. It is not hard at all to sell everything. Both of them are making the deal of their lives.

How, then, does God's omnipotence reach its goal in the world?—only through people and their freedom. It happens only through the fact that people are drawn and moved by *that* which they can desire with their whole hearts and with their whole might. But apparently it is only possible for them to desire in freedom what God also desires if they see, vividly, the beauty of God's cause, so that they experience joy and even passionate desire for the thing that God wills to do in the world, and this passion for God and God's cause is greater than all human self-centeredness.[69]

The merchant holds the pearl he has finally found to the light; the day-laborer plunges his hands into the silver coins his plow has hit upon. For Jesus the reign of God is tangible and visible. It does not simply exist in human hearts, nor is it hidden somewhere beyond history. It can be seen already, touched, acquired, traded. For that very reason it can fascinate people and move them to give up everything for the sake of this new thing without thereby losing their freedom. The sparkle and joy of the reign of God are at the same time its power of gravity, which ultimately moves all things and brings about the victory of God's grace in the world.

---

[67] Joachim Jeremias, *The Parables of Jesus* (rev. ed. New York: Scribner, 1963) 201.

[68] This is true, at least, of the original Jesus parable. The element of selling everything may be more strongly accented in Matthew's version.

[69] Cf. the comprehensive work of Ludwig Weimer, *Die Lust an Gott und seiner Sache. Oder: Lassen sich Gnade und Freiheit, Glaube und Vernunft, Erlösung und Befreiung vereinbaren?* (Freiburg: Herder, 1981), especially 429–98, which illuminates the problem from the point of view of systematic theology.

God is thus revealed as omnipotent precisely in the fact that God stakes everything on the intelligence, free will, and trust of human beings, thus surrendering all power and yet achieving the divine purpose in the world. God attains the goal desired because in this world joy in God's story is ultimately stronger than all inertia and greed, so that this joy continually seizes people and gathers them into the people of God.

What about the victims who do not survive to see the victory of God's cause?—the countless people who died too soon, when God had not yet found enough lovers for this divine cause, or who were deprived of their joy by false lovers? Would the apocalyptic way not be better—the realization that this world cannot sustain the promise, and therefore we should hope for its end? For the number of these victims is terrifying, and the total is far from being reckoned up.

Still, can one charge God with these victims? Are we not then on the same ground where Adam also made his excuse: "The woman *whom you gave to be with me*, she gave me fruit from the tree, and I ate"? That means, of course, that someone else is guilty, not I, and God is guilty of the whole situation and thus of everything.

False excuses are deeply rooted in us. They grow out of the darkening of our vision through original sin. In light of the Holocaust one sometimes hears from German theologians, "God was silent in Auschwitz," and then they develop a mysticism of the incomprehensibility of God. Why do they think about the nature of God in that context? Why do they not simply say, instead, "*we* were silent—when the windows of the Jewish shops were broken by the S.A., when the synagogues were set afire and when the Nazis gassed and burned our Jewish brothers and sisters"?

It is true that the price of freedom is fearful, the costs that arise from the fact that a human being can say "yes" or "no" to God. One dare not speak of the success of the divine plan without looking at all these victims. They show that the history of our freedom is not a cheap game. Countless human lives hang on our choice to come to the aid of the people of God or not. For when the cause of God lives and grows in the world, so do peace and justice, but if God's cause remains weak because of our rejection, then war, hatred, and violence grow.

We dare not charge God with the fearful victims that line the path of history as the price of the freedom that is given to human beings; we can only regard them as an appeal to us to turn back and join in the task of seeing to it that God has a people in the world in which God's will is done. That six million Jews were murdered is an event so appalling that it is beyond any kind of superficial interpretation. But if the Church's interpretation of the Holocaust were to be a provocation to itself to repent—out of sorrow over its own complicity—even the Holocaust could bear fruit.

It would seem to be part of the Church's repentance that it come to a deeper understanding of its own origins. The Church is not only rooted in Israel; it belongs to Israel. It cannot understand itself at all if it does not continually look back to its origins, beginning with Abraham. In Part I we dealt with the question: why does God need a special people? Now we must proceed to examine the way of that people, and its experiences on the way.

# II

# The Characteristic Signs of Israel

## 1. Gathering as a People of God

The title of this chapter may seem surprising. "Gathering" is not one of the classic theological categories. One would seek in vain for a corresponding term in a dictionary of essential biblical terms or a theology of the Old Testament.[1] This must be related to the onesidedness with which biblical phenomena are perceived, for the "gathering of the scattered people of God" has been, since the Babylonian exile, one of the fundamental statements of Israel's theology. Consider, first of all, Deut 30:1-6, a central text of deuteronomistic theology:

> When all these things have happened to you, the blessings and the curses that I have set before you, if you call them to mind among all the nations where the LORD your God has driven you, and return to the LORD your God, and you and your children obey him with all your heart and with all your soul, just as I am commanding you today, then the LORD your God will restore your fortunes and have compassion on you, *gathering* you again from all the peoples among whom the LORD your God has scattered you. Even if you are exiled to the ends of the world, from there the LORD your God will *gather* you, and from there he will bring you back.
>
> The LORD your God will bring you into the land that your ancestors possessed, and you will possess it; he will make you more prosperous and numerous than your ancestors. Moreover, the LORD your God will circumcise your heart and the heart of your descendants, so that you will love the LORD your God with all your heart and with all your soul, in order that you may live.

[1] In Horst Dietrich Preuss's two-volume *Theologie des Alten Testaments* (Stuttgart: Kohlhammer, 1991) this term appears neither in the index of terms nor in the index of Hebrew words.

Although in the literary fiction of the book of Deuteronomy the exile is still far in the future, this text presumes it: the curses that are threatened, in case the people do not follow the Torah that is laid before them,[2] have already been fulfilled. Israel was driven from its land and scattered among the nations.

However, the catastrophe of the exile is not the end of the people of God. If through its exile it comes to its senses and repents God will restore its fortunes. "Restore" here refers to the gathering of those scattered and their being led back to the land of Israel. The text emphasizes that this restoration does not merely put things back the way they were before the exile; rather it brings a blessing that far surpasses all the earlier demonstrations of God's favor. It introduces a new state of things for which the book of Jeremiah uses the term "new covenant."[3] God will circumcise the heart of the people so that it can live the Torah for sheer joy, and it will then be happier and more prosperous than in the time of its ancestors. It will truly come to life.

In Isaiah, Jeremiah, and Ezekiel the concept of "the gathering of Israel from those who were scattered" appears in many places, always with serious theological weight. "Gathering," in Hebrew *qbṣ* (parallel *'sp*), even becomes a soteriological *terminus technicus* in these prophetic books; that is, it is a fixed term for the bringing of salvation. "Gathering Israel" often parallels "help," "liberate," "rescue," "heal," and "redeem."[4]

The one who gathers the people is always God.[5] It is never said that Israel will gather itself. In most cases the background image is that of the shepherd who gathers the flock and leads it home,[6] and it is well known that scattered sheep cannot gather themselves together. In any case it is true that, just as the liberation from the house of slavery in Egypt was the work of God, so is the bringing back of the people from exile God's work, and God's alone.

It is often emphasized that God gathers the people from afar: from all lands, from all nations, from the ends of the earth, even from the ends of the heavens.[7] Obviously the goal of this gathering is a renewed dwelling in the land of Israel.[8] The gathering of the people of God of course means

[2] Deut 28:15-68; 29:20-28.

[3] Jeremiah 31:31. For the connection between Deut 30:1-10 and Jeremiah 29–31 cf. Georg Braulik, *Deuteronomium*. NEB (Würzburg: Echter, 1992) 2:216–17.

[4] Cf. Pss 106:47; 147:2-3; Isa 43:3-5; 54:5-7; Jer 31:10-11; Zeph 3:19; Zech 10:8-10.

[5] Cf. Neh 1:9; Pss 106:47; 107:3; 147:2; Isa 11:12; 40:11; 43:5; 54:7; 56:8; Jer 23:3; 29:14; 31:8; 32:37; Bar 4:37; Ezek 11:17; 20:34, 41; 28:25; 34:13; 36:24; 37:21; 39:27-28; Mic 2:12; 4:6; Zeph 3:19; Zech 10:10.

[6] Cf. Isa 40:11; Jer 23:3; 31:10; Ezek 34:13; Mic 2:12.

[7] Cf., for example, Jer 23:3; 29:14; 31:8; Bar 4:37; Ezek 11:17; Zech 10:10.

[8] This is especially frequent in Ezekiel. Cf. Ezek 11:17; 20:41-42; 28:25; 34:13; 36:24; 37:21; 39:28.

more than an external bringing together. It always means, in addition, that Israel achieves an internal unity:

> [The LORD] will raise a signal for the nations,
>     and will *assemble* the outcasts of Israel,
> and *gather* the dispersed of Judah
>     from the four corners of the earth.
> The jealousy of Ephraim shall depart,
>     the hostility of Judah shall be cut off;
> Ephraim shall not be jealous of Judah,
>     and Judah shall not be hostile towards Ephraim. (Isa 11:12-13)

Ephraim here stands for the northern kingdom, Judah for the southern kingdom. The division between the two kingdoms will be healed by the gathering of the people of God. The rivalry of the tribes will come to an end. The northern kingdom is no longer jealous of Jerusalem and the Temple; the southern kingdom buries its enmity toward the north.[9] Gathering thus aims at reconciliation. Something similar is said in Ezek 37:21-22. The purpose of gathering the exiled people is not only their return to the land, but also the overcoming of the divisions within the people of God:

> Thus says the LORD GOD: "I will take the people of Israel from the nations among which they have gone, and will gather them from every quarter, and bring them to their own land. I will make them one nation in the land, on the mountains of Israel; and one king shall be king over them all. Never again shall they be two nations, and never again shall they be divided into two kingdoms." (Ezek 37:21-22)

Especially in Ezekiel it is clear that the gathering of Israel in the post-exilic period has become a central statement of salvation, comparable with the leading out from Egypt, the original confession of the people of God. With "a mighty hand and an outstretched arm" God will lead the people out from among the nations just as God once led them out of Egypt.[10] In Jer 23:7-8 we even read:

> Therefore, the days are surely coming, says the LORD, when it shall no longer be said, "As the LORD lives who brought the people of Israel up out of the land of Egypt," but "As the LORD lives who brought out and led the offspring of the house of Israel out of the land of the north and out of all the lands where he had driven them"!

---

[9] Cf. Hans Wildberger, *Jesaja.* BK X/1 (Neukirchen-Vluyn: Neukirchener, 1972) 1:466, 471.

[10] Ezekiel 20:34. Cf. also the Exodus typology in Isa 11:16, in Isa 43:16-20 (and in all of Deutero-Isaiah), and in Zech 10:11.

In fact, this bringing of the people back from the diaspora gradually became a fundamental statement about God, who God is and how God acts. This is evident from the relative clause in Isa 56:8: "Thus says the LORD GOD, who gathers the outcasts of Israel . . . ." This is prayer language, a praise of divine action that has already become a fixed formula.[11] In the Tefillah, the eighteen-clause daily prayer of Israel formulated in the first century C.E., this development came to its conclusion. The tenth petition is: "Blow the great trumpet for our freedom, and lift a banner to *gather* our exiles, and *gather* us into one body from the four corners of the earth; blessed be thou, O Lord, who *gatherest* the outcasts of his people Israel."[12] It is clear that in this prayer the dispersal of Israel has long been an enduring situation. Correspondingly, the gathering of Israel remains an unremitting task. It is also clear that this is not merely a matter of external gathering; it involves the removal of everything that tears apart the people of God.

In addition, when considering the idea of the gathering of the people of God one should never entirely lose sight of the image of the scattered flock.[13] In that context "gathering" always includes an end to being cut off, and leading back into the community of the people of God. Thus Jesus was in a position to adopt the idea quite separately from the context of the Jewish diaspora and apply it to his own activity in Israel: "Whoever is not with me is against me, and whoever does not gather with me scatters."[14] The idea of the gathering of the people of God could also be separated from the special situation of the exile because it expressed something essential about Israel that was much older than the exile. To appreciate this situation it is necessary to go back some centuries before the time of the exile and take a look at the way in which Israel became a people.

In the Bible this process of Israel's becoming a single people is narrated in a very simple and orderly way: God calls Abraham, Abraham begets Isaac, Isaac begets Jacob, Jacob begets twelve sons who become

---

[11] Cf. also Ps 147:2.

[12] Lewis N. Dembitz, *Jewish Services in Synagogue and Home* (New York: Arno Press, 1975) 131. Translator's note: Dembitz describes this as a Sephardic prayer and gives it as the seventh benediction. The tenth, as given in a modern Jewish prayer book, reads: "Sound the great horn to proclaim freedom, inspire us to strive for the liberation of the oppressed, and let the song of liberty be heard in the four corners of the earth. Blessed is the Lord, Redeemer of the oppressed." (Central Conference of American Rabbis, *Gates of Prayer: The New Union Prayerbook* [New York: C.C.A.R., 1975]). The author quotes, in the sense given in the text above, from Hermann Strack and Paul Billerbeck, *Kommentar zum Neuen Testament aus Talmud und Midrasch* (3rd ed. Munich: Beck, 1961) IV, 1, 208–49.

[13] See n. 6 above. Especially important is the "shepherd chapter," Ezekiel 34.

[14] Matt 12:30; cf. 23:37. Jewish documents from this period could also say that the Messiah would gather the people of God: cf. Ps. Sol. 17:26.

the patriarchs of the twelve tribes. Jacob's family is brought to Egypt and there grows into a great people. At the Exodus from Egypt it already numbers 600,000 men,[15] therefore with women and children about three million people. After forty years in the desert the twelve tribes then march as a single force under Joshua's leadership into the promised land, conquer its cities, destroy those who oppose them, and take possession of the whole land.

This, somewhat simplified, is the course of the biblical narrative in the books of Genesis through Joshua. It is theology speaking in the form of a saga about how Israel became a people. We must ask ourselves what this description really intends to say, but first we must recognize that it does not coincide *in its surface details* with the historical facts. Archeology and historical criticism compel us to begin by looking at the origins of the twelve-tribe nation of Israel in a different way from that presented in the books of Genesis through Joshua.[16]

The book of Judges contains texts that draw a much more differentiated picture of the so-called "conquest of the land." Thus Judg 1:18-36 presents a long list of cities and districts in the midst of the land that Israel was unable to conquer even as late as the time of David. Biblical archeology has given us even more powerful counterarguments. For the period of the "conquest of the land" it cannot offer evidence that a single Canaanite city was destroyed by the Israelites. On the other hand, however, it does show that beginning with the thirteenth century B.C.E. there were new settlements at many places in the high country, and these settlements could not have been established by people coming from the desert, for the farmers who founded them already possessed an amazing skill in house construction, they paved streets with cobblestones, they knew how to build grain silos and waterproof cisterns, they used highly developed agricultural tools, and they terraced their fields to counter erosion. The occupation and settlement of the hill country of Palestine during the early Iron Age was evidently the work of a population well versed in agricultural technique. Where did they come from?

In the fruitful valleys of Palestine there had been numerous city states from the fourth millennium B.C.E. onward, with an established

---

[15] Exod 12:37. This number is certainly not to be interpreted realistically.

[16] In what follows I will follow primarily the essays by Helmut Engel, Hans-Winfried Jüngling, Philip J. King, and Norbert Lohfink in *BiKi* 38 (1993). The theme of the entire number is the origin of Israel. Cf. in addition Sebastian Bock, *Kleine Geschichte des Volkes Israel: von den Anfängen bis in die Zeit des Neuen Testamentes.* Herder Taschenbuch 1642 (Freiburg: Herder, 1989) 32–66; Rainer Albertz, *A History of Israelite Religion in the Old Testament Period.* Translated by John Bowden. 2 vols. (London: S.C.M., and Louisville: Westminster/John Knox, 1994) 1:40–103.

division of labor, a money economy, active mercantile contacts, monopolies on weapons, and religiously legitimated systems of government. The power of these cities was not restricted to the small compass of their walls. In the surrounding territory citizens without full civic rights and lesser tenants lived in undefended settlements; these were economically dependent on the cities and were forced to pay high taxes and perform military service. They were ruled and exploited by the cities.

There is much to favor the theory that Israel arose out of parts of this agrarian population: people who dared to withdraw from the rule of the cities, to build new settlements in the mountainous regions that were inaccessible to the chariots of the Canaanites and Philistines, and to live there in deliberate contrast to the oppressive system of the cities. Much also favors the proposition that during the same period social outcasts from the cities even dared an exodus and joined with the rebellious people of the land. Besides the archeological evidence there are two particular reasons for accepting this version of the origin of Israel, though at first it may appear very strange to us:

1. In Israel's early period God was called "El." This is shown not only by many biblical texts, but also by Israel's own name. *Isra-el* means "El reigns" or "may El reign," and perhaps "El fights" as well. El, however, was the highest god in the Canaanite family of gods. The fact that Israel has within its own name the name of a Canaanite god presupposes that the origin of the people lies within Canaan.

2. Israel had a deep-seated aversion to monarchy.[17] It was active for centuries but was especially apparent at the time when Saul and David began to introduce monarchy into Israel. This was a freedom-loving, anti-feudalistic, anti-monarchical impetus that broke through repeatedly. It must have been very old, and it is best explained on the basis of experiences of the agrarian society at the beginning, which had arisen out of opposition to the kings of the cities and their power.

Of course what has been said so far is not an adequate explanation for the origins of Israel. Israel worshiped its God not only as "El," but also under the name YHWH. Where did that name come from, and the experience connected with it? In addition, the narrative thread in the books of Exodus to Joshua that presumes that Israel came from the desert is much too strong to be simply set aside. It could have happened this way: The newly forming society coming out of the Canaanite cities or their sphere of dominance was joined by other groups of people who were not settled or only resident for part of the year, and who brought their own tribal and

---

[17] Cf. Judg 8:22-23; 9:8-15; 1 Sam 8:1-18; 12:12; Hos 13:9-11.

familial narratives with them. They must have included an Abraham group, an Isaac group, and a Jacob group, but the crucial element was the Moses group that had fled from Egypt and who to an extraordinary degree brought with them to the community the experience of a social exodus and a longing for freedom. Their God was YHWH, who was experienced as a God who saves followers from the hand of the powerful and leads them into freedom.

These groups, so diverse in themselves, gradually assembled as a social unit, a federation of tribes. They took over fundamental experiences from each other, especially faith in YHWH as a God who leads and saves those who are YHWH's own. The fact that this faith in YHWH that the Moses people brought with them succeeded so rapidly in Israel, a society that was Canaanite at the outset, must be connected with the circumstance that the groups that emerged from the Canaanite cities' sphere of dominance rejected their old gods as symbols of an unfree and feudally structured society, while in contrast they saw in YHWH the guarantor of the new society they sought. Add to this that in their exodus from the cities they had an experience that corresponded in many ways to that of the Moses people. Thus the old religion of El and Baal was overlaid by the YHWH-faith and in the process underwent a basic transformation.[18] When the book of Joshua describes how at the assembly at Shechem the twelve tribes were confronted by their leader, Joshua, with the question whether they would choose YHWH or the gods of the land (Josh 24:15), the scene certainly has a historical foundation: The Isra-El groups in Canaan freely adopted YHWH from the Moses group as their God.

This new grouping was "acephalous," that is, there was no central organ of government and no social stratification—hence the long, deeply rooted skepticism in Israel toward the later monarchy! People lived in extended families and tribes that were for the most part self-sufficient. In spite of this there was a strong sense of community between the individual groups. This was shown in common festivals at the various sanctuaries, in common narratives in which YHWH's saving deeds were recalled, in the strict separation from the social systems of the Canaanite cities, and finally in the common ethos. The formula "such a thing is not done in Israel"[19] clearly expresses the profound conviction of the tribes at that time.

The confederation of tribes thus did not constitute a political state. Compared with Canaanite rule it was a "stateless society," a society in the interstices of thoroughly established systems of rule. This experience

---

[18] This is formulated in agreement with Sebastian Bock, *Kleine Geschichte* 36, 61.

[19] 2 Samuel 13:12; cf. the formula "an outrage in Israel" (and various similar translations) in Gen 34:7; Deut 17:4; 22:21; Judg 20:6, 10.

would also remain fixed in Israel, and many centuries later, after the final destruction of any kind of independent statehood, it would help the people of God to survive as a "society among the nations."

The tribal confederation of Israel thought in passionately egalitarian terms. The phrase "liberty, equality, fraternity" was not an invention of the French Revolution. It stems from Christianity's Jewish heritage, and by its nature it goes back to the beginnings of Israel. After the experiences the originating groups in Israel had had with Egypt and the Canaanite cities they had no desire for another class society. This intent would be clearly recorded later in the Torah and there especially in the deuteronomic Law.

Thus at Israel's beginning—and that is the main point to be made here—there was a definite process of gathering, in fact a process of gathering quite different ethnic groups. These groups assembled themselves into a single nation, the people of God. We would do better to say that they were gathered into one people by God, for what is normal for human beings is scattering and isolation, not gathering. The individual groups thus entered into the sphere of experience of others, especially the Moses group, took over the experiences in the other group's past as their own, and from that point onward underwent those experiences themselves.

The fact that the Bible then incorporates the gathering of all these different ethnic groups into the artificial schema of Abraham, Isaac, Jacob, twelve sons of Jacob—thus converting existence side by side into a genealogical succession, a series of generations—is not a historical misrepresentation, but an eminently theological statement. At depth Israel certainly knew that it had many tribal ancestors and had come from many different directions. This knowledge is glimpsed when the book of Exodus says that at their departure from Egypt the Israelites were joined by "a mixed crowd."[20] When Israel's theology, despite this, derives the whole people of God from a single family it means to say that while there may have been many different groups at the beginning, YHWH made of them a single people, a new community of brothers and sisters and thus a "new family," and this was done through YHWH's action in the form of intervention and leadership. The genealogical tracing of all Israel to a single family seeks to inscribe this knowledge in terms of metaphoric language.

It is true that the concept of the gathering of Israel originated in the period of the exile, but the knowledge that the process of gathering is indispensable to the nature of the people of God is much older. This knowledge must have accompanied Israel from the beginning, from the time when it became a people. The people of God became what it was through a

---

[20] Exodus 12:38; cf. Num 11:4. On this see Albertz, *History of Israelite Religion* 1:44 and 257 n. 19.

process of gathering of many groups, and the necessity of assembling the people continued to accompany it through history, for Israel was constantly in danger of falling apart. King Josiah sought to bring the people together through his reform.[21] The prophets repeatedly attempted to gather the people. Jesus wanted nothing more than to gather Israel anew in light of the approach of the reign of God.[22] Since Easter the name of the Israel gathered around Jesus is *ekklēsia* (congregation, assembly), and wherever in Judaism the knowledge emerges that Israel must come together there suddenly appears the word "kibbutz," from the old theological concept of *qbṣ*, "gather."

In what is probably the finest of the eucharistic prayers the Roman Catholic Church possesses the idea of the gathering of the people of God occurs at the very beginning:

> Father, you are holy indeed,
> and all creation rightly gives you praise.
> All life, all holiness comes from you
> through your Son, Jesus Christ our Lord,
> by the working of the Holy Spirit.
> From age to age you gather a people to yourself,
> so that from east to west
> a perfect offering may be made
> to the glory of your name.[23]

This should give us pause for thought. "The gathering of the people of God" is not just one concept that can be added to a whole list of others but that we can just as well get along without. It is an essential concept. The people of God cannot exist without constantly gathering from all the corners of the universe. It cannot exist without bringing together all its strengths and abilities, and it cannot live without constantly reconciling itself. When that happens it is not simply preparation for service to the world that can only begin after this has happened, but it *is* the service that the people of God does for the world. For the world experiences separations and divisions at all times and everywhere. Scattering is an ancient

---

[21] For more detail on Josiah's reform movement see Norbert Lohfink, "Gab es eine deuteronomistische Bewegung?" in idem, *Studien zum Deuteronomium und zur deuteronomistischen Literatur III.* SBAB 20 (Stuttgart: Katholisches Bibelwerk, 1995) 65–142, at 111–17.

[22] Cf. Gerhard Lohfink, *Jesus and Community: The Social Dimension of Christian Faith.* Translated by John P. Galvin (Philadelphia: Fortress, 1984), Part I: Jesus and Israel.

[23] *Vere sanctus es, Domine, et merito te laudat omnis a te condita creatura, quia per Filium tuum, Dominum nostrum Iesum Christum, Spiritus Sancti operante virtute vivificas et sanctificas universa, et populum tibi congregare non desinis, ut a solis ortu usque ad occasum oblatio munda offeratur nomini tuo.* (Eucharistic Prayer III)

phenomenon. On the other hand, gathering into a free, equal, and reconciled society is something ever new. Only in the real, visible existence of
such a society is the world served, only in it does genuine divine service
happen, only in its existence is God praised.

Therefore the newly popular paired concepts of "gathering and sending" represent a falsehood if they are understood in such a way that the
gathering of the people of God is only the precondition for its true task:
being sent into the world. Those who think this way show how foreign the
Bible has become for them,[24] for in the Bible the prophets and apostles are
sent precisely *in order to* gather the people of God.[25] "Mission to gather
the people of God" would be a biblical idea, for it is certainly clear that
only a people of God that has allowed itself to be gathered into unity and
unanimity could convince the world.

## 2. A People of Faith

The experience of God's having drawn together some very different
groups into a "new family" of brothers and sisters could be illustrated in
Israel's early history only in terms of a genealogical system. Today we
have to translate into our own language what the sequence Abraham,
Isaac, Jacob, twelve sons of Jacob is meant to say. But does this sequence
of generations really mean a "new family," a new band of people who
originally had nothing to do with one another but had allowed themselves
to be brought together to form something new? Is this really a matter of a
new kind of solidarity that rests not on ethnic connections but on common
experience—the experience that God acts, saves, gathers a people and
gives it a future?

Is it not a fact that in Israel blood and natural descent play the critical
role? Doesn't everything depend on having the right connections? Didn't
Abraham's slave have to make a long and perilous journey to Mesopotamia
to bring back a wife for Isaac out of Abraham's kindred (Genesis 24)? And
didn't Jacob, too, have to go to Mesopotamia to find his wife (Genesis

---

[24] Medard Kehl, *Die Kirche. Eine katholische Ekklesiologie* (3rd ed. Würzburg: Echter,
1994) 93 rightly opposes such an ordering of mission as a second step in contrast to gathering.

[25] Cf. the central biblical mission texts: Exod 3:14-15; Isa 6:8; 61:1; Jer 1:7; Ezek 2:3-
4; 3:5-6; Matt 10:5-6; 15:24; 23:34; Mark 3:14; 6:7; Luke 4:18; 9:2; 10:1; Acts 3:20. They
speak without exception of a mission to the people of God. Very seldom does the Bible
speak of a sending "into the world" or "to the Gentiles," but when it does (cf. John 17:18
or Acts 22:21) this is in the sense of John 11:52 ("to gather into one the dispersed children
of God") or in that of Matt 28:19, where the disciples are sent to all nations to gather communities of disciples ("make disciples"). Obviously none of this in any way minimizes the
Church's mission in the world. The only question is: how is it carried out?

28–31)? Must one not be a physical descendant of Abraham to receive the blessing given to Abraham?

Obviously the natural family and physical relationship play a dominant role in Israel. We may take it for granted that especially in the first centuries of the people's history the solidarity of the extended family, the clan, and the tribe held the society together and empowered it in a number of ways. After the return from exile there was a similar situation once again.[26] And yet the biblical tradition shows from the outset that the existence of the people of God did not depend on blood or natural relationship, and certainly not on any automatic consequence of genealogy.

Abraham, the figure in whom Israel concentrated experiences stretching over centuries in its past, was brought by God "from [his] country and [his] kindred and [his] father's house" (Gen 12:1). These three phrases draw the circle smaller and smaller. The "country" is the homeland as a whole, the "kindred" are the clan, the "father's house" the family. Abraham is ripped away from all these roots, and the people of God, like its ancestor, must continually allow itself to be torn away from all national and relational ties.

It was not enough for the patriarchal narrative to concentrate this cutting loose in the figure of Abraham. It goes on. Abraham and Sarah could no longer have children, for Abraham was a hundred years old and Sarah ninety (Gen 17:17). The fact that Sarah nevertheless becomes pregnant and brings forth an heir is due solely to the gracious intervention of God (Gen 21:1). In this connection the text says explicitly: "Is anything too wonderful for the LORD?" (Gen 18:14). The narrator's interest is not in a biological miracle but in the fact that the continuation of God's cause from Abraham and Sarah to the next generation can by no means be achieved by the begetting, bearing, and raising of a son in a pious family; it is the work of God, which in turn presupposes people's faith that God will act.

All this is led to a still more profound level in the story of the "sacrifice of Isaac" (Gen 22:1-19). God means to test Abraham. God commands him to sacrifice Isaac, his heir, his beloved son, as a burnt offering on a mountain. The Enlightenment took enormous offense at this most accomplished and inscrutable of all the patriarchal narratives. Immanuel Kant wrote in his "Quarrel of the philosophical faculty with the theological faculty":

> But he [the human being] can certainly be convinced that in some cases it cannot be God whose voice he [the human being] thinks he hears; for if what [the voice] commands is contrary to the moral law, no matter how majestic

---

[26] Cf. the problem of mixed marriages in the time of Nehemiah and Ezra (Neh 13:23-31; Ezra 9:1-4; 10:1-44).

and surpassing all nature the vision may seem to be, he must regard it as an illusion.[27]

Kant explains this in a note:

> We may take as an example the myth of the sacrifice that Abraham was supposed to make, at divine command, by slaughtering his only son (and the poor child in his ignorance carried the wood, besides). Abraham should have said to this supposedly divine voice: It is quite certain that I should not kill my good son; but that you, who appear to me, are God, is something I cannot be sure of, nor can I be, even though the voice thunder from heaven.

Kant had not seen that humanity does not simply have at its disposal "the moral law" as a rational standard for every action. Certainly that law is written in the world and in the human heart, but even moral and religious people are in the habit of deceiving their consciences, and so themselves, in the craftiest ways when their own desires are at stake. That the "moral law" can be recognized, obeyed, and handed on depends on the fact that there is a people in the world that has made the will of God the center of its existence, its very sanctuary. And that such a people was possible at all depended on the fact that there were people like Abraham who surrendered themselves to the will of God by binding their own wills entirely to the will of God.

Abraham was ready to give up the dearest and most precious good he possessed for the sake of his God. Consider, after all, that Isaac was not only Abraham's natural hope. Isaac was at the same time the bearer of the promise for the sake of which Abraham had left his homeland. He gave him up, and with him all his hope and his entire future. The story says that Abraham did not withhold his only son from God (Gen 22:16). That means that he did not exclude him from his faith in God. Abraham did not say, "I will believe you, my God, and do your will, but there are some things that even you may not touch. My son I will not give up."

Abraham silently surrendered himself to God. He sacrificed his own ideas and plans and handed himself over to the will of God, even though for the moment he could not understand that will. However, Abraham's obedience was not blind. It was founded on God's assurance. Abraham, in his testing, believed anew in God's promise. He let himself be led by God. He entrusted himself to God without reservation. Thus Isaac experienced his father, in the midst of this terrible event, as a person of faith. He learned from his father's behavior what faith means. And therefore he, too, could believe.

---

[27] Quoted by Claus Westermann, *Genesis: A Commentary* (Minneapolis: Augsburg, 1984–1986) 2:432–33.

Thus faith can only be successfully handed on if children see in their parents that God is more important to them than anything else in the world, even more important than their own child. Abraham was ready to hand over his son, and therefore he received him back from God. He received him back as his child, but at the same time as a son who had seen his father's faith and thus himself became a believer.

It should already be clear that the patriarchal narratives intend to show that Israel did not arise out of natural descent, but from God's election and from faith in the promise: Abraham had to leave his father's house. Isaac could only be conceived because his parents believed God. And even then the next generation of the people of God was not assured. Abraham had to give up his child and receive him anew, now really as a child of faith in the promise.

The stories of the patriarchs continue with the biblical narrators demonstrating that not only the transition from the first to the second generation shows that Israel is something more than an automatic succession of natural generations. With the transition from the second to the third generation the readers receive the next clue: Isaac's natural heir would have been Esau, Rebecca and Isaac's firstborn son, but Esau sells his right as the firstborn to his brother Jacob for a pot of lentils. His urgent hunger, his momentary greed was more important to him than the line of the promise (Gen 25:27-34), and so Jacob became the heir, the father of the twelve tribes, the one who carries forward God's history with God's people. Of course both he and Isaac first have to learn to believe. At any rate that is how Jacob's years of service to Laban, his reconciliation with Esau, and his struggle with God are understood.[28]

At the transition from the third to the fourth generation the story repeats itself. Leah's son Reuben is Jacob's firstborn (Gen 35:23), but Reuben does not become the primary actor in this part of Genesis; instead it is Joseph, the son of Rachel. It is Joseph who saves his father and brothers from famine and thus secures Israel's survival.

Still, this is not enough: with the sons of Joseph, at the transition from the fourth to the fifth generation, the story shows again that among the people of God the line of the promise does not coincide with the natural sequence of inheritance—that is, that Israel arises out of divine action and its reliance on that action, and not from physical birth: before his death Jacob gives the firstborn's blessing not to Manasseh, Joseph's elder son, but to Ephraim, the second in order of birth (Genesis 48). Joseph's protest is fruitless.

---

[28] Jacob's service to Laban is described in Genesis 29–31, his reconciliation with Esau in Genesis 32–33, and his struggle with God in Gen 32:23-33.

Centuries later Paul was faced with the question whether the Gentiles, without being born in Israel and without circumcision, could become children of Abraham. His answer was that belonging to Israel could not be defined by physical descent.

> . . . not all Israelites truly belong to Israel, and not all of Abraham's children are his true descendants . . . . it is not the children of the flesh who are the children of God, but the children of the promise are counted as descendants. (Rom 9:6-8)

For this view of things Paul rightly appeals to the stories of the patriarchs in Genesis,[29] for what he writes only brings to verbal expression what is encountered in those stories as a persistently recurring narrative motif.

What the stories of the patriarchs illustrate in narrative form the Torah validates in its own way. It determines that every firstborn Israelite male belongs in a special way to YHWH and is only returned to his own family through redemption in the Temple. Through this repurchase in the Temple he is at the same time received anew from the hand of God (Exod 13:2, 11-16). He is not to be idolized as a "son and heir," but is to be led into faith. He is not to serve the clan but the upbuilding of the people of God.

The idea that the firstborn son is God's property received special importance in Israel because this idea was given a salvation-historical foundation in the Exodus from Egypt and was theologically connected to the levitical institution. The Levites lived without any connection to a clan or tribe. Instead, they were bound to YHWH.[30] They remained YHWH's property throughout their lives to make visible in themselves, as enduring real symbols, what was in fact true of all Israel. In Num 3:11-13 this symbolic connection between the Levites and the firstborn was explicitly formulated:

> Then the LORD spoke to Moses, saying: I hereby accept the Levites from among the Israelites as substitutes for all the firstborn that open the womb among the Israelites. The Levites shall be mine, for all the firstborn are mine; when I killed all the firstborn in the land of Egypt, I consecrated for my own all the firstborn in Israel, both human and animal; they shall be mine. I am the LORD.

What is at stake in such a legal text, which at first appears extremely odd to people of the present time? In being required to dedicate the firstborn males to God Israel has it called to its attention, again and again, how necessary it is, from generation to generation, to break through the private

---

[29] Rom 4:19-22; 9:6-13; Gal 4:21-31.

[30] Cf. Albertz, *History of Israelite Religion* 1:82–83. Important texts are Exod 32:26-29 and Deut 33:9.

interests of the natural family, which continually draw people away from God's cause. And so that this obligation will be brought to the attention of the families in Israel not only when a first son is born, but constantly, there are the Levites, whose whole existence is meant to express the primacy of God's cause over all natural interests. The stories of the patriarchs demonstrate the same thing in their own way: The people of God is not a natural entity. It lives solely out of its free election by God, and it lives from faith in the promise.

The same thing is demonstrated in a completely different way in an event narrated in the book of Numbers. Israel is still in the wilderness, on the borders of the land of Canaan. Twelve messengers are sent out to explore the promised land. They come back laden with produce and report on the fruitfulness of the land, but at the same time they bring back rumors about the size and dangerous nature of the inhabitants. There is a loud outcry and all the Israelites begin to grumble: "Would that we had died in the land of Egypt!" (Num 13:1–14:4).

This narrative also summarizes experiences that the people of God had to go through again and again: The land into which God leads them is a good and beautiful one, but it is maligned even by the pious as a land in which no one can live, a land that devours its inhabitants. According to the theology of the Priestly writing this constitutes "slandering the land," and is the true sin of the people of God.[31]

What is crucial for our context is that God punishes the slandering of the promised land by causing the generation that grumbled to remain in the wilderness and die there. They will never see the land (Num 14:22-23). Thus it is again clear that the natural sequence of generations cannot secure the promise. A whole generation dies in the wilderness because they did not believe and trust. The people of God appears to be at an end, and yet God does not let this history with Israel be broken off. God maintains the promise, making a new beginning out of pure graciousness. God promises to lead the *children* of this lost generation into the land. They will learn to know the land that their grumbling parents slandered and defamed. They will discover that it really does flow with milk and honey (Num 14:31).

Thus it is not enough to be a physical descendant of Abraham. God cuts, so to speak, the genealogical connection. The promise must be grasped anew by each generation.[32] John the Baptizer would tie his preaching of repentance to the story at precisely this point: "Do not presume to say to yourselves, 'We have Abraham as our ancestor'; for I tell

---

[31] Cf. Norbert Lohfink, "Original Sins in the Priestly Historical Narrative," *Theology of the Pentateuch* (Minneapolis: Fortress, 1994) 96–115.

[32] Deuteronomy 1–2 takes up this context again; cf. especially 1:26-39.

you, God is able from these stones to raise up children to Abraham" (Matt 3:9). The reference to the stones, of course, is connected with the fact that John preached in the wilderness. Why did he go there? Why did he call Israel into the wilderness to himself rather than appearing in the towns and villages, as Jesus would do a little later? Why did he lead the people into the water of the Jordan to immerse them? And why did he baptize at a particular point on the lower course of the Jordan, on the eastern bank, opposite Jericho, exactly where, according to the old stories, Joshua once led the children of the wilderness generation through the river into the land?

There is only one sensible answer to these questions: The Baptizer wanted to put the people of God back into the situation of Israel in the desert so that it could learn there once again to trust in its God, and he wanted to bring them back from the wilderness through the water of the Jordan once more to the borders of the promised land. That is: John reproduced for the people of God the situation of their beginnings, the situation of a new generation that no longer grumbles, but believes in the promise. All Israel is subject to the wrath of God. It is useless to appeal to one's physical descent from Abraham. Only a completely new beginning corresponding to the passage through the Jordan of old can yet save the people of God.[33]

All this throws an intense light on Christian baptism, which originates in John's baptism.[34] On the basis of its origins it is utterly different from what it became in the Christian West when everyone was a Christian and there was no alternative, so that obligatory baptism became an almost natural process by which the birth of a child was sanctified. Certainly the Church's baptismal liturgy and theology envisioned something completely different from the outset, but factually baptism has all too often become a religious ornament to natural birth. And yet, against the background of John's baptism, Christian baptism is a break with everything that had gone before, a rescue from the coercive forces that continue from generation to generation, entry into the land of promise, inclusion in the new society of the Church. Baptism makes visible the fact that no one can be born or begotten into the Church by natural means. "A person is a Christian not because of descent or belonging to a particular nation or a particular culture; a person is a Christian, rather, because of God's free, gracious election and the free decision of faith that responds to it."[35]

---

[33] Cf. Hartmut Stegemann, *Die Essener, Qumran, Johannes der Täufer und Jesus: ein Sachbuch.* Herder Spektrum 4128 (Freiburg: Herder, 1994) 294–99.

[34] Cf. Gerhard Lohfink, "Der Ursprung der christlichen Taufe" in idem, *Studien zum Neuen Testament* (Stuttgart: Katholisches Bibelwerk, 1989) 173–98.

[35] Walter Kasper, "Natur—Gnade—Kultur. Zur Bedeutung der modernen Säkularisierung," *ThQ* 170 (1990) 81–97, at 82.

## 3. The Exodus Experience

At the beginning of this second part of the book we inquired about the origins of the people of God. It appeared evident that Israel arose through a process of gathering and not from the biological potency of a particular tribe. Even the patriarchal narratives, which apparently have as their theme the descent of Israel from a single tribal ancestor, tirelessly indicate that the line of election is not coincident with the right of inheritance and descent. The genealogy Abraham, Isaac, Jacob, twelve sons of Jacob is meant to emphasize the constancy of God's action, God's firm fidelity to the promise, but not the purity of blood and race. However, not only the call of Abraham but also the Exodus from Egypt played a crucial role in this story of the unfailing care of God for this new beginning now being made in the world.

The Exodus was Israel's primeval experience, the founding event of the people of God. We do not know how the oldest stories about this event may have sounded, but there must have been some. They were handed on by the Moses group, the people who had fled from Egypt. Other groups of the tribal alliance then forming in Palestine took over the Exodus stories of the Moses group and discovered in them a reflection of their own history. At some point, then, the Exodus experiences were combined with the *pesaḥ* festival, and they live on in this combined form in Israel's memory. Every year all Israel remembers the Exodus in this way. In every Passover night the youngest child asks: "Why is this night different from all other nights?"[36] Every year the participants in the Passover meal hear the story of the Exodus from Egypt, and every one of them is, as the Mishna explicitly says, "required to see oneself as one who has come out of Egypt."[37] The central text of this making-present of the past event, which may be regarded as Israel's *credo,* is Deut 26:5-10. In the "I" and "we" of this text the past of the people of God is drawn into the speaker's present:

> A wandering Aramean was my ancestor; he went down into Egypt and lived there as an alien, few in number, and there he became a great nation, mighty and populous. When the Egyptians treated us harshly and afflicted us, by imposing hard labor on us, we cried to the LORD, the God of our ancestors; the LORD heard our voice and saw our affliction, our toil, and our oppression. The LORD brought us out of Egypt with a mighty hand and an outstretched arm, with a terrifying display of power, and with signs and wonders; and he brought us into this place and gave us this land, a land flowing with milk and honey.

[36] Cf. *m. Pesaḥ.* X, 4.

[37] Cf. *m. Pesaḥ.* X, 5: "In every generation each one is required to regard himself or herself as though he or she had come out of Egypt."

The Exodus narratives would not have been able to found a festival if they had been nothing but dry accounts of the departure from Egypt. They quickly became much more. As they were told and retold they became a river whose stream flowed more and more powerfully. They were concentrated into magnificent pictures and stylized through powerful symbols that interpret the historical event. Thus in Exod 15:1-18 the water of the Reed Sea became a mythic symbol of the underworld, death, chaos, nothingness, and YHWH became a terrifying war hero who, to save his people, seized Pharaoh's chariots and hurled them into the sea.

It is wrong to be suspicious of such expansion and stylization, for in this very way the Exodus texts became a *figura,* an enduring figure to support memory, the original image for all generations.[38] In this very way, and only in this way, they were enabled to summarize within themselves all Israel's later exodus experiences. They retain not only the experiences of the Moses group, and not only the experiences of those groups that extracted themselves from the sphere of influence of the Canaanite city states. They also condensed Israel's experience with its own lack of freedom and the compulsions that it created within itself in the course of its later history, as well as the continually renewed exodus from that state of unfreedom. What kind of unfreedom are we talking about?

The group that had been in Egypt was living there within a closed social system.[39] Society, state, culture, nature, cosmos, religion, rule, wholeness, and salvation were melded within this system into a grandiose unity, and the unity of all these areas was visible in the person of the Pharaoh. He was the focus of meaning for the entire country. He was the divine king. He was the real image of the Sun God. He secured the fullness of life for the whole land, and even for the cosmos itself. Every time a new Pharaoh ascended the throne he brought the disordered cosmos back into working order, enabled anew the cooperative action of the cosmic powers, and restored the old fullness of blessing.

The Pharaoh was even the measure of the immortality of his inferiors, that is, their eternal life, for he defended and secured all the graves in the land. The artisans and artists were organized in quasi-military fashion and were all in the royal service, or more precisely in the service of the royal cult of the dead. Thus all salvation came from the state. The flight of a

---

[38] For an extensive discussion of the typological structure of Exod 15:1-19 see Norbert Lohfink, *The Christian Meaning of the Old Testament.* Translated by R. A. Wilson (Milwaukee: Bruce, 1968) 67–86.

[39] For what follows on the society and world of meaning in Egypt I am indebted to the work of Jan Assmann, *MA^{c}AT. Gerechtigkeit und Unsterblichkeit im alten Ägypten* (Munich: Beck, 1990); cf. especially 18–24, 52–55, 218–22, 230, 244–45.

slave or an escape from the public work brigades was something that was nearly unthinkable, not only because the state system of planning and control was perfect, but because every Egyptian would have regarded such a flight as a "criminal disruption of the public order of well-being."[40]

Now of course all this does not mean that there was no system of morality in Egypt. There was indeed such a system, symbolized by the goddess Maʿat, a highly developed ethic of humanity and solidarity, of listening to one another and acting on behalf of one another.[41] But this ethic was also fully integrated into the state theology: From Pharaoh through his civil servants justice flowed over the land, and in turn all his inferiors were required to act justly.

When the Moses group broke out of Egypt that closed social system was probably already undercut and weakened, for since the period of the New Empire, especially beginning in the thirteenth century B.C.E., Egyptian texts reveal a shift to "personal piety," which for the first time placed human beings immediately before God, and no longer through the mediation of the Pharaoh.[42]

In any case this new form of piety would not have changed anything in the situation of the Moses people. They must have continued to experience the symbols of sacralized power in the most vivid fashion: the pyramids, the gigantic cities of the dead, the central granaries, the forced recruiting for the royal labor corps, the planned economy, the bloated bureaucracy, the border police, the perfect organization of power. The biblical Exodus stories still show awareness that the Israelites had to build "supply cities, Pithom and Rameses, for Pharaoh" (Exod 1:11) and report the existence of taskmasters and inhuman work rules.

The Moses group fled from this system, but the groups that set themselves in opposition to the power of the kings of the Canaanite cities at the same period were fleeing similar systems. They also made an exodus and could therefore find their experiences reflected in the stories of the Moses people. And when, two hundred fifty years later, Israel itself became a state and its own kings introduced forced labor and built up a royal administrative apparatus[43] the recollection of the departure from Egypt took on new contours. The Exodus stories now became a critique of their own state, which was in the process of betraying the ancient ideals of the tribal

---

[40] Cf. Erich Zenger, *Der Gott der Bibel. Sachbuch zu den Anfängen des alttestamentlichen Gottesglaubens* (Stuttgart: Katholisches Bibelwerk 1979) 97.

[41] The real purpose of Jan Assmann's book, *MAʿAT*, is to show this. Cf. there especially 58–121 (89!).

[42] Cf. Jan Assmann, *MAʿAT* 252–72.

[43] Cf. 2 Sam 20:24; 1 Kings 4:6; 5:13-14; 12:18 (!). On this see Albertz, *History of Israelite Religion* 1:218–19.

alliance, namely freedom, equality, and fraternity, and assuming for itself a quasi-divine rule.

From this point of view it is clear how many-layered the Exodus narratives are as we now find them in the Bible. Their final form reflects the experiences with Egypt, but also the experiences Israel had to go through in its own existence as a state. Once we have understood that, we can read these narratives once more anew, without constantly trying to reconstruct the first Exodus out of them, but with a sharpened eye for their true theological concerns.

If we look at the Exodus texts in this way, purely at the level of narrative, we notice at once that the departure itself is told much more briefly than the history that precedes it. "Only after a positively torturous long-drawn-out tension" is Israel's liberation finally successful.[44] There are a number of reasons for this drawing out of the narrative. One is that before the event of the Exodus actually happens the narrative tries out various possibilities, exploring ways in which the Israelites could act in confrontation with an over-powerful state.[45] The first possibility is that they do as the Hebrew midwives did:

> The king of Egypt said to the Hebrew midwives, one of whom was named Shiphrah and the other Puah, "When you act as midwives to the Hebrew women, and see them on the birthstool, if it is a boy, kill him; but if it is a girl, she shall live." But the midwives feared God; they did not do as the king of Egypt commanded them, but they let the boys live. So the king of Egypt summoned the midwives and said to them, "Why have you done this, and allowed the boys to live?" The midwives said to Pharaoh, "Because the Hebrew women are not like the Egyptian women; for they are vigorous and give birth before the midwife comes to them." So God dealt well with the midwives; and the people multiplied and became very strong. And because the midwives feared God, he gave them families. (Exod 1:15-21)

We could entitle this first possibility "passive resistance." It is not yet as thoroughly thought out and organized as passive resistance in modern liberation movements; it is more like the craftiness of the sly soldier Schweik. This resistance is successful at first, but in the long run it fails, as the continuation of the narrative shows: at some point the state sees

---

[44] Helmut Utzschneider, *Gottes langer Atem. Die Exoduserzählung (Ex 1–14) in ästhetischer und historischer Sicht.* SBS 166 (Stuttgart: Katholisches Bibelwerk 1996) 118.

[45] Norbert Lohfink has pointed this out in a number of essays. Cf. especially "Gott auf der Seite der Armen" in idem, *Das Jüdische am Christentum. Die verlorene Dimension* (Freiburg: Herder, 1987) 122–43, at 133. Helmut Utzschneider, *Gottes langer Atem,* also takes the position that this long preparatory narrative is meant to describe "false approaches, dead ends, and tensions into which the hope for liberation can wander" (p. 8). However, his interpretation has some different emphases.

through the midwives' strategy and takes charge of the infanticide itself. All the newborn Israelite boys are drowned in the Nile.

How are the Israelites going to deal with an all-too-powerful state that acts as if it were in fact omnipotent, a state that knows no mercy and has begun the genocide of Israel? The Exodus narrative explores a second possibility. The child Moses is saved from death in the Nile by human cunning and divine guidance. He is brought into Pharaoh's court and comes to manhood there. Then the following happens:

> One day, after Moses had grown up, he went out to his people and saw their forced labor. He saw an Egyptian beating a Hebrew, one of his kinsfolk. He looked this way and that, and seeing no one he killed the Egyptian and hid him in the sand. When he went out the next day, he saw two Hebrews fighting; and he said to the one who was in the wrong, "Why do you strike your fellow Hebrew?" He answered, "Who made you a ruler and judge over us? Do you mean to kill me as you killed the Egyptian?" Then Moses was afraid and thought, "Surely the thing is known." (Exod 2:11-14)

Here it is no longer a question of passive resistance, but of "counter-violence." But it, too, is depicted by the narrative as useless. Moses finds no solidarity among his own kindred people. The Israelites are at odds, and the system is stronger. Moses must flee. Egypt cannot be changed by counter-violence or counter-terror.

As the narrative continues a third possibility is played out. One could take advantage of a "free space" within a system that cannot be changed. This free space appears in the form of a festival. Moses, who in the meantime has acquired the assistance of Aaron, asks Pharaoh to give Israel permission to celebrate a festival far out in the wilderness:

> Afterward Moses and Aaron went to Pharaoh and said, "Thus says the LORD, the God of Israel, 'Let my people go, so that they may celebrate a festival to me in the wilderness.'" But Pharaoh said, "Who is the LORD, that I should heed him and let Israel go? I do not know the LORD, and I will not let Israel go." Then they said, "The God of the Hebrews has revealed himself to us; let us go a three days' journey into the wilderness to sacrifice to the LORD our God, or he will fall upon us with pestilence or sword." But the king of Egypt said to them, "Moses and Aaron, why are you taking the people away from their work? Get to your labors!" (Exod 5:1-4)

Probably this third possibility is the most tempting and the one most frequently put into practice: The people of God is in mortal danger. It cannot accept the structures and models of the society in which it lives, but it does not want to escape them, either. The "fleshpots of Egypt" have their effect. The people of God accommodates itself and believes that it can survive as long as it has some free space. That was the case then, and it is so today.

In Europe at the present time we are experiencing a dreadful accommodation of Christians to society. Certainly this society preserves freedom, but it may be that its models are more dangerous to the people of God than the Egyptian overseers. The worst of it is a widespread mentality within the Church itself that even makes a theology of accommodation: Christians must be all things to all people and therefore live like all others. That, of course, is only possible even for a Church that accommodates itself to the greatest possible extreme if it preserves some free space for itself by which to affirm its own identity. Undoubtedly the liturgy constitutes such a free space in the current situation of the Church. At least within the special space of the liturgy, or minimally the Christian feasts, the true form of the Church is still visible, if only distantly. But then daily life returns, and there Christians live like all their contemporaries.

The narrative rejects this third possibility as well. It is not only that Pharaoh spurns the request to allow Israel some free space, and instead raises the work quotas.[46] The narrator does not even present the possibility of a festival as a real effort, as had been the case with the cunning of the midwives and the violent action of Moses. The petition to Pharaoh to permit the celebration of a festival liturgy in the wilderness is already a preparatory symbol of Israel's departure: it is only a deception of the political authority, a pure pretext for the Exodus.[47] In reality the festival will take place at the mountain of God[48] when Israel receives the Torah there.

If one were to ask what unites these three possibilities, all so vividly portrayed in the Exodus narratives and in each case rejected, one would have to say that without exception they remain within the system of the existing society. They do nothing to oppose it; they simply want to soften it. They adapt themselves and attempt to avoid its worst consequences through deception, counterforce, or the creation of free spaces, but they remain within the system. Therefore the narrative rejects these three possibilities from the outset and shows that God has an utterly different solution: God leads the people out of the system and gives them a new land, a new pattern of society.

It is remarkable that the society of historical Egypt also sought, at the same time that the Moses group dared its Exodus, a way out of the state

---

[46] That is what is at issue when the Israelites from this point on must obtain their own straw to make bricks for the royal buildings. Cf. Exod 5:6-19.

[47] Cf. especially Exod 3:17-22.

[48] For the liturgical character of the events at Sinai cf. the consecration of the people (Exod 19:10-11, 15), the drawing of a boundary around the mountain (19:12, 23), the procession of the people to the mountain (19:17), the sound of the trumpets (19:16; 20:18), the burnt offering (24:5), the eating and drinking (24:11). The festival even takes place twice: it is repeated a second time, in perverted fashion, in the story of the golden calf. Cf. Exod 32:5.

system of subordination and unfreedom. It was a flight into personal piety, the privatization of religion and life. Egyptologists refer to this period as one in which the concept of the state was undermined for the sake of a new immediacy in religion.[49]

Israel's Exodus, however, was something entirely different in its significance. It was not about the soul or a flight into the private realm. It was about society, and its goal was a new social project. The symbol for this is the mountain of God at the foot of which Israel would gather, after its departure from Egypt, to receive the Torah, the new social order, from God. Israel's being led out of Egypt and immediately afterward being given the Torah show that God alone is the founder of the new society. By human strength alone this new thing could not be accomplished. The Exodus from the Egyptian system into a free, fraternal and sororal society is such an astonishing event that the Bible can only depict it as a pure miracle, something accomplished by God alone.

The ancient Church understood this fundamental structure of the Exodus in the most profound fashion. The night in which it recalled the rescue from Egypt coincided with the night when Jesus was rescued from the power of death, and that night's purpose is not simply the private blessedness of the individual, but the resurrection of the people of God from sin and death. In the Easter night the new members of the people of God are born through baptism, and the others recall what happened in their own baptism: They were snatched out of the old society and rescued for the possibility of a new life; they were transported into a new land, into a new society, into the eschatological people of God.

We should first recall this fundamental structure of the Exodus memories. Obviously, however, many questions will remain. There may be situations in which a geographic or spatial exodus will be lifesaving for a whole group. So the Moses group fled Egypt some time in the thirteenth century B.C.E., probably during the reign of Pharaoh Ramses II. The primitive Christian community in Jerusalem fled during the Jewish War, probably in October of 66 C.E., when the first Roman troops appeared before Jerusalem, to the land east of the Jordan. Modern Israel would not have been possible without the lifesaving exodus of many Jews from Europe. From 1919 until the founding of the state of Israel in 1948, 324,200 Jews saved themselves by moving from Europe to Palestine. At the end of May 1991 in "Operation Solomon" the Israelis brought 14,400 of their fellow believers out of Ethiopia. Within only thirty-seven hours they were flown by the Israeli air force in forty flights from Addis Ababa to Tel Aviv. The

---

[49] Cf. Jan Assmann, *MA<sup>c</sup>AT* 19, 266–67.

seats had been taken out of the planes, and the Ethiopian "fellaheen" sat close-packed on the floor. Thus an exodus of this geographic or spatial type happens repeatedly, and yet it is not the norm.

The ancient Church, for example, did not move outside the Roman empire in spite of all the persecutions it endured. The communities remained where they were. They even prayed regularly for the state, or more precisely for the emperor and his officials. Of course they did not sacrifice to the state gods, but instead held fast to their own social project within the Roman state. This is exactly the reason why they did not need to leave: they lived their own form of society in the midst of the state. Baptism removed them from paganism and gave them, as they themselves said, a new homeland. That was also a form of exodus. It was very real. It could cost your life. But it was not "geographical."

We see in all this that Israel's Exodus and its typology did not present a fixed model of how the people of God had to behave in face of a pagan society that threatened them. The "geographical" exodus is only a special form, and yet it is precisely the figure of this "spatial" departure in the history of the people of God that even to today has developed an unbelievable power. Whenever following Jesus has been taken seriously and not misinterpreted it has also had a spatial dimension, whether it was called departure or simply "moving." The power of the Exodus narratives stems from their very concreteness. But the Exodus does not describe a journey of the soul, an emigration into pure inwardness, but conflicts on the soil of real, concrete societies. Augustine's wonderful saying, *incipit exire qui incipit amare* ("the one who begins to love begins to leave")[50] shows the spiritual dimension of the Exodus. Where genuine love, which comes only from God, begins, the one who loves abandons the self he or she loves above all things, goes outside the self and turns to God and the neighbor. That, too, is always concrete, and yet spiritualizing or narrowing to the private sphere is a continual threat.[51] The biblical Exodus, which constantly kept the concrete departure from the old society and the entry into a new land before its eyes, is proof against any kind of false spiritualizing. It has something disturbingly visible about it.

## 4. The Torah as Social Project

Exodus does not happen for its own sake; it is not solipsistic. A departure simply for the sake of departure would be absurd. The Exodus

---

[50] Augustine, *Enarrationes in Psalmos* 64, 2 (CCSL 39) 824.

[51] Augustine could not deal theologically with the historical Exodus from Babylon, of which the title of Psalm 64 (Vetus Latina) speaks. He immediately spiritualizes: "The feet of the departing are the affects of the heart." Ibid. 824, 43.

brought the people out of Egypt in order to bring them into a new society, and the Torah furnishes the model for that new society. Hence in their final form the "five books of Moses" locate the Sinai event almost immediately after the departure from Egypt, so that the Torah itself becomes a figure of rescue. It is, so to speak, the other side of the Exodus.[52] The ten commandments show how closely Exodus and Torah are united. They are introduced by the statement:

> I am YHWH, your God,
> who led you out of the land of Egypt,
> out of the house of slavery. (Exod 20:2)[53]

Then come the commandments. With their introductory statement they constitute "ten words" (Greek "decalogue"), so that every member of the people of God can count them off on ten fingers. The "ten words" are thus not pure demands. They are preceded by God's fundamental act of salvation for God's people; indeed, they are themselves a lifegiving act of salvation.[54]

The salvation-historical beginning of the ten commandments in itself confirms that the notion of the Old Testament as nothing but law and demand, while the New Testament in contrast is a message of salvation, is a dangerous misreading of biblical reality. Still more clearly than the opening sentence of the Decalogue, Deut 6:20-25 formulates the connection between God's saving deed and the fulfillment of the commandments. The question of the son, during his upbringing, about the meaning of the commandments is there answered with a reference to the rescue of Israel from Egypt. The commandments are thus part of the history of the freedom of the people of God:[55]

> When your son asks you tomorrow: "Why did you keep the decrees, statutes, and ordinances under which the LORD our God has placed you?" you shall answer your son: "We were Pharaoh's slaves in Egypt, and it was the LORD who brought us out of Egypt with a mighty hand. The LORD displayed before our eyes great and awesome signs and wonders against Egypt, against Pharaoh and his whole state. But he brought us out from there in order to bring us into the land that he promised on oath to our ancestors, and to give it to us. Then the LORD commanded us to direct our lives according to all these commandments, out of reverence for the LORD our God. Then it will go well with us as long as we live, and he will care for our well-being, as we now see. Righteousness will rule among us as long as we keep this whole

---

[52] Frank Crüsemann, *The Torah: Theology and History of Old Testament Law*. Translated by Allen W. Mahnke (Minneapolis: Fortress, 1996) 42–43.

[53] Cf. Deut 5:6.

[54] Crüsemann, *Torah* 27. Cf. also the theology of Psalm 119.

[55] Crüsemann, *Torah* 203.

social order in the presence of the LORD our God and make it a reality, as the LORD has commanded us. (Deut 6:20-25*)[56]

The Church has had its problems with the Torah. Its first decades were marked by a struggle concerning "the Law." But even after that the conflicts within the Church about the meaning and validity of the Law have never ceased.[57] The Church's problem with the Torah can be reduced to a single question: How can the Law bring salvation; how can it be salvation if Jesus Christ alone is the Savior? The solution seems simple: Anyone who believes in Christ is saved. Faith alone saves, and the form faith takes in life is love. Therefore love is the Christian's "Torah."[58]

As true as these statements are they diminish the full response of the New Testament and provoke misunderstandings. We have to ask in concrete terms how a person comes to believe in Christ, and the answer can only be that one becomes a member of the Church and so of the one people of God, the people that began with the faith of Abraham, the Exodus from Egypt, and the gift of the Torah at Sinai. To put it still more clearly: Faith in Christ happens precisely through a person's entering, through baptism, into an exodus from the old society and being saved into the new society of the people of God, which through the preaching, death, and resurrection of Jesus has received its eschatological form; and there is no such thing as a society without a model, a social order, a system of law and justice.

Paul, who reflected most extensively on the relationship between faith and the Law, was far from doing away with the Torah. Instead he says quite clearly that we do not abrogate the Law by believing; on the contrary, we uphold it (Rom 3:31), for through life in the Spirit of Christ we are enabled to fulfill the demands of the Law (Rom 8:4). The Sermon on the Mount formulates this still more succinctly. Jesus says:

> "Do not think that I have come to abolish the law or the prophets; I have come not to abolish but to fulfill. For truly I tell you, until heaven and earth pass away, not one letter, not one stroke of a letter, will pass from the law until all is accomplished." (Matt 5:17-18)

Nor has the Church ever rejected the Torah as a whole. It made the commandment to love God in Deut 6:5 and the commandment of love of neighbor from Lev 19:18 the center of all commandments. In its catechisms it has elevated the ten commandments to the status of fundamental

---

[56] From a translation by Norbert Lohfink.

[57] Cf. the survey in O. H. Pesch, "Begriff und Bedeutung des Gesetzes in der katholischen Theologie," in *"Gesetz" als Thema Biblischer Theologie. JBTh* 4 (1989) 171–213.

[58] This is formulated in connection with a selection of Pauline texts: cf. especially Rom 1:17; 3:21-22; 5:1; 10:9; Gal 2:16; 5:6, 14; 6:2.

principles of its moral teaching, and it has always presumed that the Torah, to the extent that it reflects the "natural moral law," continues in force.

The problem with this Christian reception of the Torah, of course, is its selective nature. The Church has made choices. It has accepted some parts of the Torah, but not others. It rejected the cultic and purity laws while retaining the "moral law." Unconsciously it even made a selection within the moral law. Thus the commandment of love of *neighbor* from Lev 19:18 is constantly cited, while the commandment to love the *strangers in the land* in Lev 19:33-34 has, with disastrous consequences, played scarcely any part in Christian instruction, even though it follows almost immediately after the former commandment and is undoubtedly intended as an extension of the commandment to love the neighbor.

Much more serious than this sometimes conscious, sometimes unconscious selection, however, was the denigration of the Torah, beginning with the Enlightenment and the era of German Idealism, as abstruse, repellent, spiritless, even unspiritual, and—long before that—the fundamental condemnation of Torah devotion by many Christian theologians as "self-righteousness" and "legalism." Together with the accusation of "murdering God" this defamation of the Torah has constantly nourished Christian anti-Judaism. What can we do to counter it?

One could point out what a comfort and joy the Torah is for many Jewish families who live in the traditional way. One could, with Clement of Alexandria,[59] recall the humanity and benevolence of the Torah. One could show, with Eusebius of Caesarea, that the Jewish Law "like a fragrant breeze penetrated to every corner of the world."[60] One could propose that many apparently new achievements of modern law were already formulated in Israel's Torah, such as the inviolability of the home or the division of powers within the state.[61] Finally, one could point out that a good deal of the Torah has not been achieved even today: for example, that a newly married man may not be called to military service because in such a case his service to his family takes priority and he is to give joy to his wife (Deut 24:5).

We could list a great many more things in order to evoke sympathy for the Torah, but ultimately that would not solve the problem of Christian dealings with it. In the Pentateuch, the "five books of Moses," there are legal complexes that really have become foreign to us because they have

---

[59] *Stromateis* II, 18, 82–96.

[60] *Eccl. Hist.* I, 2, 23.

[61] For the inviolability of the home see Deut 24:10-11; for the division of powers in the laws of office in Deuteronomy cf. Norbert Lohfink, *Great Themes from the Old Testament* (Chicago: Franciscan Herald Press, and Edinburgh: T & T Clark, 1982) 55–75.

no *Sitz im Leben* any longer, no life-setting in which they fit: the ritual and purity laws, for example. Besides, a purely humanistic view of the Torah can furnish no ultimate standard for us.

We need to seek out the center of the Torah, the thing that holds it together. That central point can be clearly established. Here in particular the methods of scientific exegesis, especially form criticism and literary criticism, can be of great assistance. Biblical scholarship can show how the Torah grew over the centuries, how further laws were added to a crystallizing core, or how legal texts that were already in use were replaced by new ones. In the fifth century B.C.E. existing historical works were woven together with some major collections of laws in a highly sophisticated process; so the Pentateuch was created, and the gigantic structure of the Torah that is identical with it. This may even have been done at the command of the Persian government, which demanded a binding law in its provinces, one of which was Judea.[62]

The crystallizing core and focus of meaning of all the layers of the Pentateuch, however, is the commandment to worship YHWH alone. Thus in Exod 34:11-26, the so-called "law of YHWH's privilege," probably the oldest collection of laws transmitted to us in the Pentateuch, all the ordinances center on the command ". . . you shall worship no other god, because the LORD, whose name is Jealous, is a jealous God" (Exod 34:14). In the "book of the covenant," a somewhat later collection of laws (Exod 20:22–23:33), all the laws are framed by this claim of YHWH to exclusive worship, and in the middle of the book is the demand: "Be attentive to all that I have said to you. Do not invoke the names of other gods; do not let them be heard on your lips" (Exod 23:13). But the formulation of exclusive worship of YHWH best known to us is the first commandment in the Decalogue:

> You shall have no other gods before me. You shall not make for yourself an idol, whether in the form of anything that is in heaven above, or that is on the earth beneath, or that is in the water under the earth. You shall not bow down to them or worship them; for I the LORD your God am a jealous God . . . . (Exod 20:3-5)

What is at issue in this exclusive worship of YHWH? For the nations around Israel, the world was full of gods. Everything was divine. Anyone who wanted to take the reality of the world seriously, at its numinous depths, had therefore to serve many gods. That did not mean that in particular places, at particular times, and in special situations one could not concentrate on a single god; it did not even mean that one could not then

---

[62] For more detail see Crüsemann, *Torah* 329–39.

revere in that one god (or goddess) the sum total of all the divine elements in the world. One can appeal to a single god while subjecting oneself, in that god, to all the divinities of the universe.[63]

On this very point Israel was different. YHWH was *not* the sum total of all the divine elements in the world. YHWH was experienced in leading the people out of Egypt and in many other deeds of salvation as the God who alone saves. Therefore the worship of YHWH could not be combined with the worship of other gods. Therefore YHWH alone could be worshiped, in complete exclusivity. The texts often formulate this exclusivity in the image of jealousy. YHWH is a jealous God, different from the gods round about Israel. The numinosity of the world is not concentrated in YHWH, for YHWH is utterly different from the world. For a long time Israel was unable to formulate this Absolute Other who is its God *monotheistically,* as strict belief in one God. For the time being it could only say that there may be many gods in the world but we may not serve them; we may serve only YHWH.

Having YHWH alone as Lord and serving only YHWH also means orienting every aspect of life to YHWH. If YHWH were responsible only for certain parts of life, particular situations or particular times, YHWH would not be the only Lord. In that case the people of God would have to have other lords as well. The multiplicity of Israel's laws, the constantly expanding field of its Torah had no other purpose than to subject the whole world of the people of God, all the realities within which it lived, to the rule of this one God. The six-hundred-thirteen commandments of the Torah (according to Jewish reckoning)[64] are meant to show what it means to serve YHWH alone. Thus the exclusive worship of YHWH is the genuine shaping element of the Torah. When its commandments repeatedly go into detail and leave no sphere of life untouched it is only because the rule of God is to be present everywhere and all things are to honor God. This rule of God over the whole land of Israel is developed in three aspects in the Torah:

1. The Torah is concerned not only for the "inner side" of the human being but for the "external side" as well.

There are religions that concentrate entirely on the "inner side" of the human person. Matter appears to them as something strange or even evil.

---

[63] For this section, cf. Norbert Lohfink, *Great Themes* 135–53.

[64] According to the rabbis the 613 commandments of the Torah (= 248 positive commands and 365 prohibitions) correspond to the 248 organs in the human body and its 365 blood vessels. This construct is meant to express the idea that the Torah is entirely fashioned for human beings, and human beings entirely for the Torah, and thus for the worship of God alone. Cf. Peter Stuhlmacher, *Biblische Theologie des Neuen Testaments* (Göttingen: Vandenhoeck & Ruprecht, 1992) 1:258.

They urge detachment from the world. Israel, in contrast, accepted the world passionately as the gift of God, knowing that its faith would be narrow and divorced from reality if it did not subject the external, material world to God's rule as well. Therefore the Torah speaks of fields and how to till them, of vineyards and fruit trees, of birds' nests, of cattle, of houses, of parapets around roof terraces, of the human body and its diseases, of shaving and cutting hair, and even prohibits putting a muzzle on an ox when it is pulling the threshing sled over the grain on the threshing floor.[65] The Torah is for the whole creation: people, animals, plants, even lifeless things. Israel's whole life and the whole world in which it lives its life are to be saturated and formed by faith.

Georg W. F. Hegel, like Voltaire before him, sneered because the Torah even concerns itself with the burying of excrement in the vicinity of the camp (Deut 23:13-14). "It would have been better," he wrote, "if God had given the Jews some definite instruction regarding the immortality of the soul, rather than to have taught them [to go to the toilet]."[66] But the Torah is not shy of what is disgustingly material, and it is persistently this-worldly. There are no exceptions. The whole human world is to be subjected to the rule of God so that everything may receive its dignity and identity—in this particular instance, quite simply so that hygiene may be preserved and people will be healthy.

2. The Torah is concerned not only with space, but also with time.

It is not only the spaces with which people surround themselves that influence their lives. Time is just as influential. In fact, its rhythms are stronger formative forces than people realize. In Israel's religious environment it was the annual rhythm of sowing and harvest, processions to the sanctuaries and festivals for the gods that structured the year. For that very reason the Torah pays extraordinary attention to the festival calendar

---

[65] For the fields see Exod 23:10-11, for the vineyards Deut 22:9, for the fruit trees Deut 20:19-20, for the birds' nests Deut 22:6-7, for the cattle Deut 22:10, for houses Lev 14:33-53, for parapets on roofs Deut 22:8, for the body and its diseases Lev 13:1-46, for shaving and cutting hair Lev 19:27, for the threshing ox Deut 25:4.

[66] Georg W. F. Hegel, *Werke in 20 Bänden. Theorie Werkausgabe* (Frankfurt am Main: Suhrkamp, 1969) vol. 16: *Vorlesungen über die Philosophie der Religion I*, 211. Hegel quotes Voltaire, entirely accepting his opinion: "Voltaire's bitterest attacks are directed against the demands of a faith of this kind. Among other things he says that it would have been better if God had given the Jews some definite instruction regarding the immortality of the soul, rather than to have taught them how [to go to the toilet] *(aller à la selle). Latrinae* thus become a content of faith (Deut. xxiii. 13-15). The non-spiritual, from its very nature, is not a content which can belong to faith. If God speaks, it is spiritually, for Spirit reveals itself to Spirit alone." For this English translation see Georg W. F. Hegel, *Lectures on the Philosophy of Religion.* Translated by E. B. Speirs and J. Burdon Sanderson (New York: Humanities, 1962) 1:219–20.

and the divisions of time. Even the "Privilege Law" in Exod 34:11-26 speaks of three great pilgrimage festivals: the seven-day feast of unleavened bread (the matzoh feast), the feast of weeks (our Pentecost) and the vintage feast (the later Feast of Booths). All three of these festivals are connected with the annual rhythms of agriculture: in each of them the first fruits of the barley, the wheat, and the grape harvest respectively were brought to a sanctuary.

There were also harvest festivals in Israel's Canaanite environment. From all that we know they followed the rhythms of the moon (days of the new moon, days of the full moon). In Israel, however, a rhythm of sevens was established. The "Privilege Law" required that the matzoh festival should last seven days, and these seven days of the feast were extended in a rhythm of sevens (seven weeks, each with seven days) to the Feast of Weeks (Exod 34:18-22). This led inevitably to a dating of festivals that differed from that among the pagan population. The purpose of this is clear: precisely where the Canaanite world of the gods held its strongest position—in the fruitfulness of the fields, in rain and harvest—Israel set itself apart, giving itself a different festival rhythm and thus also in this field, so sensitive for an agricultural people, giving all honor to YHWH. The first fruits are brought before *YHWH;* it is YHWH, and not Baal, who is thanked for being the giver of fruitfulness.[67]

Later, during the great reform movement at the time of King Josiah (640–609 B.C.E.) whose results are recorded in Deuteronomy, the sacrifices were centralized in Jerusalem. This centralization of the cult meant as well that the great annual feasts became pilgrimage festivals to Jerusalem. The suppression of pilgrimages to Dan, Bethel, Gilgal, Mizpah, Hebron, and other sanctuaries was again intended to promote the exclusive worship of YHWH. The provincial sanctuaries with their popular customs and easily misunderstood cultic symbols could more easily fall under the influence of foreign cults.

However, the centralization of the cult meant more than that: Whenever possible all Israel was to gather in Jerusalem at the three great annual festivals and worship YHWH in one great assembly. At these festivals and their festal meals it should be visible to everyone, on the basis of its social project, what Israel is: a people drawn together and assembled by God in which the differences between rich and poor, master and slave were eliminated; a people mindful of the saving deeds of its God; a people joyful before God and grateful for the gift of the land in which it can live. At the festivals in Jerusalem "the one liberated people of God was to appear

---

[67] For these last two paragraphs see especially Crüsemann, *Torah* 115–17.

in solidarity before its God."[68] "Nowhere else and at no other time could Israel be more thoroughly itself."[69]

At the same time, every pilgrimage festival was like a new Exodus, for as a high point in the running course of time, a celebration of the history of God with God's people, such a festival took place not in the normal sphere of life but in the place that was Israel's center, a place to which one had to make a journey. Deuteronomy 16:1-17 gives an impressive description of this sense of the pilgrimage festivals. It says of the Feast of Weeks:

> You shall count seven weeks . . . . Then you shall keep the festival of weeks for the LORD your God, contributing a freewill offering in proportion to the blessing that you have received from the LORD your God. Rejoice before the LORD your God—you and your sons and your daughters, your male and female slaves, the Levites resident in your towns, as well as the strangers, the orphans, and the widows who are among you—at the place that the LORD your God will choose as a dwelling for his name. Remember that you were a slave in Egypt, and diligently observe these statutes. (Deut 16:9-12)

However, it was not only the great festivals that created a new structure for the year and even placed time itself under the rule of YHWH. The week, with its Sabbath, was an equally decisive structure. It appears that the institution of the Sabbath existed nowhere outside Israel. If that is true, the Sabbath is one of Israel's greatest and most beautiful inventions. Through this day of rest that cuts periodically into life God draws the people out of its work every week anew, so that it cannot lose itself in world and work. It is to shape the world through its work, of course, but not to enslave itself to the world and its gods.

The caesura that the Torah makes in the course of time with its rhythms of seven, however, goes much deeper. It is not only that every single year is divided into weeks, each with its Sabbath, and so subjected to God's rule. The course of the years is also subjected to a rhythm of sevens through the institution of the sabbatical years. Every seventh year the world is to pause. All debts must be forgiven, all male and female slaves liberated. Every debtor is granted a new beginning. The just society of the beginning is restored:

> If a member of your community, whether a Hebrew man or a Hebrew woman, is sold to you and works for you six years, in the seventh year you shall set that person free. And when you send a male slave out from you a

---

[68] Albertz, *History of Israelite Religion* 1:223.

[69] Norbert Lohfink, "Opferzentralisation, Säkularisierungsthese und mimetische Theorie," in idem, *Studien* 3:219–60, at 243.

free person, you shall not send him out empty-handed. Provide liberally out of your flock, your threshing floor, and your wine press, thus giving to him some of the bounty with which the LORD your God has blessed you. Remember that you were a slave in the land of Egypt, and the LORD your God redeemed you . . . . You shall do the same with regard to your female slave. (Deut 15:12-15, 17)

Of course one can object to such a text that it is pure utopia; no society could permit itself the practice of forgiving all debts every seven years. However, one should be careful with that word "utopia." We have secure evidence that the kings of ancient Babylon occasionally called for a general forgiveness of debts. This usually happened when a king ascended the throne. The deuteronomic law makes this occasional and unpredictable year of release a seven-year rule. Moreover, we need to distinguish between one utopia and another. The Greeks located the "righteous nations" they imagined on the borders of the known world, namely on the islands in the Indian Ocean. Israel, in contrast, took into account at least the *possibility* that a just society could be realized by God and through the divine deeds of liberation in the midst of this world, in the concrete "place" that God had chosen.[70] Therefore it proposed laws for a just society and shaped an entire social project on the basis of the liberating impulse of the Exodus. Hence

3. The Torah is not aimed at righteous individuals; its aim is to produce a righteous society.

The deuteronomic law proposes a carefully crafted system of individual laws meant to prevent the existence of classes of poor and enslaved people in Israel. It quite soberly takes into account that society continually drifts apart into rich and poor, masters and slaves, and it works against that drift, not in dreamy utopian constructions, but in very clear directives.[71]

For example, if a farmer gets into trouble through bad harvests or bad management and needs a loan in order to be able to continue farming, the law in Deut 15:7-11 steps in, urging fellow Israelites to provide an interest-free loan. However, if the debt is too great and the debtor is forced to work for someone else as a day-laborer, the law in Deut 24:14-15 secures the worker a daily wage. If the person in question is still not able to pay back the debt owing, Deut 24:12-13 requires a humane way of dealing with the deposit given: For example, if a poor man has given his cloak as a deposit it must be returned to him at sundown so that he can cover himself in the

---

[70] Cf. Norbert Lohfink, "Das deuteronomische Gesetz in der Endgestalt—Entwurf einer Gesellschaft ohne marginale Gruppen," in idem, *Studien* 3:205–18, at 218.

[71] In the next paragraph I am following Norbert Lohfink, *Studien* 3:211–12.

cold hours of the night. If the debt becomes so enormous that the result is seizure of the person, that is, debt slavery, one of the most commonplace and yet severe institutions found everywhere in the ancient Near East, according to Deut 15:1-6 this may not be imposed during a sabbatical year. And if this enslavement for debt occurs outside the sabbatical year, according to Deut 15:12-18 the debt slavery must end in the next sabbatical year, and the freed Israelite must, as we have seen, be equipped with cattle and seed in order to build a new life.

All this is directly connected with the exclusive worship of YHWH. According to the plan of the book of Deuteronomy the two tables with the ten commandments, in which the whole Torah is concentrated, lie in the Ark of the Covenant in the Temple at Jerusalem.[72] This means that for Israel YHWH's cultic presence is unconditionally connected with the Torah. It is precisely in the commandments that God is present among God's people, that God intervenes, saves, and gives life. If there are poor people in Israel whose rights are trodden underfoot, and if they cry out to God in their misery, YHWH is no longer being properly worshiped; then Israel's worship is distorted or even completely in vain. For all worship only brings to expression in words and concentrates in symbols what is to be done constantly throughout Israel: being a just society in the world, to the honor of God.

Another point should be noted: The Torah's law of punishment is much more powerfully directed to the reconciliation of opponents than ours. "In no place do we find prison terms, fines imposed solely to punish or any kind of payment to the state instead of the victim. They are unknown and inconceivable."[73] The principle modern readers find so shocking, "eye for eye, tooth for tooth, hand for hand, foot for foot, burn for burn, wound for wound, stripe for stripe" included in Exod 21:24-25 by no means demands that the only punishment for putting out someone's eye should be putting out the eye of the doer, but that a compensation with the value of the lost eye should be paid to the victim. The Torah's intention is that hatred and aggression should not be allowed to proliferate among the people of God. The deed should be done away with through a just compensation. The opponents should be able to live together, reconciled. Here, as with many other directives, it is clear that the Torah makes it possible for people to live together in Israel. It creates community. It makes people capable of community, and thereby also—and only thereby—capable of worship.

---

[72] Deuteronomy 10:1-5. According to Deut 31:24-29, the documentation of the deuteronomic Torah lies *alongside* the Ark of the Covenant.

[73] Crüsemann, *Torah* 169. Cf. Rainer Albertz, "Täter und Opfer im Alten Testament," *ZEE* 28 (1984) 146–66.

Everything we have here described is given its right name, collected, and summarized in the commandment of *agapē,* love of God and neighbor. Therefore the New Testament rightly sees *agapē* as the center and fulfillment of all the commandments.[74] Of course this *agapē* is not first and foremost an honorable sentiment, but helpful action, entirely in the sense of Exod 23:4-5: "When you come upon your enemy's ox or donkey going astray, you shall bring it back. When you see the donkey of one who hates you lying under its burden and you would hold back from setting it free, you must help to set it free." This text from the book of the covenant shows that the Torah also prescribes love of enemies, even if it does not use the word itself. Beyond that it makes clear how soberly and concretely the Torah speaks about *agapē.* For Israel love is an appropriate and supportive action and therefore requires the concrete basis of the people of God; it needs its love for detail and its penetrant desire for immanence, that is, its unbroken, not-to-be-discouraged will to shape and transform this earthly sphere.

History has shown that the idea of love for God and neighbor always needs the people of God as its basis. "You shall love your neighbor as yourself" (Lev 19:18) transfers the solidarity that is proper within the family to the whole of Israel. This is not about romantic or individual affection, but rather the mutual responsibility of all who live within the faith community of Israel.[75] Where this basis in the people of God was no longer a living reality, "love" very often descended to mere inwardness, a noncompulsory love for humanity ("You millions, I embrace you")[76] or provision for almsgiving. What the Bible means by *agapē* presupposes the social project of the Torah. Without it love becomes otherworldly and blows away like chaff in the wind.

For that very reason not even the New Testament gives us permission to regard whole chunks of the Torah as "finished." Obviously through Jesus the Torah was again placed on a new basis. Through him it was entirely fulfilled, and thereby it has received its eschatological form. Matthew painted this fundamental significance of Jesus for the Torah in an impressive scene: As Moses went up the "mountain" to receive the Torah, so Jesus ascends a "mountain" to give his messianic-eschatological interpretation of the Torah (Matt 5:1); and just as once the whole people of God was assembled around the mountain, so now representatives from all parts of the land of Israel are gathered around the mountain (Matt 4:25). In his "Sermon on the

---

[74] Cf. Matt 22:34-40; Mark 12:28-34; Rom 13:8-10; Gal 5:14.

[75] Cf. Erhard S. Gerstenberger, *Das 3. Buch Mose. Leviticus.* ATD 6 (Göttingen, 1993) 248.

[76] The phrase is from Schiller's "Ode to Joy."

Mount" Jesus teaches the fundamental rules for eschatological obedience to the Torah. It is a question of the right way to obey the Law, the "true righteousness" (Matt 5:20), but not of a "new law."

How could the Sermon on the Mount be a "new law" when it does not even touch many areas of human life? Jesus does not proclaim a new law; he brings the unique social project of the Torah, given once for all, to its fulfillment by formulating examples that show how this social project is to be understood and carried out *radically,* that is, in relation to its roots, and that means in conformity with the true will of God.

Jesus not only gives examples. Through his life and death he will himself become the definitive interpretation of the Torah. It is one of the central themes of the New Testament that Jesus in his death has become the place of eschatological atonement,[77] that the communities, as his "body in the world," have become an eschatological temple built of living stones,[78] and that therefore all worship has received a radically new form.[79] Thereby the Pentateuch's ceremonial law has been given a new location, and in that new place its form changes. But that does not mean that it is rejected, only that it is transformed.

No section of the Torah can be regarded as "finished" and eliminated, but the whole Torah must repeatedly be interpreted anew from Jesus and toward the will of God. When that is done it can indeed happen that parts of the Torah that at first seemed strange to us reveal a new meaning, or we might better say the meaning they were intended to have from the beginning. For example, the Torah contains extensive purity laws.[80] They apply primarily to the house, clothing, the body, and food. Clean and unclean animals are distinguished. The laws prescribe what types of meat can be eaten and what cannot. Jesus and the early Church formulated some strict measures precisely with regard to the purity laws and their later expansion by the scribes:

> There is nothing outside a person that by going in can defile, but the things that come out are what defile. . . . For it is from within, from the human heart, that evil intentions come: fornication, theft, murder, adultery, avarice, wickedness, deceit, licentiousness, envy, slander, pride, folly. All these evil things come from within, and they defile a person. (Mark 7:15, 21-23)[81]

---

[77] Rom 3:21-26; cf. Hebrews 9.

[78] 1 Corinthians 3:16; 6:19; 2 Cor 6:16; Eph 2:21; 1 Pet 2:5.

[79] Cf. the Last Supper texts, as well as Rom 12:1.

[80] Cf. Leviticus 11–15; Deut 14:3-21a.

[81] Cf. also Matt 15:1-20; Luke 11:37-41; Acts 10:9-16; Rom 14:14; 1 Cor 8:8; Col 2:21-22; Titus 1:15, and elsewhere.

Are the purity laws and holiness code of Israel thereby dissolved or reduced to pure ethics?[82] Christian theologians have judged that the jesuanic distinction between "inside" and "outside" removes all external and ritual holiness from the pre-personal sphere and refers it to internal, personal holiness. One should, however, be careful with such statements, for even holiness released from the external sphere means decidedly more in the New Testament than simply a quality internal to the soul or the moral person.

The whole people of God is supposed to be a holy people. Holiness thus always includes the social dimension that is indissolubly attached to the individual person. Not only must the human heart be holy, so must the conditions of life, the social structures and the forms of environment in which the person lives and into which he or she is constantly moving. Precisely that is what the ritual purity prescriptions of the Torah always had in mind.

Faith in one God who is the ruler of *all things* must also shape the world that surrounds people. It is not a question of believing with mind and heart while at the same time despising the body, letting the places we live fall apart, and destroying the environment. According to a saying of the prophet Zechariah, in Israel at the end time even the horses' bells and the cooking pots in the house of the Lord will be holy: "On that day there shall be inscribed on the bells of the horses, 'Holy to the LORD.' . . . and every cooking pot in Jerusalem and Judah shall be sacred to the LORD of hosts" (Zech 14:20-21). This means that a day is coming when all Israel—not only the people in it, but all objects and all the conditions of life—will be in a condition willed by God and will reflect the divine rule. To the extent that they correspond to the will of God and are shaped by God's nearness they will then find their identity and promote life. This is just what the biblical idea of purity and holiness is about. The purity Torah in the book of Leviticus is intended to promote the formation and transformation of the world by faith. From that perspective the purity Torah is something we are far from grasping as yet. It deserves to be read anew, considered anew, and questioned about its original meaning.

Obviously it is not possible to do this without making constant distinctions. But that in itself is also the purpose of the Torah: Its intention is to teach Israel to make distinctions. To regard all things in the world critically through the power of faith, that is, in a differentiating way, has become a fundamental feature of Jewish existence. Because Israel, in light of the Torah, unremittingly learned to make distinctions—which means,

---

[82] For more detail on what follows, see Gerhard Lohfink, *Wem gilt die Bergpredigt? Beiträge zu einer christlichen Ethik* (Freiburg: Herder, 1988) 110–19.

for example, not mixing things and matters that are different[83]—it could preserve its identity among the pagans. While Assyria and Babylon, once victorious states standing on the ruins of Israel, collapsed and dissolved into new nations, defeated and continually persecuted Israel, although scattered throughout the whole world, has remained a nation.

The American writer Walker Percy expresses it this way:

> Why does no one find it remarkable that in most world cities today there are Jews but not one single Hittite, even though the Hittites had a great flourishing civilization while the Jews nearby were a weak and obscure people? When one meets a Jew in New York or New Orleans or Paris or Melbourne, it is remarkable that no one considers the event remarkable. . . . But it is even more remarkable to wonder, if there are Jews here, why are there not Hittites here? Where are the Hittites? Show me one Hittite in New York City.[84]

Part of the miracle of Israel's identity is its ability to make distinctions. The *ekklēsia* needs this constant distinguishing as urgently as the synagogue does. It dare not fall into that sickened state of the spirit in which everything is the same, everything is equally valid, nothing makes any difference. Where distinctions are no longer made, the old gods return.

The Torah is the undertaking, put into motion by God and never to be surpassed, beginning on the basis of the people of God, to view all the things of the world with the eyes of God, to distinguish what is right from what is wrong, to change what is wrong, and thus to place all things under the governance of the one God.

Frank Crüsemann, as a Christian theologian, has ventured to say that "the identity of the biblical God is dependent upon the connection with his Torah."[85] He is right. Therefore the Church can and may never abandon the Torah. Of course it must live it in the spirit of Jesus—that is, in the power of the new thing that came into the world with his death and resurrection, out of his freedom and understanding, out of his radicality and fear of God.

### 5. A History of Resistance

The very first song of the Iliad tells how the Greeks brought an ox to sacrifice to the god Apollo. The sacrificing priest was an old man named Chryses:

> And soon as the men had prayed and flung the barley,
> first they lifted back the heads of the victims,

[83] Cf. the prohibitions on mixing in Lev 19:19 and Deut 22:5, 9-11.

[84] Walker Percy, *The Message in the Bottle. How Queer Man Is, How Queer Language is, and What One Has to Do With the Other* (New York: Farrar, Strauss, and Giroux, 1975) 6.

[85] Crüsemann, *Torah* 366.

slit their throats, skinned them and carved away
the meat from the thighbones and wrapped them in fat,
a double fold sliced clean and topped with strips of flesh.
And the old man burned these on a dried cleft stick
and over the quarters poured out glistening wine
while young men at his side held five-pronged forks.
Once they had charred the thighs and tasted the organs
they cut the rest into pieces, pierced them with spits,
roasted them to a turn and pulled them off the fire.
The work done, the feast laid out, they ate well
and no man's hunger lacked a share of the banquet.[86]

The full relish with which the sacrifice and sacrificial meal are described is characteristic of Homer. The battles before Troy and many other episodes are just as visually chanted. Nevertheless the text reflects something that goes far beyond Homer and his style: the ancient peoples loved serving their gods. The Egyptians, the Assyrians, the Babylonians, the Greeks, and the Romans all made loud and vocal public prayers, built countless temples, made vows, inquired of oracles, brought their gods the old, customary sacrifices, and celebrated their religious festivals with joy. Plutarch writes in his essay *De superstitione:* "Nothing is more pleasant for human beings than festivals and sacrificial meals in the temples, and initiations and mystical rites and prayers and worship of the gods."[87] The only exceptions to this rule are atheists and scrupulous people.

Of course there were scarcely any true atheists in antiquity.[88] The Greek adjective *atheos* referred primarily to activities like robbing temples, vandalizing images of the gods, violation of the right of asylum, deviation from the prescribed sacrificial rites, and the like; it had nothing to do with atheism in the modern sense.[89] During the Enlightenment phase of antiquity there was an intensive critique of religion, but it did little to detract from the fixed world of religious symbols and rituals. In Egypt and Mesopotamia there were at an early period something like "reproaches against God," but the texts in question are extremely restrained and belong to the genre of Wisdom writings.[90] On the whole being religious was a

---

[86] Homer, *The Iliad*. Translated by Robert Fagles (New York: Viking Penguin, 1990) I, 458–68.

[87] Plutarch, *De superstitione* 169d.

[88] Cf. Martin Schmidt, "Atheismus" I/2, *TRE* 4:351–64, at 351.

[89] Cf. Wolfgang Müller-Lauter, "Atheismus" II, *TRE* 4:378–436, at 390.

[90] Cf. recently Dorothea Sitzler, *Vorwurf gegen Gott. Ein religiöses Motiv im Alten Orient (Ägypten und Mesopotamien).* StOr 32 (Wiesbaden: Harrassowitz, 1995) 231: "The laments and reproaches are at no point authentic testimony to personal extremity with regard to religion; they are components of a literature developed for the use of teachers of Wisdom in their reflections on the role of Wisdom and the sage in the world." A characteristic

matter of course for people in antiquity. We may say without exaggeration that the ancient peoples lived in harmony with their gods.[91]

In contrast Israel, the chosen people of God, lived in constant rebellion against its God. The history of Israel as told in the Old Testament is in fact a history of resistance to YHWH. As soon as they were delivered from Egypt the people rebelled against the conditions of their life in the wilderness and wanted to go back to the country where they had been enslaved. Even in the land of promise they showed no sign of fidelity. They rejected the prophets who ceaselessly sought to prevent them from falling away from God. Again and again idols were erected in the land. Israel wanted to worship its God the way other nations worshiped theirs. The whole is an unbroken history of stubbornness, obstinacy, rebelliousness, and rejection of God.

This history of Israel's stubbornness is concentrated in an exemplary and even archetypal form in the stories of "murmuring" in the books of Exodus and Numbers. Almost all of them employ a verb that seldom appears elsewhere in the Hebrew Bible: the word *lûn,* translated "murmur," "revolt," "rebel." It can describe the deep growling of a dog before it attacks.[92]

According to the account in the Pentateuch this rebellion on the part of the people of God began even during the Exodus. When Pharaoh's army approached the Reed Sea the people cried out to Moses:

> "Was it because there were no graves in Egypt that you have taken us away to die in the wilderness? What have you done to us, bringing us out of Egypt? Is this not the very thing we told you in Egypt, 'Let us alone and let us serve the Egyptians'? For it would have been better for us to serve the Egyptians than to die in the wilderness." (Exod 14:11-12)

This text summarizes in anticipation the constant grumbling that begins here. The people cries out for rescue from Pharaoh's army, and it is rescued. It cries piteously for water and it is given water. It calls for bread and bread is given it. It demands meat and receives meat.[93] In spite of all

---

example is the lament in the Babylonian poem *Ludlul bēl nēmequi* II, 4-5: "I called to the god, but he did not turn his face to me; I prayed to my goddess, but she did not lift up her head to me" (ibid. 221).

[91] One striking exception seems to be the myth of Prometheus. But we should not forget that Prometheus was originally a god, and his rebellion against the Olympian gods probably reflects the historical conflicts between different classes of divinities within the development of Greek religion. (Cf. Walter Pötscher, "Prometheus," *Der kleine Pauly* 4:1174–77, at 1176.) Israel's grumbling had very different roots.

[92] As in Ps 59:15. For the fundamental meaning "rebel" cf. Rolf Knierim, *lûn, THAT* 1:870–72.

[93] Water: Exod 15:22-25; bread: Exod 16:1-15; meat: Exod 16:1-15.

this the rebellion goes on. On the surface it is directed against Moses and Aaron,[94] but Moses uncovers the truth: it is really rebellion against God:

> [YHWH] has heard your complaining against the LORD.
> For what are we, that you complain against us? . . .
> Your complaining is not against us but against the LORD. (Exod 16:7-8)

This murmuring is deep-seated. It is not merely external discontent with the conditions in the wilderness, but ultimately a lack of trust in God's saving actions. The people of God is not prepared to regard its history as something directed by God and leading to salvation. It interprets the story of its liberation as the story of its destruction. It does not trust God. It cannot believe that God is good and a keeper of promises. Because of this fundamental distrust it cannot appreciate the precious value of God's marvelous gifts—water from the rock, manna, quail—but instead longs for the fleshpots of slavery.[95] The realities of the oppressive state appear like tempting phantoms to them. Egypt is described with a naïve nostalgia as if it were the promised land:

> "If only we had meat to eat! We remember the fish we used to eat in Egypt for nothing, the cucumbers, the melons, the leeks, the onions, and the garlic; but now our strength is dried up, and there is nothing at all but this manna to look at." (Num 11:4-6)

This defamation of the story of liberation culminates in the narrative of the spies, which we encountered earlier.[96] Israel is on the threshold of the promised land and sends out twelve spies, one from each tribe. After forty days they return bringing huge grapes, pomegranates, and figs, and they report: "We came to the land to which you sent us; it flows with milk and honey, and this is its fruit. Yet the people who live in the land are strong, and the towns are fortified and very large . . ." (Num 13:27-28). This first report of the spies is accepted only selectively by the Israelites. They do not listen to the first part at all, but only to the news of the size and strength of the Canaanite cities. Most of the spies are infected by the fearful reaction of the people, so that they now slander the promised land and spread false rumors. As in their nostalgia for Egypt, so also here distrust gives birth to fantasy; reality is distorted and normal people are transformed into giants:

---

[94] Cf. Exod 2:14; 4:1; 5:20-21; 6:9; 14:11; 15:24; 16:2; 17:2-3; Num 14:2; 16:41 [MT 17:6-7]; 20:2-3.

[95] Cf. Exod 16:3; Num 11:4-6; 20:4.

[96] See above, II 2.

"The land that we have gone through as spies is a land that devours its inhabitants; and all the people that we saw in it are of great size. There we saw the Nephilim . . . and to ourselves we seemed like grasshoppers, and so we seemed to them." (Num 13:32-33)

This second account by the spies is followed by a fateful rebellion. The people want nothing more to do with the promised land and beg to return to Egypt:

And all the Israelites complained against Moses and Aaron; the whole congregation said to them, "Would that we had died in the land of Egypt! Or would that we had died in the wilderness! Why is the LORD bringing us into this land to fall by the sword? Our wives and our little ones will become booty; would it not be better for us to go back to Egypt?" So they said to one another, "Let us choose a captain, and go back to Egypt" (Num 14:2-4).[97]

Only Joshua and Caleb hold to what they have seen:

"The land that we went through as spies is an exceedingly good land. If the LORD is pleased with us, he will bring us into this land and give it to us, a land that flows with milk and honey. Only, do not rebel against the LORD; and do not fear the people of the land . . . . (Num 14:7-9)

But Joshua and Caleb cannot prevail. The community of Israel threatens to stone Moses and Aaron. God is forced to intervene. Although Moses succeeds, by his intercession, in preventing God from destroying the whole nation and starting over again with a new one, the generation that has slandered and despised the promised land is told that it will not be able to enter it. It will die in the wilderness, and only the children of this generation will see the land, forty years later (Num 14:20-35).

The story of the spies is not the last of the "murmuring" narratives in the Pentateuch, for the grumbling of the wilderness generation continues,[98] but it is an unsurpassed distillation of Israel's constant rebellion against its God. The author of the Priestly document, from which major parts of this narrative are taken, used this material to depict the specific sin of those chosen and rescued by God—the fundamental sin, so to speak, of the people of God throughout its history: its distrust of God, its lack of faith in God's promises, its low opinion of God's saving gifts, and its slandering of the land. Those rescued and gifted by God will again and again assert that "the land . . . devours its inhabitants." The Pentateuch's stories

---

[97] In the deuteronomistic version of the spy narrative the murmuring of the people of God becomes a wicked "anti-credo": "It is because the LORD hates us that he has brought us out of the land of Egypt, to hand us over to the Amorites to destroy us" (Deut 1:27). Cf. Georg Braulik, *Deuteronomium I*. NEB (Würzburg: Echter, 1986) 27.

[98] Cf. especially Numbers 16–17.

of murmuring thus do not refer to the historical situation of Israel after the Exodus, but are much wider in scope: They are meant to show why Israel has lost its land and been forced into exile.

These stories are by no means alone in offering this interpretation. Many other biblical texts say similar things.[99] In Ezekiel 20, for example, there is a long historical retrospective beginning with the election of Israel in Egypt and extending to the period of the exile. God personally recapitulates this long process, stage by stage, and repeatedly says "but they rebelled against me."[100] Israel wanted to be like the other nations (20:32) and therefore it is cast by God into "the wilderness of the peoples" (20:35), that is, the Diaspora. This is truly, from beginning to end, a history of resistance, stubbornness, and rebellion against God. In one of the latest texts of the Old Testament, the Prayer of Azariah,[101] Israel says:

> by a true judgment you have brought all this upon us because of our sins. For we have sinned and broken your law in turning away from you; in all matters we have sinned grievously. We have not obeyed your commandments, we have not kept them or done what you have commanded us for our own good. (Dan 3:28-30)

How can we explain this permanent history of resistance and rebellion? Was Israel worse than the other nations? Was it less pious? Was it lacking in religious sense? No. Israel, in fact, wanted to be religious—and God wanted something completely different.

It is of the essence of religion that human beings make gods of everything they find mysterious, everything that shocks them and causes them to shudder, everything that fascinates them and that they want to do and experience themselves: love, fertility, Nature, longing, exhilaration, power, war. All these things are experienced as divine and are divinized and adored. And it is not difficult to serve the gods of power and the goddess of love. That is something people enjoy doing. It suits them. They even long to do it and take pleasure in it.

Israel, however, had encountered the *true* God in the course of its history, and it very quickly discovered that the will of this God did not coincide with human willing. This God's will is very different. It is often counter to human plans, ideas, and intentions. It is a strange and foreign will. And so, throughout its history, Israel battled over the will of God. On the one hand it was constantly resisting that will. It preferred to live like

---

[99] This is especially true of Psalms 78 and 106, as well as the entire deuteronomistic history.

[100] Ezek 20:8, 13, 21; cf. 20:16, 24, 28, 38.

[101] Dan 3:26-45. The Prayer of Azariah exists only in the Greek tradition. The translation follows the text of Theodotion.

the other nations: hence the continual falling away from YHWH, and hence the constant grumbling. On the other hand Israel had certainly sensed that the will of its God was more beneficial and reasonable than its own will. It was better to follow YHWH than the other gods. So it undertook the tremendous attempt to fix the will of its God in written form in order always to have that will before its eyes, never again to forget it, and never again to fall away from it. The Torah, which the theologians of Israel worked on for centuries, is the attempt to unite the people of God forever with the true will of God.

However, the effort was a failure. Israel itself expressed it in an image: the Law had scarcely been engraved on the stone tablets when the people were dancing around the golden calf, and even uttering the cultic shout: "These are your gods, O Israel, who brought you up out of the land of Egypt!"[102] That is: Israel wanted to worship its God as the other nations worshiped their gods, and it wanted to transform its historical experience back into the nature religions of Canaan.

The story of the golden calf, like the stories of grumbling, reflects concrete history. In 931 B.C.E. Jeroboam I withdrew the northern tribes from the dynasty of David. He made Bethel and Dan his national sanctuaries and set up in each of them gold-covered statues of steers as symbols of YHWH.[103] Originally the steers were probably understood to be YHWH's footstools, and the cultic shout attested at Bethel and Dan, "Here are your gods, O Israel, who brought you up out of the land of Egypt!" in truth praised YHWH's deed of salvation.[104] However, the people must quickly have come to regard the steers in Bethel and Dan as images of the Canaanite fertility god Baal and worshiped them as such. Hence after the catastrophe of the exile the worship of the golden steers in the northern kingdom could become a symbol of Israel's ceaseless falling away from its God.[105] The deuteronomistic history speaks repeatedly of the "sin(s) of Jeroboam."[106]

There is no people in the world that has interpreted its own history in this way, as an unending succession of uprisings and rebellions against God; and there is no people that has so uncompromisingly revealed its

[102] The engraving of the Book of the Covenant on the two tablets of stone is described in Exod 31:18; cf. 32:15-16; the dance around the golden calf is in Exod 32:1-6.

[103] 1 Kings 12:26-32.

[104] 1 Kings 12:28. For Jeroboam's original intention see Albertz, *History of Israelite Religion* 1:140–46.

[105] Thus 1 Kings 14:9; 2 Kings 17:16; Neh 9:18; Ps 106:19-21; cf. Deut 9:12, 16; Hos 8:5-6; 13:2.

[106] 1 Kings 15:30, 34; 16:2, 7, 19, 26, 31; 21:22; 22:52; 2 Kings 3:3; 10:29, 31; 13:2, 6, 11; 14:24; 15:9, 18, 24, 28; 17:21-22; 23:15.

own lack of faith and fidelity. However, we should speak more precisely: stubbornness, faithlessness, and infidelity can only exist where a people, in the course of its history, has encountered the true God and God's will. In the religions of the people surrounding Israel there was nothing resembling "faith" or "falling away from faith." They lived in harmony with their gods, for their gods were largely the world itself and projections of the world.

We are here face to face with the difference between religion and faith. Religion does not require faith. It imposes itself on people and is in some sense evident. It is the thing that is clear to everyone. The powers of the world and their numinous strength could be perceived and venerated by every person in antiquity. Therefore the religions of the ancient world in general were often open to foreign cults,[107] and their gods were interchangeable; that is, Greek Zeus could be equated with Roman Jupiter, and both of them with the principal gods of the Eastern religions.[108] From this point of view Israel brought the world something new. Its God was not interchangeable with others, but instead demanded an allegiance that excluded all other gods.

We can also describe the difference between religion and faith, which is at the same time the difference between religion and revelation, as follows: religion asks about the great mysteries of existence. Ernst Bloch's chain of questions in the introduction to his book, *The Principle of Hope*,[109] is a prime example of religious inquiry: "Who are we? Where do we come from? Where are we going? What are we waiting for? What awaits us?" Such questions arise from human beings themselves, from their wishes and desires. The faith of Israel posed different questions: not what people seek and expect, but what is God's plan and will for the world.

Religion seeks to satisfy human interests; faith asks about God's interests because it has found that God desires nothing other than the salvation of the world. We could also say that religion constantly seeks to bring our own plan for our lives under the blessing of God or the gods, while faith, in contrast, sets aside our personal plans and only asks how it may serve God's plan for the world. Religious people are concerned for themselves; the faithful are anxious about God's concerns.

Of course religion in its complexity cannot be reduced to simple formulae. It can certainly happen that there comes a moment in what is here

---

[107] One striking exception was the Egyptian king Akhnaton (1360–1340 B.C.E.).

[108] Cf. Jan Assmann, *MA'AT* 22–23.

[109] Ernst Bloch, *The Principle of Hope*. Translated by Neville Plaice, Stephen Plaice, and Paul Knight. 3 vols. (Cambridge, Mass.: M.I.T. Press, 1986) 1:1.

described as religious concern and seeking when everything shifts and one's own interests fall silent. In all religions it can happen that an hour arrives for every individual when he or she forgets the self and simply stands adoring, in pure openness, before infinite holiness. But what we normally experience as religion, especially in its concrete manifestation within ourselves, is not like that.

To begin with people desire themselves and not God. At first the will of God is strange to them. To open oneself to a foreign will is difficult; it makes the constant rebellion of the people of God quite understandable. Grumbling was by no means limited to the time of the Old Testament. It continued in the Church. The authors of the New Testament books repeatedly warn against it.[110] Paul writes to the community in Corinth:

> I do not want you to be unaware, brothers and sisters, that our ancestors were all under the cloud, and all passed through the sea, and all were baptized into Moses in the cloud and in the sea, and all ate the same spiritual food, and all drank the same spiritual drink. For they drank from the spiritual rock that followed them, and the rock was Christ. Nevertheless, God was not pleased with most of them, and they were struck down in the wilderness. Now these things occurred as examples for us . . . . And do not grumble as some of them did, and were destroyed by the destroyer. (1 Cor 10:1-6, 10*)

As shocking as the rebelliousness of the people of God and its weakness in faith appears, it was still a sign that since the call of Abraham and the leading of Israel out of Egypt something astonishing is happening in the world: there is visible within the world a will that is not merely the projection of human concerns and desires. The story of Israel's stubbornness is also a story of the discovery of truth: the face of the true God appears.

Is it necessary to say again, at the end of this section, that we have no reason to despise Israel because of its rebelliousness? What is archetypically narrated in the stories of the wilderness is the tale of our own resistance to the history of God's guidance; concretely it is the story of our resistance to exodus from the Egypt of our desires and projections and to entry into the land God has promised us. Probably we should judge still more harshly. In Israel at least there was a struggle over the will of God, and out of its experiences of catastrophe Israel ventured to subject its own history to revision, to look at it entirely through the eyes of God, and so to acknowledge that it was a history of unceasing resistance to and rebellion against God. Could we say that a comparably shocked retrospect on its own history, coupled with a will to repent, is occurring in the Church at the end of the twentieth century? Hardly.

[110] John 6:43; 1 Cor 10:10; Phil 2:14; 1 Pet 4:9; cf. Matt 20:11; Luke 5:30; 15:2; 19:7; John 6:41, 61; 7:12, 32; Acts 6:1; Jude 16.

On the contrary: The faith for which Israel still struggled and over which it wrangled is dissolving in the current decades—at least in Europe—almost without resistance, and unnoticed by a great many, into religion: a religion that permits everything, that surrenders to everything, that has countless gods but no longer a history with the biblical God. The rescue of the people of God from the old society and its travels through the wilderness to the land of promise are something in the dim and distant past, but no longer a present reality. On balance, in terms of faith Israel's situation in exile was better than the current situation of the Church.

## 6. The Scarlet Thread of Salvation History

And what does God say about the grumbling, the constant rejection, the continual apostasy of God's people? What God says is heard in many voices within the Bible. In the book of Exodus God's initial response to Israel's stubbornness is patience. God gives them water, manna, and quails. Only after God has given the Torah and concluded a covenant with the people, and still Israel's grumbling continues, does God respond with wrath. God's desire is now to end the history of Israel and destroy the nation. We may interpret that to mean that God will leave the people to their own devices, which means that they will destroy themselves. Only because Moses entreats for Israel and reminds God of the promises sworn to Abraham, Isaac, and Jacob does God's wrath abate (Exod 32:7-14).

Similar constellations of events are frequent in the Bible. Perhaps the voice of God's wrath is nowhere so clearly heard as in the book of the prophet Hosea,[111] and there especially in Hos 4:1-3. These verses introduce a long diatribe against Israel in which the voice of God alternates with authorial commentary. The wrathful speech extends to the end of chapter 11. It begins:

> Hear the word of the LORD, O people of Israel;
> for the LORD has an indictment against the inhabitants of the land.
> There is no faithfulness or loyalty,
> and no knowledge of God in the land.
> Swearing, lying, and murder,
> and stealing and adultery break out;
> bloodshed follows bloodshed.
> Therefore the land mourns,
> and all who live in it languish;

---

[111] For the following interpretation of Hosea I am following Norbert Lohfink, "'Ich komme nicht in Zornesglut' (Hos 11:9). Skizze einer synchronen Leseanweisung für das Hoseabuch" in *Ce Dieu qui vient. Mélanges offerts à Bernhard Renaud*. LD 159 (Paris: Cerf, 1995) 163–90.

> together with the wild animals
> and the birds of the air,
> even the fish of the sea are perishing. (Hos 4:1-3)

These three verses are incredibly radical. In the whole book of Hosea there is no sterner judgment on reality. It is a genuine summary of divine wrath. All the attributes that had formerly been positive are taken from the inhabitants of the land: fidelity, love, knowledge of God. Everything the decalogue forbids is attributed to them: they are blasphemers and betrayers, murderers, thieves, and adulterers; blood guilt follows blood guilt. The wrath this evokes can only lead to an end of the universe. There will be an end even of the animals, the birds, and the fish.[112]

What then follows in the next eight chapters of Hosea in the way of wrathful words from God and the corresponding commentary by the author is only a development of the theme thus announced. The first verses of chapter 4 are like an overture introducing and anticipating the horror to come. However, God's wrath is not the last word. By the beginning of chapter 11 wrath has turned into lament. God cannot forget the first love:

> When Israel was a child, I loved him,
> and out of Egypt I called my son.
> The more I called them,
>   the more they went from me;
> they kept sacrificing to the Baals,
>   and offering incense to idols.
> Yet it was I who taught Ephraim to walk,
>   I took them up in my arms;
> but they did not know that I healed them. (Hos 11:1-3)

Then, in 11:8-9, there is a total reversal in God; the burning divine wrath collapses and is transformed into love. God halts the judgment that is already in progress. The cosmic catastrophe threatened in 4:3 does not take place:

> How can I give you up, Ephraim?
>   How can I hand you over, O Israel? . . .
> My heart recoils within me;
>   my compassion grows warm and tender.
> I will not execute my fierce anger;
>   I will not again destroy Ephraim;
> for I am God and no mortal,
>   the Holy One in your midst,
>   and I will not come in wrath. (Hos 11:8-9)

---

[112] Ibid. 188.

This transformation of wrath into mercy, of judgment into salvation, is by no means unique to Hosea. There are similar texts in the other prophetic books, and in the whole of the Old Testament. In spite of the people's unfaithfulness and rebellion God responds with fidelity. God's heart beats for Israel, and only mercy will suffice. Thus Isa 54:6-8:

> For the LORD has called you
>   like a wife forsaken and grieved in spirit,
> like the wife of a man's youth
>   when she is cast off,
> says your God.
> For a brief moment I abandoned you,
>   but with great compassion I will gather you.
> In overflowing wrath for a moment
>   I hid my face from you,
> but with everlasting love I will have mercy on you,
>   says the LORD, your Redeemer.*

Of course in citing such texts one must not fall into the error of removing them from their contexts. It has been fashionable for some time now to talk unceasingly, in sermons and catechesis, of the love of God and thereby to conceal the fact that the Bible speaks of that love primarily in the context of judgment and catastrophe.

This kind of isolating extraction falsifies the meaning of the biblical texts. The God who thus appears is not the God of the Bible but simply the projection of an ideology that is currently widespread in Western society and in the Church as well, one that considers itself enlightened and humane: it claims to acknowledge everything, to tolerate every opinion, to assign guilt to no one and to exclude no one. But what is thus proclaimed as tolerance and love is really indifference, and the "loving God" is misused as the legitimation for individual desires and dreams, for as regards individual lifestyles everything, in fact, is tolerated.

Society is less tolerant toward the "different." If it does not apply physical force it attacks with moral weapons, and it does so tirelessly. Our media drip morality and attributions of guilt, but always claim at the same time to be displaying the most enlightened tolerance and unlimited openness. This pseudo-tolerance has long since lapped over into the Church, where it has led to an inflation of talk about "love." The theme of "judgment," on the other hand, is taboo.

Against this background one is almost afraid to quote Hosea 11. Hosea's verses on the endless, profound affection of God for God's people exist in a completely different context. They do not depict a God of cheap love who accepts everything, but the "nevertheless" of divine fidelity in

the face of the infidelity of the people of God. That infidelity has consequences that not even God's fidelity can magically eliminate. Ultimately
they will bring Israel into exile.

Thus in the book of Hosea God's love appears when the divine wrath
collapses. The prophet can only speak of it in light of Israel's infidelity
and in connection with the terrible losses caused by that infidelity. God's
fidelity prevents the final destruction of the people, which is simply self-
destruction, but it does not set aside judgment in favor of salvation. The
consequences of sin cannot be bypassed. God cannot wave a wand and
produce Paradise, and God's love cannot magically transform the people
of God. Instead the divine love and fidelity make it possible for the work
that began with Abraham to continue instead of being broken off—provided, of course, that there are people in Israel who respond to and take
hold of this divine fidelity. Out of the "nevertheless" of God's fidelity and
the opening of themselves on the part of those who believe comes the history of salvation; the world is changed, and the divine plan appears like a
scarlet thread running through the history of Israel and the nations—visible in many places, but very often invisible.

In fact God has repeatedly found people who recognize God's fidelity,
stake their lives on God's promises, and trust in God's plan for the world.
Abraham and his faith in the promise worked themselves deeply into the
consciousness of the people of God, and this produced new successors of
Abraham in every age. Of course there were often only a few who understood. God has usually had to continue this history with only a tiny number of people, often only a single individual. The Bible summarizes this
experience in the figure of Elijah.

His very name is programmatic: "Eli-Ja" means "My God is YHWH
(and no other)." Elijah fights for the uniqueness of YHWH. He is convinced
that the God whom Israel had experienced throughout its history must not
be absorbed into the world of the Baals and thus equated with them. Worshiping YHWH alongside other gods already constitutes an apostasy from
the ancestral faith. Therefore the Elijah legend, playing on the cultic leap-
ing dance of the prophets of Baal, relates that "Elijah . . . came near to
all the people, and said, 'How long will you go limping with two different opinions? If the LORD is God, follow him; but if Baal, then follow
him.' The people did not answer him a word" (1 Kings 18:21).

The people do not answer because they do not want to abandon their
worship of Baal. They know that the king himself has built a temple to
Baal in Samaria and established an official cult of Baal there. Elijah, by
clinging to the confession of "YHWH alone" against all Israel, finds himself
utterly isolated. His loneliness culminates in the lament: "I have been very

zealous for the LORD, the God of hosts; for the Israelites have forsaken your covenant, thrown down your altars, and killed your prophets with the sword. I alone am left, and they are seeking my life, to take it away" (1 Kings 19:10).

This lament by Elijah is corrected in the course of the narrative. God says to the prophet: "I will leave seven thousand in Israel, all the knees that have not bowed to Baal, and every mouth that has not kissed him" (1 Kings 19:18). So Elijah was not completely alone. There were more who had remained faithful than he knew. Nevertheless, his lament touches an essential point: God's history with this people does, in fact, hang at this moment on Elijah's passionate zeal. The silent people in the land would not be enough by themselves, no matter how important they are.

"I alone am left." If we see Israel's faith as religion and the history of that faith as the history of a religion we can only regard Elijah's lament as a complete exaggeration. The religious element lies deep in the human psyche and can never be extirpated because it takes its origin from human needs. It does not depend on the fidelity of an individual. That this is the case is clear from the free forms of religion that have arisen since the decline of Christianity in the West: they all center on self-discovery.

But Israel's faith is not located within the sphere of religion. Its first concern is not with human needs but with the will of God, with God's plan for the world. Therefore Israel's faith is also unconcerned about what has always been and what has always moved people, but with what God began with Abraham contrary to all human possibilities. This new thing was from the beginning the most extreme danger in a world that revolves around its own interests. It always hangs by a thin thread. It is like walking on water. It depends, again and again, on the faith of a few, and it depends on those few finding successors. Therefore it is entirely consistent that in the cycle of Elijah narratives the next thing that happens is the calling of Elisha:

> So [Elijah] set out from there, and found Elisha son of Shaphat, who was plowing. There were twelve yoke of oxen ahead of him, and he was with the twelfth. Elijah passed by him and threw his mantle over him. He left the oxen, ran after Elijah, and said, 'Let me kiss my father and my mother, and then I will follow you.' Then Elijah said to him, 'Go back again; for what have I done to you?' He returned from following him, took the yoke of oxen, and slaughtered them; using the equipment from the oxen, he boiled their flesh, and gave it to the people, and they ate. Then he set out and followed Elijah, and became his servant. (1 Kings 19:19-21)

In this text Elisha is depicted as the son of a well-to-do farmer, for he is plowing with twelve yoke of oxen. He himself is working with the last, the twelfth pair, and so he can see how the eleven servants ahead of him are plowing their furrows. Elijah calls him by throwing his mantle over him. So Elisha is commandeered for God's cause. He knows immediately what that means for him: leaving his family and his previous occupation. The rest of the story only describes how the rich heir leaves everything behind him.

First Elisha asks for permission to take leave of his parents. He knows that he is no longer his own master, but has entered the service of Elijah. Elijah allows him to take his leave. With the question "what have I done to you?" he gives him complete freedom. One who is called can only follow in utter freedom. But it is precisely this gift of freedom that makes Elisha fully aware of what has happened to him. Probably the text means to say that he does not return to his house at all, but improvises a farewell dinner for his servants right there in the field. At any rate he uses the yokes of one pair of oxen to make the fire as a sign that he is giving up his previous occupation and that the cause of God brooks no delay.

However, the narrative not only describes the immediacy of discipleship; it also shows that the new thing that God has begun with Israel can only be handed on from person to person. There is no automatic transfer of faith to the next generation. Faith and charism must be transmitted face to face. Elisha must feel the mantle of Elijah on his own body, so to speak.

This narrative makes a third statement as well: Elisha, of his own accord, had probably never thought of becoming a prophet. He had something quite different in mind: his parents' farm, the business, the family. Probably he was called for that very reason. Religious functionaries often close themselves to the new thing that God desires. God needs the religious non-professionals who are experienced in their craft. God needs people who are able to plow with twelve yoke of oxen or work with square and plumbline—and who can also apply the plumbline to the situation of the people of God. So it will be with many other people in the course of salvation history, including Jesus and the fisherfolk he called to follow him.

The prophet Amos, for example, was a landowner who bred animals and dealt in mulberry figs.[113] His financial independence distinguishes him in a fundamental way from the professional prophets who depended on people's paying them for their prophetic words. He came from Tekoa, south of Jerusalem, but emerged in Bethel in the northern kingdom and prophesied its destruction:

---

[113] To be precise Amos was a "tender of mulberry figs" (7:14). The farmer punctured the immature fruit on the tree to cause it to produce a resinous juice to protect the wound, which made the fruit sweeter. Amos probably organized this slitting of the fruit on a grand scale and then sold the figs.

Then Amaziah, the priest of Bethel, sent to King Jeroboam of Israel, saying, "Amos has conspired against you in the very center of the house of Israel; the land is not able to bear all his words. For thus Amos has said,

> 'Jeroboam shall die by the sword, and Israel must go into exile away from his land.'"

And Amaziah said to Amos, "O seer, go, flee away to the land of Judah, earn your bread there, and prophesy there; but never again prophesy at Bethel, for it is the king's sanctuary, and it is a temple of the kingdom."

Then Amos answered Amaziah, "I am no prophet, nor a prophet's son; but I am a herdsman, and a dresser of sycamore trees, and the LORD took me from following the flock, and the LORD said to me, 'Go, prophesy to my people Israel.'

"Now therefore hear the word of the LORD.
You say, 'Do not prophesy against Israel,
   and do not preach against the house of Isaac.'
Therefore thus says the LORD:
'Your wife shall become a prostitute in the city,
   and your sons and your daughters shall fall by the sword,
   and your land shall be parceled out by line;
you yourself shall die in an unclean land,
   and Israel shall surely go into exile away from its land.'"
   (Amos 7:10-17)

Normally we know little about the situations in which the words of the prophets were originally uttered. Hence this text is especially revealing. It shows that Amos had no chance against the alliance of Temple and state, but it also shows his self-confidence. Amos knows that he is not dependent on the state. He knows that God had called him and that ultimately it is not he who is being accused and expelled by Amaziah; it is God.[114] Amos is an outsider, but God often uses outsiders to advance the history of the people of God. Amos became the first of the "writing prophets." He himself, or his followers, made a collection of his prophetic sayings. There had never been anything like it before, and prophetic books of this sort would be of crucial importance for Israel's future.

Of course it does not follow from all this that salvation history is only advanced by outsiders. In contemplating God's history with God's people we must avoid any kind of anti-institutional romanticism, which would by no means do justice to the story. The prophet Isaiah, for example, was a member of the governing elite of Judah. "He is surprisingly well informed

---

[114] Cf. Hans-Walter Wolff, *Dodekapropheton 2. Joel und Amos*. BK XIV, 2 (Neukirchen-Vluyn: Neukirchener Verlag, 1969) 354.

about events on the diplomatic plane, even in the secret sphere of foreign treaties,"[115] and that presumes a close relationship to the royal court in Jerusalem. It is possible that Isaiah was even related to the royal family.

Something similar can be said of the reform movement under King Josiah, who ruled in Jerusalem from 640–609 B.C.E., a reform that was so decisive for Israel's history.[116] The priest Hilkiah and the secretary Shaphan played an authoritative role in the reform movement.[117] They were the most important of the king's officials. Apparently it was possible at that time to unite the Davidic royal house, portions of the Jerusalem officialdom, the priests of Jerusalem, and the middle class in Judah in a coalition for a few years.[118] This coalition's purpose was to bring the people of God together anew, to restore to it the whole land that once belonged to the twelve tribes, and to make Jerusalem the place where Israel's faith would be expressed in common festivals.[119]

Here, then, we find no outsiders at work, but officials who represent the authoritative institutions of the royal period: the Temple and the royal court. What is crucial is not the origin of those who carry forward God's story, but whether they recognize and represent the cause that is at stake. Such a recognition involves, before anything else, a memory—the memory of what God has already done. It is characteristic of the reform movement under Josiah that it looks back to the history of Israel and subjects that whole history to a revision. The history that had already happened and been interpreted was looked at anew and reinterpreted. The theological basis of the movement was a prior stage of our book of Deuteronomy. That early stage then quickly became the core of a sweeping retrospective extending from Moses to King Josiah: the so-called "deuteronomistic history" embracing the books from Deuteronomy through 2 Kings.

To see Israel's prophets merely as predictors of the future would be to mistake their nature most gravely. Obviously predictions about things to come play a considerable role in the work of the prophets, but more important than all prognoses is their diagnosis of the present, and that diagnosis was impossible without a constant recollection of what had happened in the past between Israel and its God. Ancient Israel, unlike modern western people, did not look to the future. It always imagined the

---

[115] Hans Wildberger, *Jesaja*, vol. 3, BK X,3 (Neukirchen-Vluyn: Neukirchener Verlag, 1982) 1586–87.

[116] For what follows see Norbert Lohfink, "Gab es eine deuteronomistische Bewegung?" in idem, *Studien* 3:65–142, at 111–17.

[117] There is a condensed version of the events in 2 Kings 22–23.

[118] Cf. Albertz, *History of Israelite Religion* 1:201–02.

[119] Norbert Lohfink, "Gab es eine deuteronomistische Bewegung?" 115.

future as *behind it*. It had the future at its back. The Hebrew word for future is "behind" *('aḥar)*. The past, on the other hand, is "before" *(qedem)*. The Israelites would not have said "Auschwitz is behind us," but "it is before us, it lies before our eyes." So even when Israel was moving into the future it did not look forward, but back to what had already happened, and it moved, still turned backward, another step into the future. Its progress was therefore not directed by conjectures about things to come but by reflection on what had already occurred. Because the past appeared like a coherent trace in which right and wrong steps, detours and false ways were reflected, the next step was possible. We could compare the whole process to the progress of someone rowing a boat, always seated with back to the direction of travel and orienting oneself on points that have long been left behind. God leads God's people in the same way, by unfolding the past to them. Nowhere in the Bible is that clearer than in the book of Deuteronomy and the deuteronomistic history.

The great historical retrospect that began in Israel especially under Josiah reached its climax in the exile. At first it seemed that with the people's banishment from the land everything was at an end, the thread of their history with God irrevocably broken. But in fact the catastrophe of the exile proved to be a *saving* history and a step into the future, for the hour at which Israel's existence as a nation-state, the form created by David, came to an end proved to be a productive crisis. It led to a rebirth of the people of God.

The most extensive sections of the Old Testament arose out of reflection on the crisis of the exile, out of looking back, turning back, understanding their own failure as a "happy fault." The exile, in fact, was a "qualitative leap" in Israel's ability to comprehend. A great deal of what for us seems an obvious part of the faith of the Old Testament people of God only came to Israel's full awareness through the exile. Only through the exile was it possible for the Old Testament as canon to come into existence.

Perhaps we could even make this into a rule: The decisive advances in the history of God with God's people happen only when the people are in crisis, when in their affliction they recognize their guilt and turn back to God, thus correcting the direction they are going. The very crisis of the people of God would then be one of the reasons why God's cause does not fail, but instead goes forward as a history of salvation.

All this makes it clear that what is said in the books of Exodus and Numbers about Israel's resistance and rebellion cannot be the last word. In fact these two books tell not only of the grumbling of the people of God. They contain other images as well. One of the loveliest is that of the cloud under whose protection Israel encamps and by whose fiery light the people are led:

> Whenever the cloud was taken up from the tabernacle, the Israelites would set
> out on each stage of their journey; but if the cloud was not taken up, then they
> did not set out until the day that it was taken up. For the cloud of the LORD
> was on the tabernacle by day, and fire was in the cloud by night, before the
> eyes of all the house of Israel at each stage of their journey. (Exod 40:36-38)

This image of the "cloud" may stem from a very early period, when YHWH
was still only a desert god who came from Seir and was described as a vol-
cano whose fiery light was visible from afar. Ancient texts of Israel still
reflect this early experience of God, which the Moses people may have
brought with them.[120] In the period when the book of Exodus was completed, however, the image of the fiery cloud had long since passed beyond being merely a naïve image. Instead it condensed the long history of
Israel's experience of being led.

Israel is a society arising out of constantly renewed leading by God.
Throughout its existence it is continually in danger; its faith is often sustained by only a few, and those few are frequently outsiders. God's cause
always hangs by a thin thread. But the thread does not break. God's fidelity is equal to the weight of infidelity. God remains in the midst of the
people. Israel is a people living beneath the fiery light of the cloud.

## 7. The Quest for the Form of the People of God

Only the crisis of the exile made the Old Testament possible. But that
crisis also made something else possible: a new form of existence for Israel.
The history of the people of God is not only a constant struggle to hand on
the faith. It is also an unbroken quest for the proper form of the people of
God. Now, at the end of this second chapter, we must speak of that quest.

The question about the "form" of the people of God may seem strange,
but it is necessary. It would only be superfluous if faith was something
purely internal or otherworldly. But Israel's faith is always about "the
world." Its desire is to bring more and more of the world under the rule of
God. Its wish is to transform the world entrusted to it by living the Torah,
God's social order, so that it will be clear to everyone how the will of God
intends the world to be. Hence faith necessarily takes on a social dimension. But what form of society is adequate to it?

We need not spend much time demonstrating what a burning question
this was and is. Many Christians are quite uncertain what the Church's
place in society ought to be. Is it a kind of club? or some kind of umbrella
organization for Christian interests? or is it, within a society in which

---

[120] Judg 5:4-5 and Psalm 68; cf. Deut 33:2.

there are innumerable jurisdictions, the regional office for matters of religion and transcendence?

The Church itself, despite all attempts to restrict it to spiritual matters, has always regarded itself as a "society."[121] Vatican II still defined it as a *societas*.[122] But in what sense is it a society? What does the Old Testament have to say about it? It does not theorize, but describes the long road that the people of God traveled in their search for the right form, even into the misery of the exile and the Diaspora. Out of its experiences of catastrophe, then, Israel gradually, and with many backslidings, came to understand its relationship to the rest of society and to the state.

### The People of God as a Tribal Society

For a long time Israel was not a state. During a period of two hundred years, roughly from 1200–1000 B.C.E., it had no central government; in concrete terms this means that it had no king. However, we should not refer to those two hundred years as Israel's "pre-national period," as many do. By doing so they portray this period as something preliminary, while the national period is the genuine article, and in so doing they have already distorted the picture. The fact that all around Israel there were reigning monarchs while Israel itself for two hundred years had no king must be taken seriously in theological terms.[123]

For the ancient Near East the king and his central government were not only a matter of course; the king also saw to it that the order at whose pinnacle he stood had primeval legitimacy. In the Tigris-Euphrates region the epic describing the creation of the world, *Enuma Elish*, proposed that the Babylonian kingship resulted from the originating events of the world and thus, as part of the order of creation, was sacrosanct. The state theology of Egypt was much the same: the monarch and his system of government had always existed and would endure forever. In contrast to this it was simply revolutionary for biblical Israel to say of itself that in its early period it had existed for a long time without a royal institution.[124]

At the beginning of this second part we spoke at length about Israel's origins, and it was already clear that Israel's tribal society was not a primitive precursor of the state, as if in the beginning the people were unaware

[121] Cf. Gerhard Lohfink, *Wem gilt die Bergpredigt?* 104–07.

[122] *LG* 8.

[123] Cf. Norbert Lohfink, "Das Königtum Gottes und die politische Macht. Zur Funktion der Rede vom Gottesreich bis zu Jesus von Nazaret" in idem, *Das Jüdische am Christentum* 71–102, at 77–79.

[124] Cf. Joachim Jeremias, "Schöpfung in Poesie und Prosa des Alten Testaments. Gen 1–3 im Vergleich mit anderen Schöpfungstexten des Alten Testaments," *JBTh* 5 (1990) 11–36, at 13.

of other possibilities or were unable to fashion a better form of government. Instead it was a deliberate counter-model over against the monar-
chically organized Canaanite city states.[125] The people of Israel did not
want the kind of life practiced in Canaan or in Egypt. What was decisive
for them was their free association. There was unconditional and obligatory solidarity only within the family, and to a certain degree within the
clan. At the tribal level and that of tribal alliances, in contrast, nothing
could be compelled. This was especially evident in crisis situations, particularly when external enemies attacked Israel's territory. There was then
no mobilization by a central authority; it had to happen "from below,"
through a free decision of the clans and tribes to go to war.

The book of Judges mentions not a single war against external enemies in which all the tribes took part. It is true that for the battle against
the coalition of Canaanite kings that is celebrated in the Song of Deborah
two charismatic figures, Deborah and (at Deborah's instigation) Barak,
took the initiative. The tribes of Ephraim, Benjamin, Manasseh, Zebulon,
Issachar, and Naphtali joined them. The tribes of Reuben, Gilead (= Gad),
Dan, and Asher are reprimanded because they remained at home and did
not join the struggle:

> Among the clans of Reuben
>   there were serious searchings of heart.
> Why did you tarry among the sheepfolds,
>   to hear the piping for the flocks?
> Among the clans of Reuben
>   there were serious searchings of heart.
> Gilead stayed beyond the Jordan;
>   and Dan, why did he serve in foreign ships?
> Asher sat still at the coast of the sea,
>   settling down by his landings. (Judg 5:15-17*)

The same song gives the troops that answered the call to join the armies
the honorable title "people of YHWH" *('am jhwh)*.[126] We have here the oldest form and one of the oldest interpretations of the familiar expression
"people of God": where people freely join in common solidarity and fearlessly put themselves at the service of YHWH, there is the people of God.

The Song of Deborah also shows that there were as yet no clan offices
or any other positions of authority over more than a single tribe. Only the

---

[125] Albertz, *History of Israelite Religion* 1:76, 78–79.

[126] Judg 5:11, 13. Cf. Norbert Lohfink, "Beobachtungen zur Geschichte des Ausdrucks
*'am jhwh*" in idem, *Studien zur biblischen Theologie. SBAB 16* (Stuttgart: Katholisches
Bibelwerk, 1993) 99–132, at 102, 106, and 120; Albertz, *History of Israelite Religion*
1:125–26.

charism of Deborah and other judges succeeded in each case in bringing together some of the tribes to fight the Canaanite threat. After the victory their charism fades and they return to their families. The fundamental egalitarian situation is restored.

What is impressive about the tribal society is its voluntariness coupled with equality. The problem is violence. Nothing is more pugnacious than the will to freedom of a society without a state. The absence of supra-regional offices leads repeatedly to uncontrollable outbreaks of violence. The book of Judges depicts such an outbreak in exemplary fashion in the story of the shameful action of the inhabitants of Gibeah toward the wife of a foreign Levite, and in the unbridled vengeance that all Israel then takes on the tribe of Benjamin, followed by the brutal action designed to provide the surviving Benjaminite men with wives (Judges 19–21). Could the people of God survive in the long run without superior offices? Were charismatic figures like Ehud, Deborah, Gideon, or Jephthah enough?

### The People of God as a Nation

The great experiment of the state begins in Israel with David, who was acknowledged as king by all the tribes in about the year 1000 B.C.E.[127] The kingdom ended for the North with the fall of Samaria in 722, and for the South with the fall of Jerusalem in 586. It is understandable that this experiment, which was to end so terribly, should at least have been tried: in about 1050 B.C.E. the Philistines, who had arrived with the "tide of seafarers" from the North and gradually established themselves in the coastal lowlands, decisively defeated the Israelites at the city of Aphek. In the long run the ponderous and poorly equipped army of the tribal alliance was not equal to the military force of the Philistines.

The rapid rise of David and the fact that Israel became a state almost overnight is thus understandable enough. However, we must see that David built up his own powerful troop of mercenaries and with the conquest of Jerusalem created for himself a power base independent of the tribes; this constituted a radical break with the past.[128] Now Israel had a central government with the corresponding apparatus of civil officials and a system of taxation that was steadily improved. There were professional officers and a professional army in addition to the conscripted troops. The loosely defined tribal territories now became a large, cohesive territorial state. And with the territorial state there began, for the first time in Israel's history, a series of wars whose sole purpose was conquest. In 2 Sam 8:1-2 it is reported that

[127] 2 Samuel 5:1-5. Under Saul Israel was not yet a political state. Saul was indeed anointed and was acknowledged as king by acclamation (1 Sam 10:24), but he was unable to establish a central power.

[128] Albertz, *History of Israelite Religion* 1:105–11.

> David attacked the Philistines and subdued them; David took Metheg-ammah out of the hand of the Philistines. He also defeated the Moabites and, making them lie down on the ground, measured them off with a cord; he measured two lengths of cord for those who were to be put to death, and one length for those who were to be spared. And the Moabites became servants to David and brought tribute.

Still more questionable, however, is the fact that with David's successor, Solomon, a *sacral* kingship was introduced into Israel. The king now functioned as the supreme judge of the people and also as the highest priest of the Jerusalem Temple. YHWH became a state god. For the first time there appeared and established itself within the people of God what later Europeans called the "union of throne and altar." Israel now resembled the Near Eastern systems of government. In 1 Sam 8:19-20, when the prophet Samuel for good reasons objects to the introduction of kingship, the people declare that "we are determined to have a king over us, so that we also may be like other nations."

With the sacral kingship and the centrally-governed state Israel acquired some civilizing progress, but also the unjust structures of the neighboring peoples; forced labor was introduced under Solomon[129]—the very system of human degradation that caused Israel's ancestors to leave Egypt. And very quickly, on the basis of the severe Near Eastern law of credit, there developed a pronounced class society.

Against all this there arose a massive resistance in the name of the ancient tradition of freedom in Israel. We can still perceive it behind many Old Testament texts. Thus, for example, a political satire in the form of the fable of the trees ridicules the kingship (Judg 9:8-15). It goes like this: the trees want to have a king, too. They offer the kingship first to the olive tree, then to the fig tree, and finally to the vine, but all three refuse. They do not want to sacrifice their usefulness to humanity just for the sake of "sway over the other trees."

> So all the trees said to the bramble,
> "You come and reign over us."
> And the bramble said to the trees,
> "If in good faith you are anointing me king over you,
> then come and take refuge in my shade;
> but if not, let fire come out of the bramble
> and devour the cedars of Lebanon." (Judg 19:14-15)

---

[129] Cf. 1 Kings 5:13-16; 11:28; 12:1-19. It is pointless to adduce 1 Kings 9:20-22 as a counterargument.

Mocking satire was not the last of it. David had to put down two rebellions, both of them broad-based. The head of one rebellion was his own
son Absalom, and the leader of the other, much more dangerous, was a
Benjaminite named Sheba.[130] Apparently both Absalom and Sheba envisioned the creation of a kind of constitutional monarchy that would pay
more heed to the traditions of the egalitarian tribal society.[131]

When, after the death of Solomon, the northern tribes separated from
the tribe of Judah, criticism of the lack of freedom under royal government played a crucial role alongside the ancient tribal rivalries. Significantly, the signal for the rebellion was the murder of Adoram, the
taskmaster over forced labor,[132] and the rebels' shout was:

"What share do we have in David?
We have no inheritance in the son of Jesse.
To your tents, O Israel!
Look now to your own house, O David." (1 Kings 12:16)

The political resistance of the early royal period was continued, on a
different plane, in the resistance of the prophets. Their sharp social critique,
condemning contempt for and exploitation of the poor, was mixed from the
very beginning with a critique of the state and the system of government.

Later, when the kingship collapsed before the power of Assyria and
Babylon, the way was open for a recollection of the past. The deuteronomistic history, in a comprehensive revision, looked back once again to the
royal period, weighed the positive and negative elements, sought the
causes of the catastrophe, and came, on the whole, to a highly critical view
of the national period. It culminates in a scene in which the whole history
of the kingship in Israel was interpreted in anticipation of the reality. It begins with Samuel being confronted by a kind of popular petition in favor
of a king:

". . . appoint for us . . . a king to govern us, like other nations." But the thing
displeased Samuel when they said, "Give us a king to govern us." Samuel
prayed to the LORD, and the LORD said to Samuel, "Listen to the voice of the
people in all that they say to you; **for they have not rejected you, but they
have rejected me from being king over them.** Just as they have done to me,
from the day I brought them up out of Egypt to this day, forsaking me and
serving other gods, so also they are doing to you." (1 Sam 8:5-8)

---

[130] For Absalom's rebellion cf. 2 Samuel 15–18; for the rebellion of Sheba cf. 2 Sam
20:1-22.

[131] For details see Albertz, *History of Israelite Religion* 1:122–24.

[132] 1 Kings 12:18. On the separation of the northern tribes from Judah see Albertz, *History of Israelite Religion* 1:138–43.

The criticism of the royal period could scarcely be sharper, and yet the text contains a hook. God says to Samuel, "Listen to the voice of the people!" That means: "Give Israel a king!" The authors of the deuteronomistic history could not write otherwise, for after all, there was the prophecy of Nathan assuring that David's kingship would exist forever: "Your house and your kingdom shall be made sure forever before me; your throne shall be established forever" (2 Sam 7:16). When the authors of the deuteronomistic history emphasized this promise, in spite of their criticism of the royal period, they made clear that the phase in which the people of God existed as a state was not without purpose. For at that time a hope was placed in Israel that could never again be extinguished: the hope for a successor of David who would live entirely according to the will of God and would introduce a society that is truly just.

### The People of God as a Temple Community

Israel's state had collapsed before the power of Assyria and Babylon, but it was precisely under the pressure of these great empires that would henceforth rule the land that the people of God found a new shape. It is not easy to describe it correctly. The phrase "Temple community" is only a makeshift device. It emphasizes one important aspect, but it by no means exhausts the reality. What form did Israel take in this third phase of its existence?

One crucial fact is that Jerusalem, or rather the tiny province of Judea (only about fifty kilometers wide) no longer had any political independence. Judea fell successively under the overlordship of the Babylonians, the Persians, the Ptolemys, the Seleucids, and the Romans. I say "overlordship" to indicate that the great powers accorded the province a kind of self-government and even its own legal system. The titles for the agents of this self-government changed from time to time, and the extent of self-government could be greater or less depending on the political constellation of a given time. Nevertheless, Judea and all the other former territories of Israel ultimately remained governing units under foreign domination.

The Maccabean revolt against the Seleucids did succeed in driving the wheel backward one turn. Under the Hasmoneans Judea even achieved, for a moment, an expansion approximating that of David's empire. But that was only an interlude. On the whole it remained true that for many centuries Israel lost its political sovereignty. Inasmuch as it lived under the protection of the great empires it became, in sociological terms, a "sub-society"; that is, it practiced its own form of society within the territory of a larger state. Of course we cannot speak of a "sub-society" if there are no symbols and organizational structures that form a genuine *society*. In Judea the most prominent of these was the Temple. It was rebuilt in 515 B.C.E. under the Persian governor Zerubbabel, then enlarged and decorated from 19 to 9 B.C.E. under Herod the Great. In the year 70 C.E. it was finally destroyed by the Romans.

The Second Temple was no longer under the supervision of a king as it had been in Israel's national period. Therefore the priests succeeded in establishing an independent governance of the Temple, extending, in fact, far beyond the duties of the Temple itself. The high priest also assumed organizational and political functions, even becoming the representative of the whole commonwealth. For the first time in Israel's history the priesthood became a genuine power factor.[133] In Jesus' trial the ruling high priest Caiaphas and the former high priest Annas would play a crucial role.

The Temple was an exalted symbol not only for the homeland but also for the Diaspora. To finance the cult and the salaries of the priests it demanded a relatively high burden of taxes, which was produced each year with an astonishingly willing compliance. But above all it continually brought the people together for the great festivals. The Temple is the theological center of a whole series of writings from the post-exilic period, including Ezekiel, Haggai, and the Chroniclers' history. In Ezekiel 40–48 it appears as the embodiment and center of a renewed society that would freely place itself under God's rule.

Although the significance of the real and the hoped-for Temple in holding together the post-exilic people of God was extraordinarily great there now arose another entity that in the long term would be as important as the Temple in forming Israel as a society, and that in fact surpassed the Temple in significance: namely the Torah, the first five books of Moses. It is possible that the Torah was created because the Persian government demanded a codified law for its province of Judea. In any case it was constructed at the beginning of the fifth century B.C.E. out of older historical and legal works and was received by all Jews as the normative text defining Israel's concept of itself. The Torah is the one thing that made a society in the true sense of the word out of that entity, frayed as it was on all sides, that we have called a "Temple community." For it formulated the historical origins of Israel in a framing narrative and at its center set forth the social order of the people of God. The following elements are worthy of notice:

The historical framing narrative, after a short primeval history of the world and the nations (Genesis 1–11) restricts itself entirely to the experiences of rescue in the early period of Israel, from Abraham to the time

---

[133] Cf. Albertz, *History of Israelite Religion* 2:448–49.

immediately before the entry into the promised land. Only the *state* period was excluded from Israel's fundamental text. Obviously this was intentional. It was meant to say: "Israel had not first assumed its essential character under David and Solomon, but already under Moses, as a result of its liberation and the covenant with its God Yahweh on Sinai."[134]

Also worthy of note is that the laws that are contained within the framing narrative—that is, the social order proposed by the Torah—deliberately reach back to the traditions of the period before the kingship and avoid any kind of state-connected legal tradition.[135] In the complex of laws connected with Sinai (Exodus 20–Numbers 10) the state plays no part at all, although a considerable amount of other legal material derived from a later period is incorporated there. Sinai represents a place beyond the nation-state.[136] It is not Egypt and it is not Jerusalem; that is, it is far away from the divine state of Egypt and also far from the power structures of the Davidic empire. According to the Torah Israel is not David's empire, but "a priestly kingdom and a holy nation" (Exod 19:6).

Above (II, 4) we have spoken about the social project that stands behind such a statement. The people of God the Torah has in mind is a just and egalitarian society. Structures of poverty must repeatedly be eliminated. Foreigners must be given the same kind of help as one would offer one's own brother or sister. The gods of might and oppression are to have no place among the people of God. God is to be Israel's sole and freely accepted ruler, and Israel, with every aspect of its life, is to be God's realm.

All that did not remain merely letters on a page. The Torah gradually became a holy text that formed Israel and gave it its identity. When the Temple was finally destroyed, the Torah enabled Israel to survive. It marked not only Israel's piety but its whole existence at the very deepest level. From now on doing the will of God would also mean studying the Torah and living according to it.

### The People of God as a Federation of Synagogues

The fourth and definitive form of the people of God is a confederation of synagogal communities. Of course synagogues did not originate with the destruction of the Temple in the year 70 C.E. and the end of the "Temple community." The form of the synagogal community had developed some time before that. It was one of the most creative of Israel's inventions and one with the most significant consequences.

---

[134] Ibid. 472.
[135] Cf. Norbert Lohfink, *Das Jüdische am Christentum* 252 n. 89.
[136] Cf. Frank Crüsemann, *Torah* 57.

Many scholars believe that synagogal communities originated in the Jewish Diaspora. By far not all the exiles returned to the homeland, and many left the land even after the great deportations under Sargon II, Sennacherib, and Nebuchadnezzar II. Important Jewish settlements were created in Mesopotamia and these were important for the later development of rabbinic Judaism. More Jews lived in Egypt than in Judea.[137] The Jewish philosopher Philo says there were about a million.[138]

The existence of the Torah must have played an important part in the origins of synagogal communities. Jews living in the Diaspora could only rarely or perhaps never visit the homeland and its Temple. In the Torah they found a second home. For that reason Heinrich Heine called the Torah the "portable fatherland," the movable home of the Jews. Of course the Torah could only be a precondition for the formation of synagogal communities because it was not primarily a book of instruction for private devotion, but aimed at the construction of a society.

We do not know when Jews in the Diaspora or in the homeland apart from the Temple first gathered as a "community" around the Torah. Precise dating is so difficult in this matter because such gatherings did not have to have, from the very beginning, a name that could be literarily attested, and because the initial places of assembly left no obvious clues for archaeologists. The oldest inscriptional evidence for a Jewish place of prayer comes from Egypt, from the time of Ptolemy III Euergetes (247–221 B.C.E.). The oldest synagogue excavated thus far is on the island of Delos and dates from about 100 B.C.E.[139] But there must certainly have been synagogal communities and gathering places for them even earlier. We simply have no evidence of them.

An older name for the Jewish synagogue is *proseuchē* (house of prayer). But was the synagogue really established so that there would be a place for worship everywhere? Recently it has been suggested that the congregations in the synagogues developed out of the "assembly at the gate."[140] The city gates and the nearby space were, in ancient Israel, the center of public life, where news was exchanged, business dealings discussed, and

---

[137] For more detail see Aryeh Kasher, "Diaspora I/2: Frühjüdische und rabbinische Zeit," *TRE* 8:711–17, at 712.

[138] Philo, *Flacc.* 43.

[139] For this information see Martin Hengel, "*Proseuchē* und Synagoge. Jüdische Gemeinde, Gotteshaus und Gottesdienst in der Diaspora und in Palästina" in Gert Jeremias, Heinz-Wolfgang Kuhn, and Hartmut Stegemann, eds., *Tradition und Glaube. Das frühe Christentum in seiner Umwelt. Festschrift K. G. Kuhn* (Göttingen: Vandenhoeck & Ruprecht, 1971) 157–84, at 158 and 167; also Wolfgang Schrage, *synagōgē*, *TDNT* 7:798–852, at 811–12.

[140] Lee I. Levine, "The Nature and Origin of the Palestinian Synagogue Reconsidered," *JBL* 115 (1996) 425–48.

legal judgments administered. Only when more and more Hellenistic types of city layout, with different styles of gates and the surrounding spaces, made their appearance in Israel was there need for a new locality for the "assembly at the gate," and so the synagogue was established.

There is archaeological evidence to support this proposition. In any case it would offer a good explanation for the manifold functions of the synagogue; it was certainly available for worship, but it had many other purposes as well. People gathered in the synagogue for councils and judicial assemblies; official documents such as divorce decrees were prepared and delivered there; lost-and-found announcements were made, witnesses called for, notices posted, business done, wakes for the dead conducted, and public mourning held. Most synagogues contained a community archive and a kitchen for the service of the poor. Often there was even a bath so that the people need not go to the Gentile bathhouses. Finally, the synagogue offered shelter for traveling members of the faith and a place for instruction. The oldest epigraphic witness for a synagogue in Jerusalem, the famous Theodotos inscription, reads:

> Theodotus the son of Vettenus, priest and *archisynagogos,* son of the *archisynagogos,* grandson of the *archisynagogos,* built this synagogue for the reading of the Torah and the study of the commandments, and the hostel and the rooms and the water installations, for needy travellers from foreign lands. The foundation of the synagogue was laid by his fathers and the elders and Simonides.[141]

The Jewish synagogue was thus more than a house of prayer. It was a community center, and it was unthinkable without a community. But what was the form of such a community? In terms of its internal form it cannot be regarded as a "club" or "association" (*thiasos, collegium*). Clubs were widespread in antiquity, especially in the Hellenistic-Roman period. In their formal aspect they were almost always "cultic clubs"; that is, their purpose was the worship of a particular deity. In fact, however, they were always based more on a common interest, frequently mere social clubs as we know them today. The purpose of such a club could be, for example, an annual banquet in memory of a certain individual who had died, or simply a monthly drinking party.[142]

The flourishing system of clubs in antiquity was, in fact, a considerable aid to the sub-political existence of the synagogal communities. It

---

[141] *CIJ* II, 1404. Translation in S[hmuel] Safrai and M[enahem] Stern, *The Jewish People in the First Century.* 2 vols. (Philadelphia: Fortress, 1974) 1:192.

[142] On clubs in the Hellenistic-Roman world see especially Placid Hermann, Jan Hendrik Waszink, Carsten Colpe, and Bernhard Kötting, "Genossenschaft," *RAC* 10 (1978) 83–155.

provided them with a kind of cover. The Roman officials, and certainly not only they, regarded the Jewish synagogal communities simply as clubs. When Caesar forbade all *collegia* in the city of Rome he expressly permitted the Roman Jews to establish clubs. They were allowed to assemble "according to the manner and customs of their ancestors."[143] Nevertheless, the Jewish communities were in fact something different. This is clear from the very wording of the permission: they were allowed to live according to the "laws of their ancestors."[144]

The precise difference, however, can scarcely be determined by using the categories of ancient law. We can only get close to it by reflecting on what Aristotle said about the nature of "association" *(koinōnia)*. In the Nicomachean Ethics he distinguishes between the commonwealth of the *polis* (that is, the state) and the forms of community within it (the associations and clubs). The *polis* is the whole, while the associations and clubs seek their own advantages in a restricted sphere.[145] At this very point the difference is evident. The synagogal community was not only concerned with special interests (such as Sabbath devotion or the securing of a dignified burial). Its concern was for the whole of life in all its aspects, in accordance with what Torah really is.

An eloquent indication of this "wholeness" is the ability to govern in civil affairs; another is exemption from Roman military service and later from the Roman imperial cult as well.[146] The synagogal community was a society of a different order and cannot be fully comprehended in the forms of ancient club life.

Added to this is the fact that the individual synagogal communities were by no means isolated; they maintained constant communication with each other, and above all they were concerned for their ties to the "land of Israel" and regarded Jerusalem as their native city. Philo writes that Jerusalem was the true native city *(patris)* of all Jews, no matter where they were.[147]

If we take all this together it is clear that here a new form had been created for the people of God. The synagogal association was no longer a state, although it gratefully acknowledged the existence of the (legal) state and prayed for its rulers. On the other hand it was not a cultic club based on

---

[143] An important source is Josephus, *Ant.* XIV, 10, 8 (215). Cf. Helga Botermann, *Das Judenedikt des Kaisers Claudius. Römischer Staat und* Christiani *im 1. Jahrhundert.* Hermes Einzelschriften 71 (Stuttgart: F. Steiner, 1996) 52 n. 138; 119–20 n. 373.

[144] Cf. Aryeh Kasher, "Diaspora" 714–15.

[145] Aristotle, *Nicomachean Ethics* VIII 11 (1160a).

[146] Cf. Emil Schürer, *The History of the Jewish People in the Age of Jesus Christ (175 B.C.–A.D. 135).* Translated by T. A. Burkill et al. Revised and edited by Geza Vermes and Fergus Millar. 3 vols. (Edinburgh: T&T Clark, 1973) 3:114–25.

[147] Cf. Philo, *Leg. Gai.* 281; cf. *Flacc.* 46.

territorial bonds and worshiping the god of the homeland. It was certainly not a mere *societas in cordibus*, a spiritual union of the silent people of the land. Instead it was an association of communities, each of which was a fragment of public life, each a tiny commonwealth, each a *politicum.*

In any case the definitive form of the people of God began to take shape in these Jewish synagogal communities. In early Judaism that form remained somewhat amorphous, for as clear as the deuteronomistic criticism of the royal period is, early Judaism nevertheless reveals an elementary impulse toward statehood. We need only think of the restorationist politics of the Hasmoneans. The Zealots, too, fought for a form of constitution in which faith and society would coincide. In our own time the whole problem has broken out anew with the founding of the state of Israel.

It is important for us to note that the association of communities discovered by Israel became the formative principle of the early Church. Here appeared with full clarity what the people of God is: a network of communities spread over the whole earth and yet existing within non-Christian society, so that each person can freely choose whether to be a Christian or not; it is genuine community and yet not constructed on the model of pagan society, a true homeland and yet not a state.

How difficult that is to imagine and how new such a construct was to the world is evident from the fact that Christianity, when it had scarcely survived the era of persecutions and been acknowledged by the Edict of Milan (313) as a publicly recognized religion, joined itself to the Roman state and only a few decades later became the official state religion. The Church then, in the form of the "imperial Church," went through the experiment all over again that Israel had long ago suffered through, with enormous sacrifices, and this new experiment, too, brought with it costs that no one can calculate.

Perhaps it was necessary. Perhaps without that process Christianity would have become a sect and forgotten that its concern is "the world" and the transformation of society. And yet, for the Church as for Israel, the experiment with statehood was an enormous detour. It was radically ended only in our own time. Joseph Ratzinger wrote in 1965:

> Few things have damaged the Church so much in the last century and a half as its stubborn clinging to antiquated state-church positions. The attempt to shelter the faith threatened by modern science with state protective measures of its very nature hollowed out that faith from within. . . . That the Church's laying claim to the state . . . is one of the most questionable burdens of the Church in today's world is something that those who think historically can no longer refuse to acknowledge.[148]

[148] Joseph Ratzinger, *Ergebnisse und Probleme der dritten Konzilsperiode* (Cologne: Bachem, 1965) 31–32.

The search for the proper form of the people of God is apparently an endlessly wearisome process. From a theological point of view it reveals God's concern for the transformation of human society. This transformation can only occur in freedom. That is why it is such a difficult path through history, in fact a drama that extends throughout the entire history of Israel and the Church.

Through "trial and error" and through bitter experience the people of God have come gradually to understand their proper form. The community-church was not something born from the brains or created on the desks of theologians. Instead, from the time of Abraham the people of God has been a gigantic field for experiment. Salvation was a construction site from the beginning. The question has always been: What brings life to human beings, and what brings death? What causes society to succeed, and what causes it to fail? What brings the world more freedom and redemption, and what casts it into misery?

*

In this second part we have considered the characteristics of Israel as the people of God. It is clear that much more could be said. But instead of adding further chapters let us in closing this section simply allow the Jewish sages to speak once again. They asked themselves, among many other things, why God created the world and what the real purpose of creation was. The answer, as so often among the rabbis, could have a laconic brevity:

> Rav said, "The world was created solely for David's sake." And Schmuel said: "For Moses' sake." And Rabbi Johanan said: "For the sake of the Messiah."[149]

What does this text mean?[150] First of all, it says that the fact that David and Moses existed, and that one day the Messiah will come, the one who will fulfill Nathan's prophecy, is sufficient reason for the creation of the world. But beyond that the text subsumes within those great figures in Israel the realities for which they stand. David is here regarded as the author of the Psalms. He stands for prayer, the praise of God. The first Jewish voice, that of Rav, is saying that at the moment when true prayer to God happened in the world, in the linguistically perfected form of the Psalms, the meaning of creation had been realized. There can be no greater thing for the world than to have the praise of God lifted up within it.

---

[149] *b.Sanh.* 98b.

[150] The following interpretation was inspired by Emanuel Lévinas, "Textes messianiques," in idem, *Difficile liberté. Essais sur le judaisme.* biblio essais 4019 (1976) 89–139, at 123–24.

The second Jewish voice, that of Rabbi Schmuel, is not content with that answer, even though it is correct. He says: no, the praise of God is not enough to define the meaning of creation. Prayer by itself can be uncommitted. The goal of creation is only achieved when the Torah is in the world, the seriousness of morality, the yoke of the commandments, the acknowledgment of God's rule in action. Only then will God be utterly glorified, when there is a people in the world that lives according to the divine will in all things.

The third Jewish voice, that of Rabbi Johanan, agrees with both the others. Prayer and Torah are decisive and indispensable. And yet they do not adequately define the world's goal. For the creation to be perfected it needs the Messiah, the powerful helper. For human moral strength is not enough to transform the world. Only in the fullness and splendor of a *messianically* transformed people of God will the meaning of creation shine forth, only then will praise and the fulfillment of the Law find their rightful place. The second half of this book is about that messianic fulfillment.

# III

# Jesus and the Figure of the Twelve

## 1. What Is "New" About the "New Testament"?

We are standing on a threshold. Where does the Old Testament lead? In what direction does it flow? Christians say: to the New Testament! But in that case, what does this word "new" mean? What is new about the New Testament? Does it contain something strange to the Old Testament, something that had not yet been thought of there?[1]

Many Christians have encountered a formula going around that gives an apparently simple answer to this question: "The time of the old covenant was a time of fear; the time of the new covenant is a time of love."[2] This statement feeds on a number of misunderstandings, especially misreadings of Pauline theology.[3] And it is simply false. In the Torah the love commandment already has a central place. In Deut 6:4-5, which became Israel's

---

[1] For parts 1 and 2 of this chapter I will refer to my essay, "Das Neue am Neuen Testament" in *"Wenn das Salz seine Kraft verliert." Ein Kirchenjahr mit der Integrierten Gemeinde in Paderborn* (Urfeld: Integrierte Gemeinde, 1992) 2:11–39. The text has been expanded and revised.

[2] In *Gotteslob,* the official prayer- and hymnbook of the German-language dioceses, there is a eucharistic hymn by M. L. Thurmair containing the verse: "The law of fear must give way when the new covenant begins; incomparable meal of love: now in faith partake of it" (No. 544, verse 5). In the model text, the Latin *Pange lingua* by Thomas Aquinas, the sense was quite different: *et antiquum documentum novo cedat ritui; praestat fides supplementum sensuum defectui.* There *documentum* refers to the ritual of the paschal lamb, *novus ritus* to Jesus' last supper. It may be that the schema Old Testament = fear, New Testament = love can be traced to Augustine, although he qualifies it with a famous formula: *Multum et solide significatur ad vetus testamentum timorem potius pertinere sicut ad novum dilectionem, quamquam et in vetere novum lateat et in novo vetus pateat.* There are many solid indications that fear is more relevant to the Old Testament, while love is more relevant to the New. However, just as the New Testament lies hidden in the Old, so the Old Testament comes to light in the New (*Quaest. in Hept.* 2.73, CCSL 33, 106).

[3] The "fear" in Rom 8:15 is not the consequence of the *Law,* but of *sin,* which, of course, is brought to light by the Law.

daily confession of faith, we read: "Hear, O Israel! YHWH our God, YHWH is one. Therefore you shall love the LORD your God with all your heart, and with all your soul, and with all your might!" But not only love of God is part of Israel's instruction; so are love of neighbor and care for the enemy.[4] And the Old Testament not only demands love of God and neighbor; it also speaks of the boundless love of God for God's people and God's world. On the other hand, the idea of fear of God is firmly entrenched in the New Testament and cannot be removed from it. Paul writes to the community in Philippi: "work out your own salvation with fear and trembling" (Phil 2:12).

Old and New Testament speak equally of God's wrath. Why not, since wrath is something different from rage or hatred? God's wrath is that of a judge who can no longer bear the injustice happening on earth and therefore intervenes to condemn and rescue. Those who deny God's wrath and regard fear of God as passé intolerably reduce God's significance and make God an absent god who wants nothing to do with the world. The wrath of God is the very sign of God's absolute care and concern for the world, for as the world now is there is no way to approach it rightly except with wrath and love combined.

What is new about the New Testament, then, is not love, and what is characteristic of the Old Testament is not fear. Still, the contrasted pairing of fear and love is not the only mistake that is made in asking the question about the relationship between the Old and New Testaments. It is often asserted that the religion of the Old Testament was one of law and that its only concern was with the external fulfillment of commandments. Jesus, in contrast, is said to have placed religion within the human heart, within our inmost spirit. The sovereign authority with which Jesus abrogated the distinction between clean and unclean foods has, in fact, impressed every reader of the gospel. Kosher or not, what goes into the mouth does not make one unclean. What makes a person unclean is what lies within the human heart and from there infects every human word and action: greed, malice, envy, pride (Mark 7:1-23).

It is understandable that all those who stumble at the apparent superficiality and provocative materiality of the Old Testament readily welcome texts like Mark 7:1-23. They allow themselves to be misled by such passages into thinking that what is important in the New Testament is only the heart, the inner self, the spirituality of the human being, and that this very thing is the breakthrough in contrast to the Old Testament. At last the turn from everything that is purely external and to the "inner person" has been accomplished. In reality this, too, is completely twisted. Even the Old Testament prophets opposed a faith that lay only in externals. They demanded

---

[4] For love of neighbor see Lev 19:18; for care of the enemy, see Exod 23:4-5.

conversion of the heart: "rend your hearts and not your clothing. Return to the LORD, your God," wrote the prophet Joel (2:13). And in the book of the prophet Hosea is recorded as the words of God: "I desire steadfast love and not sacrifice, the knowledge of God rather than burnt offerings" (Hos 6:6).

The struggle against an externalized faith, then, did not begin with Jesus. It had long existed in the Old Testament. On the other hand it is a fact that the New Testament, like the Old, is concerned for the redemption of the *whole* person and everything that belongs to the human world. New Testament faith is no more otherworldly than that of the Old Testament. It, too, intends to saturate every part of the life of believers. It pushes for the transformation of relationships in society and the shaping of the material world. The world-connectedness of Old Testament faith is retained, simply as a matter of course, in the New Testament, and therefore "inwardness" is neither the essence of the New Testament nor what is "new" about it.

Another thing that is not "new" about the New Testament is the discovery of the individual. This position is also frequently defended.[5] It is said that in the Old Testament the dominant entity is the collective, the society, the nation. In the New Testament, by contrast, the infinite worth of the individual is discovered. Jesus directed his attention only to individuals. That, it is said, is the real progress in contrast to the Old Testament.

In reality the Old Testament had long been acquainted with the overcoming of a falsely-understood collectivism and the discovery of the individual. The whole question is explored in the book of Ezekiel in terms of the theme of "collective guilt." In Judea, and probably in the Diaspora as well, there were Jews who accused God, after the collapse in 586 B.C.E., of punishing an innocent generation for the sins of their ancestors. They had a highly memorable saying that encapsulated this accusation: "The parents have eaten sour grapes, and the children's teeth are set on edge" (Ezek 18:2). Ezekiel counters:

> A child shall not suffer for the iniquity of a parent, nor a parent suffer for the iniquity of a child; the righteousness of the righteous shall be his own, and the wickedness of the wicked shall be his own (Ezek 18:20).

Thus the individual and his or her own responsibility had long been known in the Old Testament.[6] In turn the New Testament holds firmly to

---

[5] For more on this see Gerhard Lohfink, *Jesus and Community* (Philadelphia: Fortress, 1984) 1–5; idem, "Die Korrelation von Reich Gottes und Volk Gottes bei Jesus" in idem, *Studien zum Neuen Testament*. SBAB 5 NT (Stuttgart: Katholisches Bibelwerk, 1989) 77–90, at 77–83.

[6] Cf. also Jer 31:29-30. Jeremiah and Ezekiel are writing about personal sins. That the consequences of sins indeed fall on the next generation is something of which we have become aware again since being confronted with the problems of environmental pollution. Exodus 20:5; 34:7; Num 14:18 all refer to the consequences of sin.

the theme of the "people of God." Of course the people of God in the Bible are more than a "theme." This idea is the basis, the ground of all biblical theology in both the Old and New Testaments.

In summary we may say that what is new about the New Testament is not love or inwardness or the discovery of the individual. Then what is it?

The answer is by no means simple, for at first glance it is difficult to find anything in the New Testament of which we might say: nothing was said about that in the Old Testament. In the Old Testament are election and salvation history, healing and forgiveness, mercy and compassion, festive gatherings and worship of God, representation and atonement, faith and discipleship, love of neighbor and love of God, critique of the Temple and critique of merely external fulfillment of the Law. There is even the justification of sinners by grace alone,[7] and there is openness of the people of God to all nations.

This list could easily be expanded. It shows that we are on the wrong track from the outset if we begin to play off the theological content of the New Testament against that of the Old. In this way no one can either discover what is new about the New Testament or do justice to the Old. We need a different starting point. We must take seriously the fact that the Old Testament is not only the vehicle for theological ideas, but tells a real history: the history of God with God's people, and beyond that people with the peoples of the world. The prophets say of that history that in it, in the end, the saving will of God will reach its goal despite all resistance. But when and how that will come to pass remains an open question.

That, in fact, is the decisive characteristic of the Old Testament: its radical openness to the future. The last sentence in the Old Testament, standing (in the order of books in the Christian Bible)[8] immediately before the gospels, is a statement by the prophet Malachi:

> Lo, I will send you the prophet Elijah before the great and terrible day of the LORD comes. He will turn the hearts of parents to their children and the hearts of children to their parents, so that I will not come and strike the land with a curse. (Mal 4:5-6)

Here is a promise to Israel that in the end time, represented by the returning Elijah, the alienation between generations will come to an end. The generational conflict that continually breaks out anew is in fact an ob-

---

[7] Especially in Deut 9:1-8. Cf. Georg Braulik, "Gesetz als Evangelium. Rechtfertigung und Begnadigung nach der deuteronomischen Tora," *ZThK* 79 (1982) 127–60. Cf. also Otfried Hofius, "'Rechtfertigung des Gottlosen' als Thema biblischer Theologie" in idem, *Paulusstudien*. WUNT 51 (Tübingen: Mohr/Siebeck, 1989) 121–47.

[8] In editions that place the so-called "Old Testament Apocrypha" between Malachi and Matthew this ordering is rendered invisible.

stacle to the genuine handing on of the experiences stemming from the history of salvation and failure that belongs to the people of God, without which justice and peace cannot bloom. Every generation makes the old mistakes all over again. Society continually has to begin again from the beginning. But, says the book of Malachi, there will come a time when parents and children will finally be of one mind, and that eschatological reconciliation will rescue the land from destruction. Now, however, Elijah is not yet come, alienation continues, everything is still open; the goal has not been achieved.

This openness to the future is still more obvious in the arrangement of books in the Hebrew Bible, where it is not the "minor prophets" that are placed at the end, but the books of Chronicles. Second Chronicles ends with a decree of Cyrus:

> Thus says King Cyrus of Persia: "The LORD, the God of heaven, has given me all the kingdoms of the earth, and he has charged me to build him a house at Jerusalem, which is in Judah. Whoever is among you of all his people, may the LORD his God be with him! Let him go up." (2 Chr 36:23)

Thus the Hebrew Bible ends with the word "go up" *('ālāh),* the biblical term for the return and entry into the land of promise. Obviously that is not accidental. At the end of the Hebrew Bible must stand the crucial word representing Israel's hope: arrival in the Land.

The whole subject acquires greater depth and focus if we consider how the Torah ends.[9] It closes, in the last chapter of Deuteronomy, with the death of Moses, who was not allowed to enter the Land himself but whose people were hopefully awaiting the moment of their entry into it (Deuteronomy 34). When the reading of the Torah in the worship service in the synagogue arrived at this point it did not continue with the book of Joshua and the entry into the Land; instead, the reading began again from the beginning with Genesis 1 and the creation of the world. Not only the Torah, but the reading of the Torah in the synagogue and the entire Hebrew Bible thus end with a fundamental status of Israel: the people stand on the threshold of the land of promise, but they are not yet in the Land itself. Everything remains open. The threshold has not yet been crossed.

*And the New Testament takes up this very situation. Here the threshold is crossed.*

It is indispensable that we consider this crucial point at greater length, and that we begin with the appearance of John the Baptizer, Jesus' baptism, his temptation in the wilderness, and his proclamation of the reign

---

[9] For what follows cf. Norbert Lohfink, "Moses Tod, die Tora und die alttestamentliche Sonntagslesung," *ThPh* 71 (1996) 481–94.

of God. Of course we cannot comment on these pericopes in full detail. We can only show how deeply they as a whole are rooted in the Old Testament, but how within them, at the same time, the threshold is crossed and the "new" in the New Testament comes to light.

The ordering of the New Testament writings is by no means accidental. Clear compositional lines can be discerned.[10] The New Testament begins not with the letters of Paul, though they are the oldest of its writings. It begins with the four gospels. The message and praxis of Jesus, his death and resurrection as related in the gospels constitute the basis of the New Testament. Everything that comes afterward is commentary on the gospels, just as everything in the Old Testament after the book of Deuteronomy is commentary on the Torah.

The four gospels do not begin immediately with Jesus' public activity. First of all, before his appearance, they tell of John the Baptizer. He, however, as we have already said (in II, 2 above) draws Israel (which has apparently been in the Land for a very long time already) back into its threshold situation before its entry into the Land. He appears in the wilderness, dressed like a desert-dweller and eating what the desert has to offer. Matthew and Mark emphasize all this quite pointedly.[11] They do so not by any means to characterize the Baptizer as an ascetic—after all, honey from wild bees and roasted locusts were delicacies[12]—but to call attention to the significant locus in salvation history that the Baptizer is establishing. He brings the people back to the wilderness again and immerses everyone who is ready to convert in the water of the Jordan at the very place where Israel stood before, under Joshua's leadership, it crossed over into the Land.

The synoptic gospels then tell how Jesus came from Galilee to John. He, too, enters into the wilderness situation the Baptizer has created, and he, too, lets himself be baptized in the Jordan.[13] The earliest Christian tradition very quickly attached to the event of Jesus' baptism a scene that condensed all its experiences with Jesus and gathered them into a single image so as to interpret Jesus' person and mission. Mark describes the scene as follows:

---

[10] Cf. now especially David Trobisch, *Die Endredaktion des Neuen Testaments. Eine Untersuchung zur Entstehung der christlichen Bibel.* NTOA 31. Fribourg: Universitätsverlag, and Göttingen: Vandenhoeck & Ruprecht, 1996.

[11] Cf. Matt 3:1-4; Mark 1:4-6.

[12] The key point is that one would not constantly discover wild bees' nests or large numbers of locusts in the desert. The emphasis therefore lies on the fact that the Baptizer, like Israel in the desert before him, lives entirely from the hand of God.

[13] Matt 3:13-17; Mark 1:9-11; Luke 3:21-22. In the Fourth Gospel Jesus' baptism is not narrated directly, but is indirectly indicated by the Baptizer: John 1:29-34.

> And just as he was coming up out of the water, he saw the heavens torn apart and the Spirit descending like a dove on him. And a voice came from heaven, "You are my Son, the Beloved; with you I am well pleased." (Mark 1:10-11)

It should be clear that this text is not a documentary report. It is structured of elements from the Old Testament, and without the Old Testament as background it cannot be understood at all. In particular it alludes to a passage in the book of Isaiah where God points to Israel, crushed, abducted, and staggering,[14] and says: This Israel is my servant.[15]

> Here is my servant, whom I uphold,
> my chosen, in whom my soul delights;
> I have put my spirit upon him;
> he will bring forth justice to the nations. (Isa 42:1)

The presentation of Israel here as "Servant of God" is meant to say that Israel is at the service of God, and God's "delight" in Israel is more than mere sympathy. The underlying Hebrew word means not only "to delight in," but also "joy," "desire," "longing for." That there should be a people in the world that brings justice for all nations was always the divine plan and God's whole desire. "Justice" (really "just judgment") ultimately means God's social order, that is, the saving knowledge that Israel obtained through a long history of progressive enlightenment. It creates justice. Israel's task, given by God, is to show to all nations how a just society would look. Because it will live as a just society its mere existence will become a statement of justice and judgment between the nations.

At the center of this public accrediting of Israel and its induction into the divine service is the Hebrew word *'ebed*. It means "servant." The oldest Greek translation of the Bible, the Septuagint, translated it with *pais,* which can mean both "servant" and "son." The primitive Church from the beginning applied Isa 42:1 and all the other Servant of God texts in Isaiah to Jesus and said: in him they were fulfilled. Jesus is the Servant of God and also God's beloved Son. He is the person for whom God has always been waiting with eager longing. Now, at last, God has found him. On him rests all God's delight. He has been, from eternity, the one sought and chosen.

---

[14] Isa 42:1-4. In terms of genre this text is a presentation of the Servant of God before the heavenly council. This signifies the irrevocable nature of the divine decision and its "publicness" at the same time.

[15] In current Old Testament exegesis the Servant of God in the so-called Servant Songs, which include Isa 42:1-9, is more frequently interpreted as an individual (for example, a particular prophet) than as a collective referring to Israel. However, this interpretation is by no means certain, at least for the final form of the text, for in the context of the Servant Songs the "Servant of God" is always Israel. Cf. Isa 41:8-9; 42:19; 44:1-2, 21; 45:4; 48:20.

However, because Isa 42:1 originally spoke of *Israel* this created a tension-filled theological perspective that is often overlooked. What I mean is that the Jesus of the baptism scene can no longer be seen in isolation. In him Israel is gathered together. In fact all Israel is the faithful servant and beloved Son through whom God is now definitively acting in the world for the fulfillment of the divine plan, but here again God must begin with an individual as once God began with Abraham. Now everything depends on Jesus. He is representative for all Israel.

This theological perspective, which incorporates the whole of Israel, is then consistently developed by the synoptic gospels after the baptismal scene: as Israel was in the wilderness forty years Jesus remains for forty days in the Jordan wilderness. As Israel was hungry in the wilderness, so is he. As Israel was tested in the wilderness, so he is tested. But from him comes no grumbling or rebellion. He trusts in God. He knows that God is good. Three times he resists the Tempter with a saying from the Torah;[16] he thus lives in entire obedience to the commandments from Sinai. In Matthew's gospel the repulsion of the Tempter culminates in Jesus' unconditional confession of the center of the Torah, the worship of YHWH alone: "Worship the Lord your God, and serve only him" (Matt 4:10). And at that moment, when Jesus shows himself to be the one who lives in absolute union with the will of God so that his very food is to do the will of God, the wilderness is transformed into Paradise. Matthew expresses this by saying: "angels came and waited on him" (Matt 4:11).[17]

Jewish legend proposes that in Paradise human beings were served by angels.[18] So when angels come and bring Jesus food Paradise shines forth in the midst of the wilderness of the world. Mark also plays on the theme of Paradise when he says that Jesus was "with the wild beasts" for forty days (Mark 1:13). Obviously that does not mean that he lived primitively in the wilderness or that he was in danger like a wild beast, but that peace between people and animals, and thus the ultimate eschatological peace, has begun.[19]

When Mark and Matthew cause Paradise motifs to echo at the end of the temptation story they are already anticipating what will happen after Jesus' time in the wilderness: he does not continue the Baptizer's work. He does not remain in the Jordan steppe but instead returns to Galilee; that is, he enters the Land, but under entirely different circumstances. He

[16] Cf. Matt 4:4 = Deut 8:3; Matt 4:7 = Deut 6:16; Matt 4:10 = Deut 5:9; 6:13.

[17] Matt 4:11 par. Mark 1:13.

[18] Cf. Ulrich Mell, "Jesu Taufe durch Johannes (Markus 1,9-15) – zur narrativen Christologie vom neuen Adam," *BZ* 40 (1996) 161–78, at 177.

[19] Cf. Mell, "Jesu Taufe" 176; Helmut Merklein, *Die Jesusgeschichte – synoptisch gelesen.* SBS 156 (Stuttgart: Katholisches Bibelwerk, 1994) 19.

passes through the Galilean villages. Instead of having the people of Israel come out of their villages and cities and go into the wilderness, as the Baptizer had done, he himself comes to them in the context of their normal life. He frees possessed people from their demons and cures the sick. Mark, however, prefaces all that with a proclamation that summarizes Jesus' preaching: "The time is fulfilled, and the kingdom of God has come near; repent, and believe in the good news" (Mark 1:15). This proclamation[20] also refers to the book of Isaiah, specifically to Isa 52:7. The concepts of "good news" *(euaggelion)* and "reign of God" *(basileia tou theou)* are fundamental elements of that text:

> How beautiful upon the mountains
>   are the feet of the messenger who announces peace,
> who brings good news,
>   who announces salvation,
>   who says to Zion, "Your God reigns."

"Your God reigns" must have been a confessional formula, probably even a liturgical acclamation in the worship service of the Temple. It is found repeatedly in the Old Testament. But in Isa 52:7 the confessional formula has acquired a new layer of meaning. It no longer means only "God reigns forever," but also that God's eternal reign is now being made manifest in the world in a radical historical transformation, an act of salvation for the people of God. To be precise, one should translate it: "God *will* reign." A message of good news can, after all, only be about something that was not previously known. That God reigns over Israel and is sovereign over the world is something that had long been celebrated in Israel's worship, but that God's reign is now being proved victorious in history is a new message.

How, then, will God's reign be manifested in history? Isaiah 52 gives a clear answer: it will happen when God gathers Israel, scattered in exile, and leads it home to the Land. The following description (v. 8) follows immediately after the proclamation that "your God reigns":

> Listen! Your sentinels lift up their voices,
>   together they sing for joy;
> for in plain sight they see
>   the return of the LORD to Zion.

Obviously God does not return to Zion alone, but accompanied, as if in procession, by liberated Israel, which can take possession of its land anew (Isa 52:11-12). God's coming and the restoration of Israel coincide.

---

[20] Mark 1:15 *par.* Matt 4:17. In Luke's gospel the proclamation takes place, in a different form, in the context of Jesus' inaugural preaching in Nazareth: cf. Luke 4:21.

This vision from the book of Isaiah is the background for Jesus' proclamation. Jesus himself is the messenger of joy. He proclaims an "evangel," a message of good news, and the content of the message is that God is now definitively beginning to reign. But what does that mean in concrete historical terms? For Isaiah, as we saw, this inbreaking of the reign of God is by no means something to be celebrated in the hiddenness of heaven, away from human sight. That God begins to reign means quite concretely that Israel will now be gathered and brought home to its land. Therefore we must also understand the content of Jesus' proclamation as concretely as possible.

It is a peculiar phenomenon, the causes of which one might long ponder, that in New Testament exegesis the concept of *basileia* often remains strangely abstract. Of course there is a lot of talk about Jesus' preaching of the reign of God, but then the discussion turns to the question whether it is entirely otherworldly or at least in small part here-and-now; whether it is entirely in the future or already infiltrating the present; whether it should be interpreted more dynamically as the "reign" of God or more statically as the "kingdom" of God; to what extent it is pure grace and to what extent human beings must do something in order to achieve it. All that leaves the reign of God in a strangely diffuse light. It is simply impossible to imagine how anything so nebulous could have brought any people in Israel to change their lives. Neither Jesus nor his Jewish contemporaries pictured the reign of God in such a vague and abstract fashion.

If we take seriously the background of the proclamation in Mark 1:15, which is quite clearly the book of Isaiah, we cannot avoid understanding the coming of the reign of God that Jesus announces as a quite concrete, visible event: the eschatological gathering of the people of God is beginning; Israel is being definitively given its land; it is becoming a sign for the nations—and none of this by its own strength, but in an event that reveals God's glory and the fullness of God's power. The book of Isaiah described this event as the re-creation of Israel, and Jesus must have understood it in the same way.

Thus the eschatological gathering and re-creation of the people of God by Jesus is the necessary corresponding event to his proclamation of the *basileia*.[21] If we speak abstractly about the concept of the reign of God without at the same time taking into account God's action in and for Israel in its total social concreteness the whole thing remains diffuse and ultimately incomprehensible.

---

[21] Cf. the clear and precise position of Peter Stuhlmacher, *Biblische Theologie des Neuen Testaments* (Göttingen: Vandenhoeck & Ruprecht, 1992) 70: "The *basileia* exists in the reign of God over the people of God at the end time, whom Jesus, as the messianic Son of Man, himself begins to gather."

How, then, does this re-creation of the people of God happen with Jesus? Let us hew exactly to the course of the gospel! After Jesus' baptism in the Jordan, his testing in the wilderness, and his proclamation of the reign of God, Mark immediately tells of the calling of the first disciples. Matthew follows exactly the same order, and John's is similar.[22] The gathering of disciples is thus the first thing Jesus does in Galilee, according to the gospels. We should not take this as an obvious move. It would have been entirely natural for the evangelists to precede this action with an example of Jesus' preaching and an account of his healing miracles. Luke reordered the older gospel tradition available to him in exactly that way.[23] But even for Luke, as for the other three evangelists, the calling of the disciples is of decisive importance. In the gospels the disciples are not mere figures put in place to fill the stage. They do not make constant appearances in the narrative so that, against the background of their listening and asking questions, the person of Jesus can be that much the more impressively developed. Next to Jesus they are the principal actors in the gospel drama. They are called to follow Jesus, and their following culminates in the installation of the Twelve and their mission to all Israel: "And he appointed twelve to be with him, and to be sent out to proclaim the message, and to have authority to cast out demons" (Mark 3:14-15).

The Twelve are chosen out of a much larger number of disciples. They represent the twelve tribes; they are the beginning and center of growth for the renewed, eschatological Israel. All discipleship is thus aimed at Israel and at the gathering of the whole people of God. With the disciples begins the eschatological re-creation of Israel, and in the re-creation of Israel the reign of God is revealed.

We will have to discuss the circle of disciples and especially the Twelve at greater length below. Here, at the outset, it should be clear that for Jesus the coming of the *basileia,* that is, the acquisition of a space for the reign of God in the world, was the center of his existence. Jesus announces the reign of God; better still, he calls it forth. But never did it remain at the level of mere words. It had to take on flesh. It requires not only the ear, but the eye and the taste buds. That God is Lord in Israel is not a fact to be derived from great words. It would not even be visible if many individuals repented at Jesus' call but remained alone. The inbreaking of the reign of God can only be known if people in Israel dare an exodus from their old situation and join their lives together, or rather allow them to be joined together by Jesus' power.

[22] Cf. Mark 1:16-20; Matt 4:18-22; John 1:35-51. Only Luke deviates from this sequence. He inserts before the call of the first disciples in 5:1-11 a day in Capernaum (4:31-44).

[23] See the previous note.

All this takes place concretely and before the eyes of all: those who follow Jesus leave their families and relatives and travel throughout the land with him. More important: they allow themselves to be gathered by Jesus into a "new family" that stands entirely under the sign of the reign of God. Jesus explicitly connects the existence of his disciples with the reign of God: "Do not be afraid, little flock, for it is your Father's good pleasure to give you the kingdom" (Luke 12:32). This promise contains the same word as the baptism scene. Just as God "delighted" in Jesus, God's true servant and beloved Son, so God "delights," "takes pleasure" in the little group of disciples. They are what God has been seeking and longing for through all eternity. To them is promised the *basileia,* that is, they will have a share in it, and they will have it now, today. This share is not only a hope implanted in their hearts. It is visible and tangible:

> "Truly I tell you, there is no one who has left house or brothers or sisters or mother or father or children or fields, for my sake and for the sake of the good news, who will not receive a hundredfold now in this age—houses, brothers and sisters, mothers and children, and fields, with persecutions—and in the age to come eternal life." (Mark 10:29-30)

In this precisely formulated text every word is vital. If we read it carefully we notice two things: first, "fathers" are not mentioned in the second half of this balanced parallelism. That cannot be accidental. They represent patriarchy, the old society in which the man alone ruled and decided. In the new family of Jesus into which the disciples are to grow there can no longer be anyone who dominates others. All are to be like brothers and sisters to each other.

Another striking thing is that for the comparison of the natural family and the new family it sufficed to list the categories of fathers, mothers, children, brothers, and sisters, but this series is framed by the additional mention of houses and fields. That is also intentional. What is at stake is not only the family, but a share in the "Land." Luke reports in the Acts of the Apostles that Barnabas, who came from Cyprus, sold a field (Acts 4:36-37). He had probably moved to Jerusalem, like many Diaspora Jews, and had obtained a piece of land near the city in order to make his belonging to Israel a concrete fact and to receive a share in the blessings of the messianic era. However, he sold that field to benefit the young Jesus community in Jerusalem, because it was more important to him to build up that community than to possess the field. That event makes clearly visible what is meant in Mark 10:29-30: the houses and fields that Jesus' disciples will leave are their share in the "Land." Those are lost to them. But their share in the land of promise is not lost, because their "Land" is the new family that Jesus gathers around himself. There they will find everything again a hundredfold; in it they will truly enter the Land; in it the promise of the Land to Israel is fulfilled. The promise of the Land, which has an enormous significance in the Old Testament, is by no means ignored in the New Testament, nor is it transferred to a purely spiritual plane. It is fulfilled on new ground: that of the new family.

Now, after this long digression, let us return to our initial question: What is new about the New Testament? We can now say, with great confidence, that what is new is not some aspect of its content that was unknown to the Old Testament. Instead, what is new is that now the openness of the Old Testament arrives at its goal. What had been hoped for has arrived. The promises are fulfilled. The Jordan is crossed. The Land is found. What was promised shines forth—and with such power that only the word "new" is adequate to describe the fulfillment of the old. "A new teaching—with authority!" the crowds say (Mark 1:27).

This new thing does not enter the world as pure instruction, a mere idea, a brain wave, a bolt from the blue. It appears in a concrete person. That person is Jesus Christ. The baptism scene is meant to make clear that he is the beloved Son, the Promised One whom God has desired from of old. His testing in the wilderness is meant to show that he lives in complete union with the will of God. He was the first to fully understand what God desires. He has carried out God's intention completely. In his person he will be the perfection of all Israel's enlightenment. His words, his deeds, his complete surrender to God's cause compel the disciples, all of whom are Jews, to say: He is the fulfillment of the long history that began with Abraham. He is the definitive appearance, the full clarification of everything that has heretofore happened in Israel.

The early Christian heretic Marcion said that Christ himself was the reign of God.[24] The great early Christian theologian Origen used a very similar formula when he said that Christ was the *basileia* in person.[25] Both sayings have been frequently repeated since.[26] They are not false. But what is false is not to add immediately: The reign of God requires a space in which to exercise its sovereignty; it needs a people. To put it very simply: a monarch without people is no monarch, or rather such a sovereign has abdicated. To say it more subtly: The reign of God means justice; but justice cannot exist in a single person: it can only exist in society. If there is

---

[24] Tertullian, *Adv. Marc.* IV, 33, 8: *in evangelio est dei regnum Christus ipse.*

[25] Origen, *In Matt. Comm.* XIV, 7 (on Matt 18:23): "And as he is Wisdom itself and Righteousness itself and Truth itself, so perhaps is he also the royal reign itself."

[26] Helmut Merklein formulates carefully and well when he says that Jesus appears as the "representative of the *basileia*" in idem, *Jesu Botschaft von der Gottesherrschaft. Eine Skizze.* SBS 111 (2nd ed. Stuttgart: Katholisches Bibelwerk, 1984) 65, 72.

any sense at all in talking about God's royal reign it needs a society in which God is sovereign, and in which God's sovereignty transforms people and things. Hence the reign of God simply cannot come in an isolated individual. It either appears in the form of a society or not at all.

This sheds new light on the matter-of-fact way in which Jesus, in the gospels, immediately begins to call disciples to follow him. What is new about the New Testament is Jesus, but he would not be that new element in its completeness without the disciples he gathers around him as the beginning of the eschatological Israel.

In 1990 Joseph Ratzinger said, in a talk to the Bishops' Synod on the subject of the priesthood, that what is new in the New Testament is the person of Jesus. But he added something else: another thing that is new is the "figure of the Twelve."[27] In the following sections our purpose will be to examine this new thing with regard to Jesus and the Twelve.

## 2. The "Todayness" of the Reign of God

Jesus had crossed the threshold. This was evident from the very beginning of his public life. The proclamation with which Jesus' entire preaching was summarized in Mark 1:15 claims that Isa 52:7-12 is now fulfilled. However, what is important about Mark 1:15, this summary of Jesus' proclamation, is not only its background in the book of Isaiah. Equally important is the linguistic structure that shapes the whole statement:

> "The time is fulfilled,
>      and the kingdom of God has come near;
>    repent,
>      and believe in the good news."

The proclamation does not begin with a challenge to Israel to repent and believe in the gospel; instead conversion is the consequence of what has already happened: that the time is fulfilled and the reign of God has come near.[28] Thus, as throughout the Old Testament, the action of God comes first, not the acts of human beings. God has taken the initiative. God alone gives the *basileia*. It is for the people of God to respond. God's action makes human action possible.

The structure of Mark 1:15 reveals still more: Exegetes have continually pondered the precise meaning of "has come near." Does it mean to say that the reign of God, in the dimension of linear time, is now closer

---

[27] Joseph Ratzinger, *Called to Communion: Understanding the Church Today.* Translated by Adrian Walker (San Francisco: Ignatius Press, 1996) 111–16, at 113.

[28] The same is true of Matt 4:17. It is true that the appeal to conversion comes first there, but the following "for" indicates the priority of the reign of God.

than before? That would inevitably mean that it is not yet present. In that case the threshold would by no means have been crossed, and Jesus would not have differed at all from others before him who had preached this "imminent expectation" in Israel.

The problem is solved if we take the first clause of the proclamation seriously: "The time is fulfilled." This clause gives the accent and clarifies the question of time. Certainly it appears clothed in solemn biblical language, but it means nothing more than we do when we say "now is the time" or "the time has come." The biblical linguistic raiment simply shows that the statement refers to the prophetic promises: now they are being fulfilled. Paul means the same thing when he writes: "See, now is the acceptable time; see, now is the day of salvation!" (2 Cor 6:2).

After this fundamental statement the second clause, "the kingdom of God has come near," cannot mean that the time of fulfillment has not really come yet. It is true that "has come near" contains an element of "not yet," but that has to do not with God's action but with Israel's response. At this moment Israel has not yet repented. It must still decide for or against the gospel. Hence the *basileia* is indeed near, but not yet present. It has been offered to the people of God; it has been laid at their feet. It is at their disposal, there for the taking. But as long as it has not been accepted it is only near, and it is still necessary to pray: "Thy kingdom come" (Matt 6:10).

There is no scene in the gospels that sets this tension between "already" and "not yet" more clearly before us than Jesus' preaching in the synagogue at Nazareth as Luke's gospel portrays it in 4:16-30. Jesus has returned for a short time to his home town, Nazareth. On the Sabbath he goes to the synagogue, is asked to speak, reads a text from the book of Isaiah that describes the eschatological restoration of Israel by the Messiah appointed by God (Isa 61:1-2), and interprets the prophetic text by saying: "Today this scripture has been fulfilled in your hearing" (Luke 4:21).

Ultimately, of course, this statement, which turns everything inside out, is not simply about the text of Isa 61:1-2. Luke means to say that in Jesus' appearance, his proclamation and his saving deeds, the book of Isaiah is beginning to be fulfilled, and with it all of Scripture. Now, today, at this moment the promised future is beginning. Now is the time of fulfillment! But the story goes on, revealing more and more clearly that it summarizes Jesus' whole public activity. At first Jesus receives joyful acclamation, but then the wind shifts. Suddenly the people of Nazareth take offense at Jesus. The offense lies in the concrete character of the proclaimer: "Is this not Joseph's son?" (Luke 4:22). That is: although the eschatological action of God has been prayed for and dreamed of by all, at the hour when it happens the people discover that they had imagined it would be different. Not like this. Not so concrete. Not so fixed in space. Not, of all places, in Nazareth, and above all not at this moment. Jesus' hearers would prefer to put everything off to some future time, and the story comes to no good end. The time is indeed fulfilled, but God's basileia is not accepted. The "today" God offers is disputed, and so that "already" becomes "not yet."

It is not only in Nazareth that the "today" of the gospel was not accepted. Later, in the course of the Church's history, it has been repeatedly denied or minimized, and for the same reasons as in Nazareth. Apparently it makes people uncomfortable to have God appear concretely in their lives. It puts all their desires and favorite ideas in danger, and their ideas about time as well. It cannot be today, because in that case we would have to change our lives *today*. So we prefer to delay God's salvation to some future time. There it can rest, securely packed, hygienic, and harmless.

Often this process of repression effects an intensification of *otherworldly* hope. But it can be directed against the concrete Church itself. There is a particular form of contempt for the Church that arises directly out of a rejection of Jesus' "today." I am not referring to disbelief or hatred on the part of outsiders. I mean a kind of contempt for the Church that comes from the inmost circles of the Church itself and that is so destructive because the baptized, who have been called to witness to the presence of God, no longer believe that God desires to bring salvation in the here and now of this concrete, offensive Church. What went on in the synagogue at Nazareth continues in the Church.

For that reason we have to concern ourselves with this "today" of Jesus, not only because otherwise what is new about Jesus and the New Testament will only appear in unclear fashion, but also for the sake of the Church's renewal. It cannot be renewed if it does not finally accept the "todayness" of what has happened to it. For the Church's future everything depends on whether it can again believe that the promises can be fulfilled already, and that God is at work *today*. For Jesus this "today" of God was the center of his existence. What was behind this present eschatology of his?

For as long as there has been a theology of history in Israel there must also have been a hope for the future, but it first appears with full force in the writing of the prophet Amos. His proclamation was entirely in terms of the immediate future, the impending judgment. Later the exilic and postexilic prophets spoke in glowing images both of the approaching judgment and the coming salvation. God will come to reign on earth and to restore the people of God. From the second century B.C.E., especially after the persecution of the Jews by the Seleucid emperor Antiochus IV, this expectation was consolidated in the so-called "apocalyptic" writings.[29]

The phenomenon of "imminent expectation" may also be quite old,[30] but it later became especially characteristic of apocalyptic. Particularly in times of persecution many Jewish groups were convinced that Israel was so threatened that God's intervention must be imminent. In the following period there were many types of such expectation, even including entire apocalyptic "timetables" that attempted to determine from the increase of eschatological suffering how close the last day had come. But even when there was nothing like this massive apocalyptic many devout persons expected the imminent revelation of the sovereignty of God and prayed for it daily. For example in the Kaddish, which was probably already being prayed in Jesus' time, the central section reads:

> May He establish his kingdom
> during your life and during your days,
> and during the life of all the house of Israel
> speedily and soon.[31]

The "today" in Jesus' proclamation has to be heard against this whole background. It breaks through all distant expectations and even all imminent expectations. Jesus knows with absolute certainty that the promised, longed-for, prayed-for future has arrived. The reign of God is breaking forth. That is the only explanation for his unshakable confidence of fulfillment, and for his blessing of his disciples: "Blessed are the eyes that see what you see! For I tell you that many prophets and kings desired to see what you see, but did not see it, and to hear what you hear, but did not hear it" (Luke 10:23-24).

Probably it was not only in Nazareth that people took offense at Jesus' "today." Many others would have shaken their heads and said: the world keeps going on just as before; nothing has changed; therefore the reign of God has not yet come! Jesus' response was: you are wrong; something has changed. "If it is by the finger of God that I cast out demons, then the kingdom of God has come to you" (Luke 11:20).

---

[29] In the Old Testament the experiences under Antiochus IV were recorded primarily in the apocalyptic passages of the book of Daniel. On the phenomenon of apocalyptic see especially I, 7 above.

[30] Cf. Marius Reiser, *Jesus and Judgment. The Eschatological Proclamation in its Jewish Context*. Translated by Linda M. Maloney (Minneapolis: Fortress, 1997) 26–27; Kurt Erlemann, *Naherwartung und Parusieverzögerung im Neuen Testament. Ein Beitrag zur Frage religiöser Zeiterfahrung*. TANZ 17 (Tübingen and Basel: Francke, 1995) 53–79.

[31] Jewish Reconstructionist Foundation, *Sabbath Prayer Book* (New York: J.R.F., 1945).

There are many kinds of demons. Perhaps we should translate this: if people who cannot escape from possession, obsessions, destructive compulsions that have built up within and around them because of the evils in society and the history of distress within which they find themselves—if such people, through the power of Jesus, which is nothing other than the power of God, can begin to breathe again, to be free, to trust, then the dominance of evil has already been crushed and the reign of God has come for those people. For God's *basileia* does not come as a thunderstorm that breaks over the world, a universal scene of majesty descending from heaven; it comes into the world like a grain that is sown and grows. In Jesus' deeds of healing the "today" of the reign of God was already visible and tangible.

Ultimately Jesus' present eschatology is about who God really is. Jesus lived in a revolutionary new relationship with God. For him God is so powerful in graciousness and so present in power that *as far as God is concerned* there is nothing lacking, nothing still wanting. Because Jesus lived in complete union with the will of his heavenly Father he knew that when God comes it is not by halves, but totally. And God does not come sometime, even if that sometime be tomorrow; God comes today. We simply do not do justice to Jesus' message if we speak as if God gives the *basileia,* but not altogether at this moment, as if God would allow it to dawn, but only partially, as if it were revealed, but only in anticipation. We cannot say such things any more than we can say that God was revealed in Jesus, but only in anticipation, only partially, and certainly not entirely and definitively.

We can only do justice to the New Testament if we maintain that God's being was entirely uttered in Jesus. Jesus is the definitive presence of God in the world. Who sees him sees the Father (cf. John 14:9). He is "the Son" in a sense that cannot be predicated of any other human being. Ultimately the limitless "today" that Jesus proclaims is based on his limitless participation in God's eternal "today." Those who set limits to Jesus' present eschatology are in danger of reducing the mystery of Jesus' person. It is no accident that it is in the Fourth Gospel that the statement "The Father and I are one" (10:30) is found, for that gospel contains the most decidedly present eschatology in the New Testament.

The "not yet" of the reign of God thus does not result from God's holding back, but from the hesitant conversion of people. They prefer not to have God too near. They would rather dance at their own weddings than at the wedding to which God invites us. So Jesus had to tell a parable (Luke 14:15-24) about how a man prepared a feast, giving much thought to an outstanding menu and doing everything to please his guests. At last everything was ready—but the guests did not come, even though they had been invited long before. Instead he receives one excuse after another:

"I have bought a piece of land, and I must go out and see it; please accept my regrets."

"I have bought five yoke of oxen, and I am going to try them out; please accept my regrets."

"I have just been married, and therefore I cannot come."

The parable is not about individual salvation or about salvation after death. It is about the feast of God with the people of God, which is to take place now, with Jesus' arrival. The event is as much at issue now as it was then. Those who are invited continually find new excuses in order to shield themselves from the closeness of God and the gathering of the people of God. For the most part the excuses are honorable. They almost always come down to: "I would like to, but at the moment I just can't!" But Jesus' "today" says: there is no more time because the world is already on fire. You have to act *now* because you have encountered God's cause. You must stake your whole existence *this very day* because God's invitation has reached you.

Of course if we formulate it that way we see at once that this "you must!" cannot stand in isolation. Otherwise it is not faithful to Jesus' preaching. Otherwise Jesus would have been nothing but an eschatological moralist. The point of Jesus' "today" is not first of all obligation, an imperative, a moral "must," but rejoicing at the feast that is offered, joy over the treasure and the pearl that are ready to be found.

We spoke earlier (in I, 7) about the buried treasure and the pearl of great price. Here let me refer only to the uncompromising present eschatology of that parable. It does not say: "It is with the reign of God as with a treasure that someone found, then buried it, went home rejoicing, and lived ever afterward with the joyful knowledge: the treasure exists, and at some point in the future I will hold it in my hands!" Instead, the parable tells how the finder seizes the treasure immediately: "in his joy he goes and sells all that he has and buys that field" (Matt 13:44). The hidden treasure of the reign of God is even now being dug up. The pearl of great price is already being bought. The feast is ready to begin, and it all depends only on this: will the invited guests come?

## 3. Salvation Superabundant

The only reason for the "not yet" of the reign of God is human resistance. From God's point of view one can only speak of the "already" of fulfillment. Everything has been offered. Everything presses toward the revelation of the glory of God. The "not yet" caused by human beings in fact stands in opposition to a "still more" from God's side, for God's gracious goodness is beyond all measure. When at last the *one* human being appeared who was entirely open to God and completely at one with God's will the reign of God also appeared in a surprising and even alarming fullness.

Mark illustrates this overflowing salvation immediately after his account of the call of the first disciples, in a short narrative composition that is often called "the day at Capernaum" (1:21–39). It is a Sabbath. Jesus goes to the synagogue, teaches, and heals a possessed man. After the synagogue worship service he returns with his disciples to Simon Peter's house, where he heals Peter's mother-in-law who is lying sick in bed with a fever. As soon as the Sabbath is past and it is again permitted to carry the sick, the people come together in front of Peter's house:

> That evening, at sundown, they brought to him all who were sick or possessed with demons. And the whole city was gathered around the door. And he cured many who were sick with various diseases, and cast out many demons . . . . In the morning, while it was still very dark, he got up and went out to a deserted place, and there he prayed. And Simon and his companions hunted for him. When they found him, they said to him, "Everyone is searching for you." He answered, "Let us go on to the neighboring towns, so that I may proclaim the message there also; for that is what I came out to do." And he went throughout Galilee, proclaiming the message in their synagogues and casting out demons. (Mark 1:32-39)

Mark deliberately compresses the beginning of Jesus' healings into a single long day extending from one morning through the evening and into the next morning. This is the "day of the Messiah." It extends beyond the Sabbath to the morning of the first day of the week. To begin with, however, it is a Sabbath, the day when, according to the biblical picture, creation was brought to perfection. Genesis 2:2-3 says of the Sabbath, the seventh day, that God blessed it and rested on that day "from all the work that he had done" in creating. The Sabbath is a day of fulfillment in just that sense, when the goal of creation is made visible. It is a day on which people and relationships are made whole, when they enter into rest and recover their equilibrium. The Sabbath then merges into the first day of the week, the day of the resurrection and the new creation, and it is also filled immediately with messianic salvation.

Like Mark, the Fourth Evangelist also places an event of messianic fullness at the beginning of Jesus' activity (John 2:1-12). It happens in Cana, at a wedding that threatens to end miserably because the wine has run out. The messianic superabundance is made visible here in a wine miracle Jesus performs. The narrative carefully demonstrates that he gives the

wedding party a superfluous amount of wine,[32] for it is not the clay jars or-
dinarily used to store wine that Jesus orders to be filled with water, but six
stone vessels used for ritual purification and therefore hewn out of stone
and unusually large. According to the evangelist each of these vessels contained two to three *metrete,* or about one hundred liters. Altogether between five hundred and seven hundred liters of water were changed into
wine. The narrator is not content with this detailed calculation of the
amount, however; he adds: "they filled them up to the brim" (John 2:7).
The evangelist's intention is evident from such details. He means to say
that Jesus' gift is lavish. Here is no restriction, measuring, limitation, or
stinginess. All the large vessels that can be found are filled to the brim.

However, it was not enough that the superabundance of the wine
should thus be made so plain. The narrative points just as clearly to the
quality of the wine. It even introduces for that purpose a special person,
namely the *architriklinos,* the one who supervised banquets, and especially the mixing and pouring of wine. The *architriklinos* does not know
the source of the abundant wine in the stone vessels and he is greatly displeased to learn of it only now. The "rule for wine" that he pronounces
(one offers good wine at the beginning, not at the end of the feast!) serves
the function within the narrative of saying discreetly that the wine that is
now being poured is a good wine, in fact an outstanding wine of the best
quality. Near the end of the narrative the evangelist interprets the whole
by saying: "Jesus did this, the first of his signs, in Cana of Galilee, and revealed his glory; and his disciples believed in him" (John 2:11). Readers
are thus to associate the superabundance of wine and its quality directly
with the "glory of Jesus." Jesus' glory does not remain in a supra-sensual
realm nor is it something inward, purely spiritual, transcendent: it is visible and tangible, can be tasted and enjoyed. It is as real and earthly as, according to the book of Isaiah, the "glory of the LORD" will be in Israel at
the end time.

Isaiah speaks very often of "seeing" the glory of the Lord.[33] The Fourth
Evangelist deliberately adopts the same expression.[34] The glory of Jesus
that is visible at the Cana miracle is the reflection of the glory of God in
which, according to the theology of the Fourth Gospel, the "Son" has always shared.[35] At the same time, however, it is the visible inbreaking of

---

[32] The next paragraphs on the Cana pericope follow Gerhard Lohfink, "The Glory of the
Works of God (John 2:1-12)" in idem, *The Work of God Goes On.* Translated by Linda M.
Maloney (Philadelphia: Fortress, 1987) 29–45.

[33] Cf. Isa 35:2; 40:5; 60:1, 5; 62:2; 66:18.

[34] Cf. John 1:14; 12:41.

[35] Cf. John 1:14; 17:5, and especially 12:37-43.

that glory into history, more precisely into the history of Israel, the people of God, to whom now, with the appearance of Jesus, the eschatological fullness of the "glory of the LORD" has been given.

Of course one has to believe in this "glory." The "seeing" that John speaks of is not any kind of superficial consumption with the eyes; it presupposes a believing surrender to the work of God. Hence the narrative distinguishes sharply between those who believe and those who do not comprehend what is happening. The steward of the feast is the prototype of all those who are immediately present and involved in the whole story, who even taste the magnificence of the wine, and still do not know "where it came from" (2:9). Thus the *architriklinos* is one of those who hear but do not understand, who see but do not recognize. In contrast it is expressly said of Jesus' disciples that they believe: Jesus "revealed his glory; and his disciples believed in him" (2:11).

Because the disciples believe, the gathering of the eschatological people of God begins with them. Because they believe they themselves receive, from the fullness of Jesus' glory, "grace upon grace" (John 1:16). With the wine miracle at Cana begins, in the scheme of Johannine theology, the great, eschatological "work of God." God reveals in Israel the glory promised by the prophets, and does so by revealing the glory of the Son in which all those who believe in Jesus share.

The overflowing abundance of the reign of God appears in many other gospel texts. Especially in his parables Jesus was continually painting its portrait:

The land on which the wheat is sown in the parable of the abundant harvest, despite all the enemies who threaten the harvest from beginning to end, brings a mighty yield: the wheat that fell on good ground bears thirtyfold, sixtyfold, and a hundredfold (Mark 4:1-9). The tiny mustard seed brings forth a great bush under whose branches the birds of the air build their nests (Mark 4:30-32). A poor laborer at the plow stumbles over a treasure buried in a field (Matt 13:44). A great merchant who deals in pearls is offered, one day, a pearl beyond all price, the like of which he has never seen before (Matt 13:45-46). A man who has wasted his inheritance and thrown away his rights as a son remembers that in his father's house even the day-laborers "have bread enough and to spare." He returns home and is immediately taken back into the family by his father. The father runs to meet him; the lost son receives a signet ring and a new garment; the fatted calf is killed and a feast begins (Luke 15:11-32). A king forgives a desperate debtor whose existence is completely destroyed the gigantic sum of ten thousand talents (equal to a hundred million denarii). In those days a laborer had to work a whole day to earn a single denarius. The king thus forgives a sum corresponding in value to a hundred million days' work (Matt 18:23-35). A landowner treats the laborers he has hired only in the late afternoon to work in harvesting grapes in his vineyard as if they had worked the entire day: in the evening he gives them a full day's wages (Matt 20:1-16).

Wherever we look the gospels are speaking of an overflowing abundance, of profligacy and superfluity—and not only in the parables.

In Bethany, in the house of Simon the leper, a woman pours out an alabaster jar of the most expensive nard over Jesus' head, so that his disciples are in consternation and talk about senseless waste, but Jesus defends the woman (Mark 14:3-9). Peter and his companions, after working all night and catching nothing, put out into the lake again at Jesus' command, and soon afterward they bring to land a net filled with fish to the point of bursting (Luke 5:1-11).

However, the prime example of superabundance is the story of the miraculous multiplication of loaves, related no less than six times in the gospels.[36] It is worth tracing the structural lines of this narrative somewhat more closely, taking Mark 6:30-44 as our textual basis.[37]

The superscription found almost universally nowadays, "feeding of the five thousand," is not a particularly happy choice. "Feeding" smacks of sufficiency, school lunches, soup kitchens, and not of feasting, banqueting, and festivals. Mark is apparently telling of a festal banquet, for according to 6:39 Jesus tells the disciples to be sure that all those present *recline,* that is, make themselves comfortable for a festive meal.

People in antiquity had two different ways of eating. Normal, everyday meals they took, as we do, while seated. But whenever they celebrated a festival or invited guests to a special dinner they *reclined* at table. They lay on pillows and bolsters, leaning on their left arms and eating with the right hand. So when the disciples were sent to invite everyone to recline on the ground it meant that now an evening meal was about to begin at which people would take time for a banquet at which everyone could eat his or her fill. The bolsters and pillows were lacking, but they were replaced by plenty of green grass, which Mark expressly mentions (6:39).

---

[36] Feeding of five thousand: Mark 6:30-44; Matt 14:13-21; Luke 9:10-17; John 6:1-15. The feeding of four thousand is a variant: Mark 8:1-10; Matt 15:32-39.

[37] For the interpretation of Mark 6:30-44 I am largely following my essay, "Wie werden im Reich Gottes die Hungernden satt? Zur Erzählintention von Mk 6,30-44" in Johannes J. Degenhardt, ed., *Die Freude an Gott—unsere Kraft. FS Otto Knoch* (Stuttgart: Katholisches Bibelwerk, 1991) 135–44. For Mark 6:30-44 cf. especially also Rudolf Pesch, *Über das Wunder der Brotvermehrung, oder: Gibt es eine Lösung für den Hunger in der Welt?* (Frankfurt: Josef Knecht, 1995).

Finally, the end of the story shows that this really was a banquet. There it is clearly stated that the disciples collected the remaining fragments. This, too, was a fixed ritual at a Jewish banquet: after the main course the dining room was "cleansed" by gathering up all the bits of bread larger than an olive that had fallen to the floor. In Mark 6:43 the disciples gather twelve baskets full of the remnants of the meal.

Why is so much left over? Not because the diners had not enjoyed the food or because they had not eaten their fill, but because it was a banquet. When there is a banquet there are always leftovers. Every householder knows that. For a special meal one always cooks, broils, and bakes more than is really needed, because it is part of celebration to be wasteful and a festal meal requires abundance. It is not right to be stingy on such occasions; it is better to put too much on the table than too little. The fact that in the story of the multiplication of the loaves there are twelve baskets left over is meant to indicate that Jesus is a good host: he prepared a glorious banquet; he spread a feast. The result is similar to that at the wedding in Cana.

Why did the early Christian communities tell such stories? What did Jesus have to do with banquets, and what did banquets have to do with the reign of God? According to biblical theology, a great deal! In Isa 25:6-8 we read:

> On this mountain the LORD of hosts will make for all peoples
>   a feast of rich food, a feast of well-aged wines,
>   of rich food filled with marrow, of well-aged wines strained clear.
> And he will destroy on this mountain
>   the shroud that is spread over all peoples,
>   the sheet that is spread over all nations;
>   he will swallow up death forever.
> Then the Lord GOD will wipe away the tears from all faces,
>   and the disgrace of his people he will take away from all the earth,
>   for the LORD has spoken.

This text from Isaiah presumes that God's eschatological, royal reign has begun. This is clear from the context, from what has gone before in Isa 24:21-23. God's enthronement is followed by a glorious banquet that God spreads on Mount Zion. At this feast Israel glows with new dignity. All nations are invited to share in this enthronement banquet. At the meal the shroud of sorrow and suffering that lies over the nations is torn away. Eschatological joy gleams throughout the whole world, and it will never end.

For the prophets that is all in the future, but Jesus proclaims that the future has arrived. It is present. The joy of the end time has already begun. God's festal banquet with God's people, Israel, which is to expand into a feast for all nations, is beginning. Jesus is so certain that the reign of God is now a reality, a richly abundant meal, that he calls his poor, hungry hearers blessed: "Blessed are you who are hungry now, for you will be filled" (Luke 6:21). As a consolatory promise of a reign of God that will come some day this part of the Sermon on the Plain would have been a shocking piece of cynicism, even a sneer at the people present. One may only promise the hungry that they will be filled if one expects the promise to be fulfilled not after death and not in some uncertain future, but in a future that is already beginning.

But how will the hungry be filled in the reign of God? The solution is evident in the central section of the narrative of the multiplication of the loaves, so carefully composed by Mark (6:35-41). Jesus had spoken to the crowds for a long time about the reign of God. The text says expressly that he had taught them "many things." But then the disciples come and ask him to stop teaching the crowd: "send them away so that they may go into the surrounding country and villages and buy something for themselves to eat" (v. 36). We must grant that the disciples' words are sober and realistic. It is good to preach about the reign of God, but people have to eat, too. For the disciples these are two things that can be clearly separated. Jesus' task is preaching; the people must see to their food themselves.

Mark presents this so concisely and simply that we can scarcely fail to see that the disciples are here clearly dividing reality into two spheres: that of the reign of God and that of the rest of life. Both spheres—we could even say both "realms"—are as cleanly separated in the disciples' suggestion as they would later repeatedly be divided in the course of the Church's history. In reality the modern isolation of faith from life, the separation of reality into autonomous parts, is already anticipated here. What is fascinating, of course, is that Jesus erases this clean division, which appears so sober and realistic, with a single command: "You give them something to eat" (v. 37). That destroys the convenient tactic of simply preaching to society and otherwise leaving it to fend for itself. Jesus will not participate in separating reality into separate spheres. He emphatically tells his disciples that everything is part of the reign of God: the entirety of human existence, and eating by no means least.

The disciples think they have understood. It is also their business to see to it that the crowd do not go hungry. As practical people they quickly envision a new solution: if the multitude cannot be sent away to provide for themselves privately, but are to be provided with something to eat right here, the meal has to be organized immediately. They will have to estimate how many people are present, calculate how many loaves they will need, figure out how much the bread will cost, and then as quickly as possible a group of disciples will have to go and buy bread. This is a clear plan of organization! Hence their precise question to Jesus: "Are we to go and buy two hundred denarii worth of bread, and give it to them to eat?" (v. 37).

The precision of the calculation is evident from the fact that the Mishnah gives the value of a poor person's daily bread as one-twelfth of a denarius.[38] Thus two hundred denarii will purchase 2,400 daily rations or 4,800 rations for half a day. That will be just about adequate for 5,000 to eat. We can only admire the initiative and organizational ability that lie behind the disciples' second solution. The text presumes that it would be possible for them, after this swift calculation, to collect two hundred denarii from the crowd and then go immediately to make the purchase.

The Church would later tackle the misery in the world with the same zeal and enthusiasm for organization—once it had comprehended that they must give poor people not only the gospel but bread as well. At the present time we see how the great Church aid missions organize help for starving people in impressive ways. In the meantime the disciples' second solution, as then proposed, has become the usual model for providing bread for the world. It is no accident that the names of such aid programs, including "Bread for the World" and "Misereor" (Latin for "I have compassion," cf. Mark 6:34) are derived from this very text, the "multiplication of the loaves."

What is disturbing is simply that Jesus did not accept the second solution either. He was apparently convinced that the poor could not really be satisfied by that method. Four thousand eight hundred rations for half a day distributed among five thousand—with that the worst hunger could be allayed; at best the people could be minimally fed. But the reign of God is far more than that! In it not only will need be satisfied; its essence is superabundance. In the reign of God the divine fullness will shine forth. But above all: an act of well-organized aid such as the disciples suggest would not really change the world. Society would remain what it is. It would constantly produce new structures of misery and the disciples would have to run panting back and forth non-stop to organize help for the hungry without ever putting an end to suffering.

Therefore in our story Jesus does not take the disciples' second solution seriously, no matter how well-meant it was. For him the satisfaction of the hungry in God's *basileia* looks different. He had greater things in mind with his beatitude. Jesus steadily pursues a third solution, that of the reign of God. And because he knows that his disciples can, of themselves, not

---

[38] *m. Peʾa.* VIII, 7. On this cf. Arye Ben-David, *Talmudische Ökonomie. Die Wirtschaft des jüdischen Palästina zur Zeit der Mischna und des Talmud* (Hildesheim and New York: Olms, 1974) 1:300, 306.

even begin to comprehend this true solution that arises out of God's generous fullness he takes the initiative himself. He asks: "How many loaves
have you?" (v. 38). It is not necessary to send the people away, nor is it necessary to organize a meal for them from elsewhere. The festive banquet of
the reign of God will appear as a miracle—a miracle drawn from what is
already present. But in order for the miracle to happen something crucial
has to occur first. Jesus orders the disciples to tell the crowd to organize itself in "dining groups." The next statement explains what is meant by that:
"So they sat down in groups of hundreds and of fifties" (v. 40). This is a
clear reference to Exod 18:25, which describes the order of the camp of the
people of God on their journey through the wilderness. As we know from
Qumran, the organization of the camp in Exodus 18 was deliberately reproduced at their community meals, and this was so because it was expected to
be the order at the messianic banquet in the end time.[39] Against this background the Markan text can only mean to say that Jesus is forming the
crowds of people, who were wandering without purpose or orientation, like
sheep without a shepherd (v. 34), into the end-time people of God.

It is apparently necessary for that end-time people of God to be organized in a clearly visible manner into dining communities. Only when the
scattered people of God allows itself to be gathered and comes together in
a visible way around Jesus, its eschatological shepherd, can the miracle
take place. Only then can the festive banquet of the reign of God happen.
Only then can the glory of the meal shine forth. But then everyone will
have enough. Then they will not only be given an adequate portion, but
will experience a feast. Then there will even be twelve baskets of bread
left over—the symbol of the people of the twelve tribes in its eschatological fullness.

Only when the structural lines of the text are clarified in this way can
we legitimately ask whether that all really happened. The answer can only
be: yes, it all happened, and it continually happens anew. It really happened that the Church only preached and afterward sent people home hungry. It really happened, and it constantly happens, that the Church
concerns itself for human hunger in admirable aid campaigns but does not
thereby change the world's sick society; in fact it cannot hope to change
it in this way. But it also happened, and continues to happen, that the
Church becomes what in God's terms it should be: the eschatological
people of God that allows itself to be gathered by Jesus into that new society in which the abundance of the reign of God shines forth. This eschatological form of the people of God was already inaugurated by Jesus,

---

[39] The citations can be found in Joachim Gnilka, *Das Evangelium nach Markus* 1, EKK
II/1 (Zürich: Benziger, and Neukirchen-Vluyn: Neukirchener Verlag, 1978) 260–61.

and after Easter it became a reality through the Spirit of the Crucified and Risen One. After Easter the Church would gather with eschatological rejoicing for festive meals (Acts 2:46) at which all shared with one another—not only bread, but their whole existence. Luke dares to say of that Church: "there was not a needy person among them" (Acts 4:34). At these festive meals of the first communities they would also have told the story of that *one* miraculous festal banquet at the very beginning. It interpreted the unique experience of those communities.

However, it appears that the story of the festive banquet of the reign of God corresponded completely to the experiences of Christian communities even decades later when Mark wrote his gospel. There are many indications that Mark may have written his gospel at Rome, and it appears that there were already a number of Christian house churches in that city. Mark could by no means have overlooked the correspondence between the miracle story handed down to him and the gatherings of the Roman house churches. The best thing about the story of the multiplication of the loaves was that it was still going on and does so until now.

Running through all the texts cited here from the gospels, from the day in Capernaum to the meal with the five thousand, is a scarlet thread, a fundamental law of salvation history. Joseph Ratzinger, in his *Introduction to Christianity,* in an excursus entitled "Christian Structures," calls it the "law of excess or superfluity."[40] It runs throughout the whole of salvation history but finds its clearest expression in Jesus. He himself, says Ratzinger, "is the righteousness of God, which goes far beyond what need be, which does not calculate, which really overflows; the 'notwithstanding' of his greater love, in which he infinitely surpasses the failing efforts of man."[41]

This fundamental law of salvation history is brought to expression above all in the parables of the lost son (Luke 15:11-32) and the laborers in the vineyard (Matt 20:1-16), but it echoes also in the sayings tradition in the gospels, for example when Luke 6:38 says "give, and it will be given to you. A good measure, pressed down, shaken together, running over, will be put into your lap." The imagery comes from the marketplace. The seller has filled a measure with wheat to the brim, but then presses the grain down with a hand so that there may be no empty space, shakes the

---

[40] Joseph Ratzinger, *Introduction to Christianity.* Translated by J. R. Foster (London: Burns & Oates, 1969; New York: Herder & Herder, 1970) 193–98. Cf. also Hans Urs von Balthasar, *The Glory of the Lord: A Theological Aesthetics.* 7 vols. Translated by Erasmo Leiva-Merikakis; edited by Joseph Fessio and John Riches (San Francisco: Ignatius Press; New York: Crossroad, 1983–1991) 423–31.

[41] Ratzinger, *Introduction* 196.

whole thing so that the kernels fall together, adds more, and at the end pours an overflowing measure of wheat into the buyer's outstretched garment. The Fourth Gospel says, not in such a clear image but with the same underlying idea: "I came that they may have life, and have it abundantly" (John 10:10).

Excess, wealth, and profligate luxury are thus the signs of the time of salvation—not economy, meagerness, wretchedness, and neediness. Why is that so?—because God is overflowing Life itself, and because God's whole desire is to share that life. God's love is beyond all measure, and God's gifts to human beings are not measured by their good behavior or deservingness.

Hence the principle of superfluity is evident even in creation itself. Biologists long ago noticed that quantitative and qualitative waste play a striking role in nature, and that evolution cannot be entirely explained by a calculus of utility. Nature "luxuriates." What an opulence of flowers and butterflies alone! What a superfluity of seeds to produce a single living thing! What an expenditure of solar systems, Milky Ways, and spiral nebulae! An entire universe is squandered in order to produce more and more costly forms of life on a *single* planet and to prepare a place for the human spirit.[42]

Perhaps we can also say, though shocked and almost faltering: What a squandering of human beings and entire nations before God finally found the *one* people in which to anchor the superabundance of divine grace in the world. In the book of Isaiah God speaks quite clearly about this squandering of peoples for the sake of a single nation:

> I give Egypt as your ransom,
>   Ethiopia and Seba in exchange for you.
> Because you are precious in my sight,
>   and honored, and I love you,
> I give people in return for you,
>   nations in exchange for your life. (Isa 43:3-4)

Of course it is also part of this side of the divine profligacy that God gave the *one* best and most precious human being, squandered him for the world's sake. In light of the death of Jesus it is also clear that the profligate fullness of salvation cannot be understood as some kind of never-never land or "table-deck-yourself" for consumers. This overflowing grace can only reach people when they allow themselves to be taken into the service of the plan of God. The glory that illuminated Israel through Jesus was not for the purpose of creating a better life for the privileged, but was to bring the divine brilliance, through Israel, to the whole world.

---

[42] The above is derived from Ratzinger, *Introduction* 197–98.

Finally: the disciples were promised a hundred brothers and sisters, a hundred houses and fields, and the whole joy of the reign of God, but only "with persecutions."[43] And in the course of the Fourth Gospel the glory of Jesus that the miracle at Cana tells of is explained as a glory that first comes to its true expression at Jesus' "hour," that is, in his Passion.[44] Moreover, Paul developed a whole theology of the superabundant grace of God that appears precisely in the weakness and distress of the faithful in order that it may be clear that the overflowing fullness of glory comes not from human strength, but from God alone.[45]

### 4. The Basic Sacramental Structure of Jesus' Actions

Many New Testament texts speak of the overflowing salvation that breaks out in Israel with the coming of Jesus. These include the parable of the workers in the vineyard (Matt 20:1-16). It is worth looking more closely at the "world" of this parable.

The story apparently takes place at harvest time. The grapes are ripe and must be gathered as quickly as possible. Otherwise it would be inexplicable that the owner of the vineyard is looking for workers all day long. It is true that there is no trace in this parable of the joy that filled the days of the grape harvest in ancient Israel. There is nothing about the glad shouts that rang out over the vineyards, nothing of the blessings that passersby called out to the harvesters.[46] The parable presumes a grey, sober work world in which work is nothing but toil.

The reason for this should be clear: Jesus' parables give us an astonishingly accurate portrait of the social conditions in Palestine in the first century C.E.[47] The days when free farmers in Israel harvested with joy in their own vineyards were in the past. Most of them had long since lost their land to great landowners. The Romans demanded such heavy taxes that every business had to produce a higher profit and was thus forced to economize. This meant that agricultural enterprises had to be large and employ cheap labor: either slaves or people who worked for wages. Individual family farms could no longer maintain themselves. Thus the majority of the formerly independent farmers worked as day-laborers. They

---

[43] Cf. Mark 10:30.

[44] Cf. especially John 12:23-24; 13:31-32; 17:1.

[45] Cf. Michael Theobald, *Die überströmende Gnade. Studien zu einem paulinischen Motivfeld*. FzB 22 (Würzburg, 1982). Theobald's book gave me the title for this section.

[46] Cf. Isa 9:3; Pss 126:6; 129:8.

[47] For this social development in Palestine cf. Hans G. Kippenberg, *Religion und Klassenbildung im antiken Judäa. Eine religionssoziologische Studie zum Verhältnis von Tradition und gesellschaftlicher Entwicklung*. StUNT 14 (Göttingen: Vandenhoeck & Ruprecht, 1978) 146–55.

were hired in the marketplace in the morning and paid off in the evening. The workday lasted from sunup to sundown, and on such a day an agricultural laborer earned barely enough to feed the family for the next day, namely one denarius. Anyone who was not hired in the morning faced the prospect of hungry children on the next day. The parable reflects this situation: a merciless and joyless world.

Consequently we have no reason to look down on the "workers from the first hour" who demanded a just wage system. From their standpoint they were entirely in the right. For the last, who had worked only an hour in the cool of the early evening, to be paid exactly as much as they, who had toiled for many long hours in the burning heat, was not only unjust but also inhuman. Their work was thereby robbed of its dignity.

Every society, even the worst slavocracy, depends on preserving at least some measure of justice. Otherwise it will collapse. To that extent the workers from the first hour are right to protest, and to that extent the action in the parable is "impossible" to begin with. Only when we realize that can we gain access to the real meaning of the story. In it two worlds collide; we could also call them two different forms of society.

On the one hand the parable soberly and realistically depicts the *old society* that continually gains the upper hand, even among the people of God, in which it is "every man (and woman) for him/herself." In it each individual must struggle for her or his own existence and that of the family. In it there is envy when someone has more than others, and an endless conflict between those "above" and those "below," but there is just as much, perhaps even more rivalry between those belonging to the same social stratum. Their constant comparison of their own lot with that of others leads to continual mistrust and ongoing struggles for power. The law exists to hold these struggles within some kind of bounds, and law is one of the most valuable human inventions. It is quite just for workers in such a society to fight for their rights. In a world built on mistrust and rivalry they have no other choice.

The mastery of this parable consists in the way it reveals, with a minimum of words, how God's new world suddenly breaks into this old society. The story turns out differently from what the hearers expect. They suppose that the last, who were idle all day, will receive only a few pennies. That they receive just as much as the first must have been a shock to Jesus' hearers. The ground is pulled out from under their feet; they are robbed of all their accustomed rules. But if they open themselves to the parable they do not fall into the abyss; instead their feet stand on the ground of the *basileia,* the new society of God.

In the reign of God there are different rules. It is true that people work from morning to evening; God's world is not never-never land. But work has value and dignity, and no one need go home in the evening burdened by care and anxiety. No one is left alone. Above all, it is possible to live without rivalry, and that is because there is now something greater and more just than all individual desires: work for God's cause. It is precisely this common cause, desired by all, that creates a deep solidarity, that in turn makes it possible for each to participate in the suffering of others and rejoice in the others' joy.

Of course in the parable this new society has not yet developed. It is only apparent, in preliminary fashion, in the employer who, contrary to all the experiences of the old society, is "good" (Matt 20:15). The Greek word for "good" here is *agathos*. It is usually translated at this point by "generous." "Are you envious because I am generous?" says the vineyard owner to a grumbling worker according to the *NRSV* and *NAB*. The Greek text, translated literally, says "is your eye evil because I am good?"—which is not exactly the same thing, for the basic meaning of *agathos* is "good" in the sense of "useful," "suitable," "excellent," "appropriate." When the owner gives the last as much as the first he is acting appropriately, reasonably, and therefore well. Of course he is not "reasonable" according to the rules of a society regulated by a struggle for the division of goods, but reasonable according to the rules of the reign of God. Jesus was the first to fully understand the rationality of the reign of God.[48] Therefore in the eyes of God he was the suitable person.

Once again: at the moment when Jesus tells the parable the new thing has not yet developed. It is visible in preliminary form only in himself, the one person most suitable for the reign of God. Only after his death will that revolutionary new thing take shape beyond him, in the communities of those who follow him. There will happen again and again what was told in the story of the workers in the vineyard: the old world is turned on its head. The last receive just as much as the first. Although they have only just come they have a share in the new community life whose greatest wealth is trust and solidarity.

It should by now be clear that we miss the point of the parable if we see its theme as simply and only the overflowing generosity of God. Obviously it speaks, ultimately, of the boundless and undeserved generosity of God; after all, according to biblical theology no one is good "but God alone."[49] But if the parable was only about that it would be completely non-binding. Every believer nowadays speaks about God's generosity;

---

[48] For the "rationality" of Jesus' ethics see Gerhard Lohfink, *Wem gilt die Bergpredigt? Beiträge zu einer christlichen Ethik* (Freiburg: Herder, 1988) 128–32.

[49] Mark 10:18. The Matthean version (Matt 19:17: "there is only one who is good") is in the immediate context of the parable of the workers in the vineyard.

that costs nothing and changes nothing. If Jesus had only talked about a generous God he would not have been crucified. The grumbling of the workers from the first hour reflects the grumbling of Jesus' contemporaries who were outraged at the new thing he was beginning with his disciples: a common life that grew out of constant forgiving and in which, therefore, there was room even for sinners. After all, it was a common complaint about Jesus that he ate with tax collectors and sinners.[50]

The parable, then, is not about some abstract attribute of God. Jesus speaks of the limitless generosity of God solely from the point of view that now, since his appearance, that generosity has become a reality in the form of a new society that is beginning to grow around him and because of him. The parable tells how this new reality breaks through the weariness and hopelessness of the people of God. It is an enormous event. It turns the lowest into the highest, awakens deep anxieties, evokes revulsion. But it also permits hope to bloom and gives indestructible joy.

Thus Jesus describes, in the parable of the workers in the vineyard, what is happening *at this moment:* the coming of the reign of God. He explains what is already happening before the eyes of his audience, its momentum still hidden and yet visible. The parable does not offer any kind of timeless teaching. It reveals things that are happening *now,* and by doing so it sets them free. A new possibility for living becomes imaginable. The hearers can surrender themselves to the truth of the parable. They can enter into the story it tells and through Jesus' word permit themselves to be given a new basis on which to stand. Jesus' words are active; they create reality.

This brings us to a phenomenon that is simply crucial for Jesus. If one fails to see it one has not comprehended the fundamental structure of his public life. Jesus not only speaks words; his words are at work, they reveal reality, and therefore his proclamation is imbued with and accompanied by powerful action:

After being tested in the wilderness Jesus goes to Galilee. There he calls men and women to follow him. From among them he chooses the Twelve and sends them into all parts of Israel. He founds a "new family." He drives out demons. He cures sick people. He does not effect these cures just any way; he touches the people. He takes them by the hand. He lays his hands on them. He puts his fingers into deaf people's ears. He makes mud out of dirt and saliva and spreads it on the eyes of the blind. He sets a child in the midst of his disciples. He blesses children. He eats and drinks with tax collectors and sinners. He feeds the hungry. He enters Jerusalem seated on a donkey. He curses a fig tree. He takes a whip and

---

[50] Mark 2:16; cf. Luke 7:34; 15:2; 19:7.

drives the sellers of animals out of the Temple and overturns the tables of the moneychangers. He washes his disciples' feet. At his last meal he hands them bread and wine and interprets both of these in light of his death.[51]

All that is not mere superficial activity or simply a series of incidents. It is deliberate action, and each single action has a dimension that bestows meaning, that constitutes a new reality. Scholars have therefore rightly spoken of Jesus' "sign-actions" or "symbolic actions."[52] These acts reach deep down into human physicality and take it seriously. The human being is dust and earth, and therefore Jesus can make a paste of dirt and rub it on a blind person's eyes. It is more than a simple act of natural healing, and it has nothing at all to do with the practice of magic. It makes clear that healing and liberation are not purely spiritual or interior. The earth comes to people's aid, and the body is just as much to be redeemed as the soul.

Jesus takes the body and its needs seriously. No one could have said of him what was said in antiquity about the pagan philosopher Plotinus, or what Athanasius said of the Christian hermit Anthony: Plotinus "lived as one ashamed to have been born into a human body,"[53] and Anthony "'blushed' when he had to eat."[54]

In Jesus' very acts of healing the incarnational nature of his work becomes visible: God's salvation must enter the world and penetrate every part of reality. It is not simply a question of opinion; it is matter itself that is equally at stake. Nothing can be left aside. Redemption is for the whole creation. The history of revelation is not a matter of progressive desecularization but of a more and more comprehensive incarnation, a deeper and deeper saturation of the world with the spirit of God.[55] God has come uncomfortably close to each of us for our own good. One of Jesus' witnesses would later

---

[51] Return to Galilee: Mark 1:14; discipleship: Mark 1:16-20; Luke 8:1-3; choice of the Twelve: Mark 3:13-19; sending of the Twelve: Mark 6:6-13; new family: Mark 3:31-35; touching the sick: Mark 1:31, 41; 5:41; laying hands on them: Mark 6:5; fingers in the ears: Mark 7:33; saliva: Mark 7:33; John 9:6; child in their midst: Mark 9:36; blessing of children: Mark 10:13-16; eating with tax collectors: Mark 2:13-17; multiplication of loaves: Mark 6:32-44; entry into Jerusalem: Mark 11:1-11; fig tree: Mark 11:12-14; action in the Temple: Mark 11:15-19; John 2:13-22; washing disciples' feet: John 13:1-20; last meal: Mark 14:17-25.

[52] German "Zeichenhandlungen." Cf. especially the work of Maria Trautmann, *Zeichenhafte Handlungen Jesu. Ein Beitrag zur Frage nach dem geschichtlichen Jesus.* FzB 37 (Würzburg: Echter, 1980).

[53] Peter Brown, *The World of Late Antiquity, AD 150–750* (London: Thames and Hudson, 1971) 96.

[54] Ibid.; cf. Athanasius, *Vita Antonii* 45.

[55] Cf. Joseph Ratzinger in the *Pastoralblatt* (Cologne, March 1988), quoted by Rudolf Pesch, *Über das Wunder der Brotvermehrung* 40.

express it this way: "We declare to you what was from the beginning, what we have heard, what we have seen with our eyes, what we have looked at and touched with our hands, concerning the word of life" (1 John 1:1). This opening sentence of the first letter of John says in the most powerful fashion that Jesus is no phantom, no product of fantasy, nor is he a pure spirit whose bodiliness is but a shell. The matter of faith is available to the senses. It is a tangible reality that affects the whole human person. Only in the flesh is the "word of life" perceptible.

That word, after all, is what really matters. Jesus' physical gestures are always accompanied by a word, for the human being only becomes human through language and the free rationality that imbues language. It is the spirit that breathes life into the clay, and only the word born of the spirit takes from things their indeterminacy and multiple meanings. Thus all Jesus' sign-actions are accompanied by effective and powerful words:

"I do choose. Be made clean!" (Mark 1:41)

"Your sins are forgiven." (Mark 2:5)

"Stand up, take your mat and go to your home." (Mark 2:11)

"Those who are well have no need of a physician, but those who are sick." (Mark 2:17)

"Your faith has made you well." (Mark 5:34)

"Little girl, get up!" (Mark 5:41)

"Ephphatha. . . . Be opened." (Mark 7:34)

"You spirit that keeps this boy from speaking and hearing, I command you, come out of him, and never enter him again!" (Mark 9:25)

"Lazarus, come out!" (John 11:43)

"Take; this is my body." (Mark 14:22)

In each of these cases the sign and the words constitute a complete unit. Moreover, Jesus speaks commandingly and with an assurance that only he can have because he knows in his deepest being that in him God is acting, in person and with finality. This is especially clear when Jesus forgives sins. His opponents are right to say: "Who can forgive sins but God alone?" (Mark 2:7). When Jesus nevertheless does it he claims to be standing in the place of God.

However, we should also note that the works of Jesus done for the sick and the possessed, the outcasts and the socially marginalized did not take place in a vacuum. They happened in Israel. They served the restoration of the people of God. They were intended to make clear that the fulfillment of the prophetic promises had begun. In the time of salvation proclaimed by the book of Isaiah God will heal God's people and lead them (Isa 57:18), bind up their wounds (30:26), and in those days no one in Israel will say "I am ill" (33:24). Jesus' sign-actions are therefore eschatological signs, signs of the end time in which the promises are to be fulfilled.

If we take all that together—the unity of sign and word in Jesus' actions, his authoritative acts, his deeds for the people of God, and the eschatological structure of these actions—we cannot avoid speaking of a "sacramental structure." Sacraments take their being from the unity of sign and word. Still more: they are eschatological signs. With them new creation is already beginning. Paul, referring to baptism, says: "So if anyone is in Christ, there is a new creation: everything old has passed away; see, everything has become new!" (2 Cor 5:17). It is true that sacraments require the faith of the recipient, but it is not the recipient's faith that brings salvation: it is granted to the believer beforehand. He or she is integrated into the new creation that began with Jesus in Israel.

Obviously the Church's sacraments presuppose Jesus' death and resurrection. In that respect we can only speak of a "fundamental sacramental structure" in the actions of the earthly Jesus. But we must speak of it if we are to give a correct description of his salvific, eschatological-creative action in and for Israel. Even before his death, Jesus founded a new reality in Israel. He prepared the ground for the thing that would arise in the midst of Israel as "church": he gathered Israel as the eschatological people of God.

Two objections have often been raised against what has just been said. The first insists that Jesus acted primarily through his *word*. He desired to do nothing more in his preaching than to point out to the people the impending arrival of the reign of God. Even his undeniable sign-actions were only *pointers* to what was to come. The gathering of the people of God and the formation of the eschatological community of salvation, however, he left entirely in the hands of God. He expected these to happen in the near future, as the sole and exclusive actions of God.[56]

This objection fundamentally overlooks the real meaning of "actions of God." God desires to act in the world only and always through creatures. When we say that God has "acted" in history it means that God has found people who placed themselves at God's disposal, who died to their own plans and life projects and entrusted themselves entirely to the plan and the will of God. They allow God to be the sole actor, and yet God will not do the least thing in the world without them. The prime image of this

---

[56] See the references in Gerhard Lohfink, "Jesus und die Kirche," in Walter Kern, Hermann Josef Pottmeyer, and Max Seckler, eds., *Handbuch der Fundamentaltheologie* 3, tractate "Kirche" (Freiburg: Herder, 1986) 49–96, at 85 n. 141.

attitude of allowing God alone to work is Jesus himself, but in him it has become possible for believers as well.[57]

To say that God would bring about the divine reign and the eschatological people of God without human cooperation would mean ultimately that God would have to stage a divine show that would break into the world from outside, perverting the creation in its integrity, making people nothing but puppets, and destroying all freedom. It is true that there are many apocalyptic images in the Bible that appear to suggest such a conception, but they are images that must be interpreted in their theological context. If we look closer we see that biblical theology opposes such a notion of the exclusion of humanity with the greatest acerbity. According to the theology of the Fourth Gospel God works, but does so entirely through the Son, and believers enter into Jesus' work and in the power of his spirit will do even greater works.[58]

Precisely in this context it must strike us that Jesus only cured individuals. He did not heal all the sick in Israel, nor could he. In Nazareth he could do no miracles, or scarcely any, because he found no faith there (Mark 6:5-6). This again shows that the inbreaking of the reign of God is not a spectacle. God's action is bound up with the faith of concrete individual people. The reign of God needs believers who can open themselves to it freely.

A second objection begins in the same superficial way, saying that Jesus gave no organization, constitution, or social structure to the group of those who followed him. In that very fact one can see that he was not the least bit interested in the gathering of Israel or the formation of an eschatological community of salvation.[59] He simply preached the reign of God—and oddly enough, what resulted was the Church. Those who raise this objection apparently understand the reign of God as something ephemeral and free-floating, a kind of counter-world opposed to anything social or institutional.

It is true, of course, that Alfred Loisy, with his often-quoted aphorism, "Jesus foretold the kingdom, and it was the Church that came," meant something entirely different: he intended his statement positively and was speaking against Adolf von Harnack's religious individualism. His concern, in fact, was to affirm the continuity between Jesus' preaching and the Church.[60] What is so superficial about the second objection is that it is

---

[57] For more detail on this topic see Gerhard Lohfink, "Die Not der Exegese mit der Reich-Gottes-Verkündigung Jesu," *ThQ* 168 (1988) 1–15, at 12–14 (= idem, *Studien* 383–402, at 397–400).

[58] For the interpenetration of the "work of the Father," the "work of the Son," and the "works of believers" see John 5:19, 20, 36; 9:3, 4; 10:32, 37; 14:10, 12; 17:4.

[59] For these authors see Gerhard Lohfink, "Jesus und die Kirche" 93 n. 172.

[60] Alfred Loisy, *The Gospel and the Church*. Translated by Christopher Home (New York: Charles Scribner's Sons, 1904) 166. For the interpretation of this statement, usually

founded on enthusiasm and a quite irrational suspicion of everything institutional. Institutions, however, are not evil in and of themselves, just as what is charismatic is not good in and of itself.[61] There is no society, no community, not even a movement that can exist without some institutional structure. The assertion that Jesus gave his followers no constitution and no social structure obscures the facts.

Jesus, after all, was a Jew. From the beginning of his life he was part of the living community of Israel. His disciples, like him, were themselves part of Israel and entirely oriented toward Israel, and Israel, as a community gathered around the Torah, had for a long time had a comprehensive social order. So Jesus did not have to start from scratch. He could simply take for granted a great many rules and norms, rituals and traditions. Consider, as one example, the pilgrimage of Israel to the great festivals in Jerusalem. Jesus took part with his disciples in these pilgrimages as a matter of course.[62]

On the other hand Jesus brought Israel's social order under a new eschatological constellation that certainly drew social changes in its wake. Here we must necessarily speak about Mark 3:20-35. This group of pericopes could be entitled "the founding of the new family."[63]

The text group in Mark follows immediately after the account of the choosing of the Twelve. The three-part narrative is meant to illustrate first of all the nature of the opposition Jesus encounters when he begins to gather Israel from a new center. The resistance comes from two sides: first of all from Jesus' own relatives, who call him "crazy." In addition it comes from the Jerusalem authorities who have sent theologians to Galilee to observe Jesus. These latter demonize Jesus, asserting that he is possessed by an evil spirit and is doing his miracles with the aid of the supreme evil spirit. Jesus warns these theologians with a saying about sins against the Holy Spirit. His relatives, on the other hand, who have come to bring him

---

understood wrongly, cf. Gerhard Heinz, *Das Problem der Kirchenentstehung in der deutschen protestantischen Theologie des 20. Jahrhunderts.* tts 4 (Mainz: Matthias Grünewald, 1974) 122–39.

[61] For the meaning and necessity of the institutional element in the people of God cf. Medard Kehl, "Kirche als Institution," in Kern, Pottmeyer, and Seckler, *Handbuch der Fundamentaltheologie* 3:176–97.

[62] Probably Jesus went to Jerusalem with his disciples many times during his public ministry (cf. John 2:13, 23; 5:1; 7:10; 11:55; 12:1).

[63] What follows is treated in more detail in Gerhard Lohfink and Rudolph Pesch, "Volk Gottes als 'Neue Familie,'" in Josef Ernst and Stephan Leimgruber, eds., *Surrexit Dominus vere. Die Gegenwart des Auferstandenen in seiner Kirche. FS Erzbischof Johannes Joachim Degenhardt* (Paderborn: Bonifatius, 1995) 227–42. I am borrowing from that essay in a number of places.

under household surveillance, he rejects with the brusque question: "Who are my mother and my brothers?" (Mark 3:33).

However, the narrative intends more than simply illustrating the opposition to Jesus. It only reaches its goal when Jesus constitutes a "new family," the family of those who do the will of God:

> And looking at those who sat around him, he said, "Here are my mother and my brothers! Whoever does the will of God is my brother and sister and mother." (Mark 3:34-35)

The formula "doing the will of God" in Israel meant, in essence, following the Torah. But that cannot be what is meant in this situation, for Jesus' relatives certainly obeyed the Torah. The common formula has attained a new meaning. "Doing the will of God" in this context can only mean learning from Jesus what the living will of God for "today" is, the "today" that is dawning for Israel in the appearance of Jesus, and then to respond in obedience to that "today." Whoever does that will be brother, sister, and mother to Jesus, and so will belong to the new family of Jesus.

As important as a correct understanding of what is meant by "the will of God" in this passage is a serious appreciation of the linguistic form. Jesus not only formulates in high rhetorical style here, but even juridically.[64] Looking at the people seated around him,[65] he speaks a declaratory formula that was customarily used in Israel at marriages (and correspondingly in the process of divorce):[66] "Here are my mother and my brothers!" It is true that the whole episode is more a sign-action than a formal, juridical action, but in the ancient world the two were much less easily separated than they are now. We must try not to regard biblical symbolic actions as merely illustrations or demonstrative declarations of intent. A prophetic symbolic action intends more than mere explanation or illustration. There is something creative within a symbolic act; it establishes a new reality, and in that regard it has a juridical dimension.

Jesus' declaration of separation from his relatives is thus not a mere incident, and his saying about those who now follow the will of God is not mere rhetoric. Those who know what clan and family mean in the East can only see in Jesus' distancing himself from his own family an event that creates a deep rift in social relationships that is anything but trivial.

Equally revolutionary is the behavior of those who follow Jesus. His disciples also leave their families. They abandon their previous occupations

---

[64] Cf. Norbert Lohfink, *Kirchenträume. Reden gegen den Trend* (Freiburg: Herder, 1982) 40.

[65] Matt 12:49 makes this clear: "and pointing to his disciples, he said . . . ."

[66] Cf. Bernhard Lang, "Ehe," *NBL* 1:475–478, at 476.

(Mark 1:16-20) and enter with Jesus into an unstable itinerant life, wandering throughout Galilee (Mark 1:39). They live from hand to mouth, so that they must pray to God: "give us this day our daily bread" (Matt 6:11). There can be no rule of one over others according to the model of the old society. The one who wants to be great must be the servant of all (Mark 10:42-44). And because that is impossible for human beings, the disciples must forgive one another seventy-seven times a day (Matt 18:22). They are to live as a new family down to the smallest details of daily life.

This is not just a polishing of minor flaws in the models of behavior current in the old society. What Jesus begins with his disciples is a "new" behavior extending to the deepest levels of life from which society arises.[67] This new way of acting is to "fulfill" the Torah, that is, to bring to light what Israel's social order was always meant to be (Matt 5:17-20). Just as the Torah cannot be lived by isolated individuals but presupposes the community of Israel, so also the new way of life that Jesus speaks about presupposes the social structure of the circle of disciples, the "new family." Anyone who thinks that all this had nothing to do with "form" and social structure must be deeply prejudiced.

Mark, at any rate, saw it otherwise. He follows the founding of the new family with three parables of growth to show how the reign of God expands irresistibly from the tiniest beginnings, despite the resistance of its enemies. The concrete place where this growth of the *basileia* is first perceptible is the new family of Jesus' disciples, for to them "has been given the secret of the kingdom of God" (Mark 4:11).

From that alone it is clear that Mark regards the founding of the new family as fundamental to Jesus' preaching and his gathering of the people of God. His text order shows that now something new is being sown in Israel. In spite of all resistance it will bear fruit thirtyfold, sixtyfold, and a hundredfold. From the tiny mustard seed of the group of disciples will grow the great plant that gives shade and shelter to many.

This new thing in Israel, the God-given miracle of the eschatological new beginning, does not arise out of naturally existing structures: it does not come from inheritance, giftedness, good will, blood, family, or clan. It is the interruption of all processes. It is a new sowing, a new creation, and thus also a new form:

---

[67] For more detail see Gerhard Lohfink, *Wem gilt die Bergpredigt?* 119–32, and see also Jürgen Roloff, *Die Kirche im Neuen Testament.* NTD Ergänzungsreihe 10 (Göttingen: Vandenhoeck & Ruprecht, 1993) 37–46.

No one sews a piece of unshrunk cloth on an old cloak; otherwise, the patch pulls away from it, the new from the old, and a worse tear is made. And no one puts new wine into old wineskins; otherwise, the wine will burst the skins, and the wine is lost, and so are the skins; but one puts new wine into fresh wineskins. (Mark 2:21-22)

A part of this new form that, according to the gospel of Mark, Jesus founds in the midst of Israel is the creation of the Twelve. Here, still more clearly than in the founding of the new family that follows it, is an institutional act. When Jesus creates the Twelve there is already a larger number of disciples, at least according to Mark's depiction, which says in connection with the calling of Levi and the meal with the tax collectors "there were many who followed him" (Mark 2:15). Jesus chooses twelve from this larger group of disciples. The scene, with its demonstrative gesture, takes place on a mountain and is therefore all the more impressive. Mark writes:

He went up the mountain and called to him those whom he wanted, and they came to him. And he appointed twelve to be with him, and to be sent out to proclaim the message, and to have authority to cast out demons. So he appointed the twelve: Simon (to whom he gave the name Peter); James son of Zebedee and John the brother of James (to whom he gave the name Boanerges, that is, Sons of Thunder); and Andrew, and Philip, and Bartholomew, and Matthew, and Thomas, and James son of Alphaeus, and Thaddaeus, and Simon the Cananaean, and Judas Iscariot, who betrayed him. (Mark 3:13-19)

Both the carefully preserved list of the twelve, with Simon Peter in the first place, and the verb *epoiēsen* ("he made," or "he appointed") show that this is a genuine institution. The only comparably complete list of names in the primitive Church was that for the office of the "Seven" in Acts 6:5. "Making" or "appointing" *(poiein)* in the Old Testament could describe the installation of officeholders such as judges or priests,[68] and that kind of public, official procedure is what is described here.

Still, there are echoes of other things as well. Everyone familiar with the Bible would hear in the background the fixed formula about God's "making" from the creation account in Gen 1:1–2:4. Deutero-Isaiah also echoes here; it says again and again that God "made" God's people and "will make" new things for them.[69] With Jesus' creation of the Twelve a promise from the book of Isaiah enters into its phase of final fulfillment. The new creation of Israel is now taking place. The Twelve are the beginning and the center of growth for the eschatological people of God. But

---

[68] Cf., for example, Exod 18:25; 1 Sam 12:6; 1 Kings 12:31; 13:33; 2 Chr 2:17.
[69] Cf. Isa 41:20; 43:1, 19.

Jesus' symbolic action involves not only the impressive act on the mountain. The account says:

> And he appointed twelve,
>> to be with him,
>> and to be sent out
>>> to proclaim the message,
>>> and to have authority
>>>> to cast out demons.

Readers today will of course notice that Mark nowhere says that the number of the disciples singled out by Jesus (twelve) is related to the number of the tribes of Israel. For Jewish Christians, and even for the Gentile Christian hearers of the gospel, that was so obvious that it required no mention. Similarly, it was a matter of course that at that time many of the twelve tribes had ceased to exist. When Jesus nevertheless constitutes a group of twelve if can only mean that what is at issue here is the eschatological restoration of Israel in its entire fullness and completeness as willed by God. As we have said, the hearers and readers would have understood that immediately. No special commentary was necessary.

Mark is interested in something else: Jesus appointed the Twelve "to be with him." This makes clear that the sign-action is not restricted to the scene on the mountain. It continues. Wherever Jesus goes the Twelve are to live with him and always be with him, so that they will continually make visible the new beginning of the people of the twelve tribes and set it before the eyes of everyone in Israel. They are thus an *enduring sign,* a constantly visible *figura* for the cause to which Jesus devotes himself: the gathering of the people of God, its restoration, its renewal, the creation of its unity, its eschatological new creation.

The commentary goes still farther. It also says that Jesus appointed the Twelve "to be sent out to proclaim the message, and to have authority to cast out demons." In the first place Mark is referring to the sending of the Twelve that is described in 6:6-13. The twelve disciples go out in pairs into all parts of Israel, preach as Jesus preaches, and drive out demons as Jesus drives them out. They do everything he does. Matthew and Luke emphasize this strict parallelism between the actions of Jesus and those of his disciples even more strongly than Mark does.[70]

Mark, on the other hand, has something that is entirely lacking in Matthew and is much less clear in Luke's account: in Mark's version the Twelve are on mission for a rather long time. The narrative technique used

---

[70] They do this by applying the phrase "the kingdom of heaven/kingdom of God has come near" (Matt 10:7 par. Luke 10:9) from the mission discourse in the Q source.

to emphasize their absence is the insertion, between their sending and their return, of some entirely different material, namely the account of Herod Antipas's murder of John the Baptizer (Mark 6:14-29). In this way Mark avoids having to describe any activity of Jesus in the intervening time when his disciples are absent.[71] This, in fact, is more than pure narrative strategy; it is theology. Mark intends to say that Jesus no longer acts without the Twelve. Now it is *only with them* that his work has that symbolic structure that corresponds to his action in and for Israel.

On the other hand the omission of any account of Jesus' action in the absence of the Twelve shows that his power has been wholly transferred to them. They do what he would do. They act in his place, as his representatives. They are therefore not only the beginning of the eschatological Israel. They are at the same time emissaries in Christ's place. They have an eschatological office of witness: they make Jesus and his power present. For Mark this already portends the post-Easter period.

Let us now return to our starting point! The question was: why did Jesus appear in Israel? We saw that his parables already opened up a "world" in the sense of the possibility of a new way of life. On the other hand all Jesus' actions have a symbolic dimension: symbolic not in the pale, watered-down sense in which people now understand symbols, but in the sense of effective action that creates new reality. Jesus, in all his deeds of power and sign-actions, especially the founding of the new family and the appointment of the Twelve, establishes the beginning of the eschatological Israel.

What Jesus does is therefore not *immediately* directed to the Church, but to the eschatological Israel. We can only speak of "church" at a time when it is clear, after Easter, that the greater part of Israel will not come to believe.[72] However, to the extent that the post-Easter *ekklēsia*—even though incomplete because the synagogue is absent—*is* the eschatological Israel, one can and must say that Jesus laid the foundation for the Church in all his actions. What Jesus founded, when he appointed the Twelve, was not the Church but the eschatological people of God. But in that act of foundation the basis for the Church was prepared. The Church goes back to the actions of Jesus himself.[73]

---

[71] Cf. Hans-Josef Klauck, "Die Auswahl der Zwölf (Mk 3,13-19)" in idem, *Gemeinde—Amt—Sakrament. Neutestamentliche Perspektiven* (Würzburg: Echter, 1989) 131–36, at 136.

[72] That is exactly how the Acts of the Apostles portrays the situation. Cf. Gerhard Lohfink, *Die Sammlung Israels. Eine Untersuchung zur lukanischen Ekklesiologie.* StANT 39 (Munich: Kösel, 1975), especially 93–99. In Matt 16:18 the "building" of the *ekklēsia* is in the future.

[73] For more detail see Gerhard Lohfink, "Jesus und die Kirche" 94–95.

## 5. The Manifold Character of Vocation: Apostles, Disciples, People

The Twelve were the beginning and center of growth of the eschatological Israel, and the disciples constituted the new family around which
Israel was to gather. But what was the true relationship of the disciples to
the people of God? Was all Israel meant to become a nation of disciples?
Was the circle of disciples the model for the eschatological community of
salvation, so that it represented, in anticipation, what the whole people of
God was to become, namely a *discipleship?*

There are textual indices in the New Testament that appear to point in
precisely that direction. Thus the Acts of the Apostles often refers simply
to "the disciples." The series of references begins with Acts 6:1-2:

> Now during those days, when the disciples were increasing in number, the
> Hellenists (the Greek-speaking Jews in the community) complained against
> the Hebrews (the Aramaic-speaking Jews) because their widows were being
> neglected in the daily distribution of food. And the twelve called together the
> whole community of the disciples . . . .

The word "disciples" here refers to the entire community. This unique
usage, which must go back to the time of the original Jerusalem community, is found elsewhere in Acts as well. Throughout the book "disciple"
can simply mean "Christian" or "member of the community," and "the
disciples" often refers without further explanation to the community in Jerusalem or another local congregation.[74]

Add to this the fact that the gospels, which refer with great regularity
to Jesus' disciples, are not purely historical accounts but render the time
of Jesus transparent to the later time of the Church. When the evangelists
talk about Jesus they are always speaking at the same time of their own
contemporary Church. Therefore it is certainly appropriate to see discipleship as an essential characteristic of the Church.[75] One might propose
the equation Church = disciples.

But is that correct? If we read the New Testament more carefully we
find that the situation is more multifaceted. It is true that the usage in the
Acts of the Apostles indicates unmistakably that without disciples there
can be no Church in the New Testament sense. But that book is unique
within the New Testament. The letter corpus avoids the word "disciples."

---

[74] Disciple = Christian: Acts 6:7; 9:1, 10, 26b; 16:1; 21:16b; disciple = member of the
congregation: Acts 6:1; 11:29; 19:30; 20:30; 21:16a; the disciples = the community: 6:2;
9:19, 26a, 38; 13:52; 14:22, 28; 18:23, 27; 20:1; 21:4.

[75] In previous publications I myself have largely identified the Church with discipleship.
Cf., for example, Gerhard Lohfink, *Wem gilt die Bergpredigt?* 32–35, 73. The present chapter corrects the suggestions made there.

The form of expression found in Acts must ultimately stem from the initial situation of the young post-Easter Church. In that early period distinctions were not yet needed. They only came later, although the groundwork for them was laid in the gospel tradition itself.

According to the gospels, in fact, no one could be a disciple unless he or she had been chosen by Jesus, usually with the call: "Come, follow me!"[76] Jesus did not call everyone to follow him. The proclamation of the reign of God in Mark 1:15 ends with the appeal: "repent, and believe in the good news!" and not with the call: "follow me and become my disciples!" There is no saying of Jesus in which the whole people is called to discipleship or to following Jesus. Moreover, Jesus nowhere makes discipleship a condition for participation in the reign of God.[77]

Accordingly the number of those whom Jesus calls to follow him was limited. First of all there were the Twelve; beyond that group we can name the following persons the New Testament tradition clearly indicates were "disciples" or "followed" Jesus: Matthias, Joseph Barsabbas, Cleopas, Joseph of Arimathea, Nathanael, Mary Magdalene, Mary the mother of James the younger and Joses, Salome, Joanna the wife of Chuza, and Susanna.[78] Luke counts seventy other disciples besides the Twelve.[79] Seventy is certainly a round number meant to lend a biblical flavor, for in the Old Testament twelve, forty, and seventy are the most common and theologically significant numbers.[80] It may be that in speaking of seventy Luke was not very far from the actual size of the group of disciples, but however that may be Jesus did not attempt to acquire disciples at all costs. Instead he issued warnings:

> As they were going along the road, someone said to him, "I will follow you wherever you go." And Jesus said to him, "Foxes have holes, and birds of the air have nests; but the Son of Man has nowhere to lay his head." (Luke 9:57-58)

Other observations point in the same direction: Jesus goes to the home of the tax collector Zacchaeus just as he does to that of the tax collector Levi, but he does not call Zacchaeus to follow him as he does Levi. Zacchaeus

---

[76] Cf. Mark 1:17; 2:14; 10:21; Luke 9:59; John 1:43.

[77] This has often been emphasized. Cf. the fundamental book on discipleship by Martin Hengel, *The Charismatic Leader and His Followers*. Translated by James Greig (New York: Crossroad, 1981) 59–61.

[78] Cf. Acts 1:22-23; Luke 24:18; John 19:38; 1:45-49; 21:2; Mark 15:40-41; Luke 8:1-3.

[79] Luke 10:1, 17. The manuscript tradition varies between seventy and seventy-two. If the number seventy-two is original, although that is less probable, this may be a reference to the seventy-two nations in Genesis 10 LXX (seventy in the MT).

[80] For more detail see Gerhard Lohfink, *Die Sammlung Israels* 68–70; idem, *Die Himmelfahrt Jesu. Untersuchungen zu den Himmelfahrts- und Erhöhungstexten bei Lukas*. StANT 26 (Munich: Kösel, 1971) 178–81.

will change his life. In future he will give half his fortune to the poor of Israel and repay unjustly acquired sums fourfold, but he will remain in Jericho and continue to exercise his old profession as a tax collector.[81]

As in the case of Zacchaeus, Jesus does not call Simon the leper, in whose house he takes part in a festive banquet, to follow him (Mark 14:3-9). The situation is similar with Lazarus. According to the Fourth Gospel there was an especially close bond of affection between Jesus and the family of Lazarus: Jesus loved Lazarus and wept on the way to his tomb.[82] But nowhere do we read that Lazarus was one of Jesus' disciples or followers.

It is quite obvious that among those around Jesus there were curious people like Nicodemus, who came to Jesus by night in order to learn more about him (John 3:1-2); there were adherents like Joseph of Arimathea who were secret disciples of Jesus (John 19:38); there were families of friends like Lazarus and his sisters, whose house in Bethany was a kind of base of operations for Jesus close to the capital city; there were even people who traveled with Jesus for a time, like Bartimaeus, the blind man from Jericho whom he healed (Mark 10:52): in short, there were many men and women in Israel who listened to Jesus and placed their hopes in him, supported him and sympathized with him, but who were not disciples in the proper sense of the word. They did not follow Jesus in his unstable itinerant life, but remained at home. They were "locally resident" adherents of Jesus, and among them we may number in particular those who took Jesus and his disciples into their houses at night. Often Jesus did not even know in the course of the day where he would rest in the evening.

This situation is powerfully illuminated by a little scene that takes place on the road to Jerusalem. Jesus has sent out messengers to seek lodging for himself and his disciples in a Samaritan village, but the tension between Samaritans and Jews is too strong: no one will take Jesus in because he is on the way to Jerusalem (Luke 9:51-56). This was by no means a trivial matter. The historian Josephus reports that during the time of the procurator Ventidius Cumanus (48–52 C.E.) Galilean pilgrims passing through Samaria en route to Jerusalem for a festival were attacked by the Samaritans and one pilgrim was murdered.[83]

---

[81] For Levi see Mark 2:13-17; for Zacchaeus see Luke 19:1-10. In Luke 19:8 Zacchaeus is not describing his previous good behavior but is making a promise for the future.

[82] For the friendship between Jesus and the family of Lazarus cf. John 11:3, 5; for Jesus' weeping see John 11:35.

[83] Josephus, *Ant.* 20.118-136 = *Bell.* 2.232-246. Cf. Martin Hengel, *The Zealots: Investigations Into the Jewish Freedom Movement in the Period from Herod I Until 70 A.D.* Translated by David Smith (Edinburgh: T & T Clark, 1989) 346–47 n. 178: "The whole event took place in the autumn of 51 A.D. According to the *Antiquities,* several Jews were killed, but this is probably an apologetic correction."

The dangers to which Jesus and his disciples were constantly exposed are also reflected in the mission discourse.[84] The disciples, deliberately sent out penniless and unarmed (so that they would be clearly distinguishable from the armed Zealots),[85] when they had been on the road the whole day needed a roof over their heads for the night. They needed people who would give them food and shelter them during the night hours.

> "Go on your way. See, I am sending you out like lambs into the midst of wolves. Carry no purse, no bag, no sandals; and greet no one on the road. Whatever house you enter, first say, 'Peace to this house!' And if anyone is there who shares in peace, your peace will rest on that person; but if not, it will return to you. Remain in the same house, eating and drinking whatever they provide, for the laborer deserves to be paid. Do not move about from house to house. Whenever you enter a town and its people welcome you, eat what is set before you; cure the sick who are there, and say to them, 'The kingdom of God has come near to you.' But whenever you enter a town and they do not welcome you, go out into its streets and say, 'Even the dust of your town that clings to our feet, we wipe off in protest against you.'" (Luke 10:3-11)

This text shows that what was at stake in entering strange houses was not only shelter and preservation of the disciple's own life, but equally or still more the winning of new people to Jesus' message. The houses into which the disciples entered were to become bases for the Jesus movement. A net of households into which eschatological peace had entered was to extend throughout the whole land. Everywhere in Israel there were to be people who were captivated by the reign of God and therefore trusted each other to share and care for one another. Thus there would be created a living basis that would support the disciples' work of proclamation.

All this should make it clear that Jesus did not call all Israel to discipleship. Alongside the disciples there was a broad spectrum of people who opened themselves to Jesus' gospel and took his call to repentance seriously, but did not enter into his immediate circle of followers. Thus quite naturally there came to be three groups: the Twelve, already equated with the "apostles" in the gospels,[86] the group of disciples, much larger but also numbering those who were Jesus' immediate followers, and finally the people, to the extent they gave a positive acceptance to Jesus' message.

---

[84] The mission discourse is found in the New Testament in several strands of tradition and in several forms. Cf. Matt 10:5-42; Mark 6:8-11; Luke 9:3-5; 10:2-16.

[85] For details see Gerhard Lohfink, *Jesus and Community* 53–54; Iris Bosold, *Pazifismus und prophetische Provokation. Das Grußverbot Lk 10,4b und sein historischer Kontext.* SBS 90 (Stuttgart: Katholisches Bibelwerk, 1978) 88, 91.

[86] Cf. Matt 10:2; Mark 6:30; Luke 6:13; 9:10; 17:5, 22:14; 24:10. The oldest concept of apostleship was essentially much broader in scope.

This structure of three groups is evident in all four gospels, but nowhere is it so clear as in Luke's, where it is especially obvious in those who hear the so-called "sermon on the plain," Luke's version of Matthew's "sermon on the mount." Luke goes to great lengths to describe the "audience" of the sermon on the plain as carefully as possible:

> Now during those days he went out to the mountain to pray; and he spent the night in prayer to God. And when day came, he called his disciples and chose twelve of them, whom he also named apostles. . . . He came down with them and stood on a level place, with a great crowd of his disciples and a great multitude of people from all Judea, Jerusalem, and the coast of Tyre and Sidon. They had come to hear him and to be healed of their diseases; and those who were troubled with unclean spirits were cured. And all in the crowd were trying to touch him, for power came out from him and healed all of them. Then he looked up at his disciples and said . . . . (Luke 6:12-20)

In contrast to Matthew, Luke speaks of a "level place." In this way the audience of Jesus' great address can be arranged in order. Jesus himself is at the center. We are to imagine the Twelve ranged around him; for that very reason Luke has placed the appointment of the Twelve immediately before this. Around the Twelve, in turn, there is a larger circle: the "great crowd of his disciples," and finally, around the disciples, the people. Luke uses the Greek word *laos*, thereby indicating that this is not just any crowd of people but the people of God chosen from of old.[87] The people has come together out of the whole Jewish territory; even some from the Gentile districts of Tyre and Sidon are present.

Before this carefully arranged audience Jesus begins his programmatic speech. He directs his remarks particularly to his disciples, for "he looked up at" them. But at the end of the address we will read that he spoke his words "in the hearing of the people" (Luke 7:1). We can see from this distinction how carefully every nuance has been thought out here.[88] According to Luke, Jesus' first and foremost concern is the disciples. They are the audience for the sermon on the plain in a very special sense. It is intended primarily for them. But it is also directed to the people, for all Israel is to be gathered. The disciples do not lead some kind of special, separate existence; they are at the service of the whole of Israel.

Apostles, disciples, people: these structural lines running through the gospels are not there by accident. They express something that is essential to the eschatological people of God as Jesus sees them and therefore is an indispensable aspect of the Church: Not everyone can be one of the

---

[87] For more detail on the use of *laos* in Luke, see Lohfink, *Sammlung* 34–37, 49–50, 57.
[88] A fuller discussion may be found in Lohfink, *Sammlung* 64–65.

Twelve. They are, after all, in the first place a pure symbol established by Jesus to make visible the will of God for the eschatological renewal of the people of the twelve tribes. At the same time the Twelve are *sent* to Israel; they are, therefore, the bearers of an eschatological office that will continue in the Church. For that reason they are rightly called "apostles" (= those who are sent out) even in the gospels.[89]

It is equally true that not all can be disciples, for discipleship also presumes a special calling from Jesus. It does not depend on the will of the individual. It may be that someone wants to follow Jesus but is not made a disciple by him. The man from the region of Gerasa whom Jesus freed from his demons asks him specifically "that he might be with him" (Mark 5:18). That is precisely the phrase Mark uses to describe the first function of the Twelve: "to be with him" (3:14). The healed man thus in fact asks that he may remain as a disciple in the innermost circle around Jesus.

> But Jesus refused, and said to him, "Go home to your friends, and tell them how much the Lord has done for you, and what mercy he has shown you." And he went away and began to proclaim in the Decapolis how much Jesus had done for him; and everyone was amazed. (Mark 5:19-20)

Many interpreters take it that this conclusion to the narrative already has the post-Easter mission in the cities of the Decapolis in view. The narrative takes it for granted that the man was a Gentile, and he is described as the first Christian missionary to the Gentile Decapolis. Therefore, according to the logic of the narrative, he could not be a disciple in the strict sense, because the disciples of the pre-Easter Jesus were still entirely in the service of Israel.

Whether that is true or not can remain an open question. In any case the story shows that not everyone is called into the circle of disciples. The gospels allow for the possibility that someone, though wanting to be a disciple, may be sent back to his or her family; but that certainly does not mean that such a one is unimportant to the Jesus movement. The healed man from Gerasa in fact becomes a preacher of Jesus in his own locality, and perhaps he prepares it for the later mission.

Therefore not belonging to the group of disciples in the strict sense is by no means an indication of lack of faith or a sign that someone is marginal. Nowhere does Jesus say of those among his adherents whom he did not call to discipleship that they were undecided or half-hearted.[90] All those who accept Jesus' message about the *basileia* have their own

---

[89] See n. 86 above.

[90] Cf. Gottfried Wenzelmann, *Nachfolge und Gemeinschaft. Eine theologische Grundlegung des kommunitären Lebens.* CThM. PT 21 (Stuttgart: Calwer, 1994) 45.

individual callings. Each can, in his or her own way and according to the measure of his or her own possibilities, contribute to the building up of the whole. None is second-rate. The healed man of Gerasa is just as important to Jesus' cause as the disciples who travel with Jesus.

We should therefore be careful about saying that the disciples' existence is the more radical way of life. The ethos of following is certainly radical. Is there anything harder and more inconsiderate than being called to discipleship by Jesus, answering that one must first go and bury one's father—perhaps he has just died, or lies dying, or is old and sick—and being told by Jesus: "Let the dead bury their own dead; but as for you, go and proclaim the kingdom of God" (Luke 9:60)? And yet the ethos of the Sermon on the Mount, which is not only for disciples, but for everyone who is part of the eschatological people of God, is just as radical. It demands that one forswear not only evil deeds but every angry word against one's brother or sister in the faith (Matt 5:22); it demands that a man take another's marriage (and therefore, of course, his own) so seriously that he will not even look lustfully at the wife of another man (Matt 5:27-28); it demands that those who marry will not divorce but will maintain fidelity until death (Matt 5:31-32), that there be no more veiling and twisting of speech but absolute clarity (Matt 5:37), and that one give to anyone who asks for anything (Matt 5:42).[91]

Equating the lustful glance of a man at another man's wife with actual adultery is just as drastic as the demand that the disciples leave their families. Jesus demands of the one an absolute and unbreakable fidelity to the spouse (Matt 5:31-32) and of the other an absolute and unbreakable fidelity to the commission to preach (Luke 9:62). That means that Jesus takes the concrete form of one's life, whether it be marriage or standing in the service of proclamation, with the utmost seriousness. Both ways of life are only possible in their radical form in light of the brilliance and the fascination that stream forth from the reign of God. But above all, these ways of life do not exist independently and in isolation from each other. The disciples on the road depend on the help of the families who open their homes to them in the evening, and the families depend on the new family that has begun in the circle of disciples. There are constant and ongoing streams of radiation, reverse effects, overlappings. The disciples do not live for themselves but for the people of God, and the adherents resident in one place no longer live only for themselves and their children.

Thus there is no two-tier ethic: an ethic of perfection for apostles and disciples and a less perfect standard for the rest of the people of God. One must admit, of course, that there is one text in the gospels that appears to

---

[91] The following paragraph follows Gerhard Lohfink, *Jesus and Community* 40.

presume such a two-tier ethic: the story of the rich man who comes to Jesus with the question how he may attain "eternal life." Jesus points to the ten commandments and the man answers that he has kept them from his youth. Then Jesus looks at him with love and says to him:

> "You lack one thing; go, sell what you own, and give the money to the poor, and you will have treasure in heaven; then come, follow me." When he heard this, he was shocked and went away grieving, for he had many possessions. (Mark 10:21-22)

Matthew edited the Markan text slightly, altering "you lack one thing . . ." to "if you wish to be perfect . . ." (Matt 19:21). Throughout the Church's history the gospel of the rich young man has had an extraordinarily powerful reception: it has given a great many men and women the strength to abandon their bourgeois existence and undertake an alternative life of discipleship in a new kind of community. The history of the foundation of many an order of religious began with this text.

However, Matthew's "if you wish to be perfect" has also led to the idea that there must be two conditions of life in the Church: that of the perfect, who live a life of discipleship, and that of the less than perfect, for whom nothing more than the ten commandments is required. But that kind of two-tier ethic does not do justice to the text. Neither Mark nor Matthew is here formulating general norms for the people of God. The story deals with one concrete case. Jesus says "go, sell what you own" to a particular person who has come to him, restless and searching. Jesus' challenge is to him personally. It is a word that calls him to discipleship. Of course this text is also, in the minds of the evangelists, transparent for the later Church, in which there are to be many calls to discipleship and following Jesus. But these callings in turn will always be specific to individuals, not a law for everyone.

The whole matter is still clearer if we take seriously the key word in the Matthean interpretation. Behind the word "perfect" is the Hebrew adjective *tāmim,* and *tāmim* means "whole," "undivided," "complete," "intact," "sound." Being perfect in the biblical sense thus does not mean what we mean by "perfect," but living *whole* and *undivided* before God. The rich man kept his wealth separate from his relationship to God and therefore something "more" was required of him. Jesus wants his "all."[92]

This "all," in turn, is not a privilege of disciples. The poor widow who gave two copper coins gave everything she had in contrast to the rich people who gave only a portion of their surplus for the Temple. She gave

---

[92] For more on the biblical notion of "perfection" see Gerhard Lohfink, *Wem gilt die Bergpredigt?* 69–75.

her "all" (Mark 12:41-44). The "all" is different for each person. For one it can mean leaving everything. For another it can mean remaining at home and placing one's house at the disposal of Jesus' messengers. For a third it could even mean nothing more than giving a cup of fresh water to the disciples as they pass by. "Truly I tell you, none of these will lose their reward," Jesus says (Matt 10:42).

The more closely we read the gospels the clearer it repeatedly emerges that the structure apostles–disciples–people does not arise from some accidental conjunction, but is essential to the gospels. It results not only from the practical-functional point of view that Jesus could not possibly have moved through Israel with thousands of disciples, nor does it arise solely from the fact that only a few in Israel followed him. We have to begin at a deeper level. Ultimately the distinction among apostles, disciples, and people is the precondition for the freedom of every individual within the people of God.

Each person has her or his own story, with a unique ability to see and not to see, freedom and unfreedom. This individual story corresponds to the calling of each individual person. Only the one who sees is called, and no one is called to something that is outside the realm of his or her possibilities. No one can be called to everything, but the different callings can work together to form the whole.

The division of the Church between the perfect and the less perfect, between a radical ethic and a less radical ethic ignores the unity of the people of God and the ordering of all its members toward the same purpose. That from the third century onward monastic communities arose in the Church as a fixed and defined locus of discipleship and the "evangelical counsels" was an all but necessary development as soon as the congregational Church of the early period became a Church of the masses in which the contours of the gospel appeared on the verge of vanishing. Monasteries and "communities of common life" sustained the idea of discipleship in the Church through the centuries. But this was an emergency measure with new limitations, for in this way discipleship in the Church developed into a *special form of life,* a special ecclesiastical estate. For the rest of the baptized there was scarcely any opportunity to live the way of discipleship. For that one had to enter a monastery or convent.

However, discipleship and following Jesus correspond to the gospels only if they can be lived in a close companionship, in fact a unified life of apostles, disciples, and people. Only then does the eschatological people of God achieve its strength. Only then does it become a single body with many members; only then is it a heavenly edifice built up of many living stones. How this might look in concrete form, when discipleship and following Jesus are lived in normal communities in the midst of the people of God, is a topic that will occupy our attention in Part IV.

## 6. Table Manners in the Reign of God

When we are familiar with certain things and people we no longer take much notice of their individuality. Most Christians see nothing special about the appointment of the Twelve, and they take the gathering of a circle of disciples around Jesus as something perfectly normal. But we ought to be clear about the enormity of this series of events: a carpenter, an ordinary workingman, presents twelve men to the crowd and says: this is the beginning of the eschatological Israel! A theological layman surrenders himself totally to the "today" of God's action, gathers a group of disciples, and includes in it not a single priest or religious professional, but fishermen instead.

Certainly such a proceeding was not entirely unprecedented in Israel. John the Baptizer had also gathered a group of disciples. Some of Jesus' own disciples had, in fact, been John's disciples beforehand. The difference was that John pointed to the future, to one more powerful than himself who was yet to come. That one would cut down all the trees in Israel's plantation that brought no fruit (Luke 3:9) and effect the final separation of the wheat from the chaff on Israel's threshing-floor (Luke 3:16-17). Jesus, in contrast, called his disciples' attention to what was already happening: "Blessed are the eyes that see what you see!" (Luke 10:23). At the center of his message was not a wrathful judgment but a wedding: "The sons of the wedding chamber (= wedding guests) cannot fast while the bridegroom is with them, can they?" (Mark 2:19). The disciples are guests at the wedding feast because with Jesus the messianic time of salvation, the wedding of God and God's people, has already begun.[93] Hence Jesus' gathering movement stands under a different sign. It is already making the eschatological Israel visible. Only because of this can we understand why Jesus did not gather his disciples, as the Baptizer did, in the wilderness by the Jordan, but also not in the synagogues or the Temple. Israel is being given a new center, and that center is Jesus himself—and in Jesus, God, who has now become entirely present. This relativizes all "holy" places and sanctifies all profane places. It is no longer important where people gather. Everywhere in Israel, wherever Jesus' message is accepted, is holy ground.

Certainly the common meal, and therefore the common table, played a crucial role simply because a wedding is being celebrated. We can even

---

[93] Cf. Rudolf Pesch, *Das Markusevangelium.* HThK II/1 (Freiburg: Herder, 1976) 1:173.

say that the profane table at which Jesus eats with his disciples becomes the new place of salvation. Jesus dares to effect the eschatological renewal of the people of God with the simplicity and intimacy of a table around which his disciples gather as a family.

These disciples were by no means "like-minded people." There is a good deal of evidence that Jesus chose the Twelve from the most diverse groups in the Judaism of his time in order to make it obvious that he was gathering *all* Israelites. The Twelve were a colorful mixture: from the former disciples of the Baptizer (John 1:35-40) to Matthew the tax-collector (Matt 10:3) to Simon the Zealot (Luke 6:15). In a tax-collector and a Zealot the most bitterly opposed forces that existed in Israel at the time were joined within a single group, for the tax-collectors gathered revenue for the Romans while the Zealots utterly rejected the Roman occupation as incompatible with the reign of God.

We should try to imagine how such different people could sit at one table. They were like fire and water. But just there began the miracle of the eschatological people of God. If each one were to remain in his or her own corner and individual house nothing of the reign of God could be seen. Its fascination can only appear when people of different backgrounds, different gifts, different colors, men *and* women sit together at a single table—and when they join their lives so that together, undivided, they can serve God's cause.

Add to this that Jesus' disciples, male and female, were not born heroes. They were people with failings and weaknesses. Jesus had no others to work with. The Twelve were not made the center of Israel because they were holier or more perfect than the others; they were not a bit better than anyone else. They became the center because Jesus chose them and they put themselves at his service. The issue was never them as special individuals, but always and only the whole people of God, to whom they were sent.

We must note, however, that the Twelve serve the gathering of the people of God not only through their mission, but through their mere existence. In Mark 3:14 we read: "And he appointed twelve . . . to be with him, and to be sent out to proclaim the message . . . ." The fact that the Twelve were sent out led to the later equation of the group of twelve with the post-Easter group of apostles, "those who were sent out." Matthew and Luke already referred to "the twelve apostles."[94] We could call this aspect of Mark 3:14 the *missio apostolica,* the apostolic mandate. The apostolic office in the Church developed out of this sending of the Twelve. It was not invented by the Church, but had its basis in Jesus' sending of the

[94] Matt 10:2; Luke 6:13; cf. Acts 1:26.

Twelve, for sending means that there is something that does not arise from the ability and talents of human beings. In the mission something that comes from God alone is transmitted more widely. Office in the Church means ultimately that Jesus' messianic authority is carried on in the Church and remains a living thing.[95]

But what about the other characteristic of the Twelve that Mark mentions, namely that they are with Jesus? We could call this aspect of Mark 3:14 the *vita apostolica,* the apostolic life. Unfortunately, in the course of the Church's history it gradually lost its significance and power. Even though the Church never lacked apostolic office, the apostolic life faded from it. Very often it has only been the religious orders and intentional communities that handed on Jesus' call to the *vita apostolica* as the Church's "genetic information." The fact that the Church is still alive today is due to the apostolic office, but the fact that it lives only the feeble life of an invalid results from the vanishing of the apostolic life.

We are accustomed to see the model and foundation of apostolic office in the Twelve, and that is right. Every ecclesial office, that of the bishop as well as that of the priest and deacon, ultimately rests on Jesus' sending of the Twelve. But that does not exhaust the figure of the Twelve, for their mission presupposes their being with Jesus, and that being-with by no means signifies only a temporary state of togetherness that would rapidly be dissolved in their definitive mission. Being with Jesus could all too easily be understood as a limited period of preparation, a kind of retreat or workshop, only afterward to be followed by the real thing: the time in which the Twelve are to engage singly in battle. We should not underestimate the power of such images. In the Church today they shape our ideas of office and apostolate much more than we are aware. Being with Jesus is all very well—so we could describe a false idea of apostolate—but only when it is quickly followed by mission. Of course we gather now and then to deepen our common faith, but then we return to "our places," living out our mission as individuals in the world.

The sweep of Mark's gospel leads in a completely different direction. Jesus does send out the Twelve—but in pairs (Mark 6:7) and not alone, because in Judaism testimony required at least two people. And the Twelve quickly return (Mark 6:30); only then do they begin really to experience their being-with Jesus, a learning process that will turn their entire lives around, a process that is a matter of life and death.

Mark's gospel portrays this process of conversion of the Twelve, which repeatedly brings forth a misunderstanding of discipleship, at length and with precision. It is coextensive with the journey to Jerusalem,

[95] Cf. Joseph Ratzinger, *Called to Communion* 111–16.

which in Mark essentially begins with Peter's messianic confession and Jesus' first passion prediction (8:27-33).

We may therefore say that the sending out of the Twelve plays no greater role in the narrative process of the Markan gospel, but rather a lesser role than the description of the endless struggle to achieve the new common life, the Twelve's being with Jesus. The apostolic life and the apostolic mission are for Mark not two successive periods of time but two intertwined ways-of-being of the circle of the Twelve in which the second always presupposes the first.

Only when the Twelve learn this new way of being together can they proclaim the gospel and drive out demons. Weekend seminars, days of recollection, or weekly workshops are not adequate, for this learning is only possible in the common fate that is the *vita apostolica*. The apostolic life is not simply a community of souls but a being-together in all areas of life. It includes the whole of one's existence.

The disciples' learning process extends through the whole of the Markan gospel and is one of its principal themes, but it is concentrated in the second half of the gospel, from the moment when Jesus and his disciples turn toward Jerusalem and thus toward his death. This second half of the gospel begins with a kind of trumpet blast: Jesus asks his disciples who they take him to be. They respond:

> "John the Baptist; and others, Elijah; and still others, one of the prophets." He asked them, "But who do you say that I am?" Peter answered him, "You are the Messiah." And he sternly ordered them not to tell anyone about him. (Mark 8:28-30)

Israel had long held the idea that in the end time God would send anew one of the prophets of old who had been taken up into heaven and kept in readiness there.[96] This idea was by no means so abstruse as it seems at first glance. In effect it said that the people of God continually lives out of the faith of those who, like Elijah, had set themselves with the fullest clarity on the side of God, and the future redemption of Israel would be nourished by the faith of those earlier ones.

Certainly in Jesus' time such ideas, correct in themselves, were already overgrown with a great many speculations. Mark 8:28 shows clearly how people puzzled over the mystery of Jesus' person. How should he be categorized? Apparently many thought he was a prophet, or even one of the great prophets of the past who had come again. Against all speculations of this sort Peter's confession tells the truth: Jesus is the longed-for Messiah of Israel.

---

[96] Cf. Mal 3:23-24; Sir 48:10-11.

But the messianic title could also be all too easily misunderstood, for most Jews at that time were convinced that the coming of the Messiah would necessarily be connected with the eschatological revolt of Israel against the rule of the Gentiles and with a sudden reversal of all political and social relationships. The Zealots promoted a national uprising against the Romans through the use of violence. They were convinced that their struggle would force God's eschatological intervention.

Jesus clearly distanced himself from that kind of political theology and from national wars of liberation.[97] He was convinced that a victory over the Roman occupation forces would by no means answer Israel's real need. Therefore in the Our Father he does not have his disciples pray for the liberation of Jerusalem and the restoration of the kingdom of David.[98] Jesus wants revolution all right, the overturning of all relationships, but his revolution begins much more radically than the revolt of the Zealots. It begins where human beings, in the depths of their wills, seek not the honor of God but their own glory, not the work of God but only themselves. And escaping from one's own demons does not happen overnight. It is a long road that requires a new basis, a new family, a renewed people of God.

For Mark the office of the Messiah is a way of total surrender to the eschatological work of God, that is, to the new being-together that God desires to create in Israel. That way will bring Jesus to his death. Therefore no one can confess him as the Messiah of Israel without taking into account his self-surrender even to the point of death. Simply proclaiming him as the powerful and glorious Messiah, separated from the humble form that the Messianic reality is to assume through him, seemed to Mark and to Jesus himself positively dangerous. Thus it can be no surprise that Mark immediately continues, after Peter's solemn confession of Jesus as Messiah:

---

[97] Important in this connection are Matt 5:38-47; Mark 12:13-17; Mark 4:26-29 (the reign of God ripens; it is not to be forced by Zealot struggles); Luke 10:4 (going without shoes or sandals makes any kind of aggression or flight impossible and therefore signals— in contrast to the attitude of the Zealots—absolute commitment to peace). Cf. Peter Stuhlmacher, *Biblische Theologie* 1:145.

[98] Cf. in contrast the fourteenth benediction of the Tefillah: "And turn in compassion to Jerusalem, your city. Let there be peace in her gates, quietness in the hearts of her inhabitants. Let your Torah go forth from Zion and Your word from Jerusalem. Blessed is the Lord, who gives peace to Jerusalem." Translator's note: this is the text as currently in use; see Central Conference of American Rabbis, *Gates of Prayer: The New Union Prayerbook* (New York: C.C.A.R., 1975). The author quotes an older version: "Have mercy . . . on Jerusalem, your city, and on Zion, the place of your glory, and on your Temple, your dwelling, and on the kingdom of the house of David . . . ."

> Then he began to teach them that the Son of Man must undergo great suffer-
> ing, and be rejected by the elders, the chief priests, and the scribes, and be
> killed, and after three days rise again. (Mark 8:31)

Peter had spoken of the Messiah; now Jesus suddenly speaks about the
Son of Man. Why the shift? Apparently the misunderstanding regarding
the title of "Messiah" can only be removed if at the same time Jesus refers
to the "Son of Man." But what is the meaning of "Son of Man"? Again it
is worth taking a closer look at the Old Testament background.

The concept of the Son of Man comes from Daniel 7, where Daniel,
in a dream-vision, sees four gigantic beasts rising from the sea: first one
that looks like a winged lion, then one like a bear with three ribs of the
creature it is eating hanging from its jaws, then a leopard with four heads.
The fourth beast is so perverse as to be unclassifiable: it has iron teeth and
one of its horns contains human eyes. The fourth beast devours or tram-
ples everything in its path (Dan 7:1-8).

But then there is a sharp break. Daniel sees a new sequence of images,
and in the midst of these very different images is "one like a Son of Man"
(cf. *NRSV*: "one like a human being"). This figure is the counter-pole of
the beasts. They came from the sea, but this human figure comes from
heaven:

> I saw one like a human being coming with the clouds of heaven. And he came
> to the Ancient One and was presented before him. To him was given domin-
> ion and glory and kingship that all peoples, nations, and languages should
> serve him. His dominion is an everlasting dominion that shall not pass away,
> and his kingship is one that shall never be destroyed. (Dan 7:13-14)

The imagery in Daniel 7 seems bizarre to us today, but it was by no means
so for readers in the Maccabean period. It contained, in a concealed form,
a theology of contemporary history formulated out of the experiences of
the period of persecution under the Seleucids. Politically this theology of
history was very explosive; hence it had to be coded. The four beasts stand
for the successive world empires, each more bestial and wicked than the
last: Babylon, Media, Persia, and the empire of Alexander with its successor states, especially that of the Seleucids. These great powers, says the
text, come without exception from the sea; that is, they embody chaos.
They live from oppression and a violent power that has nothing but contempt for human beings.

Worst of all for Israel were the Seleucids in Syria and King Antiochus
IV. He is represented symbolically as the horn with the human eyes. With
him appears the possibility of the final destruction of Israel. And yet according to the book of Daniel even Antiochus IV was only the instrument

of divine wrath against the people of God who would not learn from their history and refused to repent. The time of divine wrath reaches its culmination under Antiochus, and also comes to an end.[99] Power has been taken from all the nations that have become bestial, and it will be taken from this one as well (7:11-12). Then the Son of Man will appear.

This figure resembling a human being stands in absolute contrast to the four beasts. Obviously this one, like the others, represents an empire, or rather a society, for this is a new kind of society. It is, at last, no longer bestial, but human. It does not feed on its own power like the four empires before it. It receives all dominion from God ("the Ancient One"), and it is, at last, the pure reflection of God's dominion. Therefore this new society will not disappear; it will remain forever. The text says that it is identical with the "people of the holy ones of the Most High," that is, with the true Israel that lives according to the will of God.[100] To it will be entrusted the divine dominion (7:27).

When the gospels speak of the "Son of Man" they of course mean Jesus. The image of God's new community drawn from the book of Daniel, the society that replaces the old world empires, has been concentrated in a single, concrete person. But as in the case of the "Suffering Servant of God," here too the original meaning continues to play a part. The Son of Man is Jesus of Nazareth, but only because with his appearance the eschatological Israel is beginning: as a truly human society coming entirely from God and no longer built on violence, but rather on nonviolence even if that should mean death. But it is precisely in this that its power is revealed. It will be mightier than the strength of all the great powers and world empires.

In one respect, certainly, the Son of Man in the Jesus tradition differs from the one in the book of Daniel: while in the latter it is said that "all peoples, nations, and languages should serve him" (7:14), Jesus says of himself that he "came not to be served but to serve" (Mark 10:45).[101]

Of course at that moment all of this was utterly incomprehensible to the disciples. Peter only sees that Jesus intends to go to Jerusalem, even

[99] Cf. Dan 8:19, 23-25, and, on this whole subject, Odil Hannes Steck, "Weltgeschehen und Gottesvolk im Buche Daniel," in Dieter Lührmann and Georg Strecker, eds., *Kirche. Festschrift für Günther Bornkamm zum 75. Geburtstag* (Tübingen: Mohr, 1980) 53–78, at 65–71.

[100] Cf. Dan 7:17-27. The "people of the holy ones of the Most High" are "the Israelites, that is, the true, understanding Israel (even if they are to be seen together with their angels, or their angel Michael, or if, in a preliminary stage, the reference may have been solely to these angelic powers)" according to Norbert Lohfink, "Der Begriff des Gottesreichs vom Alten Testament her gesehen," in idem, *Studien zur biblischen Theologie*. SBAB 16 (Stuttgart: Katholisches Bibelwerk, 1993) 152–205, at 198 n. 118.

[101] Cf. Peter Stuhlmacher, *Biblische Theologie* 1:121.

though death threatens him there. When he attempts to persuade Jesus not to go to the capital, Jesus speaks to him in the sharpest words we know him to have said: "Get behind me, Satan! For you are setting your mind not on the plan of God but on human plans" (Mark 8:33*). God's plan is not that Jesus should die.[102] How could God will the death of Jesus? What God wills is the new society, the eschatological Israel. But because Jesus remains true to this divine plan he will die, because people do not will what God wills. Jesus' death on the cross was unavoidable. "It must be so," but not because God has decided on the death of the Son. It is because God's way among human beings meets bitter resistance, and because Jesus does not turn aside from that way.

Will the Twelve and all the disciples ever come to understand the way of the Son of Man? At first it does not seem likely, for at a later point Mark describes a dispute among the disciples. "On the way" they are arguing about which of them is the "greatest" (9:34). The impulse to rivalry that human beings have inherited through their evolution from the animal kingdom and then exaggerated since the expanding intellect has enabled them to construct illusions without limit is also present among Jesus' disciples. We can by no means speak of unanimity among them. What does Jesus do in this situation? He does not address all the disciples who have been arguing among themselves; instead he calls the Twelve together and says to them: "Whoever wants to be first must be last of all and servant of all" (9:35).

That precisely at this point Mark again introduces *the Twelve* into the narrative (while otherwise he mainly speaks about *the disciples*) reveals his knowledge that unanimity in the people of God can only exist if there is at least a core group that converts to unanimity. For this very reason Jesus turns to the Twelve in critical situations and at decisive moments. For this very reason he seeks, by means of their unanimity, to achieve that same unanimity among the many.

The dispute among the disciples in Mark 9:34 was preceded by Jesus' second passion prediction, after which the text says "but they did not understand what he was saying and were afraid to ask him" (9:32). The narrative is composed in such a way that the two things are directly connected, namely the disciples' dispute about rank and their lack of understanding of this second prediction of the passion. Because they are divided

---

[102] In the kerygmatic language of the NT we find it said that God "gave" God's son up to death. Cf. especially Rom 8:32. Statements of that type do not contradict what I am saying here. They are not meant to deny the human agency in Jesus' death; rather, they assert God's refusal to manipulate history from outside through divine power. God, by allowing human beings the freedom to do evil and even to kill Jesus, surrenders God's own self and the divine Son as well, and precisely in this surrender is God's purpose accomplished.

among themselves and each is seeking only his or her own interest, namely to be "the greatest," they cannot understand Jesus' way. Those who are not part of the intimate community of the new family in which all are close to one another and where the individual's true impulses really become evident, where dying and rising are learned, cannot in the end understand the dying and rising of Jesus.

The importance Mark attaches to this connection is evident from the third passion prediction (10:32-34). Again the evangelist follows the same narrative structure: passion prediction, dispute among the disciples, instruction of disciples. This time the conflict arises out of a petition from the sons of Zebedee, John and James. They are intent on securing their positions of power in the reign of God in good time. Now, in contrast to Mark 9:34, the conflict takes on a special aspect: the old family with its private interests intrudes on the circle of the Twelve. Two men who are brothers by physical descent ally themselves against the other ten. According to Matthew their mother was also involved in this intrigue (Matt 20:20). Again Jesus speaks only to the Twelve:

> "You know that among the Gentiles those whom they recognize as their rulers lord it over them, and their great ones are tyrants over them. But it is not so among you; but whoever wishes to become great among you must be your servant, and whoever wishes to be first among you must be slave of all. For the Son of Man came not to be served but to serve, and to give his life a ransom for many." (Mark 10:42-45)

It is immediately apparent that in this little narrative composition the Son of Man and his disciples are contrasted with the Gentiles and their rulers. That is precisely the situation in Daniel 7: the world empires, whose nature it is to oppress, stand in contrast to the new world of God in the figure of the Son of Man.

Still, we must note that neither in Daniel 7 nor in Mark 10 are the nations simply called evil. It is true that they appear as beasts in Daniel, but it is also said that *God* has permitted them a certain degree of dominion (Dan 7:6). Jesus uncovers the power structures of society with equal clarity. Elsewhere he says "give to the emperor the things that are the emperor's" (Mark 12:17). His interest is not in damning all human forms of rule. He by no means questions the necessity of the state. But it is not his concern to provide assurances for the state either. His interest is solely in God's new society, which in the midst of the old world is beginning the unheard-of new thing.

This new thing extends to the deepest depths from which society originates. It can be summarized in a simple phrase: no longer desiring to rule, but instead to serve the cause of God and thereby to serve other people.

"Serving" must not, however, be understood in a faded and colorless sense. In its original meaning the word signifies nothing other than serving at table. It has its basis in the daily table service that in the ancient world was left to slaves, servants, or women.

It is precisely at table that the contrast between the superiors who recline and the slaves or women who must serve is especially palpable.[103] In Greek and Roman culture household service was always a matter of subservience. "How can a man be happy when he has to serve someone?" asks the Sophist Callicles in the Platonic dialogue *Gorgias*.[104] Thus it is no accident that Jesus shapes the new society he begins with his disciples by starting at the common table. Here the true revolution commences; here is the beginning of the genuinely classless society.

The concreteness of all this is evident at Jesus' last meal. He celebrates this Passover meal not with his natural family, in accord with Jewish custom, but with his new family; yet also not with an *ad hoc* selection of disciples, but—as Mark expressly states—with the Twelve. Again Mark brings the Twelve into the narrative. Probably in doing so he also adhered very closely to the historical facts.

Jesus celebrated his last meal with the Twelve. Because the common table is the most beautiful symbol of community it is now utterly clear how Jesus understands this circle of the Twelve: as a circle for eating together, living together, being utterly open to one another. The Fourth Evangelist would later interpret that openness as follows:

> I do not call you servants any longer, because the servant does not know what the master is doing; but I have called you friends, because I have made known to you everything that I have heard from my Father. (John 15:15)

Luke reveals a deep sense of these connections when he places the saying about service that he had found in his source (cf. Mark 10:42-45) just here, at Jesus' last meal (Luke 22:24-27), and John does likewise by inserting here the footwashing scene and a long farewell discourse by Jesus, one of the most intimate discourses in the New Testament (John 13–17). Thus serving at table and washing feet become the standard for the eschatological Israel. Jesus, the Lord, washes his disciples' feet and thus does the very kind of dirty work that is otherwise given over to the slaves or the lowest members of the household.

From that point of view one could describe the whole ethos that Jesus presents to his disciples as the "table manners in the reign of God." In that way it would be clear that this ethos is not some cloudy "world ethos" or

---

[103] H. W. Beyer, *diakoneō*, TDNT 2:81–93, at 83.
[104] Plato, *Gorgias* 491e.

some kind of thin "civil religion." It is not even a "natural moral law." It is the specific ethos of those who allow themselves to be gathered at Jesus' table.

Part of the table manners in the reign of God is that there are no more classes: all sit at the same table. Another part of those table manners is that each first looks to see that the others have everything they need; only then do they think of their own plates. It is also part of these table manners that the greatest is the servant of all; this alone shows that such a one is able to exercise an office. Finally, it is part of these manners that one does not seek the best place but the worst. In the gospel of Luke this is formulated as follows:

> "When you are invited by someone to a wedding banquet, do not sit down at the place of honor . . . . But when you are invited, go and sit down at the lowest place, so that when your host comes, he may say to you, 'Friend, move up higher'; then you will be honored in the presence of all who sit at the table with you. (Luke 14:8-10)

This text has offended many people, for it appears to recommend a sham humility that is all too transparent: The guest chooses the worst place, of course, but only in order to be complimented by being invited higher. Was the gospel really suggesting to its hearers that sort of deceitful playacting? Obviously not! The incident begins with Jesus observing how all the guests deliberately aim at the places of honor (14:7). Therefore this is about something entirely different.

What is at stake, as with all the "table manners" that Jesus speaks about, is right behavior in the *basileia*. In God's new society people no longer have to worry about the place that is rightfully theirs. They can let other people *show* them the place that is right for them. What looks like a comic rule of propriety is really the reversal of all bourgeois values: no one need any longer struggle unceasingly for his or her reputation, but instead all can be concerned about God's reputation and allow their own honor to be received as a gift.

If we consider what all that means, concretely, it will surely be clear that the "table manners in the reign of God" are anything but banal and obvious matters. They turn the world on its head. If they were lived out society would be unrecognizable. It would be made anew.

At this point we must mention another text that only Matthew and Luke have handed on to us. It is a saying of Jesus to the Twelve:

> "Truly I tell you, at the renewal of all things, when the Son of Man is seated on the throne of his glory, you who have followed me will also sit on twelve thrones, judging the twelve tribes of Israel." (Matt 19:28)

This saying is both promise and obligation. It again throws light on the community of the Twelve. For if we understand their eschatological office of judging not in an external sense as purely a matter of sovereign rule, then they must judge Israel by their behavior and their very existence. The absolute clarity of their adherence to Jesus and their unanimity in their common life have become the measure of what should be lived out in all of Israel, and therefore will be a standard of judgment for Israel.

In Luke's gospel this saying about the office of the Twelve in judging Israel is part of Jesus' discourse at the Last Supper, and Luke offers us a slightly different version from that in Matthew. In this gospel we read:

> "You are those who have stood by me in my trials; and I confer on you, just as my Father has conferred on me, a kingdom, so that you may eat and drink at my table in my kingdom, and you will sit on thrones judging the twelve tribes of Israel." (Luke 22:28)

We would not do justice to this saying if we located it within a purely future eschatology. There is no more such utterly future eschatology in the New Testament. Eating and drinking in the *basileia* begin *today,* and by the same token the judging of the people of God begins *today,* namely in the sense that the unanimity of the Twelve becomes an irritating standard for the people of God. The Lukan version of the saying again makes clear what is at stake for Jesus: God's *basileia* is not where the Temple stands, or where the Sanhedrin passes judgment; it is only present where the Twelve are gathered in unanimity with Jesus around the one table, and where the one serves the other.

Certainly at the time of the Last Supper that eschatological community among the disciples had by no means been achieved. They are still arguing (Luke 22:24) and they still cannot understand (John 13:7). The new thing is only projected in the symbol of the Eucharist. The death of Jesus was still needed to open the disciples' eyes, to bring them to genuine unanimity, and to make them understand what was meant by the new family and its table manners.

## 7. The Death of Jesus: A Death for the People of God

Mark made Jesus' journey from Galilee to Jerusalem an important part of his gospel, and Luke follows him in this. Because he has considerably more narrative material at his disposal than Mark had he even succeeds in shaping something like a "travel account." It begins with the statement: "When the days drew near for him to be taken up, he set his face to go to Jerusalem. And he sent messengers ahead of him" (Luke 9:51-52). This means first of all that the situation is becoming acute. Jesus anticipates a violent death. He begins his journey to Jerusalem in the clear knowledge of what is facing him.

Yet this is precisely what Luke does *not* say. His statement is an artistic construction formulated entirely in the language of the Greek Old Testament. There are similar expressions in the book of Ezekiel: The prophet "set[s his] face toward Jerusalem."[105] Classically educated Greeks must have found such language very odd, but Luke is using it to say that what is now about to happen has nothing to do with accident or blind fate. It is the necessary culmination of Jesus' whole activity; still more, it is the culmination and high point of God's long journey with the people of God. The "bible language" that Luke deliberately employs connects the story of Jesus with the story of Israel, and the fate of Israel with the fate of Jesus.

Jesus' public activity began in Galilee, but it must be completed in Jerusalem, for there stands the Temple. There is the center of Israel. There the people of God gather for festivals. There all Israel is represented at the Passover feast—and the proclamation of the reign of God must be as public as possible. Therefore the decision can only be made there. In Jerusalem Jesus will call the whole people of God to a decision.

Not only does Luke see it this way: Jesus himself saw the same thing. When some Pharisees told him that he should leave Galilee because Herod Antipas was planning to get rid of him he answered them:

> "Go and tell that fox for me, 'Listen, I am casting out demons and performing cures today and tomorrow, and on the third day I finish my work. Yet today, tomorrow, and the next day I must be on my way, because it is impossible for a prophet to be killed outside of Jerusalem.'" (Luke 13:32-33)

Jesus will go on his way until it ends in Jerusalem, this text says. But Jesus does not act under pressure from other people, certainly not that of a Herod who is as crafty and yet as powerless as a fox. He will go his own way because he cannot turn aside from his duty toward Israel.

Jesus knows, then, what is awaiting him in the capital city. Why is Jerusalem so dangerous for him?

All four gospels report how much hostility there was toward Jesus and how that menacing hostility continually increased. According to the narrative framework of Mark's gospel this deadly enmity toward Jesus began in the very first days of his public activity. The story of the cure of the man with the crippled hand ends with: "The Pharisees went out and immediately conspired with the Herodians against him, how to destroy him"

---

[105] Ezek 21:7; cf. also Gen 31:21; Jer 42:15, 17; 44:12; Dan 11:17, and especially 2 Kings 12:18. For the whole linguistic background to Luke 9:51-52 cf. Gerhard Lohfink, *Himmelfahrt Jesu* 212–17.

(Mark 3:6). Jesus had cured the sick man *on the Sabbath,* and that causes conflict both here and elsewhere. Of course it would never have occurred to Jesus, the Jew, to deliberately violate the Torah or to declare it outmoded. It was holy to him. It was, for him, the ordinance of God. But he inquires with the fiercest intensity, something that does not arise out of learned study of the Law but from an unfathomable knowledge of God, what the true purpose of the Torah is. And here begin the conflicts that will accompany his activity from the very beginning.

The Torah's intent is that God alone should be Lord in all things. This absolute lordship of God, however, had shown itself precisely in the *history* of Israel, and it shows itself now in the coming of the reign of God. The Torah is part of the living history of the people of God. Therefore it must now be interpreted in terms of its internal goal and purpose, the goal at which, in Jesus, it has now arrived. The message about the reign of God does not replace the Torah—how could it?—but it fulfills and encompasses it. In Luke 16:16-17 this relationship between the Torah and Jesus' message about the reign of God is tersely and intensely formulated:

> "The law and the prophets were in effect until John came; since then the good news of the kingdom of God is proclaimed, and everyone tries to enter it by force. But it is easier for heaven and earth to pass away, than for one stroke of a letter in the law to be dropped."

Thus not the tiniest letter, not even the flourish on a single letter can be removed from the Torah. But its intent, its purpose is revealed in the light of the *basileia* in a revolutionary new way, and for those whose ceaseless study of the Torah obscures their view of the present action of God this can only be alarming and offensive.

The offense lies especially in the fact that Jesus does not interpret the Torah as the scribes do. He does not compare verses and he does not refer to the interpretations of famous sages. In the narrow sense of the word he does not practice exegesis or scriptural interpretation at all. He speaks and acts with authority—and in doing so he has the Scripture on his side in a very elemental sense. He simply knows what the presence of the reign of God demands. He has a feeling that is utterly scandalous to others for what God's cause requires at a given time and where the true will of God is being avoided or, still worse, turned into its opposite, even if this is done in the name of fidelity to the Law.

Those who do not open themselves in trust to Jesus' authority and his message about the *basileia* cannot understand his way of approaching the Torah. Such people see only violations of the Law, and still worse: the seduction of Israel to lawlessness. For this very reason the conflicts begin so early, very soon after Jesus' first public appearance, and for that reason they are so sharp. It should be clear by now that these conflicts over the Torah are not about minor questions. The issue is whether God is acting now, today. More precisely: the issue is whether God is acting in Jesus anew, creatively, in a way that surpasses everything that has gone before.

Thus the conflict does not begin in Jerusalem, but that is where it reaches its climax, for in Jerusalem a confrontation with the Temple is added to the previous accusations that he is disregarding the Torah. And here the whole matter is much clearer than in the questions regarding the Law. Even in Jesus' time the "Law" had a considerable range of meaning within Judaism. It included not only the Torah recorded in the five books of Moses but also its later applications and expansions, the *halakah*. *Halakah* was also regarded as Torah, but it was much more flexible and fluid than the Torah set down in the Pentateuch. The *halakah* of the Essenes or that of the Sadducees was different from that of the Pharisees.[106] Jesus' opponents could thus argue among themselves about whether he had violated the Torah in a particular case or not.

But the Temple was a solid reality. It was Israel's cultic center. It was said of the Temple that it hallowed the city of Jerusalem and the whole land. In it the only true God was worshiped. It was the place of reconciliation for the whole nation. On the Day of Atonement, *yom kippur*, the High Priest went into the Holy of Holies and sprinkled blood for Israel's reconciliation toward the place where once the Ark of the Covenant had stood. The worship in the Temple was the beating heart of Israel.

Of course all this had its economic aspect. The Temple not only supported hundreds of priests; the whole city lived off of pilgrimages to the Temple, as did the countryside around it. To call the Temple into question was to let loose an avalanche.

Those who paid the Temple tax or donated money to the Temple had to use Tyrian coin. That is why there were moneychangers in the columned hall on the south side of the gigantic "Court of the Gentiles." There were even merchants from whom one could buy a sacrificial animal.[107] Soon after his arrival at the festival Jesus, in a prophetic symbolic

[106] Cf. Karlheinz Müller, "Anmerkungen zum Verhältnis von Tora und Halacha im Frühjudentum" in Erich Zenger, ed., *Die Tora als Kanon für Juden und Christen.* HBSt 10 (Freiburg: Herder, 1996) 257–91, especially 268–69, 283.

[107] If Jostein Adna's researches on the Herodian Temple and Jesus' action there are correct the buying and selling did not take place in the Court of the Gentiles but in the royal hall of columns erected specifically for the purpose of such business. Probably the sacrificial animals were not brought into that porch or into the Court of the Gentiles; rather the merchants sold a kind of "receipt" that could be given to the Levites, who in turn obtained unblemished animals from the markets outside the Temple and brought them to the sacrifices. Jesus' action in the Temple was intended to put an end to the entire business of sacrifice. (I am grateful to Peter Stuhlmacher for this reference. The results of Adna's research will soon be published.)

act, drove the merchants on the margins of the Temple area from their stands and overturned the tables of the moneychangers (Mark 11:15). Such an action must have created quite a stir. And it was mortally dangerous.

Did Jesus, in doing this act, set himself in a fundamental way against the existence of the Temple, or was he simply condemning the trivialization of Temple worship? There is still a third possibility: that the Temple as such was a fundamental reality for Jesus, but in light of the prophetic promises and in the context of his own eschatological preaching he saw before him the image of a very different Temple.

In Mark 11:17 Jesus accuses the merchants of having made the Temple, which according to Isa 56:7 was meant to be "a house of prayer for all the nations," into a "den of robbers" (Jer 7:11). In speaking of "a house of prayer for all the nations" the book of Isaiah referred to the eschatological Temple in which even the Gentiles, having joined themselves to Israel, would worship the true God. Mark thus means to say that Jesus, in clearing the external parts of the Temple of merchants, was giving the signal for the coming of the nations, that is, for what the Old Testament describes in a number of different ways as the pilgrimage of the nations to Zion.[108] Thus according to the understanding of Mark's gospel Jesus does not issue a fundamental challenge to the Temple any more than he had called the Torah into question; rather he uses a prophetic sign-action to show that now the hour of the eschatological Temple has come.

If we look to Jesus himself, his action in the Temple accords precisely with his message and his understanding of himself. He could have read in the book of the prophet Zechariah: "there shall no longer be traders in the house of the LORD of hosts on that day" (Zech 14:21). "On that day" means for Zechariah the eschatological day when God will be ruler over the whole earth. On that day the Temple will shine anew. Everything in Jerusalem and Judah will receive its radiance from the Temple's holiness. The ordinary cooking pots in the land will be consecrated to the Lord, just like the sacrificial vessels in the Temple (Zech 14:20). In other words: when the reign of God is finally established all the situations and relationships of ordinary life will be ordered and sanctified so that all things can give glory to God.

Jesus sets these and other promises regarding the Temple to come under the radical "today" that shapes his whole message and praxis. Because the reign of God is breaking in already and the new creation of Israel has already begun, the business of the Temple cannot go on in the way that is now customary. The time for the eschatological Temple has come.

---

[108] Cf. Psalm 96; Isa 2:2-5; 25:6-8; 56:1-8; 60; 66:18-24; Jer 3:17; 16:19-21; Mic 4:1-5; Zeph 3:9-10; Zech 2:15; 8:20-23; 14:16-17, and elsewhere.

Did Jesus have a concrete conception of this new, eschatological Temple? We do not know. All we know is that he said that not one stone of the old Temple would remain upon another.[109] We also know that after Easter the communities very quickly came to see themselves as the eschatological Temple, as a sanctuary built of living stones; this happened long before the Temple was utterly destroyed by the Romans, down to its foundations, in the year 70.[110]

The Sadducean priestly nobility who had power in Jerusalem apparently had a very clear idea of the degree to which their own picture of the Temple was called into question by Jesus. Just as in the case of the Torah the conflict was not about marginal questions of interpretation of the Law, so here it was not a matter of marginal details of the operation of the Temple—for example, whether the moneychangers and dealers in sacrificial animals should not have carried on their business in the city rather than in the outer precincts of the Temple. It was a question, rather, of Jesus' right to regard the cult in Jerusalem entirely in light of his own message about the *basileia*. That is precisely what was so energetically denied him by the High Priests, the scribes, and the elders, that is, the Sanhedrin, the highest religious authority in Israel. Immediately after Jesus' action in the Temple the Sanhedrin undertook an investigation of the affair and asked Jesus: "By what authority are you doing these things? Who gave you this authority to do them?" (Mark 11:28).

Here is the real root of the conflict. It is a question of whether God is acting in Jesus or not. This is an ultimate faith-question. Those who accuse the Jewish officials in Jerusalem of being moved by purely economic interests or mere narrowmindedness are missing the depth of the conflict. In particular this kind of analysis prevents Christians looking at the issue from posing the faith-question to themselves: do *they* really believe that God can act in a new and creative way on and among God's people? Even today?

Jesus' action in the Temple leads to the final decision that he must be executed, and for this reason: that the Sanhedrin consider him a "deceiver" of the people.[111] Jesus' death is thus no accident, not the outcome of a series of unfortunate circumstances. It is the nearly inevitable result of the appearance of Jesus and the unbelief of the people of God. At any

[109] Mark 13:2; Matt 24:2; Luke 21:6; cf. Luke 19:44.

[110] Cf. especially 1 Cor 3:9, 16-17. The Essenes also regarded their community as the eschatological Temple. Cf. 1QS 8,4-10; CD 3,19, and elsewhere.

[111] For the idea of Jesus as "deceiver" cf. Matt 27:63; John 7:12, 47; Justin, *Dial.* 1.69.7; 108.2. For the historical problem see August Strobel, *Die Stunde der Wahrheit. Untersuchungen zum Strafverfahren gegen Jesus.* WUNT 21 (Tübingen: J.C.B. Mohr/Paul Siebeck, 1980) 81–92.

rate it was clear to the early communities that unbelief was the true cause of Jesus' death. The Fourth Gospel in particular uncovers this connection. There the description of Jesus' public activity ends with the observation:

> Although he had performed so many signs in their presence, they did not believe in him. This was to fulfill the word spoken by the prophet Isaiah: "Lord, who has believed our message, and to whom has the arm of the Lord been revealed?" (John 12:37-38 // Isa 53:1)

Jesus knows what is about to happen to him. In that knowledge he celebrates the Passover meal with his own, as prescribed, within the city of Jerusalem. It is his last time to be together with those he has chosen. It is also his last opportunity to interpret his death. The pattern of the Passover meal offered an especially good frame for this, for from of old this very meal had been imbued with signs, references, and interpretations. There were the bitter herbs, the unleavened bread, the lamb, the first *(Kiddush)* cup, the second *(Haggada)* cup, the third cup (the cup of blessing), and the fourth *(Hallel)* cup. The meal made present the Exodus from Egypt and looked forward in hope to the Messiah. An ancient Aramaic interpretive word over the unleavened bread read: "See, this is the bread of affliction that our ancestors had to eat when they came out of Egypt."[112]

We have already spoken of the fundamental sacramental structure of Jesus' actions (see III, 4 above). At this last meal that structure was most concisely revealed. This meal and the constitution of the Twelve would be the most important and impressive symbolic actions of Jesus' life. Mark describes the special character of this meal in 14:17-25.

First of all, Jesus celebrates the Passover meal not with his natural family, according to the custom of the Jewish Passover ritual, but with his new family, and not with an arbitrary selection of disciples who might happen to have been available, but, as Mark clearly states, with the Twelve (14:17-18). His last meal had the familial intimacy that is proper to the Passover meal, and yet the very choice of participants emphatically points to Israel, its eschatological gathering and the new creation of the people of God that Jesus began with the group of the Twelve.

During the meal Jesus took bread, said the prayer of thanks over it, broke it and handed it to the Twelve. That was a fixed ritual surrounding the table prayer before the main course, after the appetizers had been eaten,

---

[112] Quoted freely from Gustav Dalman, *Jesus-Jeschua* (Leipzig, 1922) 127–28. The age of the saying is, however, disputed. Günther Stemberger, "Pesachhaggada und Abendmahlsberichte des Neuen Testaments" in idem, *Studien zum rabbinischen Judentum.* SBAB 10 (Stuttgart: Katholisches Bibelwerk, 1990) 357–74 thinks it is of later origin (pp. 360–61). In any case Exod 13:8 (cf. Exod 12:26-27) suggests that there existed a Passover ritual with extensive interpretation at a very early period.

when the head of the house recalled the Exodus from Egypt. Of course Mark tells us nothing of the preliminary courses, the Passover liturgy, and the other elements of the meal. The tradition he is following presumes that everyone knows about that as a matter of course. Mark and his tradition speak only of what is special and unique about this one Passover meal,[113] including Jesus' interpretation of the broken bread: "This is my body." "Body" should not be understood in the Western sense as the opposite of soul. "Body" is the person, the whole human being. Jesus is saying: "I myself am this bread, I with my history and my life. My life will be broken like this bread. I give it to you so that you may have a share in it."

Jesus' sign-action is thus a prophecy of his death. In the sign of the broken bread Jesus proclaims his death. At the same time, however, this sign-action is more than a prophecy of death, for Jesus gives the Twelve a share in his existence, his life that is now to be given up to death. Evidently his death has a deep dimension in which the Twelve, and thus Israel, must share. What that is Mark (in contrast to the Lukan/Pauline strand in the Last Supper traditions)[114] does not yet say at this point.

The Markan tradition presumes, without directly stating it, that the main part of the meal followed immediately after the table prayer and the word of interpretation over the broken bread: the eating of the lamb with the bitter herbs, bread, and the fruit mixture called *haroseth*. At the end of the main course the head of the house took the third cup, the cup of blessing, and said another prayer of thanksgiving. At this point Mark takes up the account again because another special moment occurs: Jesus makes the handing over of and drinking from the cup of blessing another sign-action, for after speaking the prayer of thanksgiving over it he interprets it as follows: "This is my blood of the covenant, which is poured out for many."

The concepts are almost too close-packed for people today. But we should not blame the ancient text for that. Today's hearers would not know that the background to the Aramaic words of interpretation was Deut 16:1-8, "this is the bread of affliction." For Jewish ears at that time it was enough to speak a few key words, often only one, in order to evoke a longer biblical text. What is Mark's text meant to say?

---

[113] For the order of the Passover meal see Joachim Jeremias, *The Eucharistic Words of Jesus* (New York: Scribner, 1966) 84–88. That Mark 14:22-25 is an integral part of a more extensive text that described Jesus' last meal as a Passover meal has been demonstrated by Rudolf Pesch, most recently in "Das Evangelium in Jerusalem: Mk 14, 12-26 als ältestes Überlieferungsgut der Urgemeinde" in Peter Stuhlmacher, ed., *Das Evangelium und die Evangelien. Vorträge vom Tübinger Symposium 1982.* WUNT 28 (Tübingen: J.C.B. Mohr/Paul Siebeck 1983) 113–55, especially 146–55.

[114] See Luke 22:19-20; 1 Cor 11:23-26.

First of all, Jesus points once more to his imminent death. He interprets the cup of red wine as his blood that will soon be shed. "Shedding blood" means "killing." Jesus will be killed. But here again he does not rest content with a prophecy of his death. The text does not speak simply of Jesus' blood, but of his "blood of the covenant." And "blood of the covenant" refers to the events in Exod 24:4-11, where Israel's founding action is told. At the foot of Sinai Moses built an altar and twelve stone pillars, sprinkled the altar with sacrificial blood, read the book of the covenant to the twelve tribes, and sprinkled the people with the blood, saying: "See the blood of the covenant that the LORD has made with you in accordance with all these words" (Exod 24:8). After this Moses and the elders of Israel were able to eat a meal with God on the mountain. We need not inquire at this point about the original meaning of this sprinkling with blood. Probably it was meant to show that Israel had become a nation of priests in the sense of Exod 19:6: "you shall be for me a priestly kingdom and a holy nation." What is crucial for the later understanding of Exod 24:8 is that here three motifs are combined: the common meal, God's covenant with Israel, and the blood with which the covenant is sealed. In the Jewish interpretive tradition of Jesus' own time this blood that was sprinkled on the altar at the foot of Sinai was understood as the means of atonement for the sins of Israel.[115]

Against this background Jesus' words over the cup of blessing in Mark 14:24 can only mean that his life will be given up to death, but his blood thus shed will not be shed in vain and without reason; it is the "blood of the covenant," for it renews and completes the covenant that God once made with Israel at Sinai. This eschatological renewal of the covenant that is at the same time the new creation and the new foundation of Israel will take place through the blood of Jesus that frees Israel from its guilt and atones for it.

If we take this background seriously the "many" spoken of in the words over the cup in Mark's gospel can only be, in the first instance, Israel. Jesus interprets his violent death as a dying for Israel, as an atoning surrender of his life for the life of the people of God.

This interpretation on behalf of Israel should be clear from the very fact that Jesus gives the cup of blessing to the Twelve, the representatives of the people of the twelve tribes whom he has chosen. But the reference to Israel is just as clearly indicated by the background of the Sinai covenant. That covenant was made with Israel, and when it is renewed it is also with Israel. Thus in the first instance the "many" are the people of the twelve tribes.

---

[115] In Targum Onqelos (and similarly in Targum Yerushalmi 1) we read at Exod 24:8: "Moses took the blood and sprinkled it on the altar in order to make atonement for the people, and he said: 'See, this is the blood of the covenant that the LORD has made with you in accordance with all these words.'" Cf. Peter Stuhlmacher, *Biblische Theologie* 1:137.

Of course we may not rest with this statement, for the reference to the "many" comes from Isa 52:13–53:12, the fourth Servant Song. The servant of God suffers as representative of the many, and in this song, where "many" is a continuing thread (Leitmotif), the many are clearly the Gentile nations.[116] Therefore in reflecting the Last Supper tradition he had received Mark must have had both Israel and the Gentile nations in view. That is not a problem, because in the theology of the Old Testament Israel is the representative of the nations. It was not chosen for its own sake but for the sake of the world. The salvation that is extended to and in Israel is to be salvation for the whole world. Therefore the "many" can be Israel in the first instance and then, through Israel, the nations. The universal statement would only be false if it omitted the reference to Israel, and that is certainly not the case in Mark, nor is it in the other New Testament authors.

Thus we can say that according to Mark Jesus, during the ritual of the Passover meal, interpreted the broken bread and the red wine in terms of his imminent death. And when he handed the bread and wine to the twelve disciples he gave them, and Israel through them, a share in the power of his death. For this death is interpreted simultaneously as atonement for Israel, which had succumbed to sin and guilt, and as a renewal of the covenant at Sinai. But through this eschatological Israel the new salvation now definitively given is to extend to the nations.

One is almost ashamed to describe the events depicted in Mark 14:22-25 in such a dry and pedantic fashion, but it is necessary if we are to come closer to comprehending the extraordinarily dense texts in the Last Supper tradition. Of course we still cannot fully understand these texts in this way. That would only be possible if the reality of our lives corresponded to them. They were, after all, embedded in a meal that lasted for a long time and in any case was full of symbols and imbued with deep significance. This meal was about making present the salvation of Israel; moreover, the death that threatened Jesus and his disciples gave every word and every gesture great weight. Even after Easter these texts were embedded in living assemblies in which the death of Jesus and his rescue from death were present realities.

Certainly what Jesus, according to the gospels, said that night and very soon afterward put into action by his death was anything but banal. The

---

[116] Within Isa 52:13–53:12 we encounter the "many" in 52:14, 15 and 53:11, 12a,e; 52:15 shows that these are the "nations." We should also consider that even within the Old Testament itself the substantive "the many" can stand both for the eschatological Israel (Dan 9:27; 11:33; 12:3) and for the "many" from among the Gentiles (Isaiah 52–53). The expression is similarly broad in the New Testament: in the Last Supper traditions its initial meaning can only be Israel, but in Matt 8:11 it clearly refers to the nations. Cf. also Mark 10:45 with 1 Tim 2:6.

Last Supper traditions, both the Markan and the Pauline, presuppose that in his dying Jesus became the place of eschatological atonement for Israel, and that means that the legitimate locus of atonement was no longer the Temple, but Jesus himself with his surrender of his life even unto death. The table around which Jesus gathered with his disciples now became the definitive center of Israel. Mark says just that when he tells us that at Jesus' death the curtain of the Temple was torn asunder (15:38).

The enormity of all this is such that many exegetes deny that Jesus spoke the words over the cup. Representation and atonement are said to be theological motifs applied by the post-Easter communities in order to interpret the execution of Jesus on the cross, an event that they could not otherwise comprehend. Jesus himself would have understood his death more simply, perhaps in the manner of the "eschatological foreshadowing" with which Mark concludes the Last Supper scene: "Truly I tell you, I will never again drink of the fruit of the vine until that day when I drink it new in the kingdom of God" (14:25). It is said that Jesus would surely have held fast, even unto death, to his message of the coming reign of God and his life *for* others, but the concise theological fabric of blood, atonement, representation, and covenant embodied in the words over the cup cannot be attributed to him. After all, he had never spoken of such a thing in the entire period of his activity before this.

There is another position that raises this objection at a still more radical level. This says that the idea of Jesus' atoning death is not only quite improbable, but is also incompatible with his preaching of the reign of God. Jesus preached a Father willing to forgive unconditionally. That this loving Father should then, one day, cease to be so generous and suddenly demand atonement is simply out of line with Jesus' message and praxis.[117]

However, this line of argument leads in the wrong direction. It reduces Jesus' preaching of the reign of God to a timeless message about the timeless being of God, and that is something as unbiblical as anything could ever be.[118] The approach of the reign of God is, for Jesus, not something outside of time. The *basileia* is not something present always and everywhere. It has its hour. It is unique, tied to Jesus, to be grasped in the present moment, not repeatable at just any time; it is God's *eschatological* offer. In this it is quite like John's baptism. Jesus was able to build on the

---

[117] Thus Peter Fiedler, "Sünde und Vergebung im Christentum," *Concilium* (D) 10 (1974) 568–71; idem, *Jesus und die Sünder.* BET 3 (Frankfurt and Bern: Peter Lang, 1976) 277–81; Werner Zager, "Wie kam es im Urchristentum zur Deutung des Todes Jesu als Sühnegeschehen?" *ZNW* 87 (1996) 165–86, at 179, 184.

[118] For what follows cf. also Rudolf Pesch, *Das Abendmahl und Jesu Todesverständnis.* QD 80 (Freiburg: Herder, 1978) 103–11.

movement that the Baptizer had begun. Without the Baptizer's call to conversion Jesus' good news would not have been possible. Like John's baptism, Jesus' proclamation was a unique address of God to Israel. The salvation offered by Jesus may therefore not be abstracted from its historical situation.

If Jesus found more irresolution than faith in Galilee, and if Israel's representatives in Jerusalem rejected him and even saw to it that he was executed, then Israel refused the reign of God. And if Israel refused the reign of God it missed the meaning of its very existence, gambled away salvation for itself and the nations, and made God's election an act *ad absurdum*. Only in this way is the dreadful seriousness of the words of judgment on Israel that Jesus spoke near the end of his public activity to be explained.[119] He must, for example, have been anticipating the definitive refusal by the people of God when he said:

> "Jerusalem, Jerusalem, the city that kills the prophets and stones those who are sent to it! How often have I desired to gather your children together as a hen gathers her brood under her wings, and you were not willing! See, your house is left to you, desolate." (Matt 23:37-38)

In the hour at which God's eschatological messenger was eliminated there had to exist a situation in which nothing was any longer as it had been when Jesus' public activity began in Galilee—a situation in which Jesus' proclamation, "the reign of God has come near" could not simply be repeated. For at that hour grace itself had been rejected.[120]

Therefore at the moment when his proclamation, taken as a whole, had proven unsuccessful and his death appeared imminent Jesus found himself faced with a new situation, and that new situation demanded a new interpretation. The argument that Jesus never spoke beforehand about his blood, or about representation and atonement, is untenable. It presumes that human life is ahistorical.

The new interpretation that Jesus gave at the very moment when the people of God was preparing to throw away its election did not happen in just any time and place. It occurred at the Passover meal, in one of the holiest hours of the Jewish year. Jesus interprets his death as God's final saving decree. Israel's guilt, concentrated in Jesus' death, is answered by God not with the withdrawal of Israel's election but instead by the full and ultimate gift of life, even though God's people have thrown away their life. That is precisely what the Bible means by "atonement."[121]

---

[119] Cf. Reiser, *Jesus and Judgment* 322–23.

[120] Pesch, *Abendmahl* 106.

[121] Cf. Hartmut Gese, "Die Sühne" in idem, *Zur biblischen Theologie. Alttestamentliche Vorträge.* BEvTh 78 (3rd ed. Munich, 1989) 85–106; Bernd Janowski, *Sühne als Heils-*

With this interpretation Jesus makes authoritative reference to the Bible. He knows, of course, the texts about the covenant at Sinai made with atoning blood;[122] he knows the texts about the new (i.e., renewed) covenant that sets aside Israel's sin after it has broken the Sinai covenant;[123] in particular he knows the texts about the Suffering Servant of God who gives up his life and takes the guilt of the many on himself.[124]

In interpreting his death in light of the Torah and the prophets did Jesus deny the good news he had preached? Quite the contrary. Jesus preached the *basileia* as a reign of mercy and divine grace. When he now, in the crucial hour before his death, presents to the participants at the meal in definitive signs the truth that God holds fast to the covenant with Israel, that God is renewing that covenant and offering God's people new life in spite of everything, he reveals the full radicality of divine mercy. One must, in fact, say that only in the interpretation Jesus gives to his imminent death does the true countenance of his message of the *basileia* appear.

If there are always exegetes who simply deny that Jesus could have interpreted his death as an existential representation on behalf of the many and as an atoning sacrifice for Israel, this is not ultimately a matter of historical-critical issues. The decision was already made beforehand, long before the historical argumentation began. Rudolf Bultmann made this clear, with the honesty so characteristic of him, when he wrote in his famous essay on "New Testament and Mythology":

> How can the guilt of one man be expiated by the death of another who is sinless—if indeed one may speak of a sinless man at all? What primitive notions of guilt and righteousness does this imply? And what primitive idea of God? The rationale of sacrifice in general may of course throw some light on the theory of the atonement, but even so, what a primitive mythology it is, that a divine Being should become incarnate, and atone for the sins of men through his own blood![125]

It is just here that the switches are laid on the tracks of self-confident historical methods of proof. People who are the heirs of the European Enlight-

---

*geschehen. Studien zur Sühnetheologie der Priesterschrift und zur Wurzel KPR im Alten Orient und im Alten Testament.* WMANT 55 (Neukirchen-Vluyn: Neukirchener Verlag, 1982); idem, *Stellvertretung. Alttestamentliche Studien zu einem theologischen Grundbegriff.* SBS 165 (Stuttgart: Katholisches Bibelwerk, 1997); Peter Stuhlmacher, *Biblische Theologie* 1:136–43.

[122] Exod 24:4-11.

[123] Jer 31:31-34; Ezek 16:59-63; 37:21-28.

[124] Isa 52:13–53:12.

[125] Rudolf Bultmann, "New Testament and Mythology. The Mythological Element in the Message of the New Testament and the Problem of Reinterpretation" in Hans-Werner Bartsch, ed., *Kerygma and Myth: A Theological Debate.* Translated by Reginald H. Fuller (London: S.P.C.K., 1953–64; rev. ed. New York: Harper & Row, 1961) 1–44, at 7.

enment can no longer reconcile ideas like representation and atonement with the autonomy they have so laboriously won for themselves. But are the two things really incompatible? Representation and atonement are only an offense when the experience of the people of God has been lost. For life among God's people representation and atonement are elementary. They detract nothing from the dignity and independence of persons.

Israel's existence always depended on individuals who *fully* believed. The fact that the scarlet thread of salvation history never broke depended on Abraham, Moses, Elijah, Amos, and Isaiah, on King Josiah, John the Baptizer, and many others. Others could enter into their faith and thus come to faith for themselves. It was not a language game to say of Abraham that those who blessed him would be blessed, and that in him all the peoples of the earth would find blessing (Gen 12:3). Jesus, acting as representative for the many, was not an exotic exception but the high point and final culmination of a long history of representation in Israel. Only by way of representation can faith be handed on at all.

Representation in this context never means dispensing others from their own believing and conversion; it is meant to make both of these possible. True representation does not abrogate the maturity of others; it desires nothing more than that the others will be free to act for themselves. It means that one person takes the place of another not to "replace" the other but to enable that other to assume his or her own place.[126]

If each individual in his or her natural existence is dependent on representatives, so is the people of God a still finer net of representations—precisely because it cannot exist at all without free, mature, and considered action. What is valid for everyone from the beginning is above all true in the life of faith: human beings depend on the help of others; left to themselves they perish. The dictum abstracted from Kant's *Critique of Practical Reason*, "you can because you shall"[127] is extremely questionable. In

---

[126] Cf. the thoroughly informative work of Karl-Heinz Menke, *Stellvertretung. Schlüsselbegriff christlichen Lebens und theologische Grundkategorie* (Einsiedeln: Johannes, 1991) 17. At this point he refers to Dorothee Sölle, *Stellvertretung. Ein Kapitel Theologie nach dem "Tode Gottes"* (2nd ed. Stuttgart: Kreuz-Verlag, 1982).

[127] Cf. Immanuel Kant, *The Critique of Practical Reason* (Chicago: Encyclopaedia Britannica, Inc., 1952) 302: "He (= one who in a difficult situation must decide according to conscience. Author's note) judges, therefore, that he can do a certain thing because he is conscious that he ought, and he recognizes that he is free—a fact which but for the moral law he would never have known." Apparently the dictum "you can because you shall" was later abstracted from this sentence. At any rate, in 1942 Walter Schmidkunz edited a collection of quotations from Kant in the series *Münchner Lesebogen*, number 11, under the title *I. Kant, Du kannst, denn du sollst. Vom Ethos der Pflicht*. The formula in the title does not appear among the quotations. I am grateful to P. Giovanni Sala, S.J., of Munich, for this information.

light of the Judeo-Christian tradition it should be "you can if you will accept help."[128]

The supposedly "autonomous individuals" who think they need no help and no representative of course have representatives all the same: for example, the media, which all too often do their thinking for them, shape them according to their own images, and thus without their noticing it abrogate their maturity. People always have their representatives; it is only a question of which ones.

The resistance shown by people today against the concept of atonement is certainly much sharper than their reaction to the idea of representation. However, atonement is nothing other than representation carried to the ultimate. Still, one can only understand what is meant by "atonement" by considering the difference between atonement in the Old Testament sense and atonement in the religious world in general.

In the realm of religion as such atonement is primarily a human action carried out to obtain the favor of the gods. A person gives up something especially dear and precious to him or her in order to bring the deities or powers who have influence over that person's life to his or her side. The initiative comes from the human side. This person desires to make his or her life secure, and to that end develops the most varied cultic mechanisms.

Israel was aware of all those mechanisms, but it had seen through them and reflected on them in light of its own experience of God. Ultimately it turned them on their head. For in Israel all atonement came from God's side. It was God's initiative. Atonement is a new opportunity for life given by God. Atonement is the gift of being able to live before the holy God, in the space of the divine presence, in spite of one's own lack of holiness and continually renewed state of sinfulness. Bringing about atonement does *not* mean appeasing God or causing God to be forgiving, but allowing oneself to be rescued by God from the death one deserves.[129] Israel knew that human beings cannot work off their guilt, and that both atonement and forgiveness must come from God. Atonement, like covenant and the forgiveness of sins, is God's gracious decree into which human beings can only enter. In this as well biblical thought is distinctly different from that of the religions, at least as far as the power of discernment is concerned.

Still, with all this the real question has not yet been answered. It could be stated as follows: If everything comes from God's initiative, why must there be atonement at all? If *God* has created atonement, just as God created forgiveness, why is simple forgiveness not adequate? Why can God not simply decree: your guilt is taken away; everything is forgiven and forgotten?

formulation to Ludwig Weimer.
ut Gese, "Sühne," 91.

The answer can only be: Because then reality would be done away with; because then the consequences of sin would not be taken seriously. Sin does not dissolve into thin air even when it is forgiven, because sin does not remain in the sinner. It has consequences. It always has a social dimension. Every sin sinks into human society, destroys a segment of the world, and creates a context of evil. Even if God forgives all guilt the consequences of that guilt are not eliminated. What Adolf Hitler let loose on the world was by no means done away with by his death in April 1945 even if he regretted it and even if he was forgiven for it. The fearful consequences of Nazism poison society even today, and they continue to fester in the lives of the surviving victims, even in the lives of their children and grandchildren.

Therefore the consequences of sin have to be cleared away, worked off, and that is something that human beings cannot do for themselves any more than they can pronounce their own absolution. A real "clearing away" of guilt is only possible on a basis that God alone can establish. God has created such a basis in God's people, whom he renewed and perfected in Jesus.

There is a text from Dag Hammarskjöld, the second Secretary General of the United Nations, who was murdered when a bomb caused his plane to crash near the border of the Congo on 17 September 1961 while he was on a mission to try to end the civil war in that country, that can help us better to understand the matters we have been discussing. It comes from his diary, published after his death under the title *Markings*. It reads:

> Easter 1960. Forgiveness breaks the chain of causality because he who "forgives" you—out of love—takes upon himself the consequences of what *you* have done. Forgiveness, therefore, always entails a sacrifice.
>
> The price you pay for your own liberation through another's sacrifice is that you in turn must be willing to liberate in the same way, irrespective of the consequences to yourself.[130]

This clearsighted text, confirmed by Dag Hammarskjøld's own life and death, makes clear what is at stake when we speak of representative atonement: namely that love forgives. But it cannot forgive the consequences of sin because they have long since burned themselves into our history. The chain of causes begun by sin grows of itself. If love is true love it therefore not only forgives but takes responsibility for the consequences of what the other does. And that costs something. It cannot happen without sacrifice. And it can only succeed if many work to heal the consequences of the guilt of others. Dag Hammarskjöld points to this when he says that one's own liberation obligates one to give oneself up for the liberation of

---

[130] Dag Hammarskjöld, *Markings*. Translated by Leif Sjöberg and W. H. Auden, with an introduction by W. H. Auden (New York: Knopf, 1964) 197.

others. Thus begins a new chain of causes that works against the causal chain of guilt.

When the New Testament tradition speaks of the atoning death of Jesus it means that through his death—a death entirely *for others,* self-emptying to the last extreme, *agapē* in the most radical sense—he has broken through the complex of evil in the world and established a new basis on which it is possible to clear away the consequences of sin.

Jesus' death thus does not bring about a magical redemption that is transmitted to those needing redemption in a secret and mysterious way. That Jesus died for our sins does not mean that we ourselves need no longer die to sin. His death is not a substitutionary action but the origin and enabling of a process of liberation that continues. But the social basis on which it continues is the eschatological people of God. It began with the constitution of the Twelve, but only with Jesus' surrender even to death for Israel was the new causal chain forged and redemption and liberation definitively established in the world. The Fourth Evangelist says this in a penetrating image:

> Meanwhile, standing near the cross of Jesus were his mother, and his mother's sister, Mary the wife of Clopas, and Mary Magdalene. When Jesus saw his mother and the disciple whom he loved standing beside her, he said to his mother, "Woman, here is your son." Then he said to the disciple, "Here is your mother." And from that hour the disciple took her into his own home. (John 19:25-27)

This scene may certainly have been intended to legitimate the Beloved Disciple as witness to the tradition.[131] But there is something much more fundamental at work beyond that: Jesus is founding a new family, that is, the basis on which people who have nothing at all to do with one another can join together in unconditional solidarity. It is the place where true reconciliation with God and one another becomes possible. But people cannot create this new possibility for themselves. It must come from the cross. It had to be grounded in the death of Jesus.

We had said that in Jesus' death his message of the *basileia* first arrived at its most profound depth. When at the Last Supper he interpreted his imminent death as a representative, atoning death he did not retract his earlier preaching of divine mercy, but instead revealed the social reality of that mercy. God is not content with mere forgiveness. In his death God gives Jesus the place where guilt *and* its consequences can be done away with.

---

[131] Thus, for example, Jürgen Becker, *Das Evangelium nach Johannes. Kapitel 11–21.* ÖTK 4/2 (Gütersloh and Würzburg, 1981) 592.

However, Jesus' death reveals something more in light of his previous preaching: It shows with the greatest clarity how hidden and humble is the reign of God. The reign of God cannot come without persecutions and sacrifices; indeed, it cannot come without daily dying.

What was already indicated in Jesus' preaching becomes fully apparent in his death: The *basileia* requires a certain resignation to events and a self-surrender; it will not come without pure receptiveness, and that receptiveness is always a kind of suffering as well. The reign of God comes just at the point where Jesus himself can do no more but can only give himself up and surrender to God's truth.

Thus through the death of Jesus the idea of the reign of God is given a final clarification and sharpening: from now on it cannot be formulated without reference, at the same time, to the death of Jesus. That changes nothing in the overflowing fullness of the reign of God that we spoke of in III, 3, but that fullness comes only through the new daily dying. The chapter to follow must show what that means for the Church's existence.

# IV

# The Characteristic Signs of the Church

At the Passover meal Jesus spoke of his impending death and interpreted it for the twelve disciples in the symbols of bread and wine. A few hours later he was hanging on the cross. The Sanhedrin had him seized during the night, condemned him as a deceiver of the people and a blasphemer, and handed him over to the Roman occupation forces. For the Roman trial the Sanhedrin altered the charge to one of political sedition. Pilate accordingly had Jesus crucified as "King of the Jews," that is, as a political messiah, between two terrorists.[1]

It looked as if it was all over, and not only in the sense that Jesus was dead within a few hours and his disciples had taken flight. Jesus and his message seemed to be finished in a more radical sense, for Deut 21:22-23 must have played a crucial role in the efforts of the Sanhedrin to have Jesus crucified. There, within a passage regarding the burial of executed criminals, we read: "anyone hung on a tree is under God's curse." This refers to the public display on a gallows of criminals who had already been executed. We know from the Temple Scroll found in Qumran cave 11 that this sentence later furnished the juridical basis for the crucifixion of Jews accused of betraying the Jewish people.[2] While crucifixion already

---

[1] For the historical questions see Josef Blinzler, *Der Prozeß Jesu* (4th ed. Regensburg: F. Pustet, 1969); August Strobel, *Die Stunde der Wahrheit. Untersuchungen zum Strafverfahren gegen Jesus.* WUNT 21 (Tübingen: J.C.B. Mohr/Paul Siebeck, 1980), especially 81–94; Rudolf Pesch, *Der Prozeß Jesu geht weiter.* Herderbücherei 1507 (Freiburg: Herder, 1988).

[2] Cf. 11Q 19 64, 6-12: "If there were to be a spy against his people who betrays his people to a foreign nation or causes evil against his people, you shall hang him from a tree and he will die. . . . If there were a man with a sin punishable by death and he escapes amongst the nations and curses his people and the children of Israel, he also you shall hang on the tree and he will die. Their corpses shall not spend the night on the tree; instead you shall bury them that day because they are cursed by God and man, those hanged on a tree

constituted for Gentiles in antiquity the most shameful and debasing form of execution it had a still more negative symbolic weight in Israel because of Deut 21:22-23: anyone hanging on a cross was cursed by God, that is, someone condemned not only by human beings but by God.

From this perspective we can see that for the Sanhedrin the Passover feast with its masses of pilgrims not only presented unwelcome difficulties for the arrest of Jesus but also offered a positive opportunity to expose him before the assembled people of Israel as a blasphemer of God. Once Jesus was hanging on the cross before the eyes of the festival pilgrims it would be obvious that by no stretch of the imagination could God be behind such a person.

Jesus on the cross and thus cursed by God: the effect of this apparent judgment of God must have been devastating. Most of his followers lost their nerve. Many of his disciples fled. The Galileans returned to their native place. Simon Peter took up his old trade and went back to fishing.[3] In reality the whole story ended at this point.

But something unheard of happened. To grasp its enormity we need to look at the events following Good Friday for a moment through the eyes of a neutral observer who only sees the externals: Jesus' disciples left the capital city and were in the process of being scattered to the four winds. But suddenly the movement turned back on itself: they regathered, and not just anywhere, but in the very place that was most dangerous for them, the city of Jerusalem. There, at the next festival, the Feast of Weeks (Pentecost), they declared publicly that God had not accepted the judgment of the Sanhedrin that Jesus was a deceiver of the people. God spoke a counter-judgment: God awakened Jesus from the dead, placed him at the right hand of God, and so justified him.

When they were asked how they knew all that, they spoke of an experience that had dramatically changed their lives once again, something that happened to Simon Peter, the whole group of the Twelve, and many other disciples: Jesus appeared to them as risen and justified by God. They expressed it in words such as:

> "The God of our ancestors raised up Jesus, whom you had killed by hanging him on a tree. God exalted him at his right hand as Leader and Savior that he might give repentance to Israel and forgiveness of sins. And we are witnesses

---

. . . ." (Translation by Florentino García Martínez, *The Dead Sea Scrolls Translated* (English translation by Wilfred G. E. Watson; 2nd ed. Leiden, New York, and Cologne: W. J. Brill; Grand Rapids: Eerdmans, 1996).

[3] Cf. Gerhard Lohfink, "Der Ablauf der Osterereignisse und die Anfänge der Urgemeinde" in idem, *Studien zum Neuen Testament*. SBAB 5 NT (Stuttgart: Katholisches Bibelwerk, 1989) 149–67.

to these things, and so is the Holy Spirit whom God has given to those who obey him." (Acts 5:30-32)

In this and similar texts every word is important: this is not a listing of just any set of events; what is being described is *God's action*. It was *God* who had raised Jesus from the dead. *God* had sent the Spirit. These were two great events that were expected in Israel at the end time: the resurrection of the dead and the outpouring of the Spirit of God on all flesh.[4] Thus these witnesses were saying that in the resurrection of Jesus the events of the end time had already begun. The Easter event is God's powerful, definitive, eschatological action.

The God who is at work here is the God of Abraham, Isaac, and Jacob, the God of the ancestors. Therefore all this is about the destiny of Israel and, through Israel, the destiny of the world. It is not merely about the rescue of Jesus, as an individual person, from death. And the fact that he hung *on a tree* says nothing at all against him. God had, precisely because of his death, appointed him Lord and Messiah.[5] But as Messiah he is also Savior. Thus what is at issue is still the salvation of Israel, just as it was for the earthly Jesus. Luke in fact defines the resurrection and exaltation of Jesus as the action of God for this very purpose: to give Israel repentance and the forgiveness of sins.[6]

The Twelve, who now open their mouths before the largest possible public audiences, refer all this to their own personal experience: they themselves are witnesses to God's action. However, there is another witness: the Holy Spirit. "We are witnesses to these things, and so is the Holy Spirit" (Acts 5:32). If we ask how this second witness can be heard and give testimony to the resurrection of Jesus we may, following Luke, point to the events at Pentecost. At that time the young Jerusalem community suddenly made its public appearance: 120 men and women as a single assembly, in unanimity, as the new family of Jesus, filled with the Spirit of God.[7] They show by appearing fearlessly before the crowd on the day of Pentecost that everything Jesus had begun with the constitution of the Twelve as the beginning of the eschatological Israel is now continuing under the Easter sign. The existence of the community of disciples becomes, together with the direct testimony of the apostolic preaching, a second witness to the resurrection of Jesus.

---

[4] Resurrection of the dead: Isa 25:8; 26:19; Dan 12:2; 2 Maccabees 7; outpouring of the Spirit: Ezek 36:26-27; Joel 2:28-29 [MT 3:1-5].

[5] Cf. Acts 2:36 with 5:31.

[6] Cf. Acts 2:36-38; 3:15-19; 5:30-31.

[7] For the number of 120 see Acts 1:15 with 1:14; a single group: Acts 1:13; 2:1; unanimity: Acts 1:14; new family: Acts 1:14; filled with the Holy Spirit: Acts 2:4. See further in section IV, 2 below.

This people-of-God aspect of Jesus' resurrection is often neglected in preaching today. For the most part it is no longer clear at all that to say "Jesus arose from the dead" is not merely to speak of his personal overcoming of death and the hope for all believers that results from it, but equally to speak of the work of God here in this world. The resurrection of Jesus is intimately bound up with the resurrection of the people of God, that is, its eschatological gathering. The Emmaus story in particular shows this with special clarity. The knowledge that Jesus is alive by no means leads the two disciples who had been departing in resignation from Jerusalem to the climactic statement of countless Easter sermons, "life has meaning," or "there is life after death for us as well." Instead it takes them back to Jerusalem, where the rest of the disciples are: "That same hour they got up and returned to Jerusalem, and they found the eleven and their companions gathered together" (Luke 24:33).

As true as it is that the resurrection of Jesus gives us hope for our own resurrection from death this is never the theme of the Easter texts in the gospels. Instead, the real theme there is the raising of the people of God, already stiffened in death in the sense of Ezek 37:1-14. In that chapter the prophet sees the skeleton of Israel scattered over a great plain and hears God saying:

> "Mortal, these bones are the whole house of Israel. They say, 'Our bones are dried up, and our hope is lost; we are cut off completely.' Therefore prophesy and say to them, Thus says the Lord GOD: I am going to open your graves and bring you up from your graves, O my people; and I will bring you back to the land of Israel. And you shall know that I am the LORD, when I open your graves, and bring you up from your graves, O my people. I will put my spirit within you, and you shall live, and I will place you on your own soil; then you shall know that I, the LORD, have spoken and will act," says the LORD. (Ezek 37:11-14)

This text is not about the dead members of the people of God; it is about the entombed existence of the present, living generation. There is no hope that they can free themselves from their *rigor mortis*. The people of God can only come to life if God awakens it and breathes life into it through the Spirit of God. The Easter narratives in the gospels and the Pentecost narrative of Acts must be read against this background. All these New Testament texts point toward the reawakening and expansion of the people of God. Their principal motif is the mission of the apostles to Israel and to the world.[8]

The fact that after Good Friday Jesus' disciples assemble as the eschatological people of God is in itself a testimony to the resurrection. As

---

[8] Cf. Matt 28:19-20; Mark 16:15; Luke 24:47; John 20:21; 21:15-17; Acts 1:8.

important as the testimony to Jesus' resurrection in the word of proclamation is—and it is as fundamental as Israel's confession of its rescue from Egypt—equally important is the testimony that lies in the very existence of an Easter people of God. In fact one really cannot speak of the resurrection of Jesus without at the same time speaking of the *consequences* of his resurrection in the Church.

Luke very deliberately depicted this connection in the Acts of the Apostles. On the one hand he tells how the apostles after Easter testified to Israel about Jesus' resurrection. On the other hand he interweaves the accounts of that preaching with reports on the life of the primitive community. In Acts 4:32-34 this interweaving is utterly palpable. There we read:

> Now the whole group of those who believed were of one heart and soul, and no one claimed private ownership of any possessions, but everything they owned was held in common. With great power the apostles gave their testimony to the resurrection of the Lord Jesus, and great grace was upon them all. There was not a needy person among them . . . .

The apostles' witnessing to Jesus' resurrection is here built into a depiction of the life of the primitive Christian community. And that the believers bound their lives to one another so that none of them suffered any need was the very thing that gave force to the preaching of the resurrection. They needed no special eloquence, for they knew whereof they spoke, and their hearers could see it.

The Risen One himself could no longer be seen by anyone, but everyone can see his communities. They are his body in the world. They are the visible body of the Crucified and Risen One. They are as real and physical as the disciples experienced the Risen One to be. The Easter communities are not something purely spiritual, any more than the Risen One is pure spirit. In the gospel of Luke, Jesus says when he appears to all the disciples: "Look at my hands and my feet; see that it is I myself. Touch me and see; for a ghost does not have flesh and bones as you see that I have" (Luke 24:39).

The early Church's theological disputes about the real bodiliness of the Risen One reflected in this text also touch on the bodiliness of the Church. It is visible, palpable, tangible. It is socially organized. Anyone who locates it only in the word of proclamation or in the hearts of the faithful, and pretends that invisibility is its true nature, takes seriously neither its existence as the beginning of the eschatological Israel nor its origins in the Risen One and his bodiliness. Because the Church is sacrament of salvation it must be as physical as its sacraments. The last section of this book is about this tangible reality of the Church.

## 1. The Exodus Continues

In the New Testament there is a unique and at first glance alienating phenomenon: In the synoptic gospels the concept of the reign of God occurs with extraordinary frequency, but in the rest of the New Testament, including the Fourth Gospel, it seldom appears. This means that the reign of God was central to Jesus' preaching, but in early Christian theology the concept quickly receded into the background.[9] Had the early Church thus abandoned something essential?

That is surely not the case. After all, the Church recalled and handed on Jesus' "language" in the first three gospels; but more than that, it made real in baptism what Jesus preached when he spoke of the reign of God, and it kept that reality alive in its baptismal theology. The early Church understood baptism as Jesus had understood the coming of the *basileia:* as the absolute, gracious action of God given to baptismal candidates without any deserving on their part. And as for the *basileia,* so also for baptism the law of "today" was in force: The baptized already have a share in the new world that has dawned with Jesus: "if anyone is in Christ, there is a new creation: everything old has passed away; see, everything has become new!" (2 Cor 5:17). And just as the reign of God does not sweep ethereally somewhere above the clouds, but is entirely earthly and creates a renewed Israel, so also with baptism: in it God creates the eschatological people of God and continually adds new members to it. Finally, it is impossible to speak of baptism or of the reign of God without speaking of Jesus' death. Accepting the reign of God is always a matter of suffering as well, even of "dying," and being baptized means dying with Christ. Paul, reflecting on the creed in 1 Cor 15:3-5, writes:

> Do you not know that all of us who have been baptized into Christ Jesus were baptized into his death? Therefore we have been buried with him by baptism into death, so that, just as Christ was raised from the dead by the glory of the Father, so we too might walk in newness of life. (Rom 6:3-4)

This text makes clear the depth at which baptism is lodged. It is not a moral uplifting or an act of heroism; it means being incorporated into something new, something that lies entirely outside the previous existence of the baptizand and that she or he could never produce out of her or his own resources. This appears to link baptism with the ancient mystery religions that had long since established themselves alongside the older be-

---

[9] In the Fourth Gospel the concept of the "reign of God" appears only twice, and in the entire NT letter corpus only nine times; in contrast it is found eighty-three times in the synoptic gospels. It appears that after Easter the concept remained a living one for a certain period of time among those who handed on the words of the Lord.

liefs in the gods of antiquity and that, roughly at the same time as the expansion of Christianity, were attracting more and more followers. In the mystery religions the individual encountered, in secret rituals consciously elaborated under the veil of mystery, a myth that promised immortality.[10]

Christian baptism, however, despite some superficial similarities, is an entirely different thing. This is apparent first of all from its origins in the baptism of John.[11] It is not only for individuals and their personal salvation, but for the eschatological renewal of the people of God. This renewal happens, unlike any mythical event, in a real history. The baptismal candidates do not encounter a mythical drama "that never happened but always is,"[12] but the historical figure of Jesus, the Messiah from Nazareth, his gospel, his praxis of the reign of God, his death, and his resurrection. By allowing themselves, through faith and baptism, to be incorporated into this very real history of Jesus and thus into the Church, his equally real body, they are placed on a new footing that makes it possible for them no longer to live according to the models of pagan society.

Those models, in fact, were not harmless ideas that one could choose to follow or not. Paul speaks of *sin* in connection with his baptismal theology, and not sin as the failure of an individual, but sin as a power that has spread through the world, that rules people like slaves and allows them no freedom at all.[13] It not only accosts them from without but has long since brought their whole existence—in Paul's language their "body"—under its power. Hence the radical nature of the baptismal event: "We know that our old self was crucified with him so that the body of sin might be destroyed, and we might no longer be enslaved to sin" (Rom 6:6). This text also indicates the enormity of the baptismal event. Baptism is more than mere repair; it is rescue from the power of sin, which is everywhere and perverts everything. But this process of rescue from the ruling power of sin must also be described as soberly and realistically as possible. No one can escape from his or her own self; no one can be a completely different person. Each of us has our own inherited traits, our genes, our history, the manner of behavior we acquired even as children. Each of us has our strengths and weaknesses. Nothing, or scarcely anything in all that can be changed.

---

[10] There is a good overview of the mystery religions in Hans-Josef Klauck, *Die religiöse Umwelt des Urchristentums I. Stadt- und Hausreligion, Mysterienkulte, Volksglaube.* Kohlhammer Studienbücher Theologie 9,1 (Stuttgart: Kohlhammer, 1995) 77–128.

[11] Cf. Gerhard Lohfink, "Der Ursprung der christlichen Taufe" in idem, *Studien* 173–98.

[12] Thus the late Roman author Sallust in his work *De diis et mundo* 4,9, with reference to Attis.

[13] For sin as power in Paul cf. especially Rom 5:12, 21; 6:15-23; 7:14-25.

But it is possible to experience a change in rulers. It is possible for people no longer to serve the gods of this world, but instead the true God and that God's plan for the world; it is possible for them to put at the service of God's cause the vitality and imagination that were previously engaged only for the self and its interests. It is even possible that the individual's very weaknesses may serve the building up of the community—and even guilt, when it leads to repentance, can be changed into a "happy fault."

Of course no one is capable of all that out of his or her own self. People prefer to make dreadful and expensive sacrifices to their own gods rather than to trust in the God of Israel. Even those who believe in God want to serve two masters: first the self, one's own plans and desires, and God as well, finally. That a single individual or a whole group of people can make the transition to the rule of the true God is therefore one of the greatest miracles in the world. It is never the result of heroic use of one's own powers; it never comes from oneself.

This transfer of rulership is only possible if God allows people to encounter salvation history within the world and gives them a taste of the new thing God is creating in the world. How could anyone change the direction of his or her whole life without having seen and tasted and entered into a joy that exceeds every other joy?

In fact the baptismal theology of the New Testament speaks not only of turning away from sin, not only of dying and being buried, but of resurrection to a new life. It does so cautiously and without false enthusiasm, so that the tension between "already" and "not yet" is preserved. It remains true that creation is still groaning in labor pains (Rom 8:22), that sin is still powerful in the world, and that the baptized can at any moment fall back into unbelief and deny Christ. But given all that, the New Testament says that the baptized are like "those who have been brought from death to life" (Rom 6:13), indeed that through baptism they have already been raised with Christ from the dead and in him have been seated in heaven (Eph 2:5-6).

Certainly such texts are always in danger of being read as beautiful thoughts or theological constructs. They can be understood as purely mental projections or subjective experiences of individuals. Therefore it is absolutely vital to take seriously their relationship to the people of God: dying and rising in New Testament theology mean very concretely the transition from the old society into the new form of life of "community." This is absolutely clear in Paul's writings.[14] He tells the communities in Galatia:

---

[14] Besides Gal 3:26-29 see also 1 Cor 12:12-13 (and Col 3:9-11).

. . . in Christ Jesus you are all children of God through faith. As many of you as were baptized into Christ have clothed yourselves with Christ. There is no longer Jew or Greek, there is no longer slave or free, there is no longer male and female; for all of you are one in Christ Jesus. And if you belong to Christ, then you are Abraham's offspring, heirs according to the promise. (Gal 3:26-29)

Thus through faith and baptism one belongs to Christ; one is as close to him as to a garment one puts on. The formula so frequent in Paul, "in Christ," however, does not mean merely the internal union of the baptized individual with Christ. It means belonging to a social body, namely the body of Christ, the Church. In the text just cited Paul explicitly describes the social novelty and revolutionary character of this body: in it the deep gulf between nations, classes, and genders is overcome. Because in the new family in which all are equally sons and daughters of God there need be no more national egoisms, no struggles between classes and sexes, the promise to Abraham is fulfilled and there arises in the ancient world a new thing that is fundamentally different from all ways of life in paganism.[15]

The awareness that acceptance of the faith means entry into a new creation, a new form of society, is evident not only in the Pauline letters. The whole of the ancient Church was sustained by that knowledge, and for that reason it was also aware of the great significance of baptism. Baptism was seen as a change of rulers, a turning away from the gods and demons of Gentile society and an entry into the Church as the space of Christ's lordship.

All that was very concrete: probably as early as the second century the candidates for baptism each had to produce a guarantor who would attest the sincerity of their conversion. They had to take part in a three-year baptismal catechesis that carefully educated them in Jewish-Christian discernment and the form of life demanded by faith. The ancient Church took it for granted that the Christian life of the baptismal candidates would not come of itself, but had to be learned. It was also assumed that evil is powerful and that every inch of the reign of God had to be fought for. Therefore the instruction of the catechumens and baptism itself was accompanied by symbolic actions that expressed the struggle: exorcism, anointing, imposition of hands, solemn renunciation of the *diabolos* and his works.

As a natural consequence, nothing in the life of the newly baptized could remain as it once had been. Many Gentile callings were no longer acceptable for Christians, or they had at least to consider whether such

[15] For more detail on this see Gerhard Lohfink, *Jesus and Community* (Philadelphia: Fortress, 1984) 87–98.

professions could be exercised: namely all those that brought them into contact with mythology and pagan cults. Teachers had to discuss texts containing stories of the gods, sculptors and painters had to depict the figures of gods, civil officers had to swear by the gods. Actors, gladiators, pimps, prostitutes, astrologers, and dream interpreters were only accepted as candidates for baptism if they abandoned their professions.[16]

Frowned upon also were viewing plays, gladiatorial contests, and beast spectacles, taking part in processions and parades connected with pagan cultic activities, or participating in public dinners at the imperial festivals. Even expressions like "by Hercules" were to be avoided. The list of things Christians were to avoid could go on and on. Much more important, of course, was that the newly baptized were gradually incorporated into a community in which people joined their lives together, bore one another's burdens, and acted responsibly toward and on behalf of each other. What the early Church called *agapē,* life no longer for oneself but for God and the brothers and sisters in the community, was experienced, in contrast to pagan existence, as a radical new beginning, a gift of new life.

We must of course admit that this new baptismal existence was by no means lived by all the baptized. The knowledge that death had already taken place in baptism and that therefore physical death from persecutors had no further power was certainly not so strong in all Christians that it entirely conquered the fear of death. During the persecution under Decius (250–251) the Church found that a great number of believers preferred to obey the emperor's edict and take part in the sacrifice to the gods prescribed for the whole empire, or at least to obtain *libelli* (certificates of having sacrificed) by bribery, than to demonstrate their loyalty to the faith. The distress about the true situation of the communities that then filled the Church shows, in any case, how vivid was the awareness, in that era still, that all believers as a body *should* have rejected the emperor's command.

From the third century onward there developed in the Church, along with the structuring of the catechumenate, another practice that in its own way promoted awareness of the salvation-historical significance of baptism: the night before Easter began to see a long vigil service, and baptism was incorporated into this Easter night. That was an extraordinarily fortunate development, because as a result not only did the liturgical place of baptism correspond entirely to the New Testament theology of dying and rising with Christ; at the same time it became still more obvious than it had previously been that baptism is *exodus.* For in the readings for the

---

[16] Cf. Adolf von Harnack, *The Mission and Expansion of Christianity in the First Three Centuries.* Translated and edited by James Moffatt (New York: Harper, 1962). Especially clear are the corresponding instructions in the *Apostolic Constitutions* 2.62; 8.32.

Easter night the Exodus theme of course plays a crucial role, just as it does at the Jewish Passover.

As Israel went out of Egypt, the land of slavery and unfreedom, and received at Sinai, in the Torah, a new social order that made possible freedom and equality, so the Church celebrated in the Easter night its exodus from the rulership of sin and death, and its rescue and translation into the new life in Christ. In the solemn creed and the baptism of the catechumens the assembled community experienced anew, each time, what had happened for it as a whole. In fact, Paul had already related Christian baptism to the passage of the Israelites through the Reed Sea in 1 Cor 10:1-13.

In II, 3 above I have already spoken at length about the fundamental significance of the Exodus in Israel's history. What is so astonishing is that there is an exodus at the beginning of the New Testament people of God as well. Luke does not speak of it directly,[17] but it must have happened, for the Twelve and most of Jesus' disciples were Galileans. In Jerusalem they gave themselves away with their Galilean dialect (Matt 26:73). It is easy to understand that they did not feel at home in the capital city. Nothing was more natural for them than to return to their Galilean home after Jesus was arrested, or at the latest after his execution. But the appearances of the Risen One brought them back to Jerusalem, and there the first community coalesced around the Twelve.

That, of course, meant that the Galileans had to find housing in Jerusalem, and it also meant that they had to find new employment. In many cases it even meant that they had to take up a new line of work, for there was no call for fisherfolk in Jerusalem. All this meant, ultimately, that they were dependent in many ways on the solidarity and assistance of disciples of Jesus who were already living in Jerusalem.

That the "community" form took on its New Testament shape arose, of course, out of the encounter with the Risen One, the power of his Spirit and the experience of Easter forgiveness, but we should not overlook the factor of the disciples' material needs. The situation almost forced them to bring into being what forms a community: the communal character of life in all its aspects and the mutual *agapē* that sees what others need and helps to bear the other's burdens.

Something of this new way of life in community still emerges in many passages of Acts. We learn, almost in an aside, that the mother of John Mark had opened her house to the community as a place of assembly. In connection with Peter's arrest by Agrippa I we are told that part of the

---

[17] For theological reasons Luke did not want to narrate this exodus. In order to point to the continuity between the time of Jesus and that of the Church he has the Twelve remain in Jerusalem. Cf. Luke 24:49; Acts 1:4 against Matt 28:16; Mark 16:7; John 21:1-14.

community had gathered in her house and were praying for Peter's liberation (Acts 12:12). This may have been the house with the upper room in which Jesus' disciples regularly met before Pentecost (Acts 1:13).

In another context Luke writes that "a Levite, a native of Cyprus, Joseph, to whom the apostles gave the name Barnabas (which means 'son of encouragement') . . . sold a field that belonged to him, then brought the money, and laid it at the apostles' feet" (Acts 4:36-37). We have already seen that Barnabas was one of those Diaspora Jews who had settled in the Holy Land and acquired land there in order to give public evidence of their belonging to Israel and so to receive a share in the blessings of the world to come (III, 1). After encountering the new community he sold that land to help the community. This set of actions shows that there was no communism in the Jerusalem community, as was often asserted in the past, but rather a "charismatic community of goods" in which individuals freely placed their houses or the proceeds of the sale of their property at the disposal of the community.[18]

For the very reason that many disciples of Jesus had dared the exodus to Jerusalem and left their homes they had to

> live and work *together* out of necessity, especially in the hostile atmosphere surrounding them, manage their affairs and finance their daily life and mission from the sale of landed property (such as Barnabas's field)—in order to be able to fulfill their eschatological task of building in Jerusalem the messianic community in which there could be "not a needy person among them" because otherwise "their testimony to the resurrection of the Lord Jesus" would have been diminished.[19]

The move of the Galileans from their homeland and the way Barnabas and the mother of John Mark placed their property at the community's disposal can again show what we should understand by Exodus: not a withdrawal from the world, not despising the world, no mere renunciation on ascetic grounds. The *biblical* Exodus was entirely for the purpose of the building of something new that God desires in the world. It is mobility for the sake of the gospel and God's new society. This can be illustrated by another set of events that took place twenty years later, when the Christian message had already reached Rome, Corinth, and Ephesus.

In Corinth during his so-called second missionary journey Paul met Prisca and Aquila, a Jewish couple. Both were tentmakers by trade and had their own shop. In antiquity tentmakers mainly made leather goods; tents were also made, for the most part, of leather. The emperor Claudius

---

[18] Cf. Rudolf Pesch, *Die Apostelgeschichte (Apg 1–12)*. EKK V/1 (Zürich: Benziger; Neukirchen-Vluyn: Neukirchener Verlag, 1986) 187.

[19] Ibid.

had driven Aquila and Prisca out of Rome, together with many other Jews. When Paul met them they were already Christians. They took him into their family in Corinth, where at first Paul worked with them in their business and also used their house and shop as the base for his missionary work (Acts 18:1-5).

Prisca and Aquila, with their family and their tent-and-leather-goods business, were of very great importance for the Pauline mission. After many months of fruitful cooperation with Paul in Corinth they moved to Ephesus, probably not least in order to secure a solid base for Paul in Asia Minor (Acts 18:18-19). In Ephesus, too, Paul would have lived and worked in their house as he needed to. It was at the same time the gathering-place for the community in Ephesus, or at least part of it. We know that from 1 Corinthians, at the end of which Paul sends the community in Corinth warm greetings from "Aquila and Prisca, together with the church in their house" (1 Cor 16:19). In Ephesus during a period when Paul was absent a highly gifted Jew from Alexandria named Apollos met Prisca and Aquila. They took him into their household as well and instructed him in the way that salvation history had taken (Acts 18:24-28).

Years later when Paul wrote his letter to the Romans as preparation for a missionary journey to Spain he asked the Roman community to give special greetings to Prisca and Aquila:

> Greet Prisca and Aquila, who work with me in Christ Jesus, and who risked their necks for my life, to whom not only I give thanks, but also all the churches of the Gentiles. Greet also the church in their house. (Rom 16:3-5)

This request shows that Prisca and Aquila had meanwhile returned to Rome, where they originally had their business. In Rome, as elsewhere, there was a Christian community in their house. That would have been in part their own extended family, but also Roman Christians who regularly gathered there.

Thus the household of Prisca and Aquila offers us a visible image of the "new family": here is a "natural" family that does not live for its own sake but places its house entirely at the disposal of the gospel. That house becomes a *base* for Paul's mission, first in Greece and then in Asia Minor, and probably the subsequent return to Rome was meant to furnish a base for Paul's intended journey to Spain. At the same time it becomes the crystallization point for new communities that grow up around this household. There they find the necessary place for their gatherings, but much more than that: they find a couple who have placed themselves, too, entirely at the service of the gospel. They instruct Apollos, and certainly many others, in the faith. They stick out their necks for Paul in Ephesus. All Gentile Christian communities owe them thanks, as Paul says.

In the early days of the Church the beginning of new communities always depended on whether there were families like that of Prisca and Aquila who were prepared to move to other cities for the sake of the gospel and there, with their families, to become the starting-point for a new community. Not only baptism itself, then, was an exodus. The life of these Christians became a continual exodus for the sake of the building up of the Church.

Since then there has always been an exodus going on in the Church. It was part of the existence of countless missionaries who left their homelands to make the gospel of Jesus Christ known in other lands, in the lives of all those who left their families to live the evangelical counsels in monastic communities and religious houses, in the lives of Catholic priests who renounced marriage and family in order to make visible in symbol something of the eschatological existence of all the baptized.

This manifold exodus was by no means intended to be a flight from the world; its aim was always to recover the complete form of following Jesus: table community, the common life of the "new family." The flight of early Christian ascetics into the desert received its "Christian form" only in those men and women who created a new kind of community of life out of the ascetic movement. All this is quite obvious in the Western monasteries: they were almost always a bit of new society, new culture, transformed world, and their influence reached far beyond their walls. Many monasteries that began as new foundations in wild places developed into successful business enterprises and shaped an entire cultural landscape.

It is true that the monasteries and their special role in the history of the West also indicate a certain loss: they indeed regarded themselves as monastic "families," but they consisted only of men or women. For married people there was, at least in the Catholic Church, for many centuries no opportunity to follow Christ in a biblically constituted way of life. Certainly there were countless mothers and fathers who lived their own exodus, for the most part in silence and hiddenness, in the form of neighborly love that very often meant the sacrifice of their own lives. But all too often the help of a Christian community was denied them.

It is a striking indicator of the situation that it was precisely at the time when the communities of the ancient Church lost their splendor and began to take on their later shape within the imperial Church that the hermits and monks began to appear. Thus the monasteries did indeed carry on the exodus character of the Church and were a blessing for the whole, but by that very fact they also contributed to the circumstance that the way of discipleship lost its community structure and thereby its openness to all the baptized.

The monasteries and charitable works became "representatives" of the Exodus. The parishes of the Middle Ages and the modern era were scarcely touched by the idea of New Testament community. Probably the guilds and brotherhoods offered more in the way of a Christian form of life than did the parishes. Later the Christian clubs and societies replaced the medieval community forms. All this had less and less to do with "exodus." Today the parishes, at least in Europe, have scarcely any power to resist the pagan models of the surrounding society. Pastoral care is more and more specialized toward the "edges" of life. Faith has become private and modest. The Exodus texts are still read in the Easter night, but less and less are they lived.

In spite of all this the history of the Church should not be read as one of decline, as if it had slowly but surely degenerated, especially since the Constantinian shift. The development toward an imperial Church and finally toward a state religion was almost a matter of necessity, given the constellation of late antiquity. Perhaps the Church had to take that road. It was a grandiose attempt to create a Christian "empire" and thus to unite faith, life, and culture.

Only a careful look at the people of God in the Old Testament, their experiment with the state and the collapse of the experiment, could have preserved the Church from repeating the old mistake. But it was not possible in late antiquity or in the Middle Ages for people to read the Old Testament so analytically. Political theology was, instead, enraptured with David and Solomon. Only the history of the modern era shattered the dream.

Today the experiment is truly at an end and can never be resumed, for it left people no chance to make a free decision for faith. And what it hoped for—the solid unity of faith and life, gospel and everyday, has a much better basis in the community Church, the form that emerged from the Jewish synagogue.

Meanwhile the Church is living almost everywhere in the world subject again to persecutions in the midst of a new paganism. It will only survive in that situation if it returns to communities constituted according to the New Testament, not in a false romanticism of the primitive Church but under the conditions of the third millennium. The word "return" is not really the right one in this context. What is wanted is a new dawn, but now with much better knowledge drawn from history.

We know today that as long as the faith was not the state religion (and later civil religion) the Christian communities through their very existence had an enlightening and even a "de-idolizing" effect. The critical probe of their faith affected everything. They claimed to be forming an opinion of their own, and still more, to be developing their own way of life. This touched attitudes toward life and death, eating and fasting, wealth and poverty, festivals and daily life, but also toward power, even the fundamentals of the *polis* and the empire. They constantly drew the distinction: to whom loyalty is owed, loyalty is given. To whom resistance is due, resistance is given, if necessary even to the point of martyrdom.[20] A Church that dares a new exodus in this sense need have no fear of the future.

## 2. The Church Gathers

Gathering, like exodus, is a fundamental feature of the Church. This is obvious from its very name. The new community in Jerusalem must have called itself the *ekklēsia* of God. Whether it was first the Hellenists in the community who did so or the "Hebrews," the Aramaic-speaking group— in their case it would have been *qāhāl* or *qᵉhālāʾ*—can remain an open question. In any case Paul, in 1 Cor 15:9 and Gal 1:13, speaks of God's *ekklēsia*, which he had persecuted:[21] "You have heard, no doubt, of my earlier life in Judaism. I was violently persecuting the church of God, and was trying to destroy it" (Gal 1:13).

But what is the *ekklēsia* of God? In Greek the *ekklēsia* is the assembly of the people, the coming together of all those with citizen rights in a given city. When the community in Jerusalem adopted this term of civil law from the life of the *polis,* the city-state, for themselves they asserted an extraordinary claim. They thus indicated that they did not see themselves as a group of like-minded friends and also not as a group of people who had joined together because of particular interests; they were a gathering created by God, one that was "public" and had an interest in all things.

Accordingly in the time that followed the Church deliberately avoided applying the manifold terminology of ancient guilds and societies to itself. The Christian community was not a *thiasos* or an *eranos* or a *koinon* or a *collegium.*[22] It was not a segment or part of a larger whole. Concretely it was not a group, or a faction, or a club, nor was it a sect. It was rather "a public assembly of the whole."[23]

---

[20] This paragraph owes much to a lecture by Arnold Stötzel at the Villa Cavalletti, 21 October 1995.

[21] Cf. also 1 Thess 2:14; Phil 3:6; Acts 8:3.

[22] Cf. Wolfgang Schrage, *synagōgē, ktl., TDNT* 7:798–852, at 829.

[23] Joseph Ratzinger, *Principles of Catholic Theology: Building Stones For a Fundamental Theology.* Translated by Mary Frances McCarthy (San Francisco: Ignatius Press, 1987) 253: "The social structure in which the Church exists is not a club, not a circle of friends, but the 'people of God' in contrast to the people of the [world]—for which reason the Eucharist is not a private celebration for special groups; it continues to be Eucharist only when it is a public assembly of the whole . . . ."

But what is this "whole"? Naturally it is not the city, and certainly not the Roman state. The "whole" is the people of God. The word *ekklēsia,* in fact, reveals something more. As a description of the Church it was certainly not derived directly from the popular assembly of the hellenistic cities. This public discourse is only part of the context. The real origin of "*ekklēsia* of God" is the Old Testament and the Jewish traditions of speech that derived from it. Ultimately *ekklēsia* points to the people of God gathered at Sinai.

In the book of Deuteronomy the day when Israel in its full number was gathered around the mountain of Horeb (= Sinai) and received the Ten Commandments "out of the fire, the cloud, and the thick darkness" (Deut 5:22) was described by a fixed formula. It was called "the day of the assembly" *(yôm haqqāhāl* or *hēmera tēs ekklēsias),*[24] for it was at Sinai, as the book of Deuteronomy sees it, that the foundational assembly of Israel took place, the event that constituted Israel as a people. When the new community in Jerusalem took up the concept of the *ekklēsia,* then, it was thus showing that it understood itself as the eschatological fulfillment of that gathering at Sinai.[25]

It may be that this self-description was already in place on that first Pentecost that, according to Luke's presentation, was the occasion of the Church's foundation.[26] Pentecost, after all, was the Jewish "Feast of Weeks," and at that festival, originally nothing more than a harvest thanksgiving, in New Testament times it was already customary to celebrate the making-present of the Sinai event.[27]

[24] Deut 9:10: "on [the tablets] were all the words that the LORD had spoken to you at the mountain out of the fire on the day of the assembly." Similarly Deut 10:4; 18:16.

[25] In the War Scroll from Qumran (1QM 4, 10) we have the first direct witness to the expression *qᵉhal ʾēl,* the Hebrew equivalent of *ekklēsia tou theou.* Something similar, however, is found in Neh 13:1 (= 2 Ezra 23:1 LXX), differing from Deut 23:4. *Qᵉhal ʾēl* in 1QM 4, 10 refers to God's eschatological troops assembled for battle. But because of Neh 13:1 it would be too hasty to posit a specific dependence of primitive Christian terminology on the War Scroll. Besides, 1QM 4, 10 refers also to Deuteronomy (cf. Deut 23:2-9) and confirms the supposition that *ekklēsia tou theou* refers to the representation of the eschatological Israel.

[26] It is true that in Luke's account this foundational character does not belong to Pentecost alone; rather, Pentecost is one in a whole series of orders and events that found the Church. Cf. Gerhard Lohfink, *Die Sammlung Israels. Eine Untersuchung zur lukanischen Ekklesiologie.* StANT 39 (Munich: Kösel, 1975) 93–99.

[27] (1) An important indication of the salvation-historical overlay of the Sinai event on the ancient harvest festival is the time designation in Exod 19:1: "On the third new moon after the Israelites had gone out of the land of Egypt . . . ." (2) In 2 Chronicles 15 it is reported that a renewal of the covenant was begun under King Asa in Jerusalem *in the third month* (cf. 2 Chron 15:9-15). (3) The book of *Jubilees* (second century B.C.E.) presumes that its community celebrates an annual renewal of the covenant at the Feast of Weeks. Cf. *Jub.*

Still, whatever may have been the case with Pentecost the word *ekklēsia* reveals that the Church did not regard itself as a *new* people appearing in the stead of the old people of God, having dissolved and replaced it, but as *Israel,* or more precisely as the beginning and center of growth for the eschatological Israel. In this point as well the post-Easter community continued what Jesus had begun.

The word *ekklēsia* reveals still more. We saw that this concept always incorporates the image of a concrete assembly: that of the people at Sinai or that of those who had civil rights in the ancient city. That means, however, that the Church lives through and in its concrete gatherings. They are the fulfillment of its existence. The Church is present in them. In them is most clearly evident what the Church is and what God desires of it. Joseph Ratzinger put it this way: "The real *locus* of the Church is not some kind of bureaucracy or the activity of a group that considers itself 'basic,' but a 'coming together'"—that is, the assembly in which the whole community comes together or is at least represented, and in which the union with the whole Church is preserved.[28]

In his second book Luke repeatedly depicts the Church's manner of existence in the form of concrete assemblies. At the beginning of Acts, immediately after telling of Jesus' departure, he paints a picture typifying what *ekklēsia* is:

> Then they returned to Jerusalem from the mount called Olivet, which is near Jerusalem, a sabbath day's journey away. When they had entered the city, they went to the room upstairs where they were staying, Peter, and John, and James, and Andrew, Philip and Thomas, Bartholomew and Matthew, James son of Alphaeus, and Simon the Zealot, and Judas son of James. All these were constantly devoting themselves to prayer, together with certain women, including Mary the mother of Jesus, as well as his brothers. (Acts 1:12-14)

This picture is so vivid that it was repeatedly painted in later centuries in connection with the Pentecost event and has brought forth an impressive iconographic tradition. Of course Luke did not intend this picture as a photographic snapshot of a single instant; in it he collected and concentrated the manifold experiences of the early Church. Nor does he show us a *model* that can simply be imitated; rather what he paints is a *archetype* comparable to the image of the Exodus that the Old Testament presents to our gaze. Arche-

---

6:1, 11, 17 (!), 20-21. (4) The Pentecost account in Acts 2:1-13 is clearly imbued with motifs from the Jewish Sinai *haggadah.* Cf. the compact summary in Rudolf Pesch, *Apostelgeschichte* 1:102. For all these reasons we may suppose that as early as the time of Jesus, at least in one part of Judaism, there was a celebration of the Sinai event at the Feast of Weeks.

[28] Joseph Ratzinger, *Principles of Catholic Theology* 252.

types have their own effectiveness. The biblical Exodus cannot be imitated in a superficial manner and yet the Exodus texts have deeply influenced the history of God's people until the present time and have continually taken on new life within that history. The same is true of Luke's texts. But what does this "picture" of the *ekklēsia* at the beginning of Acts show us?

To begin with, it shows a continuing assembly extending, we might say, from the day of the Ascension until the day of Pentecost. Obviously Luke does not mean that Jesus' disciples never separated from one another, but rather that their life had become a constant and continually renewed act of assembly.[29]

They assemble not in disparate groups but all in the same place, the same room. That, too, is important to Luke. He knows about a "room upstairs," and a little later, at the beginning of the Pentecost account, he will say that "they were all together in one place" (2:1). He takes up this "in one place" *(epi to auto)* again in 2:44, 47. The expression became in the early Church, especially in the letters of Ignatius of Antioch, a fixed expression to represent the idea that a community must not split into different assemblies.[30] The *one* place is important. It shows the unity of the *ekklēsia*.

The Twelve had assembled, a number completed by the selection of Matthias in the immediately succeeding account in Acts 1:15-26. The full complement of apostles is important because on the day of Pentecost they are to appear before Israel as the beginning of the eschatological twelve-tribe people of Israel. The Twelve are the center of the assembly, the center of the *ekklēsia*. Their names are listed individually, with Peter at the head of the list, since the cause of Jesus for which they are the public witnesses can only be handed on face to face, from person to person (Acts 1:21-22). God has built the Church of God not on principles, but on people.

But not only are the Twelve gathered; there are many others, to a total of 120. This number is mentioned by Luke immediately after 1:14. Obviously it points to the twelve tribes and the twelve apostles, but at the same time it probably expresses the experience that a community should not contain more than 120 people.[31] Only at that size can it remain a concrete

---

[29] "Where they constantly remained" (*hou ēsan katamenontes,* Acts 1:13) is an obedient response to the command of the Risen One to "stay here in the city" (Luke 24:49; cf. Acts 1:4) and therefore means more than simply "where they were staying" *(NRSV, NAB).*

[30] Cf. also Acts 1:15; 2:1, 44, 47. Paul already used the expression for the community assembly. Cf. 1 Cor 11:20; 14:23. It then becomes stereotypical for the Apostolic Fathers. Cf. *1 Clem.* 34.7; *Barn.* 4.10; Ign. *Eph.* 5.3; Ign. *Magn.* 7.1; Ign. *Phld.* 6.2; 10.1. See also Justin, *Apol. 1,* 67.3.

[31] The large numbers in Acts 2:41; 4:4; 21:20 have a different function. They are meant to show not the ideal size of a community (as in 1:15), but the constant growth of the *ekklēsia*.

assembly in which no one is invisible, in which each member can be aware of the sorrow and happiness, the cares and the joys of the others. How could it be possible to share responsibility for the faith of the others in a huge community with hundreds of baptized persons? The figure of 120 is the upper limit if a community is not to become an anonymous cultic society but remain a community of common life struggling to fulfill its prophetic calling.

After listing the names of the Twelve Luke speaks immediately of the women, including Mary, the mother of Jesus. He is apparently thinking first of all of the women who followed Jesus from Galilee and supported his cause out of their own means (Luke 8:1-3). Why do the women come immediately after the apostles? Apparently Luke wants to prevent anyone from misunderstanding the archetype of the *ekklēsia* he is presenting as a purely male Church. Later iconography reinforced his depiction when it showed Mary seated in the center of the assembly with the twelve apostles to her right and left.[32] In this way Mary herself becomes an image of the *ekklēsia,* the real symbol of faithful listening and receiving.

After Mary and the other women Luke mentions a third group: Jesus' relatives. They are also now present even though it was not long since that Jesus had to put distance between himself and them (Luke 8:19-21). But Jesus' death and resurrection had changed everything. God's eschatological creation is beginning, and in it the natural family also becomes part of the new family of the *ekklēsia.*

But with all this we still have not touched the crucial point. The nature of this assembly must still be defined: all of them, the Twelve, the women, Mary and Jesus' brothers "were constantly devoting themselves to prayer." They were praying for the Holy Spirit who was to descend on the assembly on the day of Pentecost.

The fundamental expression of the Church is thus not simply the assembly. There are countless assemblies in the world. The Church's expression of its existence happens in every assembly that is entirely an attentive plea for the coming of the Spirit because it knows that of itself it is completely helpless. In that it differs from the many assemblies in the larger society, its parliaments, councils, committees, commissions, and councils, as bitterly necessary as all of them are. Among the Church's most precious possessions is the knowledge that of itself it is incapable of bringing about even something *resembling* a community, and that when it attempts to do so in spite of that knowledge the effort yields nothing but

---

[32] This picture is found as early as the Rabbula Gospel Book, a Syriac manuscript from the year 586 (Florence, Biblioteca Laurenziana). Cf. P. Sevrugian, "Pfingsten V. Ikonographisch," *TRE* 26:395–98, with illustrations.

dead-end rivalries. The assembly of the *ekklēsia* thus has a center that sustains everything and that it cannot make of itself. It is a gift: the Spirit of Jesus. Only from this center can it find unanimity, and that unanimity is then its entire strength.

That is the image Luke presents at the beginning of his second book, based on individual reports and narratives, but especially on his own experience of church. It is not limited to Acts 1:14. Luke expands the picture, telling history through stories, and he continues to present in new imagery the archetype of the Church that he set forth at the beginning. Immediately after the events of the day of Pentecost he gives his first summary:

> Awe came upon everyone, because many wonders and signs were being done by the apostles. All who believed were together and had all things in common; they would sell their possessions and goods and distribute the proceeds to all, as any had need. Day by day, as they spent much time together in the temple, they broke bread at home and ate their food with glad and generous hearts, praising God and having the goodwill of all the people. And day by day the Lord added to their number those who were being saved. (Acts 2:43-47)

The "awe" that seized everyone is not only a reaction to the wonders and signs that were being done through the apostles. It must have originated from the Pentecost event itself. Here again we see the connection between the event at Sinai and that on the day of Pentecost, for the awe that seizes the whole people is characteristic of the "day of the assembly" at Sinai.[33]

In addition Luke shows here too that the *ekklēsia* is a continual assembly. Those who come to believe do not join a club or organization, but are added to an "assembly."[34] Thereby are they "saved." That means not only eternal life but also and primarily the rescue, the salvation, the peace they already receive. They live, indeed, in a new bond of togetherness in which each has everything he or she needs because all give everything they have.

The notion that salvation only comes to believers after death, which later fastened itself on the minds of many Christians, does not correspond to the Church's faith and certainly not to the ideas of the early Church. Those who love their sisters and brothers have already passed from death to life (1 John 3:14). The border between life and death, the real threshold, is no longer physical death, but the dying that takes place in baptism. In our text this eschatological consciousness is indicated in the "gladness" or "jubilation" by which Luke refers to the eschatological joy of the *ekklēsia*,

---

[33] Cf. Exod 20:18, 20; Deut 5:5.

[34] This must be the meaning of *epi to auto* in 2:47. The meaning must be derived in light of 2:44.

which in celebrating the breaking of bread is already sharing in heavenly joy. The "already now" is also visible, however, in the "wonders and signs" being done through the apostles. The fact that now, as formerly with Jesus, salvation and rescue are being made present in the healing of the sick is a sign of the messianic end time.

The believers are a single assembly even though the place of their assembling changes. They meet in the Temple to praise God publicly. This shows their claim to be the eschatological Israel. But they can also meet in a private house to celebrate the Lord's Supper. Again the unanimity of their assembly is emphasized.

Following this summary Luke tells how Peter heals a lame man at one of the gates of the Temple and then interprets the healing in Solomon's Portico as the work of God, who through this miracle has justified and glorified the crucified Jesus. As a result Peter and his companion, John, are arrested and the next day are brought before the Sanhedrin, who forbid them ever again to preach and teach in the name of Jesus. After their release they go immediately to "their own," a word Luke here uses for the community as the "new family":

> After they were released, they went to their friends [Greek: their own] and reported what the chief priests and the elders had said to them. When they heard it, they raised their voices together to God and said, "Sovereign Lord, who made the heaven and the earth, the sea, and everything in them, it is you who said by the Holy Spirit through our ancestor David, your servant:
>
>> 'Why did the Gentiles rage,
>>     and the peoples imagine vain things?
>> The kings of the earth took their stand,
>>     and the rulers have gathered together
>>     against the Lord and against his Messiah.'
>
> For in this city, in fact, both Herod and Pontius Pilate, with the Gentiles and the peoples of Israel, gathered together against your holy servant Jesus, whom you anointed, to do whatever your hand and your plan had predestined to take place. And now, Lord, look at their threats, and grant to your servants to speak your word with all boldness, while you stretch out your hand to heal, and signs and wonders are performed through the name of your holy servant Jesus." When they had prayed the place in which they were gathered together was shaken; and they were all filled with the Holy Spirit and spoke the word of God with boldness. (Acts 4:23-31)

There is prayer in this assembly also, just as Acts 1:14 had foretold. But now a concrete example makes it clear how Luke imagines prayer. It is not a timeless, situationless, ahistorical prayer, so general and universally applicable that it can be repeated at will. No, for Luke prayer is always new because its locus is the ongoing history of the community. In Acts 4:23-31 the assembly's prayer responds in every detail to the report of Peter and John.

The community is, after all, faced with the question of its own existence. It could obey the Sanhedrin, which had just succeeded in having Jesus executed, and dissolve itself. Or it could go underground and continue its life there. Finally, it could oppose the decision of the Sanhedrin publicly, go on working as it had before, and thus risk its life. It must therefore interpret what has come upon it in this hour and seek to recognize the will of God.[35]

That interpretation takes place in prayer. But that means that even the interpretation of the immediate situation is something that the community cannot do of its own accord. That interpretation is only possible in prayer, and that means opening itself to God, looking at what has happened and simultaneously listening to Scripture.

What has happened? When Jesus was executed there was a scarcely credible coalition in Jerusalem, one might say a counter-assembly against God and God's Messiah. Herod and Pontius Pilate had joined together against Jesus, along with the Gentiles and the tribes of Israel. But inasmuch as Israel had joined itself to the Gentiles it had become like them, and therefore Psalm 2, which speaks of the revolt of the nations against God and God's Anointed, must also be applied to that portion of Israel. The Sanhedrin does not appear to be expressly mentioned, but that is only appearance; for Luke Psalm 2 had already referred to them: "rulers" *(archontes)* is his regular expression for the members of the Sanhedrin.[36] Psalm 2 therefore illuminates the whole situation in detail; thus the first step toward interpretation has been taken.

The second step consists in the community's placing itself alongside Jesus, again through listening to Scripture. The powerful of the earth have not only assembled themselves against Jesus, the servant of God, but in exactly the same way against the *ekklēsia,* which thus also becomes God's servant (cf. Acts 4:29).

With this a theologically clear interpretation of the events, and one with the most serious political consequences, is completed: The Sanhedrin, the highest religious instance in Israel, is acting not in God's name, but against God. When the High Priests threaten the community it is nothing but the empty and fruitless "raging of the Gentiles" in Psalm 2.

[35] For more detail on this subject see Gerhard Lohfink, *The Work of God Goes On.* Translated by Linda M. Maloney (Philadelphia: Fortress, 1987) 30–35.

[36] Cf. Luke 18:18; 23:13, 35; 24:20; Acts 3:17; 4:5 (!), 8.

Therefore the prayer can now come to its conclusion. The assembly asks God to act and to accomplish the divine plan and judgment, resting on the power of God as creator alluded to at the very beginning of the prayer. This is a prayer for courage and thereby also a prayer for the Holy Spirit.

We can see how concretely and situationally this assembly prays. It lives out of an intensive theology of history. It interprets its own situation in terms of God's earlier words and deeds and joins its destiny to that of Jesus. In doing so it dares to apply Scripture directly to its here and now. In Acts 4:23-31 Luke seeks to make clear that the critical examination of its own situation and the search for the present will of God on the basis of biblical theology of history are component aspects of the assemblies of the *ekklēsia.*

As the assembly concludes its prayer the place where it is gathered is shaken, and all are filled with the Holy Spirit and with courage. Their prayer has already been heard! That is attested by the shaking of the earth. At the same time it expresses the enormous power of the prayer of a community assembled in *unanimity.* It moves mountains (cf. Mark 11:22-24).

The assembly in Acts 4:23-31 marks a turning point in the history of the community: for the first time the young Church has encountered the resistance of the Jewish authorities. Hence the first section of Acts also ends with this assembly. The next section (4:32–5:42) sharpens the picture of the mutual closeness of the Jerusalem community but also shows how the conflict with the Sanhedrin is exacerbated. Luke begins this new section with a second summary, after which he tells the story of Ananias and Sapphira, inserts a third summary, and finally reports another arrest of the apostles. Again they are forbidden to preach in the name of Jesus, and again they prefer to obey God rather than human beings. They preach the gospel of Jesus the Messiah openly (5:42).

At this point there is a deeper caesura in the narrative structure of Acts, again marked by an extensive account of a community assembly. The community has grown larger; the fascination that emanates from it is continually bringing in new people. Is the fact that strife and rivalry erupt connected with this growth?

> Now during those days, when the disciples were increasing in number, the Hellenists grumbled against the Hebrews because their widows were being neglected in the daily distribution of food. (Acts 6:1*)

We need not go into the historical questions raised by Acts 6:1-7. It is important for our discussion only to observe how Luke depicts the origins and course of an assembly.

First he describes the conflict, the depth of which he by no means minimizes, for he speaks of "grumbling" in the community. He is convinced, then, that the faithless grumbling of the people of God during its time in the desert is repeating itself. As before, so here again it is a question of food. To resolve the conflict the Twelve take the initiative, for they are especially responsible for the unanimity of the community:

> And the twelve called together the whole community of the disciples and said, "It is not right that we should neglect the word of God in order to wait on tables. Therefore, friends, select from among yourselves seven men of good standing, full of the Spirit and of wisdom, whom we may appoint to this task, while we, for our part, will devote ourselves to prayer and to serving the word." What they said pleased the whole community, and they chose Stephen, a man full of faith and the Holy Spirit, together with Philip, Prochorus, Nicanor, Timon, Parmenas, and Nicolaus, a proselyte of Antioch. (Acts 6:2-5)

The Twelve call "the whole community of the disciples" together. In Luke's intention we are to suppose that to begin with there was discussion of the conflict in all its aspects. Then the apostles make a suggestion, namely that the responsible members of the community should be more clearly designated—we might say that the structure of the community should be more refined. The community is obliged to attract more people in order that the eschatological Israel may be gathered. But it is also the community's task to live as God's just society in which there are no longer any poor people. In future the community's task of proclamation is to be undertaken primarily by the Twelve, while care for the messianic social form of the Church will be the task of the Seven.

The suggestion made by the Twelve receives the assent of the whole assembly. No vote is taken; the community must make its decision by consensus. If there were no unanimity the decision would have to be postponed. The assembly chooses, probably from a larger number of proven men, seven—very likely by casting lots, as Luke depicted the choice of Matthias in Acts 1:23-26.[37] After their election the Seven are installed in office through prayer and the laying on of hands. The concluding note that Luke adds, its language reflecting Exod 1:7, is important. It shows that the renewed growth of the community is also a consequence of the newly discovered structure: "The word of God continued to spread; the number of the disciples increased greatly in Jerusalem, and a great many of the priests became obedient to the faith" (Acts 6:7).

The next depiction of an assembly is again found at a turning point in the history of the community: the persecution of the *ekklēsia* that breaks

---

[37] For this procedure see Gerhard Lohfink, "Der Losvorgang in Apg 1,26," in idem, *Studien* 169–71.

out after the choice of the Seven has the opposite result from what had been intended: the Church expands in daughter communities throughout all Judea and Samaria and even as far as Antioch. From Antioch, then, begins the expansion of the gospel to Asia Minor and Greece, as depicted in Acts through the story of Paul's missionary journeys. This triumphal march of the gospel throughout the Mediterranean basin, the growth of the Church by leaps and bounds, something no one could have imagined at the outset, begins with a modest assembly. No one could have suspected what it would set in motion:

> Now in the church at Antioch there were prophets and teachers: Barnabas, Simeon who was called Niger, Lucius of Cyrene, Manaen a member of the court of Herod the ruler, and Saul. While they were worshiping the Lord and fasting, the Holy Spirit said, "Set apart for me Barnabas and Saul for the work to which I have called them." Then after fasting and praying they laid their hands on them and sent them off. (Acts 13:1-3)

Luke is here making use of old traditions from the Antioch community. Prophets and teachers still play an important role there. In an assembly the Holy Spirit "says" that Barnabas and Saul should be sent out to do missionary work. The text appears to leave many things in the air. Does it mean that only the prophets and teachers were assembled, or the whole community? Did this "worshiping the Lord"—which probably refers to one or more gatherings for prayer—extend over a long period of time, or does Luke envision only a single worship service? But especially: were their discussions about the community's missionary work, and was their result described as the "speaking" of the Holy Spirit, or does the text refer to a genuine prophetic speech?

Against the background of biblical prophecy we should most probably reckon with a brief, charismatic prophetic speech confirmed by the rest of the assembly. From the point of procedure alone, of course, there are many ways in which God can speak. In biblical times dreams and visions, hearing, and prophetic reception of the word were extraordinarily important. Today none of this plays much of a role in the Church except in marginal groups. In its place, as in modern society generally, we have group discussions and consultations. The cultural form of faithful attainment to insight alters in every age, and God can make use of any form for self-revelation.

Nevertheless, in living communities formed by the New Testament even today it happens that in their assemblies a word may come like a bolt of lightning to reveal the situation of those assembled, to clarify matters, or to indicate how to move toward the future. There are prophets today also, namely people who believe with their whole existence and to whom

God has given the gift of discernment. Prophecy is not just seeing the future (prognosis), but first of all and primarily discernment (diagnosis).

It continually happens that those with the gift of discernment see the true situation of Church and world. They uncover false images that individuals or the whole community have of themselves. They see the world in the laser beam of the gospel. They recognize what concrete actions are to be taken. In taking such people and their prophetic charism seriously a community formed by the New Testament is different from all the assemblies in our society, in which endless opinions collide because one's own position or that of one's own group is unconditionally defended.

However the assembly described in Acts 13:1-3 was imagined by the narrator, we must take seriously the theological statement that in it the Holy Spirit spoke. It seems certain as well that at least at the end of the events described, when Barnabas and Saul were solemnly sent forth, the whole community is thought to be present, for when the missionaries return from their work in Cyprus and Asia Minor the whole community is summoned together:

> From there (Attalia in Asia Minor) they sailed back to Antioch, where they had been commended to the grace of God for the work that they had completed. When they arrived, they called the church together and related all that God had done with them, and how he had opened a door of faith for the Gentiles. (Acts 14:26-27)

Together with what has been said Acts 13:1-3 makes clear that at that time the founding of new communities was not the affair of a Church administration with universal oversight, but the task of the communities themselves. Then, of course, they were obligated to remain in constant contact with their daughter communities, to strengthen them and to help them in need or when there was conflict.

If the conflicts became too great it could well be that one would have to call on the mother of all communities, Jerusalem, for help. Luke describes such a case, by way of example, in Acts 15:1-35. This is the last major community gathering that he depicts.[38] This assembly also marks for him a turning point in the history of the *ekklēsia*. It is brought about by a conflict that at the time threatened to split the whole Church. The question was whether the Gentiles who were crowding into the Church were required (in the case of men) to be circumcised before their reception into the eschatological Israel, whether Gentiles were bound to observe

---

[38] Cf. possibly also Acts 20:7-12. At the gatherings in Acts 20:17-38 and 21:18-25 only the elders of the communities of Ephesus and Jerusalem are present.

the whole Torah or not—a question that was more and more urgent in light of the intensive mission of the Antiochene community.

Here again we cannot occupy ourselves with historical inquiries and reconstructions, as worthwhile as they are. We will concentrate solely on the line of Luke's depiction, because Luke not only intends to show what happened at that time, but also and primarily how conflicts of that sort can be dealt with in the Church.

First of all we should say that the name "apostolic council" is not quite accurate. What Luke describes is an assembly of the Jerusalem community in which a delegation from Antioch, including Barnabas and Paul, takes part. It is true that we read in 15:6 that "the apostles and the elders met together to consider this matter," but the elders are members of the Jerusalem community, and before this the Antiochene delegation had been received by the whole community:

> When they came to Jerusalem, they were welcomed by the church and the apostles and the elders, and they reported all that God had done with them. (Acts 15:4)

Later, after agreement was reached, we read:

> Then the apostles and the elders, with the consent of the whole church, decided to choose men from among their members and to send them to Antioch with Paul and Barnabas. They sent Judas called Barsabbas, and Silas, leaders among the brothers. (Acts 15:22)

Thus it is clear that Luke intends to describe an assembly of the entire community, while at the same time emphasizing the official function of the apostles and elders.

We also see that, as in Acts 6:1-7, Luke shows no interest in concealing the depth of the conflict. It began when people from Judea (on their own initiative?) arrived in Antioch and demanded that the newly-converted Gentile men be circumcised. Luke writes that their coming caused "no small dissension and debate" (15:1-2). The community assembly in Jerusalem also begins with bitter conflict (15:7), but at the end the assembly arrives at unanimity, so that a delegation can be sent to Antioch with a letter containing the following formula of agreement: The Gentile Christian men need not be circumcised, but all the converts should hold to the things that, according to Lev 17:10-14, were to be asked of every foreigner living in Israel, namely to eat no meat from strangled animals and no food containing blood. In addition they were to eat no meat that had been offered to idols and make no marriage within the degrees of affinity prohibited to Jews (Acts 15:29). But how was this understanding and the consequent unanimity reached?

The first step toward agreement consists in Peter's speaking. He says in essence that God has already acted and thus decided the matter. With this statement Peter recalls the conversion of the Roman centurion Cornelius and his household (Acts 10). That was, of course, an individual case, but through it God's will was revealed. The Holy Spirit descended on Cornelius and his household just as on the assembly gathered at Pentecost. Whoever believes and has received the Spirit is no longer unclean, but clean. Thus God has already decided, and all that remains is for the community to accept this divine decision in obedience.

When Peter finishes his speech the assembly is silent (15:12). One should not overlook this brief sentence. Where does it happen in our society that a whole assembly debating difficult questions is suddenly silent? The silence of the community is its assent to what Peter has said, but also a silent bow to what seems very probably to be the will of God.

After Peter's speech Barnabas and Paul are also in a position to report to the assembly about the signs and wonders God has done among the Gentiles through their preaching. Their argumentation is on the same plane as Peter's: they point to things that have already taken place. God speaks through events. It is only necessary to look at them carefully and with the eyes of faith.

Then James begins to speak. He argues on a different level, but one equally necessary: James considers the disputed question in light of Sacred Scripture:

"My brothers, listen to me. Simeon has related how God first looked favorably on the Gentiles, to take from among them a people for his name. This agrees with the words of the prophets, as it is written:

'After this I will return,
and I will rebuild the dwelling of David, which has fallen;
   from its ruins I will rebuild it, and I will set it up,
so that all other peoples may seek the Lord—
   even all the Gentiles over whom my name has been called.
   Thus says the Lord, who has been making these things
      known from long ago.'

Therefore I have reached the decision that we should not trouble those Gentiles who are turning to God . . . ." (Acts 15:14-19)

This set of quotations from the prophets—a combination of Amos 9:11-12 with Isa 45:21—is meant to show that first Israel, "the dwelling of David, which has fallen," must be restored. That has happened in the post-Easter community, or at least it has begun, and therefore the Gentiles may now be added. James also adduces the pilgrimage of the nations that is promised in Scripture (cf. I, 4 above). The crucial point here is that Israel itself must first become the shining city in order that the nations may set out on the way toward it.[39] For James that pilgrimage of the nations has already begun, and therefore no one may restrain the Gentiles who are streaming toward the eschatological Israel. But such a restraint would exist if Gentile men were required to undergo circumcision.[40]

James's speech brings about the final agreement. In Luke's mind this was probably abetted by the fact that James, after his scripturally-based argument, proceeds to suggest the points in the formula of agreement listed above. All of them are intended to make it possible for Jewish and Gentile Christians to eat at a common table.

An essential factor in the success of this assembly is the narration of the things that have already happened. When the community is made aware of the events that have happened in recent months and years the ground is prepared for the resolution of the disputed question. What has happened is interpreted as the action of God:[41] "they related all that God had done with them" (Acts 14:27; cf. 15:4).

However, these past events are only seen to be the actions of God because they are viewed in light of Sacred Scripture. What James sets forth is a considered theology of history based on biblical prophecy. This theology of history is an aid to understanding the very recent past and placing it within salvation history. Therefore the scriptural quotation also ends with reference to the divine plan: " . . . making these things known from long ago." Finally, it is important that all this takes place within the mother community in Jerusalem, where the witnesses who "were there from the beginning" (cf. Acts 1:21-22) live, and that the assembly is prepared to listen to the words of those witnesses.

At this point we can end our stroll through Luke's second book. Our purpose was not to recite the history of the primitive Church or primarily to discuss the composition of Acts. What is of interest is that for Luke the Church is unimaginable without its assemblies. Therefore at the very beginning of his second book he depicts the time between the Ascension and Pentecost as a continual assembly, indeed as the archetype of all assemblies, and in chapters 1–15 he describes community assemblies at various turning points in the history of the *ekklēsia*.

---

[39] Cf. Isa 2:2; 60:1-3; Mic 4:1-2.

[40] Regarding the function of Acts 15:14-18 within Lukan ecclesiology cf. Gerhard Lohfink, *Die Sammlung Israels* 58–60.

[41] For the schema underlying Acts 14:27 and 15:4 cf. Linda M. Maloney, *"All that God had Done with Them." The Narration of the Works of God in the Early Christian Community as Described in the Acts of the Apostles.* AmUSt TR 91 (New York: Peter Lang, 1991).

These assemblies are not only eucharistic celebrations, something Luke speaks about rarely. Instead, they are assemblies in which everything that is crucial for the community is discussed: attacks from without, the perils of persecution, internal strife, care for the poor, concerns about mission, reports of returning sisters and brothers, the creation of new ministries, the elaboration of community structures. We could expand this list considerably if we included the treatment of concrete community problems in Paul's letters. Those letters reflect in amazing degree the materials of community assemblies in the new mission congregations. The letters themselves were read aloud and discussed in such assemblies (cf. Col 4:16-17).

The praxis of assemblies of this sort by no means ended with the close of the apostolic age. Ignatius of Antioch, for example, writes to the community in Philadelphia:

> Since it was reported to me that the Church which is in Antioch in Syria is in peace, in accordance with your prayers, and the compassion which you have in Christ Jesus, it is proper for you, as a Church of God, to appoint a deacon to go as the ambassador of God to it, to congratulate those who are gathered together, and to glorify the Name [of God]. (Ign. *Phld* 10.1)[42]

This section of the letter reveals the *communio* of the communities with one another as well as indicating the kinds of things that might occupy a community assembly. In the so-called *Letter of Barnabas* we read: "Do not by retiring apart live alone as if you were already made righteous, but come together and seek out the common good" (*Barn.* 4:10).[43] This kind of assembly in which all together seek "the common good," namely the things that build up the community, was only lost when the Church became a mass phenomenon. From then on there was almost no opportunity for any assemblies except for worship. Obviously the celebration of the Lord's Supper was the most important assembly from the very beginning, and the binding center of all other assemblies. And yet those other assemblies that Luke was concerned to describe at such length and for which there are many witnesses from apostolic and post-apostolic times[44] were necessary for the Church's life. They were no longer possible in the oversized communities of the imperial Church, but wherever the Church was strongly alive they reasserted themselves.[45]

---

[42] Translation by Kirsopp Lake, *The Apostolic Fathers I*, LCL (Cambridge, Mass.: Harvard University Press, and London: William Heinemann Ltd., 1912).

[43] Translation by Kirsopp Lake, *The Apostolic Fathers I*.

[44] Cf. 1 Cor 5:1-5; 14:23-25; Matt 18:17; *Did.* 16:2; Ign. *Phld.* 10.1; Ign. *Poly.* 6.2; *Barn.* 4:10; *2 Clem.* 17.1-4.

[45] We may recall only the monastic councils. Cf., for example, the Rule of Benedict 3.1-3: "As often as anything important is to be done in the monastery, the abbot shall call the

In those assemblies there is space to report what is moving the community and what has happened in it since the last gathering. Events can be told and interpreted—not merely events internal to the community, but whatever is happening in the larger society, the whole scope of world, history, and culture can and should be brought into the common discussion and thus become divine address.

In these assemblies the critical knowledge that has been gathered through the long history of the enlightenment of the people of God comes to the fore as the power of discernment, but so also does the whole potential for experience that has accumulated in the community assemblies themselves, for over generations they have accompanied and sustained multitudes of destinies and the stories of many individuals. They have lived and learned, in the most concrete manner, what makes people unfree and what frees them, why they are sick and what can heal them. The walls of the assembly are drenched with stories.

The community assembly is also the place of brotherly and sisterly correction. For the early Christian communities that was a matter of course. The New Testament letter corpus speaks of it repeatedly.[46] In what is probably the oldest New Testament letter Paul writes to the community in Thessalonica: "we urge you, beloved, to admonish the idlers, encourage the faint hearted, help the weak, be patient with all of them" (1 Thess 5:14). This little piece of the letter concretizes a fragment of the community assembly. It would not be possible without open discussion and the patient correction that encourages the fainthearted, raises up the weak, helps to bear the burdens that someone must shoulder (Gal 6:1-2), and brings those who have sinned into the right way.

Without correction there can be no serious life in faith, for isolated Christians are not in a position to free themselves from their self-deceptions. They need the experience, discerning faculty, and firm counsel of others. Any and all can allow themselves to be helped, again and again. Obviously the freedom of individuals must be taken seriously at all times. They can only be spoken to openly if they permit it, and if they themselves want to be helped.

---

whole community together and himself explain what the business is; and after hearing the advice of the brothers, let him ponder it and follow what he judges the wiser course. The reason why we have said all should be called for counsel is that the Lord often reveals what is better to the younger." Timothy Fry, o.s.b., ed., *The Rule of St. Benedict in English* (Collegeville: The Liturgical Press, 1982).

[46] Cf. Matt 18:15-17; Luke 17:3-4; Acts 20:31; Rom 15:14; 1 Cor 14:24-25; Gal 6:1-2; Eph 5:10-14; Col 3:16; 1 Thess 5:14-15; 2 Thess 3:13-15; 1 Tim 5:19-21; 2 Tim 4:2; Titus 1:9, 13; 2:15; 3:9-11. Cf. Rainer Grosse, "Zurechtweisung innerhalb neutestamentlicher Gemeinden," Diplomarbeit, Catholic Theological Faculty of the University of Munich, 1991.

The assembly must never seek a scapegoat. Every fault is shared, and each must ask himself or herself whether one's own lack of faith and one's own failure has contributed to the failure of the brother or sister.

But the assembly is not only the place of mutual correction; it is also the place of constant reconciliation. When Peter asks how often he must be reconciled with his sister or brother and is told "seventy-seven times" (Matt 18:21-22) the background of the episode is not only the word of Jesus, but also the praxis of New Testament communities that knew that without ceaseless reconciliation they would not survive a week as communities, but that also knew that such reconciliation could not be exhausted in empty formulas. The basis for mutual reconciliation is the assembly, where solutions allowing for a new beginning can be found. There genuine conversion is possible. The community assembly is the place in the Church where worship and life come together, and where reconciliation is a serious business.

Finally, the common assembly is the place where the community can ask, again and again, what its way is to be, what is its next step, what is God's concrete will for it. Week after week it must struggle in its assemblies to learn how it can be God's instrument for the world. To that extent the assembly, like the Church itself, has an eschatological quality. It makes possible an undivided existence entirely directed to the reign of God because it opens the whole lives of the members of the community to the will of God. The assembly repeatedly seeks to see the world through God's eyes, from its "end," from the point of view of God's plan. But it has to reacquire that measuring rod again and again. It is contrary to the deepest instincts of the human being, even the "faithful."

The assembly gains its strength from its unanimity. That word has become alien to today's Christians. Exegetes themselves fall silent when it turns up in their texts. For unanimity is contrary to the newly desirable image of a democratically organized Church with continual votes and majority decisions. But we cannot avoid seeing that the theme of unanimity is central to New Testament *paraklēsis,* apostolic exhortation.[47]

We have already seen the role that unanimity plays in the assemblies Luke describes. He depicts it as a miracle, a messianic sign that is possible in the power of the Holy Spirit and the common experience of the works of God. In the gift of unanimity, not in its own activity lies the theological mystery of the Church, its power and the fascination that goes forth from it. Living in unanimity is the first and most important mission of the Church. Only then will it be possible to gather the separated from all nations.

---

[47] Cf. only Rom 12:16; 15:5-6; 1 Cor 1:10; 12:25; 2 Cor 13:11; Eph 4:1-6; Phil 1:27–2:4; 4:2; Col 4:2; 3:15; 1 Pet 3:8.

It is no different for Paul than for Luke. He writes to the community in Philippi:

> If then there is any encouragement in Christ, any consolation from love, any sharing in the Spirit, any compassion and sympathy, make my joy complete: be of the same mind, having the same love, being in full accord and of one mind. Do nothing from selfish ambition or conceit, but in humility regard others as better than yourselves. Let each of you look not to your own interests, but to the interests of others. (Phil 2:1-4)

In a passage like this one it is obvious that the community is not a structure that can be adequately understood in psychological or sociological categories. Unanimity does not yet exist when "like-minded people" come together. People are not like-minded, and they will never all hold the same opinion. Nor does unanimity come about when something has been "thoroughly discussed," no matter how important community discussion is. Unanimity is certainly not the resigned withdrawal from putting one's own opinion forward.

Being in unanimity means, rather, allowing oneself to be placed by God on a new footing, what Paul in Phil 2:1-5 calls "sharing in the Spirit" and "being in Christ." This new basis is made possible by Jesus' surrender of his own life, which Paul speaks about in the so-called hymn that follows immediately in Philippians (2:6-11). Of themselves people can never be in unanimity. They can only achieve it if they allow themselves to be united in favor of something that is beyond themselves: the will of God, God's work, God's gospel, the history that God has begun in the world. The place of that kind of unity is the assembly.

With all that has been said it is surely obvious that the form of assembly here described could not be introduced by ecclesiastical decrees. Nor can it be established as one schedules an extra worship service. It can only arise where the living history of God, of which we have been speaking, exists. And that history can only be experienced in a comprehensive community of life. We may, however, feel confident that the form of assembly that was once the strength of a young Church is again being given to the communities of today.

### 3. The Church's Most Intensive Moment Is Remembering

On 16 January 1996 Israeli President Ezer Weizmann gave a speech to the German Bundestag that remains unforgettable, not only because it was the very first time that an Israeli president visited the Federal Republic of Germany, but especially because Ezer Weizmann spoke in thoroughly biblical fashion, as one who remembers. Let me illustrate with a few excerpts from the beginning and end of his speech:

. . . Every individual Jew in every generation must think of himself or herself as if he or she had been there—there in the generations, the places, and the events that lie far in the past . . . . Memory shortens distance. Two hundred generations have passed since the historical beginnings of my people, and they seem to me like a few days. Only two hundred generations have passed since a man named Abraham arose to leave his land and his home and go into a land that today is my land . . . . Only one hundred fifty generations passed between the fiery column of the Exodus from Egypt and the smoke columns of the Shoah. And I, born of the descendants of Abraham in the land of Abraham, was present for all of it.

I was a slave in Egypt and received the Torah at Mount Sinai, and with Joshua and Elijah I crossed the Jordan. With King David I entered Jerusalem, and with Zedekiah I was taken from there into exile. I did not forget Jerusalem at the waters of Babylon, and when the Lord brought Zion home again I was among the dreamers who raised the walls of Jerusalem. I fought against the Romans and was driven out of Spain; I was dragged to the stake in Magenza and in Mainz, and I have studied Torah in Yemen. I lost my family in Kishinev and was burned up in Treblinka . . . .

We are a people of memory and prayer. We are a people of words and hope. We have created no empires, built no castles and palaces. We have only set words together. We have built up layers of ideas, constructed houses of memory, and dreamed towers of longing: may Jerusalem be built again, may peace be given and come speedily, in our time. Amen.[48]

This manner of remembering moved many at the time. Others found it unapproachable. Some were offended. Benjamin Korn, a German essayist living in Paris, wrote some months later against Weizmann's speech:

What . . . would have happened if German Chancellor Kohl had followed Weizmann to the podium and said: "I was a captain in the Teutoburger forest and was in the forefront of the German tribes when we put the Romans to flight"? He would have brought down peals of laughter; he would have been diagnosed with serious schizophrenia and been taken where they put people who think they are Napoleon, Alexander, Frederick the Great, Herman the German, or Moses. The insane content of the two statements is identical, except that the one is religious and the other ordinary insanity: the one brings a straitjacket, the other gooseflesh.[49]

But are the statements: "I received the Torah at Mount Sinai" and "I was a captain in the Teutoburger forest" really identical in structure? Social

---

[48] As quoted in the *Frankfurter Allgemeine Zeitung,* Wednesday, 17 January 1996, No. 14, p. 6.

[49] From *Die Zeit,* 15 November 1996, No. 47, p. 48.

scientists nowadays speak of a "collective memory" and make a careful distinction between "communicative" and "cultural" memory.[50]

"Communicative memory" is the concrete history that is present to a given generation (not an individual). Obviously this knowledge is constantly being expanded through education and the media, but nevertheless it does not extend more than three generations into the past. Everything beyond the realm of what is "still available to be heard about" is known as fact (perhaps even interesting), but it "means" nothing. Therefore the principal mass of communicative memory moves linearly forward with the generations.

A people's "cultural memory" or that of a particular group is something different. It responds to the question: "What must we never under any circumstances forget?" It is the foundation of the identity, the consciousness of a "we" in a people or group that remembers. Cultural memory offers more than interesting facts: it offers meaning. It creates community by providing it with a common world of meaning. To do this it need not comprehend the whole course of history. Often just the beginning is enough. It does not collect events, but selects. It does not make lists, but tells stories or fixes symbols. "Only the *meaningful* past is remembered, and only the *remembered* past is meaningful."[51]

One might argue about what, at the end of the twentieth century, might constitute the "cultural memory" of Germans, but it certainly would not be the battle of the Teutoburger forest. Probably in the period of nationalist obsession, from the wars of liberation against Napoleon until Hitler, it did form part of it, but no longer. Herman the German is no longer foundational to German identity. In contrast, the stories of the liberation of Israel from Egypt and of the reception of the Torah at Mount Sinai are foundational for Jewish self-awareness. Benjamin Korn overlooked that important difference.

Perhaps he does not even know what a Jewish festival is. In Ezer Weizmann's speech the cultic making-present that happens in the Passover night forms a constant background. When Weizmann says that "every individual Jew in every generation must think of himself or herself as if he or she had been there" he is alluding to a part of the liturgy for the Passover night, where it is said: "In every generation each is obliged to see herself or himself as one who has come out of Egypt."[52] This contemporaneity of all

---

[50] The concept of "cultural memory" was introduced by Aleida and Jan Assmann (following Jurij Lotmann and Maurice Halbwachs). For the next two sections cf. Jan Assmann, *Das kulturelle Gedächtnis. Schrift, Erinnerung und politische Identität in frühen Hochkulturen* (Munich: 1992) 20–24, 34–37, 42–45.

[51] Jan Assmann, *Das kulturelle Gedächtnis* 77.

[52] *m. Pesaḥ.* X, 5.

generations with the saving events of the past, something that takes place in the feast, is already formulated in the Torah itself.[53] It is, in fact, a formative principle of the book of Deuteronomy, where "today" occurs seventy times,[54] for example in 5:2-3: "The LORD our God made a covenant with us at Horeb. Not with our ancestors did the LORD make this covenant, but with us, who are all of us here alive today." At the moment when these words in Deut 5:2-3 were spoken by Moses decades had passed since the making of the covenant at Sinai (= Horeb). A whole generation had died in the wilderness. And yet the new generation, and with it all future generations who will celebrate the festival of the renewal of the covenant, is standing at Sinai. So that the *today* will be clear in all its radicalness the text says: the covenant was *not* made with the ancestors; it is being made with us today. What once happened is happening for us. Today is the beginning of everything.

This consciousness never ceased to exist in Israel after that. For all faithful Jews, and not only for them, it is a matter of course that at the Passover meal the foundational history of the people of God is made present. To equate such a memory with German memory of Herman from the Teutoburger forest is the real insanity.

The worst of it, perhaps, is that Benjamin Korn places the national wars of liberation on the same level with the suffering of the Jews. There can be no objection to liberation movements as long as they do not trample right underfoot and degenerate into a blind fury of nationalism. There were liberation struggles of all shades in Israel as well, even to the point of fanatical hatred of the Romans. But there was also—and that is what has sustained the Jews through the centuries and kept them alive—resistance and suffering for the sake of *freedom of belief,* a faith that does not adore human power, but God. This resistance meant centuries of persecution, and often martyrdom.

If Jewish memory remained at the level of German guerilla wars there would long since have been no more Jews, or no one in the world would have anything against them. But the "dangerous memory" that Israel brought into the world reaches much deeper. It is the inextinguishable memory that there is a conscience, that there is guilt, that there is *one* God and that God acts in the world, that this God desires a just society in which might does not make right. Hitler's incomprehensible attempt to exterminate the Jews of Europe by mass-production methods was an attempt to get rid of that memory definitively. There is no other way to understand the Holocaust.

[53] Cf. especially Exod 13:8-10, 14-16; Deut 6:20-25; 29:9-14.
[54] Cf. Horst Dietrich Preuss, *Old Testament Theology.* 2 vols. (Louisville: Westminster/John Knox, 1995–1996) 1:223.

Today the Holocaust has become for Israel a new collective memory alongside the biblical foundational narratives, one that has long since acquired a "foundational character" of its own. This shows once again that the events that constitute the innermost self of Israel, its memory and its fund of remembrance, lie within history and are inextricably bound up with its faith.

The neighbors of ancient Israel founded their cultural memory on cosmic myths. In Egypt it was told how in the time before time Horus, the god of Lower Egypt, and Seth, the god of Upper Egypt, brought their two lands together into the Pharaonic empire. "The state ruled by the king is the result of a union brought about in the mythical primeval past by the two gods, and newly accomplished by every king when he enters into his rule and through its exercise."[55] The myth of Horus and Seth was Egypt's foundational myth.

Israel's memory was not founded on an event in the world of the gods, but in real history, not on an event in the mythic past but in a time when the Egyptian state had already existed for nearly two thousand years. But above all: in the minds of the ancient Egyptians the genuine event that brought their present reality into being was something that happened in their mythical time of origin, in contrast to which history itself was only a repetition, nothing more than a ritual again-and-again-bringing-to-pass of the mythical primeval event. The immediate expression of this "historical consciousness fixed on origins and circular time" is found in the late Egyptian temples with their images, texts, and rituals.[56]

In Israel, by contrast, the collective memory of the Exodus set in motion a very different kind of history. And although there was also a foundational history in Israel, in which the decisive event had already happened, the history that unfolds from it is unimaginably dynamic. It is like a sequence of explosives, a wide-open field for experimentation. It revises itself, it is criticized by the prophets in the most radical fashion, it takes utterly unexpected turns, and it is uninterruptedly directed to the future. "We have only set words together," said Ezer Weizmann, only "built up layers of ideas," but those words have changed the world.

In Jesus and the Church founded on him Israel's history again takes one of those turns that no one expects, that overturns everything. It is usually forgotten that what happened then in Galilee and afterward in Jerusalem was not something strange and alien to Israel; it was Jewish history. The actors were all, without exception, Jews. Jesus was a Jew, Mary was a Jew, all the apostles were Jews. It is banal to say it, of course, but unfortunately

---

[55] Jan Assmann, *Das kulturelle Gedächtnis* 167–68; cf. 78.
[56] Ibid. 185.

there is still good reason to say it to Christians. The *ekklēsia* came into existence in Israel, understanding itself as the eschatological Israel gathered by God, and it is therefore inextricably and forever bound to the whole of Israel. The Exodus of the people of God from Egypt is our Exodus as well; the ancestors of Israel are our ancestors; Israel's memory is our memory.

There is no more appropriate image of this state of affairs than that of the olive tree as developed by Paul in Romans 11.[57] Paul did not invent this image for the people of God. It was ready to hand in Hosea and Jeremiah.[58] But Paul makes the image of the olive tree a striking interpretation of the relationship between Israel and the Gentile Church. It is worth examining this Pauline image and the history of its reception more closely in connection with the question of the Church's collective memory. It will then appear how urgent the question of the Church's true "memory" is.

In Romans 9–11 Paul begins his reflections on God's covenant fidelity to God's people by listing all the things that God's loving choice has bestowed on Israel over time:

> I have great sorrow and unceasing anguish in my heart. For I could wish that I myself were accursed and cut off from Christ for the sake of my own people, my kindred according to the flesh. They are Israelites, and to them belong the adoption, the glory, the covenants, the giving of the law, the worship, and the promises; to them belong the patriarchs, and from them, according to the flesh, comes the Messiah . . . . (Rom 9:2-5)

All of this is then concentrated in the image of the olive tree. Its strong roots are the ancestors, especially Abraham, and all the branches of the tree derive their strength from those roots. The Gentile Christians who are Paul's primary addressees in Romans 9–11 have been taken from paganism and incorporated into the history of the people of God. In this imagery they have been grafted into the olive tree that is Israel. On the other hand the Jews who have not believed in Jesus as the Messiah have broken away from their own trunk.

> . . . if the root is holy, then the branches also are holy. But if some of the branches were broken off, and you, a wild olive shoot, were grafted in their place to share the rich root of the olive tree, do not boast over the branches. If you do boast, remember that it is not you that support the root, but the root that supports you. (Rom 11:16-18)

---

[57] The following interpretation of Romans 9–11 is more thoroughly documented in Gerhard Lohfink, "Jesus und die Kirche" in Walter Kern, Hermann Josef Pottmeyer, and Max Seckler, *Handbuch der Fundamentaltheologie* 3, tractate "Kirche" (Freiburg: Herder, 1986) 65–70.

[58] Cf. Hos 14:7; Jer 11:16.

The image of the olive tree and the branches grafted onto it shows how much a matter of course it is for Paul that the Church is *Israel.* Obviously there is no question about it as far as Jewish Christians are concerned. They are not even mentioned at this point. They were already spoken of beforehand, when Paul wrote about the chosen "remnant of Israel" (Rom 11:1-7). But of the Gentile Christians he says explicitly that through their faith they have been implanted in the ancient root and live out of its strength.

We must see, however—and a great deal depends on this—that Paul does not stop with this stage of the image of the olive tree. He does not give us a fixed image, and certainly not a still-life. The image represents a drama for him. It was already dramatic that branches were hacked out of the olive tree and other branches grafted into their place. But that is not the end of it. The Gentile Christians are sternly warned that if they should become proud they will not remain in the olive tree, but will themselves be lopped off:

> You will say, "Branches were broken off so that I might be grafted in." That is true. They were broken off because of their unbelief, but you stand only through faith. So do not become proud, but stand in awe. For if God did not spare the natural branches, perhaps he will not spare you. Note then the kindness and the severity of God: severity toward those who have fallen, but God's kindness toward you, provided you continue in his kindness; otherwise you also will be cut off. (Rom 11:19-22)

And still the drama continues. Whereas Paul has, to this point, continually formulated "against nature" (no one grafts "wild" shoots into a tree, but only "noble" ones; the roots, on the other hand, should be "wild"), now he stretches the extraordinary and unusual aspects of the whole affair to the limit: even the branches that have been cut off (the Israel that has remained unbelieving) are not to desiccate on the ground or be burned; they are to be grafted back into the old trunk:

> And even those of Israel, if they do not persist in unbelief, will be grafted in, for God has the power to graft them in again. For if you have been cut from what is by nature a wild olive tree and grafted, contrary to nature, into a cultivated olive tree, how much more will these natural branches be grafted back into their own olive tree. (Rom 11:23-24)

So we come to the very point that is crucial for Paul. His greatest suffering is the path of disobedient Israel that took offense at Jesus. He cannot be content that only a remnant of Israel has come to believe in the Messiah. What is the meaning of the unbelief of so many?

Paul gives an answer in terms of salvation history: Through their unbelief faith came to the Gentiles (11:11). The apostle to the Gentiles thinks quite concretely here. He always preached first in the synagogues. Only when the people of the circumcision would not listen to him there did he turn to the uncircumcised.[59] Thus the faith of the one group brought salvation to the others. Gentile Christian communities sprang up everywhere. The failure of the unbelieving part of Israel has enriched the world. In the image of the olive tree, many new branches were grafted in.

And yet this still is not the whole story. Paul is convinced that it is precisely the becoming-visible of the messianic salvation among the Gentiles that will cause the Israel that stands aside to see at last. He formulates it this way: "So I ask, have they stumbled so as to fall? By no means! But through their stumbling salvation has come to the Gentiles, so as to make Israel jealous" (Rom 11:11). By this Paul means that the fascination of the messianic reality that is now taking social shape in the Gentile Church will rouse Israel and inspire it to emulation. Israel will recognize in the Gentile Christian communities that the messianic transformation of the world has already begun, and that in turn will lead them to faith in Jesus as the Messiah. The crucial text toward which the whole argumentation in Romans 9–11 aims is: "hardening has come upon part of Israel, until the full number *(plērōma)* of the Gentiles has come in. And so all Israel will be saved" (Rom 11:25-26).

This talk about the Gentiles' "coming in" shows that Paul has in mind the pilgrimage of the nations that we have already considered several times before. The nations, by coming to faith, are entering into the eschatological saving community of Israel. By "the full number of the Gentiles" Paul does not mean merely a certain number, as the translation might suggest. He also means the "fullness," the moment when, through the streaming-in of the Gentiles into eschatological Israel, the fullness of the messianic reality bursts forth in its shining glory,[60] so that it will be evident that the Messiah must already have come. Then, says Paul, the whole of Israel, still faithless till now, will come to believe; then the "full number of the Jews" will correspond to the "full number of the Gentiles," and that will be for the rest of the world like a miracle that brings for them the definitive turn to life:

> Now if their stumbling means riches for the world, and if their defeat means riches for Gentiles, how much more will their full inclusion mean! . . . For if their rejection is the reconciliation of the world, what will their acceptance be but life from the dead! (Rom 11:12, 15)

---

[59] Cf. Acts 13:46-48; 18:6; 19:8-10; 28:25-28.
[60] For a fuller grounding of this see Gerhard Lohfink, "Jesus und die Kirche," 68–69.

By now it must be quite clear that Paul's concern here is not simply the salvation of individual Jews, but something far greater. This is about salvation history, about God's plan. It is about how God arrives at God's goal in the world. All this is identical with the question of the election of Israel. It is irrevocable (11:29) because on it depends the salvation of the world (11:15).

For Paul the destiny of the nations is indissolubly bound up with the way of Israel, and by the same token the destiny of still-unbelieving Israel is bound up with the way of the Gentile Church. He expected quite concretely that very soon the fullness of the messianic reality in the Gentile Church would lead the Jews to faith in Jesus as Messiah, and that very thing would change the course of the world and bring God's plan to its fulfillment.

What Paul prophetically foretold as the messianic transformation that would also come upon the Jews has not yet happened. But the thing that he warned the Gentile Church about in positively minatory fashion *has* happened: the Church became proud and for centuries has arrogantly looked down on the synagogue. Scarcely had the Church put its own time of persecution behind it and achieved its freedom when the first repressive measures against the Jews were introduced.

In February of the year 313 the Emperor Constantine agreed in Milan with the Emperor Licinius on a religious-political program that was favorable to Christianity. Two years later, on 8 October 315, he decreed that Christians were forbidden, under penalty of death, from converting to Judaism. This was preceded by another law forbidding Jews to persecute some of their co-religionists who wanted to become Christians. This shows that at the time the Jewish side was not very tolerant either:

> It is Our will that Jews and their elders and patriarchs shall be informed that if, after the issuance of this law, any of them should dare to attempt to assail with stones or with any other kind of madness . . . any person who has fled their feral sect and has resorted to the worship of God [i.e., the Christian faith], such assailant shall be immediately delivered to the flames and burned, with all his accomplices. Moreover, if any person from the people [i.e., a Christian] should betake himself to their nefarious sect *(nefaria secta)* and should join their assemblies, he shall sustain with them the deserved punishments.[61]

A few decades later, by which time Christianity had step by step become the official religion of the empire, the following occurred: In Callinicum on the Euphrates some Christians, encouraged by their bishop, burned down a Jewish synagogue. When Emperor Theodosius I, who was living in Milan,

---

[61] Codex Theodosianus XVI 8,1. Translation from Peter Schäfer, *The History of the Jews in Antiquity: The Jews of Palestine from Alexander the Great to the Arab Conquest.* Translated by David Chowcat (Australia and U.S.: Harwood Academic Publishers, 1995) 178.

angrily ordered the synagogue to be rebuilt at the expense of the guilty parties Ambrose, the bishop of Milan, forced him to annul the punitive edict.[62] That Ambrose, one of the best men of the Church, who had struggled for its freedom from the powerful influence of the emperor, could not see the difference in this matter is especially painful. Under Theodosius II the burning of synagogues became so frequent that most of that emperor's edicts were directed to the protection of synagogues and Jewish private houses.[63]

To the extent that Christian arrogance toward the Jews grew the Jewish content of Christianity was obscured. Christian faith was continually in danger of being spiritualized in a false sense; the Christian hope was in peril of being falsely projected into a world beyond death. In light of this development, and in the face of their Christian persecutors, how could the synagogue recognize in the Church the fullness of the messianic reality? What Paul saw prophetically before his eyes could not come about. His image of the olive tree and the dynamic within which he had developed it was overlooked or reinterpreted for centuries.[64]

If the Christian communities had taken the letter to the Romans seriously the relationship between Church and synagogue would have developed differently. The merciless persecution of Jews, the countless forced baptisms since the early Middle Ages, the hideous pogroms would not have been possible. The Christians would then have known that they themselves, through the mercy of God, had been grafted into the olive tree of Israel, that the Jews are their brothers and sisters and are sheltered for all time under God's covenant faithfulness, "for the gifts and the calling of God are irrevocable" (Rom 11:29).

The Second Vatican Council was the first to dare, at last, to incorporate the Pauline image of the olive tree into an official Church teaching document. In the crucial Article 4 of the "Declaration on the Relation of the Church to Non-Christian Religions" *(Nostra aetate)* we find:

---

[62] Cf. ibid. 185; Karl Baus et al., *The Imperial Church from Constantine to the Early Middle Ages.* Translated by Anselm Biggs (New York: Seabury, 1980) 87–88.

[63] Cf. Schäfer, *History of the Jews* 187.

[64] Cf. Ulrich Wilckens, *Der Brief an die Römer (Röm 6–11).* EKK VI/2 (Zürich: Benziger; Neukirchen-Vluyn: Neukirchener Verlag, 1980) 267. Of course the Church's knowledge of its character as Israel was never fully forgotten. It repeatedly glimmers through, for example in the ancient prayer for the Easter night in the Gelasian sacramentary: "O God, we know that your ancient wonders shine forth even in our time: for what your mighty arm once did for a single people when you freed it from Egyptian persecution you now bring about for the salvation of the Gentiles through the water of rebirth. We pray that the fullness of the whole world may become descendants of Abraham and belong to the dignity of Israel, your people *(ut in Abrahae filios et in Israeliticam dignitatem totius mundi transeat plenitudo)."* See the adapted form of this prayer recited after the reading from Exod 14:15–15:1 at the Easter Vigil.

> On this account the church cannot forget that it received the revelation of the Old Testament by way of that people with whom God in his inexpressible mercy established the ancient covenant. Nor can it forget that it draws nourishment from that good olive tree onto which the wild olive branches of the Gentiles have been grafted (see Rom 11:17-24).[65]

"The church cannot forget." This is true even though Romans 11 was, practically speaking, forgotten, for Romans belongs to the Church's *canon*, that is, its indispensable standard, and thus to its abiding memory. Of course we can see from the suppression of Romans 11 that it is possible for parts of the Church's memory to be obscured and in need of being uncovered. There are such things as buried memories. There are even false memories. How could Christians so quickly suppress Romans 11? This must ultimately be related to the fact that there is another text in the New Testament that impressed itself much more strongly on the minds of Christians than the Pauline image of the olive tree. In the gospel of Matthew the people cry out before the procurator, Pilate: "His blood be on us and on our children!" (Matt 27:25).

It is this passage that has truly shaped Christian attitudes. The image of the olive tree and Paul's warning to the Gentile Christians paled before it. Theologians were aware also of another text from Matthew that appeared to complement Matt 27:25. At the end of the parable of the wicked tenants Jesus, according to Matthew's version, says: "Therefore I tell you, the kingdom of God will be taken away from you and given to a people that produces the fruits of the kingdom" (Matt 21:43). This text is most probably the basis for a scheme of thought that played a dominant role in Christian theology and devotion for a long period of time. It could be briefly formulated this way: Israel, by murdering the Son of God, lost its election. Its role as people of God and instrument of salvation history was thrown away. God chose a *new people*,[66] namely the Church. This new people has replaced the old.

But is that a correct interpretation of Matthew? Who are the addressees of "therefore I tell you"? From whom is the reign of God to be taken

---

[65] *Nostra aetate* 4. Translation in Austin Flannery, ed., *Vatican Council II: Constitutions, Decrees, Declarations* (Northport, N.Y.: Costello, and Dublin: Dominican Publications, 1996).

[66] When Vatican II speaks of the Church as the "People of God" it uses both the expression "messianic people" *(populus ille messianicus)* and the words "new People of God" *(novus populus Dei)*. Cf. *Lumen Gentium* II.9; *Nostra aetate* 4. In analogy to the "new covenant" we should understand this as referring to the eschatologically *renewed* Israel, *newly gathered* by God in Jesus Christ *and newly created through his death*. This must be emphasized in order to exclude the misunderstanding that there has been a substitution (a new people *in place of* the old).

away? The text is as precise as possible, for in Matthew the discourses of Jesus that include the parable of the evil tenants (Matt 21:23–22:46) are directed exclusively to the leaders of the people. One after another Jesus speaks to the high priests and elders of the people, the high priests and the Pharisees, the Pharisees and the Sadducees. They alone are the addressees of these words.

The saying about the reign of God that will be taken away from "you" is thus not directed to the people of the city, still less to Israel as a whole, but to Jesus' opponents, the religious authorities in Jerusalem. So that this may be clear to all hearers of the gospel the text says, immediately after these words about the reign of God's being taken away: "When the chief priests and the Pharisees heard his parables, they realized that he was speaking about them. They wanted to arrest him, but they feared the crowds, because they regarded him as a prophet" (Matt 21:45-46). It could not be clearer. It is the leading authorities who are threatened with having the reign of God taken from them, not the people. The people's leaders are of course the people's representatives, but in this case they do not represent the whole of Israel. Immediately before this, in Matt 21:31, they had been told: "the tax collectors and the prostitutes are going into the kingdom of God ahead of you."

For Matthew, Israel at this moment includes as well all those who had heard and been converted by the penitential preaching of the Baptizer (Matt 21:32), the children who cried "Hosanna" to Jesus in the Temple (21:15), the disciples who follow Jesus, the women who will stand beneath the cross (27:55-56). Beyond this the saying that threatens the removal of the *basileia* also clearly makes reference to the Gentile Church, which in turn will receive a share in the reign of God. Matthew thus draws a distinction. There can be no question here of the withdrawal of the *basileia* from Israel as a whole.[67]

But does not the whole people cry out to Pilate "his blood be on us and on our children"? They do indeed shout these words in Matthew's gospel, and the saying is doubly serious because Matthew has inserted it into the Markan text he was using. But we must look closely at what these words say and what they do not say.

In terms of form this is a "conditional self-curse." Juridically it could be paraphrased: "If it should be the case that Jesus is not guilty, we take the responsibility for his blood, that is, for his execution, on ourselves."

---

[67] Matt 8:11-12 cannot be offered as an adequate basis for such an interpretation either. There are other texts in Matthew as well. The concept of a *divorce* between the believing and unbelieving parts of Israel is more adequate to the whole of Matthew's gospel. Cf. extensively on this subject Gerhard Lohfink, "Jesus und die Kirche," 53–59.

That is how Matthew must have understood the saying to begin with. But we will have to say more about the hidden meaning of the words, which he derives from Jesus' words at the Last Supper. In any case the notion of "killing God" that would soon develop in Christian brains like a dangerous virus can in no way be derived from this saying. Here again Matthew is very precise. In connection with Jesus' entry into the city he inserts a short scene describing the "people" he has in mind when he tells the passion story: "When he entered Jerusalem, the whole city was in turmoil, asking, 'Who is this?' The crowds were saying, 'This is the prophet Jesus from Nazareth in Galilee'" (Matt 21:10-11). The people of the city thus do not join in the Hosanna-shouts of the festival pilgrims[68] or the rejoicing of the children in the Temple.[69] Instead, led astray by the high priest and elders,[70] they shout to the Roman governor, "crucify him!" They know little of Jesus, ultimately no more than that he is a prophet. A little later Jerusalem's guilt is defined: this is the city that kills the prophets and is about to do so again.[71] Thus Matthew does not offer the slightest basis for the later accusation of "killing God"; in fact, he makes such a reproach impossible. For Matthew the crowds in Jerusalem do not even grasp that Jesus is the *Messiah*.[72] They are told that he is a prophet, and they treat him as Jerusalem has always treated the prophets.

That is one side of the Matthean presentation. The crowd that shouts "crucify him!" and calls Jesus' blood on itself is limited to Jerusalem[73] and does not understand the implications of what it is doing. The guilt of their leaders is greater.[74] On the other hand, Matthew no longer speaks in 27:25 of the "crowd" *(ochlos),* but of the "people as a whole" *(pas ho laos).* Apparently he is convinced that in what they are doing Jerusalem and the Temple stand for the whole of Israel. What is happening in Jerusalem is

---

[68] We can see how thoughtful Matthew is in depicting this non-agreement from the fact that the people (cf. 23:1), according to 23:39, will one day enter after all into the cry of "blessed is he who comes in the name of the Lord" when they see and recognize Jesus (at the parousia?).

[69] Matt 21:15. The rejoicing of the children is redactional in Matthew, in contrast to Mark.

[70] Matt 27:20.

[71] Matt 23:37-39; cf. 21:46 (!).

[72] Matt 21:11 speaks in favor of this interpretation. Only the children (21:15) and the festival pilgrims (21:9) greet Jesus as the Messiah.

[73] In favor of this is that the "people" *(laos)* that calls down Jesus' blood on itself in 27:25 was previously referred to as the "crowd" *(ochlos).* Cf. 27:15, 20, 24. The "people" *(laos)* is found in the immediate narrative context as actant only in 26:5, and there the text can only refer to the festival pilgrims and the residents of Jerusalem.

[74] For example, in 22:41-46 Jesus speaks with the Pharisees about the question of the Messiah. Cf. also 21:23-27.

being done in the name of Israel, and the whole people of God is taking responsibility for Jesus' execution.

It is quite in accord with this Matthean line of thought that Jerusalem and its Temple must bear the consequences of what is done to Jesus. The city will be burned to the ground[75] and not one stone of the Temple will remain upon another.[76] Matthew takes seriously the guilt that fell upon Israel through the execution of Jesus as an innocent "prophet," and he takes the consequences of that sin just as seriously.

We in turn must take Matthew seriously. For if Israel at that time had only listened to Jesus as a "prophet," for example to his saying "give . . . to the emperor the things that are the emperor's, and to God the things that are God's" (Matt 22:21) there would have been no Jewish War thirty-six years later, the war that was not only a senseless revolt against Rome but at the same time a Jewish self-laceration. The historian Josephus recounts how the rival Jewish groups fought one another to the death both before and during the siege of Jerusalem.[77]

To that extent we must say that the rejection of Jesus, the fact that people did not take seriously his power of discernment, produced consequences, and those consequences were borne by Jerusalem and by Israel. Hence there is a historical truth concealed in the people of Jerusalem's acceptance of guilt. But can that acceptance be equated with the loss of election, with the exclusion of all Israel from the history of salvation?

We must not take this question lightly. If Jesus found more indifference than faith in the people, and if the leaders of Jerusalem rejected him in Jerusalem and even saw to it that he was killed, Israel rejected the reign of God. And if it did that it missed the meaning of its existence. It was then no longer God's sign among the nations. Matthew, like many other Christian theologians of his time, was faced with this urgent question.

And yet for him there is no more question of the loss of Israel's election than there is for Paul. God had not canceled the covenant with Israel. The key text is in the Last Supper tradition, for according to Matthew, as in the other gospels, Jesus at his last meal established atonement for the many. The people before Pilate interpreted Jesus' blood as a conditional self-curse; Jesus interpreted it as atonement for the guilt of the people of God and for all who would one day belong to God's people.

There is not the slightest evidence that Matthew understood the words at the Last Supper differently from Mark (cf. III, 7 above). On the contrary!

---

[75] Matt 22:7.

[76] Matt 24:1-2.

[77] See, for example, Josephus, *Bell.* IV.3 (§135-223); V.1 (§1-38); V.3 (§98-105); V.6 (§255-257).

He even went beyond Mark in introducing the motif of forgiveness of sins in the Last Supper saying: "for this is my blood of the covenant, which is poured out for many for the forgiveness of sins" (Matt 26:28).[78] Matthew cannot have thought that this forgiveness was denied to those who were guilty of the crucifixion of Jesus. But we need not take refuge in generalities here. According to Jer 31:31-34 the motif of forgiveness of sins is an indispensable part of the "new covenant." That new covenant, after all, is nothing other than the Sinai covenant that Israel had broken and that God is renewing eschatologically, in a way that surpasses all that has gone before.[79] In that case even the breach of the covenant must be forgiven. Therefore Jeremiah concludes his proclamation of the new covenant with the statement: "for I will forgive their iniquity, and remember their sin no more" (Jer 31:34). Of course Matthew, with his knowledge of Scripture, was aware of that. It is true that in regard to the forgiveness of sins he is also thinking of the Gentile peoples who will come from east and west (Matt 8:11), but he is thinking just as much of the forgiveness of sins promised to those who have broken the covenant and for whom it will be renewed.

We could also formulate the whole thing as follows: Israel condemned itself before Pilate's judgment seat, but God did not accept that self-condemnation. God did not make the cross a sign of cursing,[80] but a sign of pardon and new life, indeed of the renewal of the covenant with Israel. The people cried "his blood be on us and on our children." In light of the Last Supper tradition that blood can only be the saving blood of Jesus.

It is precisely this divine decree that is remembered in the Church when it celebrates the Eucharist. In this very sense the Church celebrates in every Eucharist its founding event, which is not in opposition to the founding event of Israel, but presupposes it, continues it, and brings it to its goal. In this foundational event Jesus has turned toward Israel, the people of God, represented by the Twelve, in spite of its guilt; he has confirmed its election and renewed the covenant with it. The Church's most intensive moment, its unique memory, its true recollection, is a ceaseless turning toward Israel.

---

[78] Matthew prepares for this insertion by removing the motif of forgiveness of sins from his description of the appearance of John the Baptizer. Cf. Matt 3:2 against Mark 1:4.

[79] Cf. Norbert Lohfink, *The Covenant Never Revoked: Biblical Reflections on Christian-Jewish Dialogue*. Translated by John J. Scullion (New York: Paulist, 1991). The association of the "eschatologically renewed covenant" and "forgiveness of Israel's guilt" is found not only in Jer 31:31-34, but also in Ezek 16:59-63 and 37:21-28.

[80] Gal 3:13-14 does not contradict this. There Paul says that Christ has freed believers from the mortal condemnation of the Law (= curse of the Law) by taking on himself the curse of sins (though these are foreign to him).

One must be shocked to the depths of one's soul when one considers that the same Christians who in their Eucharists celebrate the pardon of all guilt through the cross of Christ have not forgiven their Jewish brothers and sisters, through all the centuries, for the death of Jesus. In late medieval iconography there was even the incredible depiction of the so-called "living cross": Jesus, hanging on the cross, thrusts a sword through the breast of the female figure of the synagogue.[81] That was certainly an extreme of perverse malice, but it would not have been possible without the broad underlying current of a false theology. On the whole the history of Christian anti-Judaism shows how crucial it is to test Christian memory again and again. It is not enough that the liturgists speak of the "anamnetic structure," that is, the memorial structure of the Church's liturgy and of the Church itself. It is a question of what is being memorialized. The memory must be the *right one*.

What took place when Jewish synagogues were burned in the fourth and fifth centuries was not the Church's true memory, even if people appealed to Matthew's gospel in support of it. It was contrary to what Jesus did at the Last Supper. What happened in the Crusades was not the Church's true memory. It was contrary to Jesus' peaceful entry into the Holy City. What happened when physical force was used against heretics was not the right kind of memory. It was contrary to the Sermon on the Mount.

The Church therefore needs a place in which it can not only hand on its own memories but continually subject them to critical examination. That place is the assembly that we considered at length in the previous section. If every organism hands on its genetic information as a "biological memory," certainly the Church itself lives from carefully transmitted, precise, and continually tested memory. Its narratives and confessions, its laws and commandments, its exhortations and promises, prayers and songs, symbols and symbolic actions are its lifegiving memory.

There is nothing arbitrary in all these concrete forms of memory, in all this "inherited information" of the faith. In them is transmitted precisely that power of discernment that the people of God has absorbed and made its own through many generations, testing it in the experiences of countless women and men, often with heavy sacrifices and long wanderings from the true path. The Church's memory is thus not simply a clinging to the old and the eternal yesterday. It is a kind of life insurance. Those who forget are condemned to repeat all the mistakes of the past.

---

[81] Cf. Willehad Paul Eckert, "Antisemitismus V," *TRE* 3:137–43, at 138. For illustrative material see especially Herbert Jochum, *Ecclesia und Synagoga. Das Judentum in der christlichen Kunst*. Exhibition catalogue (published by the editor, 1993).

The assembly is the place where the Church's memory is kept alive. Certainly the eucharistic assembly has a special importance for this, for nowhere else is it so clear that the memory of the people of God is not created by itself but given by God, according to Ps 111:4: "he has gained renown by his wonderful deeds."[82] In the memorial celebration of the Eucharist it is obvious that salvation and liberation do not happen, ultimately, through moral appeals or instruction, or through free-form meditation or mysticism falsely understood, but through a precise salvation history that is "called" into memory and by that very means brings the Church together and builds up community. Ultimately the liturgy contains everything the Church needs: there is its *genuine* memory. It only needs to live what is contained in its sacraments and memory. The long road of this chapter is meant to show how crucial such memory is. The life of the people of God depends on it.

In this sense the Sunday celebration of the Eucharist is not a luxury that the baptized can permit themselves according to their own mood or convenience, but something they can just as easily do without. The Sunday celebration is a necessity of life, for after at most a week the community is in danger of losing its memory. The continual erosion of memory and the constant danger of individual isolation work against the conscious memory of the eucharistic celebration.

In the Old Testament reading at the Eucharist we are reminded of the deeds of God in the old covenant; the Gospel reading reminds us of God's deeds in Jesus. The New Testament reading reflects God's eschatological action, and the Eucharistic Prayer recalls the Church's founding event. Moreover, that recollection is not simply a historical recall, but is so intensive that it makes present the past action of God: the participants in the Eucharist take part in what happened then. They participate in Jesus' last meal and receive a share in his death and resurrection.

Certainly there is a point in the Church's year when the memorial structure of the liturgy is even more obvious than in the Sunday Eucharist. That is the Easter Vigil.[83] In the long night of that vigil the Church's memory is brought to its highest point. In that night the Church tells itself, in more stories than are told at any other time, about how God's people were led from the darkness of the beginning to the light of Easter morning. It looks back to its own beginning with Abraham, and even beyond to the

---

[82] Translator's note: the German *Einheitsübersetzung* has "Er hat ein Gedächtnis gestiftet an seine Wunder," i.e., "He has provided a memory of his wonders."

[83] The next four paragraphs on the Easter Vigil are drawn largely from a text by Bishop Josef Stimpfle, "Das Geheimnis der Kirche," Diocesan Synod of Augsburg 1990 (Donauwörth, 1991) 496–98, at 488–90.

roots of humanity. It follows the whole road once again—the creation of human beings, the call of Abraham, the sacrifice of Isaac, the passage through the Reed Sea, the rescue from Pharaoh and his chariots and charioteers, the road home from exile, the raising of the Messiah from the darkness of the grave—and it is not ashamed to say: all that is today!

It says:[84] This is the night of Exodus and liberation! This water of baptism is the same water through which our ancestors were rescued from the power of the Egyptians, and it is also the water over which the Spirit of God swept at the beginning! As on the first day of creation it kindles light and knows that the true light of the world is Christ, and the eighth day, the day of the new creation of the world, has already begun.

In this the Church overleaps with assurance the sense of reality not only of most contemporaries but also of most Christians, and entirely reevaluates the facts by proclaiming the re-vision of all things as the logic of its memory. In the great liturgy of the Easter Vigil the Church transfers its faithful into the divine "instant." It looks at history through God's eyes and thus discovers what is revealed only in a familiarity with God's thoughts and through the constant experience of God's actions, and what is comprehensible to the Church alone. But in this night the Church is illuminated by it.

This night, it therefore says, is light as day, and it snatches the people of God out of the darkness of sin. In it heaven and earth are joined; in it what has been thrown down is built up again; the old has become new and the broken world is restored to its original beauty. The Easter night, which leads immediately to the brightness of Easter morning, is the greatest of the many feasts the Church celebrates. Like all Christian feasts it is not an empty memorial but creates the most intensive presence of what it celebrates, and by actualizing presence it also creates a future. For where the past deeds of God become the present they always open into the future. The *futurum,* what is merely yet-to-come, becomes *adventus,* the thing already arriving. Every feast can be a prophetic event that guides the steps of the community closer to what God has already begun as the overwhelming salvation of the world. The principle of memory and the principle of hope are not mutually exclusive. Each conditions and affects the other.

### 4. The Church Is to Be the Body of Christ

In the year 395 C.E. the shrine at Eleusis, near Athens, was destroyed by christianized Goths under King Alaric, who thus brought to an end a

---

[84] Cf. especially the *Exsultet* at the Easter Vigil.

thousand-year history. Countless people had, over the centuries, come to that place to be inducted into the mysteries: not only Athenians but increasingly men and women from all over Greece, and at the end Romans and even Roman emperors.[85] Eleusis promised those who submitted to its initiation ritual an internal transformation and after death a happier life than awaited noninitiates. The Eleusinian mysteries can serve as a model of individualistic salvation: the mystics returned to their daily lives without taking on new ties. No community or church was constituted at Eleusis. The initiates did not even join in cultic associations as was often the case with later mystery cults.[86]

For us the Eleusinian mysteries are instructive in a variety of ways. They show the human need for "personal religion" but at the same time they reveal the deep longing to pass beyond the limits of banal, everyday experience and to enter into mystery, to see what is hidden. By that very fact they witness to the unquenchable human drive toward inner renewal, self-rejuvenating strength, and even eternal life. Of course they also show that people prefer to achieve all that through mere ritual and with a concentration on the self. Naturally, besides the ritual purification and vision of secret things about which one was not permitted to speak the mysteries also involved solemn processions and a festive communal banquet. But salvation, so it was promised, was given directly to the individual and had no social consequences. In all this the Eleusinian mysteries are an outstanding example of the "religious," and in all of it there are points of contact to contemporary esotericism.

That Eleusis founded no "communities" and certainly no "church" was not an accident. We have already seen (in II, 7 above) that the "community" form arose out of Israel, and what was at stake in Israel was precisely *not* a purely individual salvation that could be attained independently of the life of the people of God. In the same way salvation through Christ was bound up with the New Testament people of God. Certainly individualism would be a major temptation for Christian people as well. At the extreme the Church was then seen simply as the union, after the fact, of those who had already attained salvation as *individuals* through their personal union with Christ: those who already believe simply gather as a kind of fraternal society.[87]

---

[85] I am following Hans-Josef Klauck, *Umwelt des Urchristentums I,* 95.

[86] Ibid.

[87] For Adolf von Harnack, for example, the Church was a "fraternal society" of many individuals who as individuals, through faith in the good news—that is, the good news of their immediate relationship to God the Father—had already been saved. Cf. Gerhard Lohfink, *Jesus and Community* 1–3.

Christian salvation, however, is something else, and takes a different path. It consists precisely in incorporation into the Church as a social body. Only in that way is it possible to participate in the history of liberation that began with Abraham. Salvation in Christ means inalienable incorporation in his "body," and life through his saving action is impossible apart from a common life with the members of this body. One can have communion with Christ only and always in communion with others. Paul had to struggle with the community at Corinth over this fundamental difference in biblical faith, and it was certainly no accident that the struggle took place just there. Religious individualism already had a history in Greece. In Corinth that individualism with regard to salvation appeared especially at the eucharistic celebration.

It is true that we can no longer reconstruct the details of the Lord's Supper as it was celebrated in Corinth, but it is certain that it took place in the evening and was associated with a complete dinner. That must have been true not only in Corinth but in the other early Christian communities around the year 55.[88] The dinner began with "breaking of bread," and at the end the "cup of blessing" was passed.[89] But it was in fact the dinner that revealed one of the awkward situations in the Corinthian community that Paul had to deal with: at that meal the better-off members ate their fill while the poor went away empty. Some dined richly while others went hungry (1 Cor 11:21).

How was such a thing possible? Many modern interpreters have posited that the rich began their dinner early because they did not have to work, while the slaves, artisans, and small merchants had to remain at their tasks and could only come at a later hour.[90] However, that supposition has some difficulties as regards the sequence (word over the bread, complete dinner, word over the cup) that Paul transmits in 1 Cor 11:23-25 for Jesus' last meal and thus presupposes for the sequence of the meal in Corinth.[91] If we retain this sequence and suppose that the poorer members

---

[88] Cf. Luke 24:29-30; Acts 20:7; Pliny, *Ep.* X.96,7 (?). *Didache* 10.1, 6 attests only to the combination with a complete dinner, not to the time of day.

[89] Peter Stuhlmacher attempts a description of the course of the entire celebration in *Biblische Theologie* 1:366–67.

[90] Important for this direction in interpretation was Günther Bornkamm's essay, "Herrenmahl und Kirche bei Paulus" in idem, *Studien zu Antike und Christentum. Gesammelte Aufsätze II.* BEvTh28 (Munich: Kaiser, 1959) 138–76.

[91] Otfried Hofius says correctly in his "Herrenmahl und Herrenmahlsparadosis," *ZThK* 85 (1988) 371–408 that the "text of 1 Cor 11:23b-25 gives rationale and norm for the liturgical usage of early Christian communities, while at the same time reflecting that usage" (p. 371). Therefore it is difficult to suppose that in the Corinthian community the words over the bread and cup had already been combined (contrary to 1 Cor 11:23b-25) and were both spoken after the dinner.

only arrived later it follows that they regularly missed the first part of the Eucharist—which is scarcely imaginable.

We must therefore suppose that all gathered at the same time to celebrate the Lord's Supper. The "divisions" in the assembly (11:18) did not occur because they were separated by scheduling, but because the rich had better food as part of the common meal than the poor had. It is rightly pointed out that in antiquity there was a well-known form of the common meal called *eranos* at which the host only provided the space but not the food. Each brought to the meal what she or he had and ate of what all had brought.[92] We have the same practice; it is what Americans call potluck.

There was some disagreement in antiquity about whether at an *eranos* each should eat only what she or he had brought, or whether it was better to share in common what everyone contributed.[93] In the Corinthian community it had apparently become customary for each to eat what she or he had packed. Thus the rich were sated and the poor had what was left over. Paul describes it as follows:

> When you come together, it is not really to eat the Lord's supper. For at the (common) meal each eats his or her own dinner, and one goes hungry and another becomes drunk. What! Do you not have homes to eat and drink in? Or do you show contempt for the church of God and humiliate those who have nothing? (1 Cor 11:20-22*)[94]

It is this contempt for the community that is the true misery in the Corinthian eucharistic celebration. It is by no means the case that part of the community despised the sacrament as such. On the contrary! Like baptism, the reception of the Eucharist was most highly esteemed.[95] The problem was sacramental individualism: the Eucharist was apparently regarded as an individual reception of salvation independent of the community. The poor had their Eucharist, of course, even if they had nothing

---

[92] Cf. especially Peter Lampe, "Das korinthische Herrenmahl im Schnittpunkt hellenistisch-römischer Mahlpraxis und paulinischer *Theologia Crucis* (1 Kor 11,17-34)," *ZNW* 82 (1991) 183–213, at 194–98. It is true that Lampe retains the position that the rich came earlier. But Hofius argues convincingly against this common assumption ("Herrenmahl," 384–391). He shows, on good philological grounds, that *prolambanein* in 11:21 does not refer to "going ahead" with one's own meal in the sense of anticipation, but to "taking by preference" or "taking for oneself." Correspondingly *ekdechesthai* in 11:33 should not be translated "wait," but "accept" (in the concrete case "preserve table fellowship"). These translations are not only unproblematic semantically but fit better in the context.

[93] See the discussion of this in Xenophon, *Memorabilia* III.14,1. Cf. Peter Lampe, "Das korinthische Herrenmahl," 196.

[94] For this translation see above, n. 92.

[95] The practice of baptism on behalf of the dead (1 Cor 15:29) attests to the high regard for baptism in Corinth, and in 1 Cor 10:1-13 Paul has to combat a false sacramentalism with regard both to baptism and the Lord's Supper.

from the meal. That the Eucharist was a *common* meal: still more, that it made Jesus present in his servanthood's self-surrender and therefore had to have consequences for life together within the community was not seen. Eleusis was not far away.

When Paul warns the satisfied not to receive the Eucharist unworthily and not to be guilty of the body and blood of Christ (11:27) he is thinking first of all of their attitude toward the eucharistic body of the Lord, for which they are answerable. But at the same time they are guilty with respect to the body of the community because they are dividing it (11:18). Paul does not hesitate to say that they "show contempt for the church of God" (11:22). That means that they are living schizophrenically: they have regard for the body of the Lord and at the same time disregard the community. But that cannot be, for the eucharistic body and the body of the community are closely related. In the Eucharist the Crucified and Risen One gives a share in his body and thus creates communion between himself and the community that is his earthly embodiment.[96] In another context, namely with regard to partaking of meals at which meat offered to idols is served, Paul can say:

> The cup of blessing that we bless, is it not a sharing in the blood of Christ? The bread that we break, is it not a sharing in the body of Christ? Because there is one bread, we who are many are one body, for we all partake of the one bread. (1 Cor 10:16-17)

There is thus an indissoluble union between the eucharistic body of Christ and the body of the community. If the community does not realize, even in its celebration of the Lord's supper, the serving self-sacrifice of Jesus, although it participates in it sacramentally, it is twisted at its deepest depth. Its collective sickness must then manifest itself in the sicknesses of individuals. Paul says baldly: "For this reason many of you are weak and ill, and some have died" (1 Cor 11:30). We must be careful not to set aside this statement as a kind of magical thinking. When the community has been experienced as God's eschatological new creation from the dying and rising of Jesus and then is nevertheless split by egotism, that fact can have its effects even in the bodies of its members, all the way to the somatic level.

We must also be careful, however, not to look down on or distance ourselves from the better-off in Corinth who eat the food they have brought for themselves. Is their behavior worse than the normal condition of our

---

[96] This statement is derived from Josef Hainz, "Vom 'Volk Gottes' zum 'Leib Christi.' Biblisch-theologische Perspektiven paulinischer Ekklesiologie" in idem, *Volk Gottes, Gemeinde und Gesellschaft. JBTh* 7 (Neukirchen-Vluyn: Neukirchener Verlag, 1992) 145–64, at 156.

communities, in which people of course receive the sacrament on Sundays but otherwise go their own way and scarcely have anything to do with one another?

It would, of course, be a misunderstanding of Paul's intention in 1 Corinthians 11 to interpret him as merely demanding a greater solidarity within the community. More is at stake for him here. That is clear from the section of the letter on charisms, concluding with 1 Corinthians 12–14.

When Paul began dealing with the community in Corinth he, like all the other early Christian missionaries, must have placed great emphasis on experience of the Spirit as evidence of the new life. That invited an excited atmosphere in which speaking in the Spirit, and especially ecstatic praise of God in tongues, was admired. It was an atmosphere that invited new beginnings. But it was very soon evident in Corinth that a charismatic praxis that arises entirely from individual experience of the Spirit can take on a life of its own. Under certain circumstances it leads far away from the gospel and the upbuilding of the community. In Corinth, of course, that must only have happened at a time when Paul had already left the city.

Now, from Ephesus, he attempts to make it clear to the community that the important charisms are not only those that are external, striking, and even spectacular. There are many other gifts of grace, and the greatest and most fundamental of these is *agapē*. The criterion is always whether the charisms gather the community and contribute to its upbuilding. That is the basic theme of chs. 12–14 of 1 Corinthians.[97] Within this context Paul, using the image of the body and its members, shows that all the baptized are equally valuable members of the body that is the community.

> For just as the body is one and has many members, and all the members of the body, though many, are one body, so it is with Christ. For in the one Spirit we were all baptized into one body—Jews or Greeks, slaves or free—and we were all made to drink of one Spirit. (1 Cor 12:12-13)

Paul then continues by elaborating on this image of the many members of the body, an image well known in antiquity: all are dependent on each other and none of them can say that it has no need of the others. What is distinctively Christian in this picture, however, appears only at the point when Paul says that the weaker and less presentable members of the body must receive more respect than the noble and honorable members:

> But God has so arranged the body, giving the greater honor to the inferior member, that there may be no dissension within the body, but the members

---

[97] Chapters 12–13 do not yet speak of building up the community, but the theme emerges clearly in ch. 14 (cf. 14:3, 4, 5, 12, 17, 26) and chs. 12–14 constitute an organic whole.

may have the same care for one another. If one member suffers, all suffer together with it; if one member is honored, all rejoice together with it. Now you are the body of Christ and individually members of it. (1 Cor 12:24-27)

The purpose of these statements is clear: Paul not only sets those who do the everyday and therefore often despised work in the community on an equal basis with those who are highly gifted. He places the former even above the latter ("greater honor"). Here, at the latest, it becomes clear that all this is about something more than humane ideas or social concern, however important that is. What is at issue is nothing less than the fundamental principle of community: that each esteems the other above himself or herself (Phil 2:3). This is just what Jesus wanted to show his disciples by washing their feet. This is precisely the thing with which he endowed the people of God as an unforgettable memory through his "death for the many." This is what makes the Church the "body of Christ" through the power of the Eucharist given to it.

It may be necessary to emphasize at this point that the fact that the community is the "body of Christ" does not at all mean that it can be equated with Christ. It can never equal his word, his life, his purity, his absolute surrender, and his complete unity with the will of the Father in this world. It is not only the Church of the saints, but always the Church of sinners as well. And yet it is the real and physical presence of Christ in history. To say less would be an inadequate reflection of Pauline theology.

It would also be an error to suppose that Paul's statements about the body of Christ are only a narrow sector in his theology, perhaps confined to isolated passages in 1 Corinthians. The idea of the body is anything but an island in Paul's thought. It rests on a broad textual basis, a long list of passages that speak of the baptized's being "in Christ."

Today's reader of the Pauline letters is at first inclined to read the frequently recurring "in Christ" in an individual sense. This is usually referred to as a "personal relationship to Christ." Often it is even interpreted as referring to that union with Christ that is described in such impressive imagery by Christian mystics. Such an understanding is not entirely false; it can be one aspect of Paul's intention. After all, in Gal 2:19-20 he formulates: "I have been crucified with Christ; and it is no longer I who live, but it is Christ who lives in me."

Of course, even in the case of Gal 2:19-20 the question arises: is the "I" who speaks really only the individual or is this something broader? The latter is certainly true of the majority of the texts that speak of "being in Christ." Their reference is ecclesiological: those who are "in Christ" live within the realm of Christ's Spirit, poured out since Easter, in which sin and death are no longer the ruling powers. Thus "being in Christ" does not mean a purely individual relationship between Christ and the believer. It means belonging to the realm within which Christ rules, and that realm is his body, the community. This is the basis on which every individual is wholly bound to Christ and to her or his fellow Christians.

Hence in Phil 2:1 Paul speaks of "encouragement *in Christ.*" He is not envisioning a dialogue between Christ and the soul but a strengthening *within the realm of the community,* where mutual love, the company of the Spirit, warm affection and compassion, unanimity and concord are to rule (Phil 2:1-3). Just after this Paul quotes an ancient Christian song that describes in hymnic form how Christ emptied himself of his glory, became obedient like a slave, and offered his life, even unto death (Phil 2:6-11). For Paul "being in Christ" means living in just that kind of surrender for the sake of others, and that is only possible where Jesus is Lord and where people call on his name.

Only out of the foundational event described in Phil 2:6-11 can community come to be, and only on such a basis can the divisions that continually threaten communities and the Church as a whole be overcome. Humanistic appeals to solidarity or brotherhood and sisterhood are inadequate. Rivalry between individuals, families, groups, and nations is much too powerful. But if the community lives from the dying and rising of Jesus it will become a new thing in the world. Then even the differences between people that normally destroy every community will become its wealth. For from the reality that people who are quite different and remain different can desire the same thing through Christ and the power of his Spirit can arise a variegated and multiform entity.

In such a community some are called by God to be apostles, others to be prophets, a third group to be teachers. Others have the power to believe with their whole existence, and such faith is always a miracle that releases further miracles. Some have the charism to detect sicknesses, others the charism of consolation, still others have the charism of community leadership. Some have the gift of theological insight, others the gift of handing on that insight. The gift of insight into human nature is given to some, while others have the gift of discernment, and still others the ability to bring forth the right language with which to praise God (cf. 1 Cor 12:8-11, 28).

This multitude of gifts that Paul describes to the Corinthians in the image of a body that is a living organism with many members is a response to one of the most urgent of human questions, heretofore unanswered by any form of society: How can it happen that people who are very different, who are rich indeed *because* of their differences and must not be reduced to uniformity, can nevertheless live together in peace? For people are not the same and do not want to be. Everyone desires to be unique, and rightly so. But how can they remain different and still do justice to each other without destroying society?

The solution "people of God," given a specific form in the New Testament as the "body of Christ," rests entirely on freedom and voluntariness. It also rests on the fact that the differences between people are not denied, but instead are made a means to mutual enrichment. The thing that binds together what otherwise would drive to disunion is *agapē,* something not possible from human beings alone, but a gift of the divine Spirit, and that Spirit is released through Jesus' surrender of his life.

Thus the community can become the place where the rich come to the aid of the poor, the gifted to the ungifted, the laughing to those who weep, the strong to the weak, the healthy to the sick, the married to those without family. Often within the community the contrary is the case, and that is again a sign that more is happening in it than a social institution can manage: the unmarried are a blessing to the children of the married; the weak are seismographs for developing rifts in the community that the strong have not even noticed; the sick, through their faith and joy, support those who are healthy.

It is obvious: all this is scarcely possible in a large community, so big that no one can keep track of it and consisting of a great many isolated individuals. It presumes a constant communication, a weaving together of lives, a continual assembling and reassembling, an incorporation of every individual in service to the missionary tasks of the community. But that is just what Paul meant with his image of the body. If we are honest we must say that both the Church as a whole and its individual communities are very far from realizing, even remotely, the image of the body of Christ that Paul sets before the eyes of the Corinthians. We are, instead, in danger of getting farther and farther from what Paul meant by "the body of Christ."

In fact one of the fundamental problems of the Church at the end of the twentieth century is that faith no longer saturates the whole of life, but only a narrow sector. Out of an entire week we often have no more than sixty minutes on Sunday for "faith." Our employment has long since become a world in itself with its own rules and ways of behaving. It has scarcely anything to do with Christian existence. All the efforts of Christian societies and Church efforts toward a "lay apostolate" have not changed this. In the same way leisure time has also become a world unto itself, as have education, the economy, culture, and all the other spheres of life. Faith is drying up. It no longer has any material that it can transform. It has become unworldly and therefore ineffectual.

For many Christians it would not be a turning point in their lives if they decided, one day, to stop praying tomorrow, next Sunday to leave off going to church, and at the next opportunity to stop the church paper. Their lives would continue according to the very same social rules, norms, styles of behavior, and models as before. Nothing would change because their faith would already, long before that, have become unworldly, inconsequential, and ultimately futile. It was, in fact, not faith at all. Where faith is really faith it cannot be shoved to the margins of life.

Christian faith, just like Jewish faith, subjects *all* of life to the promise and claim of God. Its nature is such that it interpenetrates all aspects of the lives of believers and gives them a new form. Of itself it demands that social relationships must change and that the material of the world must be molded. Faith desires to incorporate all things so that a "new creation" can come to be.

At the same time faith tends toward a more and more intensive communion among believers, for only in the community, the place of this communion, only in the place of salvation given by God can the material of the world really be molded and social relationships really transformed. It would therefore be essential to Christian faith that individual believers should not live alongside one another in isolation but should be joined into a single body. It would be essential that they weave together all their gifts and opportunities, that in their gatherings they judge their entire lives in light of the coming of the reign of God and allow themselves to be gifted with the unanimity of *agapē*. Then the community would become the place where the messianic signs that are promised to the people of God could shine forth and become effective.

All this is part of the tendency of faith to embodiment. Christian faith *of itself* produces an impulse to bind believers in communion and by way of that communion to draw all spheres of life into God's new creation. This integrating tendency is a property of faith itself. It is not something added secondarily at some time or place. An individual cannot first begin to believe alone and then, afterward, join the Church. The acceptance of faith is already identical with incorporation into the church. Accepting faith already means desiring the communion of believers. Accordingly the transformation of world and society is not an obligation that is added to faith as something secondary. Where faith is a living thing it is, instead, a transformed world from the very outset.[98]

The communion of believers thus is not something that is merely spiritual and intellectual. It must be embodied. It needs a place, a realm in which it can take shape. Perhaps from here one must read again, with new eyes, how often Paul's letters and the Acts of the Apostles speak of "houses." It is amazing how many houses are known to us by name sim-

---

[98] Cf. Norbert Lohfink, *Das Jüdische am Christentum* 12.

ply in connection with the apostolic work and journeys of Paul: the house of Lydia the purple-seller in Philippi, the house of Jason in Thessalonica, those of Titius Justus and Gaius in Corinth, the house of the evangelist Philip in Caesarea, and the house of Mnason of Cyprus in Jerusalem.[99]

In these and many other houses[100] of the early Christian era unfolded a crucial piece of the life of the primitive Christian communities. The *natural* family, which constituted the central focus of the several houses, was opened and joined into a broader context: the *new* family of the community. In these houses catechumens were instructed, brothers and sisters in the faith on journey were welcomed as guests, the community gathered for its meetings and the celebration of the Lord's Supper, unemployed Christians found work, and for the most part the first contacts were made with Gentiles who wanted to become acquainted with a Christian community. When they did so they did not learn merely a set of abstract principles of faith, but Christian life.

In this context we should also consider the following: the ancient house cannot simply be compared to modern houses; the function of the latter is almost exclusively to furnish a mere dwelling place. In contrast, in antiquity and for a long time thereafter the house was a larger social unit. It contained not only the family in the narrow sense but also other people who lived and worked there. Frequently the house was also a place of production. Larger production facilities separate from the house were rarely found. This meant that in Christian houses like that of Aquila and Prisca (cf. IV, 1 above) faith and life, or faith and work, constituted a unity. Prisca's family saw how Paul worked with his hands, and those to whom Paul preached the gospel in connection with his artisanal work at the same time experienced a Christian family.

Something else must be added: the houses in which Paul dwelt were often those belonging to the first converts in a given city. This was true of Lydia's house in Philippi and that of Jason in Thessalonica, and probably also of Gaius's house in Corinth. It was precisely in the houses of the first converts, then, that the community usually gathered. In that way those houses embodied a bit of living community history that was made present in every assembly—not only in the rooms themselves, but in the people as well.

Obviously in the intimate space of the primitive Christian house churches conflicts emerged much more clearly than in present-day parishes

[99] Lydia's house: Acts 16:14-15, 40; Jason's house: Acts 17:5-7; Titius Justus's house: Acts 18:7; Gaius's house: Rom 16:23; Philip's house: Acts 21:8-14; Mnason's house: Acts 21:15-17.

[100] Cf., for example, Acts 2:2, 46; 5:42; 8:3; 20:20; Rom 16:5; 1 Cor 16:19; Col 4:15; Phlm 2.

in which all too often people carefully distance themselves from one another and deflect any attempts at intrusion on their private lives. Thus in the early Christian communities mutual correction was a matter of course (cf. IV, 2 above). The conflicts between Paul and Peter in Antioch over questions of table fellowship between Jewish and Gentile Christians took place, according to the letter to the Galatians, "before them all" (2:14). What Paul wrote to the community in Corinth about the situation of the Lord's Supper among them was certainly read aloud in that assembly, probably before the eucharistic celebration. Unfortunately we do not know what happened in that assembly.

We would love to have much more detailed information about the concrete lives of those early communities, but our sources for the most part offer us little. Nevertheless we know enough that we are in no danger of glorifying the community life of those times. Above all, Paul's two letters to the Corinthians show us a community in which there was uncertainty, arrogance, slanted theology, and serious social conflicts. It would have been no different in other places.

What distinguishes those communities is not their moral integrity or the power of their faith, still less their unanimity. Nevertheless, Paul calls them "the saints" in the introductions to his letters, "the called," "God's beloved," "sanctified in Christ Jesus," the "*ekklēsia* of God."[101] He thus expresses the conviction that what is crucial is not the mistakes that are made; there will always be those. Theological foolishness is also not decisive; there will never be a lack of that. Not even sin and guilt are the most important things, however dreadful they often are; they can be forgiven.

What is decisive, after all, and everything depends on it, is that the community knows that God has called it to make the divine plan visible and to be a place of reconciliation in the world as the body of Christ. It is already that body, anterior to any of its own efforts. The Spirit of God promised for the end time, the Spirit of Jesus Christ, has already been given to it and has made it one body. Nevertheless it must know that its task is still to become that body.

## 5. Faith Must Be Learned

The early Christian witnesses from the beginning of the third century (Hippolytus, Tertullian, and Clement of Alexandria) give the first clear evidence of the establishment of a catechumenate.[102] From Hippolytus we

---

[101] Saints: Rom 1:7; 1 Cor 1:2; 2 Cor 1:1; Phil 1:1; called: Rom 1:7; 1 Cor 1:2; God's beloved: Rom 1:7; sanctified in Christ Jesus: 1 Cor 1:2; *ekklēsia* of God: 1 Cor 1:2; 2 Cor 1:1.

[102] Cf. especially Hippolytus, *Traditio apostolica* 15-20.

know that the catechumenate in Rome at that time lasted three years.[103] During that period of time the aspirants to baptism learned Christian teaching and practiced the Christian life before being admitted to the sacrament. Apparently the Church was of the opinion at that time that a faster introduction to faith was simply impossible.

At first glance it seems as if the beginning phase of the Church stood in irrevocable contradiction to this practice. After all, the Acts of the Apostles, the only book in the New Testament that offers us concrete narrative material on primitive Christian baptismal practice, does not appear to know of any kind of catechumenate. It is shocking to see how quickly people are baptized according to the narratives in Acts:

- After Peter's Pentecost sermon, on the very same day three thousand people are baptized and "added" to the community (2:41).

- The Ethiopian queen's minister of finance is taught by Philip in his chariot and immediately baptized at the first water source that appears (8:38).

- In Damascus Ananias enters the house where the blinded Saul is staying, lays hands on him (thus healing him of his blindness) and, immediately after this laying on of hands, baptizes him (9:18).

- The Roman centurion Cornelius, on the very same day on which Peter, following divine instruction, comes to see him, is baptized together with his relatives and friends (10:48).

- Lydia, the dealer in purple cloth, after hearing Paul's preaching outside the gates of Philippi, receives baptism together with her whole household, that is, her family and all those who lived in her house. Immediately afterward she welcomes Paul and his companions into her household (16:15).

It is no different for the Philippian jailer after the earthquake during the night, which broke Paul's and Silas's chains. He is so shaken by the event that he asks them:

"Sirs, what must I do to be saved?" They answered, "Believe on the Lord Jesus, and you will be saved, you and your household." They spoke the word of the Lord to him and to all who were in his house. At the same hour of the night he took them and washed their wounds; then he and his entire family were baptized without delay. He brought them up into the house and set food before them; and he and his entire household rejoiced that he had become a believer in God. (16:30-34)

---

[103] Ibid. 17: *Catechumeni per tres annos audiant verbum.*

Finally, it is the same story with the disciples in Ephesus who had only received the baptism of John. They, too, are immediately baptized in the name of Jesus (19:5-6).

Of nine baptismal texts in Acts no less than seven speak of an immediate baptism. Only in Acts 8:12-13 (conversions in Samaria) and 18:8 (conversions in Corinth) does the question of time remain open, but that has to do with the literary structure of the brief "notices" in 8:12-13 and 18:8. Immediate baptisms are not excluded in those passages either. In contrast, Luke nowhere speaks of a catechumenal period before any baptism. That cannot be pure accident. Why does baptism happen so quickly in Luke's accounts?

Of course we could say that the baptismal texts in Acts still reflect something of the original character of baptism: it was administered against the horizon of an intensive expectation of the immediate parousia; it was a sacramental sealing in view of the nearness of the end of the world, rescue from the approaching judgment. Because the judgment of the world was at the door baptism had to be administered quickly, just as John the Baptizer had baptized those who came over the Jordan to him as soon as they had publicly confessed their sins.

However, this is not a satisfying answer, because an immediate expectation of the end plays no part in Luke's interpretation of history. For him there are broad fields of action open to the Church. In Acts 1:8 the Risen One promises the apostles before he leaves them for good: "you will receive power when the Holy Spirit has come upon you; and you will be my witnesses in Jerusalem, in all Judea and Samaria, and to the ends of the earth." When space and time are so greatly extended we must raise the question in all seriousness: why this quick baptizing? A very different kind of answer would be that the immediate baptisms in Acts are literary creations. Luke tells the events in time-lapse fashion so that readers will be able to picture the events vividly and as "action scenes." The dramatic manner of narrative would, in the case of baptism, thus illustrate the power of the Spirit of God and the strength of faith in the beginning.

This would be a better answer because it remains on the level of Luke's presentation. Nevertheless, it is not really satisfying either. There is, in fact, a much simpler explanation: the possibility of immediate baptism rests, in Acts, on the fact that the candidates for baptism, like those who came to John the Baptizer, were already members of the people of God, or at least were strongly shaped by God's people.

The three thousand who, according to Luke's account, were baptized in Jerusalem on the day of Pentecost were not Gentiles, but Jews and Jewish proselytes from Gentile lands who were dwelling in Jerusalem. There were at that time many Jews from the Diaspora who moved with their families to Jerusalem in order to live and die as close as possible to the Temple.[104] Their move to the Holy City, which must have entailed major sacrifices, was a sign of their faith in the prophetic promises and an expression of their love for "the Land." They wanted to anticipate the eschatological gathering of dispersed Israel at Zion. For the most part these former diaspora Jews lived the faith of the people of God more earnestly than the longtime inhabitants of Jerusalem. After all, they had experienced the exodus from their homelands into the land of promise. But however Luke imagined the audience for the Pentecost preaching it is certain that for him they were not Gentiles, but Diaspora Jews.[105]

The Ethiopian queen's finance minister whom Philip baptized must have been a "god-fearer" who was close to Israel's faith.[106] He had undertaken the long and dangerous journey from Nubia to Jerusalem in order to worship the true God in the Temple. He loved the Sacred Scriptures, for he had with him a scroll of the prophet Isaiah and was reading it in his chariot during the return journey.

The centurion Cornelius and the purple dealer Lydia were also "god-fearers." Paul encountered Lydia on the Sabbath with her family at the river, where he expected to find a *proseuchē,* a Jewish synagogue or at least a Jewish place of prayer.[107] Thus she and her family lived consciously in the light of Israel's faith. It is still clearer in the case of Cornelius, who not only kept strictly to the Jewish hours of prayer but shared his income with the poor among the people of God and had gathered around him a group of friends who loved the faith of Israel, as he did. He was highly regarded by the Jewish community in Caesarea.[108] In the case of the disciples at Ephesus, who had received John's baptism, and in that of Saul, who as a Pharisee had lived strictly according to Torah, "as to righteousness under the law, blameless" (Phil 3:6), their rootedness in Judaism is obvious.

[104] Cf. Martin Hengel, "Zwischen Jesus und Paulus. Die 'Hellenisten,' die 'Sieben' und Stephanus (Apg 6,1-15; 7,54–8,3)," *ZThK* 72 (1975) 151–206, at 165–74.

[105] What is crucial is that in Luke's conception the Gentile mission is first begun in Acts 10 through God's intervention.

[106] "God-fearers" were Gentiles who were associated with the synagogue. While they had not received circumcision (in the case of men), they attended Sabbath services, worshiped the one God of Israel, kept the Sabbath and the food prescriptions. Cf. Marius Reiser, "Hat Paulus Heiden bekehrt?" *BZ* 39 (1995) 76–91, at 83–87. Reiser argues on good grounds that the people from Gentile society whom Paul brought to faith in Jesus Christ were not simply Gentiles, but "god-fearers."

[107] Acts 16:13: at the river because ritual washing was possible there.

[108] Cornelius kept the Jewish hours of prayer: Acts 10:2-3; almsgiving: 10:2; group of friends: 10:24, 27; high regard among the Jews: 10:22.

The picture as a whole is crystal-clear. The Christian communities of the first decades still participated immediately in Israel's knowledge of salvation. Those who were baptized, whether Jews or god-fearing Gentiles, had long been aware that the change of allegiance from the gods to the true God was a part of faith, as was a turning from pagan ways of life to a life of righteousness. They had no need to learn the right way to pray and how to worship. They had prayed every day in the Tefillah, the basic Jewish prayer, for the coming of the Messiah and the eschatological gathering of Israel. Every Sabbath in the synagogue they had heard the Torah and the promises of the prophets. They knew the story of God with God's people since Abraham.

But above all they did not need to learn what *life in community* meant, because this way of life as "community" was a matter of course for them. Believers in the early days of the Church had, because of their Jewish origins or their god-fearing attachment to the synagogue, long since taken the step from Gentile society into a very different living space. What they still had to learn was that the history of Israel had now entered definitively into the stage of fulfillment. Concretely they had to believe that in the crucified and risen Jesus the Messiah of Israel had come, that the eschatological gathering of the people of God, and with it the messianic transformation of the world, was already in progress, and that the Messiah and his messianic salvation were to be encountered in the company of Jesus' followers and nowhere else. As soon as they believed and confessed this, they were admitted to baptism.

Why, then, does Luke depict baptism as happening so quickly and why is there no catechumenate in the baptismal narratives of Acts?—because the baptismal candidates had already been living their catechumenate for many years. *Judaism was the catechumenate of the primitive Church.*

Only when there was a danger that the Church would lose its roots in Judaism was it necessary to introduce the catechumenate as a separate institution. It is only consistent that the Church then had resort primarily to Jewish tradition and Jewish methods of discernment in establishing the catechumenate. This is evident already in the so-called Teaching of the Twelve Apostles *(Didache)*. Its first six chapters are pure baptismal catechesis and consist in large measure of the Two Ways treatise, which stems from Judaism.[109] The Teaching of the Twelve Apostles begins with it: "There are two ways, one that leads to life and one that leads to death, and great is the difference between them" *(Did.* 1,1). The Church, in accept-

---

[109] For a reconstruction of the Two Ways tractate, its Jewish origins and its redaction in the *Didache* see Kurt Niederwimmer, *The Didache.* Translated by Linda M. Maloney. Hermeneia (Minneapolis: Fortress, 1998) 59–124.

ing the Two Ways tractate as part of its preparation for baptism, was saying that it is indispensable for baptism to learn to distinguish between the powers of death and the powers of life. Those who accept baptism choose the way of life. But that way demands a new manner of life. It is important, then, to avoid seeing the Church's catechumenate as purely *instruction*. It was more than that. It was an initiation of the baptismal candidates into a new way of life that was fundamentally different from the way of Gentile society. We have already discussed this above, in IV, 1.

Preparation for baptism was very soon divided into various stages, with appropriate sacramental aspects attached to each. Thus, for example, *exorcism* showed that the acceptance of faith was a change in rulership, from the powers of paganism to the rule of Christ. Such a change of allegiance was not simply a matter of good will. One had to let oneself be liberated from the demons of fear, greed, and egoism that lodge within every individual. The *salt* that was placed on the catechumens' tongues in a special ritual was to show that the new thing cannot be grasped only with reason. It must be tasted, and only the taste of truth and the beauty of faith make it possible for the baptismal candidates to go their new way in genuine freedom.

In these and other sign-actions that divided the period of baptismal preparation into stages we see clearly that the catechumenate is already the beginning of baptism. It is, as Joseph Ratzinger has written, "not a preliminary course of instruction, but an integral part of the sacrament itself. On the other hand, the sacrament is not just a liturgical act but a process, a long road that demands an individual's whole strength . . . ."[110] Thus in the early Church catechumenate and baptism constituted an organic unit. They cannot be considered in isolation and independently of each other.

But does this mean that we must return to the practice of adult baptism, as in the early Church? In fact the call for eliminating infant baptism makes itself heard again and again with some regularity. Infant baptism is described as a false development that constitutes a disturbing factor impeding what the Church should be. It has destroyed the catechumenate and with it the conscious acceptance of faith and responsible decision in favor of the Church. For that reason it shares in the responsibility for the dangerous bloating of the Church into a "Volkskirche."[111]

---

[110] Joseph Ratzinger, *Principles of Catholic Theology* 36. For the following remarks on infant baptism cf. ibid., 27–43, especially 41–43.

[111] Translator's note: this is a German concept that does not translate directly into English; hence its omission from the dictionary! It implies a situation, common in Europe but unknown in North America, in which membership in the established church, or one of only a few major churches, is a "given" from birth and is virtually coincident with citizenship. Children are baptized as a matter of course into the church to which their parents (often only nominally) belong.

It is worth our while to pursue this question of infant baptism a little farther because the question is a focal point that again assists us in seeing clearly what "church" is. We can probably get to the heart of the problem fastest by beginning with the objection of many parents today: they say that their child should decide for itself whether to be a Christian or not. To that point it should grow up in complete freedom, without indoctrination and without influence from others—in a neutral space, we might say.

That sounds enlightened, but only superficially. In reality this position ignores the reality of the world and its inhabitants. It is not only false because there are no "neutral spaces" in our society. It is also a complete mistake with regard to the nature of human existence. No child can be asked whether it wants to come into the world or not, whether it wants to live or not. Its life is simply given to it. The "givenness" for any child appears not only in the fact that its parents give it life, but also in the circumstance that for a rather long time they must take responsibility for its life. We encounter here once again the phenomenon of representation, without which life in human society is impossible. The parents have brought forth life and now act as the child's representatives, because the child cannot do it; they provide it with food, clothing, shelter, and education. The child cannot yet make decisions about any of that. It needs representatives.

Indeed, it needs representatives who will give it, in every respect, the best that they have. It must already be clear that this cannot be restricted to food and clothing. A child needs more than that. It needs love and a sense of belonging, education and training. It needs the best of all these things. But if the parents are believers and regard their faith as the best and most important thing in their lives, can they withhold from their child a life within the realm of faith? May they prevent it, from an early age, from learning to distinguish between good and evil, true and false, beautiful and ugly, human and inhuman, and finally also between the world and God? May they prevent it from sharpening not only its external senses but also the senses with which a person receives the word of God and beholds God's works? May they close to their child the manifold world of faith, which cannot be separated from the sacraments, and which reveals God's actions in the world?

The absurdity of such an idea is evident if we consider the phenomenon of speech. All parents teach their children to talk. But learning to speak is more than simply achieving command of an array of sounds. Every language conveys a world. At every stage of learning to speak the child grasps and interprets its world. The idea of letting a child grow up in a neutral space in which world and existence remain uninterpreted is a complete misunderstanding of the relationship between language and reality. Every word, every sentence, every form of speech conveys a world and interprets it simultaneously. The child constantly absorbs into itself, from its first breath, a world already interpreted (rightly interpreted or foreshortened, displaced, deprived of its meaning). And the more it matures toward understanding the more powerfully is it handed over to the currently dominant models of society, its standards and its powers.

It would therefore be entirely irresponsible for believing parents to surrender their child to the intepretations of the world that pour over it, leaving it helpless and without the ability to discern, and not to open to it the most comprehensive interpretation of the world that exists: the truth of God that has definitively entered the world in Jesus Christ. But that truth is not simply to be apprehended in concepts. It must be tasted. It must be breathed in. It is a way of life.

Baptism is the entry into this way of life. The baptism of the still *immature* child expresses the truth that the life of faith cannot be created by human effort. Faith cannot be instilled. It can only be received. It is always a gift, a grace. Therefore believing parents may not withhold baptism from their child any more than they may withhold food, clothing, play, playmates, language, or education.

If the parents want their child to learn to understand the language of God's truth they themselves need help. The family alone is not an adequate space within which God can speak and act. The parents and their children need the experiential space in which the word of God is received and lived by many. This space is the Church with its liturgy, its sacraments, its assemblies, its experiences gathered up and handed on from generation to generation. Therefore baptism should take place, whenever possible, in the presence of the assembled community. The community, together with the parents and godparents, assumes responsibility for the child's faith. They will stand at its side like a multitude of believing fathers and mothers. They themselves must be continually converted so that the child can really discover *as a free gift* a space within which faith is experienced.

The parents can learn, within this experiential space, that their child is God's creation, beloved of God and therefore sacrosanct. It is entrusted to them, but it is not their property that they can misuse to advance their own lives. The child is no more at its parents' disposal than it is at the disposal of anyone else. They do not have the right to shape it in their own image and according to their private desires. They have neither the right to make an idol of it nor to make it their tool. This inviolability of the child, its freedom given to it by God, is expressed in the sacramental action of baptism.

Being baptized means receiving a share in the history of God with the world, and only those who have a share in that history can, step by step, learn true freedom. Those who want to raise their children in a supposedly "neutral space" will certainly hand it over to a multitude of powers and very soon see it deprived of its freedom.

In fact the view was the same in Israel. No faithful Jew would ever have thought of trying to rear his or her children first of all in a neutral space. Circumcision of male children, the sign of the covenant, is performed on the eighth day after birth, and introduction to the Torah cannot begin too early. In Deut 6:4-7 we read:

> Hear, O Israel: The LORD is our God, the LORD alone. You shall love the LORD your God with all your heart, and with all your soul, and with all your might. Keep these words that I am commanding you today in your heart. Recite them to your children and talk about them when you are at home and when you are away, when you lie down and when you rise.

and a little later:

> When your children ask you in time to come, "What is the meaning of the decrees and the statues and the ordinances that the LORD our God has commanded you?" then you shall say to your children, "We were Pharaoh's slaves in Egypt, but the LORD brought us out of Egypt with a mighty hand. The LORD displayed before our eyes great and awesome signs and wonders against Egypt, against Pharaoh and all his household. He brought us out from there in order to bring us in, to give us the land that he promised on oath to our ancestors. (Deut 6:20-23)

Jewish children are therefore to hear repeatedly from their parents the Torah and the story of liberation on which it rests until it has become part of their own lives.[112] It must be no different in the Church, for it, too, lives from this story of liberation that has found its definitive fulfillment in Jesus. The story is too huge for a single family. It is only possible for them to bind their child into it if the family itself is bound up in the new family of the Church.

In recent decades the Church has seen ever more clearly how necessary a reintroduction of the catechumenate is. Its task is to place the way of life into which the child has been brought up in the full light of believing consciousness so that the young adult can really make a free decision about the form of her or his life.

Vatican Council II promoted a multi-stage catechumenate for adults.[113] We can only hope that the correct form will be found. But all who take

---

[112] Cf. Norbert Lohfink, "Der Glaube und die nächste Generation. Das Gottesvolk der Bibel als Lerngemeinschaft" in idem, *Das Jüdische am Christentum* 144–66.

[113] *Sacrosanctum concilium* 64; *Ad gentes divinitus* 14.

part in shaping it should be clear on one point: a purely superficial rein-troduction of an adult catechumenate would be insufficient, for as we have seen, a catechumenate is more than mere instruction. It is initiation into the way of life that is faith. But before anyone can be initiated into that way of life it first has to exist. Therefore what the Church needs before anything else is itself to be a concrete *society* that makes faith visible as a way of life different from neopaganism. Then the catechumenate would again have a basis. But such a concrete Christian society can exist in a world that is far along the way to becoming pagan again only in the form of communities that themselves make visible God's new world and new project for society. *Such a community is then already in itself a catechu-menate.* If it does not exist even the best "introductions to the faith" are of no avail.

Thus the real question is not what should be the model for the cate-chumenate, or whether there should be infant baptism or baptism of adults. It is certainly not a question of "Volkskirche" or "church by choice." The real question is that of the existence of living communities within the Church of which one can say: "Come and see!" (John 1:46). In such a community there can always be those who remain distant, outsiders, oc-casional visitors, guests, friends, and beneficiaries. There has never been a "pure community," and such a thing would be quite unbiblical (cf. III, 5 above). But it must be living in the gospel sense, and it should be such that one can say of it: "Come and see!"

If there are such communities infant baptism will no longer be a prob-lem. If there are none even adult baptism or the best adult catechumenate would not take us a step farther. In Luke's time immediate baptism was possible because the preparation for baptism was the lived and living ex-perience of community based in Israel.

## 6. The Church and Wholeness

There is a saying in the Bible about the relationship between God and Israel that appears repeatedly in different forms. We could call it the prin-ciple of "wholeness." God has turned wholly and undividedly toward this people, and correspondingly Israel is to live whole and undivided before its God. This "wholeness" is essential to biblical faith. It is part of the structure of the Judeo-Christian reality.

The thing itself is not encompassed in a single word in the Bible. So far as it concerns people it echoes in concepts like "holy," "righteous," "ir-reproachable," "intact," "perfect." But it need not be bound to specific terms; it can also be expressed in a whole sentence. For example, it is always part of the thought when the so-called "covenant formula" is expressed:[114] "I will be your God, and you shall be my people." In Israel's ears this "covenant formula" must have recalled the language of marriage. In a marriage contract, usually made in writing, the formula might be: "She (is hereby) my wife, and I (am hereby) her husband from this day forever."[115] A more beautiful image for "wholeness" as such a mutual transfer is scarcely possible.

Quite often the principle of "wholeness" also reveals itself quite simply in the whole course of a story. When Genesis 22 tells how Abraham is to sacrifice his son Isaac, and how he travels the long road, sets up the altar, binds Isaac—the narrative becomes progressively slower and more faltering—and then after all receives his child back from God the theme of "wholeness" is also fundamental.

However, the matter is most frequently expressed by the word *tāmim*. The word itself can be used in the Hebrew Bible to describe the unblemished condition of an animal to be offered in sacrifice.[116] If it is perfect, undamaged, and without blemish it is *tāmim*. But the word also characterizes the righteous who conscientiously fulfill the Torah and walk faithfully before God.[117] In Gen 17:1* the Priestly document formulates as follows: "When Abram was ninety-nine years old, the LORD appeared to Abram, and said to him, 'I am God Almighty; walk before me, and be single-hearted *(tāmim).*'"

With "be single-hearted!" God lays claim to Abraham's whole life. The ancestor of Israel is to walk before God in unconditional trust. The Greek Bible translates *tāmim* in this passage with *amemptos* (irreproachable), the Latin with *perfectus* (perfect). But neither the original Hebrew text nor the translations refer to Abraham's moral perfection; they speak of his relationship to God: Abraham is to live in undivided surrender before the face of this God who has been revealed to him.[118] What is said to Abraham in Genesis 17 is said to the whole people of God in Deuteronomy 18: "You must remain wholeheartedly loyal *(tāmim)* to the LORD your God" (Deut 18:13*).

The context shows what this wholehearted loyalty means concretely. This state of being "utterly with God" is illustrated against the background

---

[114] For the covenant formula cf. Norbert Lohfink, "Dt 26,17-19 und die 'Bundesformel'" in idem, *Studien zum Deuteronomium und zur deuteronomistischen Literatur I.* SBAB 8 (Stuttgart: Katholisches Bibelwerk, 1990) 211–61. All the passages containing the formula are listed there. Cf. also Rolf Rendtorff, *Die" Bundesformel". Eine exegetisch-theologische Untersuchung.* SBS 160 (Stuttgart: Katholisches Bibelwerk, 1995).

[115] Cf. Norbert Lohfink, "Dt 26,17-19 und die 'Bundesformel,'" 214.

[116] Cf. Lev 9:2-3; 22:19, 21; Num 6:14, and elsewhere.

[117] Especially in the Psalms, in Proverbs, and in Qumran.

[118] Cf. Gerhard von Rad, *Das erste Buch Mose. Genesis.* ATD 2/4 (4th ed. Göttingen: Vandenhoeck & Ruprecht, 1956) 168.

of superstition and magic. Those who practice divination or sorcery or who seek oracles from the dead have already turned away from the God of Israel. Joshua 24 tends in the same direction. There Joshua demands a decision of the people at their great assembly in Shechem:

> "Now therefore revere the LORD, and serve him wholeheartedly *(b<sup>e</sup>tāmim)* and in faithfulness; put away the gods that your ancestors served beyond the River and in Egypt, and serve the LORD. Now if you are unwilling to serve the LORD, choose this day whom you will serve, whether the gods your ancestors served in the region beyond the River or the gods of the Amorites in whose land you are living; but as for me and my household, we will serve the LORD." (Josh 24:14-15*)

The principle of "wholeness" or "wholeheartedness" thus has its ultimate basis in the exclusivity of the service demanded by YHWH and in the rejection of all other gods. Hence the great commandment also reads: "Hear, O Israel: The LORD is our God, the LORD alone. You shall love the LORD your God with all your heart, and with all your soul, and with all your might" (Deut 6:4-5). It is no accident that these and the sentences that follow it became Israel's confession, to be spoken every day, for their genius is to summarize the whole Torah in graphic form: the people in Israel are to place everything under the rule of God; their whole existence, their whole way of life, every step they take, all the things with which they have to do.

It is no different in the New Testament. If we look, for example, at Matthew's Sermon on the Mount we quickly see that *its* inmost principle is also that of "wholeness." At the end of the six great antitheses in which true faithfulness to the Law is inculcated in exemplary fashion stands, almost at the center of the Sermon, the exhortation: "Be perfect, therefore, as your heavenly Father is perfect" (Matt 5:48).

Without its background in the Hebrew Bible this saying would be almost impossible to understand, for "perfect" cannot be understood either here or in the Old Testament in terms of the Greek ideal of perfection. It does not mean an autarchic personality at the pinnacle of life, possessing all the virtues and so mature in all of them that increase is impossible.[119] Instead, "perfect" here goes back to *tāmim,* and therefore it can only mean that the audience of the Sermon on the Mount are to live the Torah, which is now being unfolded for them by Jesus in its eschatological sense, with their whole existence and without any inward division.

The perfection that is asked of them is measured by the perfection of God, which definitely shows that it is not a question of the Greek ideal of

---

[119] See the examples of the Greek ideal of perfection listed in Gerhard Lohfink, *Wem gilt die Bergpredigt? Beiträge zu einer christlichen Ethik* (Freiburg: Herder, 1988) 215 n. 19.

perfection. Being required to aim at the *perfectio absoluta* of the divine being would not be an encouragement, but instead a reason to despair. Matthew is thinking of something different: Jesus' hearers and disciples may surrender themselves wholly and undividedly to the will of God because God has already turned toward humanity, wholly and undividedly and without making distinctions. God makes the sun to rise on the evil and the good, says the text not long before this; God gives rain to the righteous and the unrighteous (5:45).

However, the principle of "wholeness" is not the background only to Matt 5:48. It is the key to many other statements in the Sermon on the Mount.[120] In 6:24 God's claim to exclusive worship from the Old Testament is directly echoed: "No one can serve two masters; for a slave will either hate the one and love the other, or be devoted to the one and despise the other. You cannot serve God and wealth" (Matt 6:24). Here again the whole matter is entirely clear: the pupils of the Sermon on the Mount can do nothing but serve God undividedly. If they make mammon, that is, their own property, their master alongside God they are already divided and split in two. The text's formulation presupposes that this division is precisely the problem of people touched by God. Evil people only want to serve themselves in any case. To that extent they are often more "whole" than the good. Believers, on the other hand, want both: certainly they want to serve God, and yet they also want to live for their own interests. The Sermon on the Mount says with clear-headed sobriety: you cannot have both. Those who want to live in the presence of God can only do it wholly and undividedly.

This "wholeness" is not only a question of money. Jesus' disciples also live divided lives if they separate their fellow human beings into those one must love and those one may hate (5:43-47). They live divided if they use two measures of judgment, seeing the speck in the other person's eye and not noticing the log in their own (7:3-5) They live divided if they pray to God as their Father but at the same time tear their lives apart because of constant anxiety about life and its needs (6:25-34). They live divided if they say "Lord, Lord!" in worship, but ignore the Law. Then they cannot be helped even if they become prophets or accomplish marvelous deeds in the name of God. They will still be "violators of the Torah" (7:21-23). They also live divided if they put their piety, their good works, their prayers and fasting on display, because in doing so they show that their primary interest is in obtaining recognition from other people. Of course they want recognition from God too; what they really desire is a double reward, from people and from God, and that very thing makes their actions divided (6:1-18).

---

[120] For what follows cf. ibid. 65–98.

The disciples will also be divided and separated if, without killing their fellow believers, they nevertheless hate them (5:21-22), or if they avoid adultery itself but relish it in their fantasies (5:27-28). The shocking statement that merely looking at another's wife with lust is adultery—and as adultery a capital crime within the meaning of Torah[121]—is addressed to a divided and separated love. The disciples can only love undividedly because their existence before God is to be whole and undivided.

What Matthew's gospel formulates in a series of individual statements Mark demonstrates with a story, the story of the poor widow's offering:

> [Jesus] sat down opposite the treasury, and watched the crowd putting money into the treasury. Many rich people put in large sums. A poor widow came and put in two small copper coins, which are worth a penny. Then he called his disciples and said to them, "Truly I tell you, this poor widow has put in more than all those who are contributing to the treasury. For all of them have contributed out of their abundance; but she out of her poverty has put in everything she had, all she had to live on." (Mark 12:41-44)

Shortly before this Jesus had been asked by a scribe about the most important commandment. As response he had cited the great commandment from Deut 6:4-5 and the commandment of love of neighbor in Lev 19:18. The great commandment is given as follows:

> "You shall love the Lord your God with all your heart, and with all your soul, and with all your mind, and with all your strength." (Mark 12:30)

For Mark the widow's offering is an illustration of the great commandment. She had two copper coins (the text mentions the smallest monetary unit of the time) and she gave not one of them but both. She gave "everything she had, all she had to live on." With this conclusion Mark 12:41-44 becomes an instrument of discernment. The widow, says the narrative with disturbing clarity, did not give as people give donations or alms. She did not give a tenth, or even half of what she had. She gave everything.

This "everything" can be illustrated with a rabbinic text, also about a poor woman. She comes into the Temple and can bring nothing as her sacrifice but a handful of flour. The priest who receives her offering ridicules her for this handful. In the following night the priest in a dream hears a voice telling him: "Do not despise her, for she is like one who has offered her very self."[122] The same is true of the widow in the gospel: she gave everything, and thereby herself.

---

[121] Cf. Lev 20:10; Deut 22:22.

[122] *Lev. Rab.* 3 (107a); quoted from Hermann L. Strack and Paul Billerbeck, *Kommentar zum Neuen Testament aus Talmud und Midrasch.* 6 vols. in 7 (Munich: Beck, 1922–1961) 2:46.

If we take Mark 12:41-44 seriously in this way we cannot avoid the question of what the widow is to eat the next day if today she gives everything she has for the Temple. Did she really follow the great commandment "with all her mind"? Does she not, rather, lack understanding?

The interpreter must pose this question because it alone can lead us to the place where the narrative can say what it wants to say. All Jesus stories and Jesus sayings continually force the question of the place where they can reveal their meaning, where they can be realized and taken at face value: that is, where they can be lived not only in a spiritual sense but physically. If those who attempted to live the story of the poor widow were destroyed by it the story in itself would be senseless and worse—it would be irresponsible and could not be retained in the Bible.

The story, like all biblical texts, presumes the basis of the people of God. Mark, in telling this story, must have had in mind the concrete mutuality of Christian communities where each can make available his or her whole self and life but where each is also sustained by the others. Where many people join their lives together in this way the widow is no longer alone. There are always sisters and brothers who will protect her and share their meal with her. There, too, she is needed. Help will not only be given *to her,* but she can also help others. We know from Jewish and early Christian literature that care for widows was something important, even essential, to those communities.[123] We also know what a crucial role the widows and unmarried played in the upbuilding of communities in the early Church. They helped not only with what they had; they were also a real symbol of "wholeness."

In connection with another Markan text, namely the narrative of the "multiplication of the loaves" (cf. III, 3 above) we have already said that alms and charitable actions, however necessary, cannot really alleviate the world's suffering. World society reproduces its structures of misery endlessly and repeatedly. We already saw that the solution must be more deeply rooted. Jesus does not have the disciples go away to obtain bread but organizes the hungry people in table groups and satisfies them himself with his messianic superabundance.

The miracle of the multiplication of the loaves continues in communities where each gives all that she or he has: property, time, abilities, but also inabilities, weaknesses, and apparently empty hands in which there is nothing but the ridiculous sum of two copper coins. Where that happens each has what he or she needs, and imagination for cooperative effort is

---

[123] There is a survey of much valuable material in Gustav Stählin, *chēra, TDNT* 9:440–65. Cf. especially 1 Tim 5:3-16; Jas 1:27; Polycarp, *Phil.* 4:3; *Herm. Man.* 8.10; Tertullian, *Ad uxorem* I.7; Eusebius, *Hist. eccl.* VI.43.11; *Const. apost.* II.26; III.1-15.

awakened so that although the community is always poor there is a superabundance available for the founding of new communities. This, God's solution to the needs of the world, is the most rational and appropriate solution there can be. It is already formulated in the double *agapē* commandment, and it is illustrated in the figure of the poor widow who takes the great commandment literally.

But when Mark speaks of the widow's sacrifice he is not only looking back to the great commandment quoted just before. He is also looking forward to Jesus' death. This is the last story in Mark's gospel before the Passion narrative begins. For him the "wholeness" of the widow already reflects the "wholeness" of Jesus' death. The widow, with her offering, wanted to aid in providing for the Temple, the place of God's presence, the glory that was appropriate for it. Jesus gave his life so that the people of God, the place of God's presence in the world, might shine forth in its eschatological glory.

But is such a reading not perhaps a wild over-interpretation of biblical texts? Can God really ask anyone to give *everything?* Would that not be a demand too great for a human being? Does the Church require its faithful to give up everything? Would anyone in Church office dare to confront Christians with anything that even remotely pointed in that direction?

If we are honest we must say that nowadays the biblical texts are more commonly interpreted in the sense of general humanity, with the result that their radicalness is blunted or denied. Previously in the Catholic Church, in preaching and parish missions, something was at least said from time to time about the radical "wholeness" of religious life, but even that has become very rare. With what result? No one is won for the gospel with this softened and accommodated message that dares to say no more than what is plausible for our society. On the contrary! The churches are emptying.

Certainly no Church official can *order* this "wholeness." It can only grow up in perfect freedom. Where it happens it remains a miracle, but the very miracle that is promised to the people of God in the messianic era. Must not at least the biblical texts be interpreted in such a way that this "wholeness" of which they repeatedly speak is put before the eyes of the faithful? For the texts do speak of it unceasingly!

Let us shift from Matthew and Mark to Paul. After speaking in his letter to the community at Rome for eleven chapters about "God's righteousness" given to human beings as pure grace because of the cross of Christ and making them whole and *righteous before God* (another term for "wholeness") Paul begins the apostolic paraenesis of his letter, which is both promise and encouragement, as follows:

> I appeal to you therefore, brothers and sisters, by the mercies of God, to present your bodies as a living sacrifice, holy and acceptable to God, which is your spiritual worship. Do not be conformed to this world, but be transformed by the renewing of your minds, so that you may discern what is the will of God—what is good and acceptable and perfect [before God].
>
> For by the grace given to me I say to everyone among you not to think of yourself more highly than you ought to think, but to think with sober judgment, each according to the measure of faith that God has assigned. For as in one body we have many members, and not all the members have the same function, so we, who are many, are one body in Christ, and individually we are members one of another. We have gifts that differ according to the grace given to us . . . . (Rom 12:1-6)

It is obvious that here Paul is alluding to the worship celebrated in the Temple at Jerusalem. At that time the Temple had not yet been destroyed; the smoke of whole burnt offerings still arose daily to heaven. But since Jesus had been made to die outside the city there was another worship for those who believe in him. It was inaugurated by Jesus himself, and it consists in this, that those who live out of his surrender of his whole existence bring their own bodies, that is, themselves, "as a living sacrifice, holy and acceptable to God."

The sacramental terminology that permeates the first part of this text of course means that it is the *whole* of life that is to be offered to God. The "body" stands for life in its totality. The concept of a *holy* sacrifice also parallels this "wholeness," because "holy" is something that belongs entirely to God. Finally, the concept of "perfection" also appears, and it too points to "wholeness."

To hand oneself over entirely to God in this sense, to place one's own life at God's disposal and to allow it to be fully incorporated into God's plan and will as Jesus did is, according to Romans 12:1-2, eschatological worship, true liturgy. For this kind of worship that seizes and encompasses the whole of life Paul chooses the adjective *logikos*. In this context we must translate it as "spiritual," but "reasonable" and "enlightened" also echo in Paul's usage. We here encounter again what we already observed in connection with the widow's offering: what she did was by no means unreasonable, but appropriate. In the same way for Paul everyone who places his or her life at God's disposal acts reasonably and in enlightened fashion. It is true that burning animals in the Jerusalem Temple was a symbol deeply grounded in human nature, but it was only preliminary and representative of what Paul has in mind: the surrender of one's whole existence.

However, Paul mentions three criteria that must be fulfilled if reasonable surrender is not to become unreasonable:

First Criterion: The surrender of one's whole life must correspond to God's will and plan. Therefore one must continually test what the will of God is at each point, what is "good and acceptable and perfect" before God. We could also say that the fact that someone surrenders her or his life is ambiguous in itself. There are many kinds of self-sacrifice in the world, and more than a few of them are perverse. For example one may blow oneself up in order to kill as many Jews as possible, or one may enslave oneself to someone else and destroy one's life through such slavery. Self-sacrifice in itself therefore means nothing. It all depends on whether one devotes one's life to the right cause, to what God really desires.

Second Criterion: Each member of the Christian community has his or her own story, his or her own abilities, and therefore his or her own calling. Therefore "wholeness" looks very different for each individual. This personal "wholeness" is in fact determined by the different gifts of grace that God has given to each (Rom 12:6). Much is demanded of one, less of another. We already encountered this different way of measuring in the words of Jesus (see III, 5 above): of some Jesus demanded unconditional discipleship, of others only that they offer his disciples a cup of cold water.

Third Criterion: To place one's whole life at God's disposal is only reasonable if it is done within a community in which the most varied charisms, a great number of services, and many life stories are woven together. For that very reason Paul speaks at this point, as in 1 Corinthians, of the "body" of the community and the many members that belong to one another. For isolated individuals it is scarcely possible to accomplish the "wholeness" of surrender in an enlightened fashion. Without the Christian community with its gathered experience and the guiding principle of the Church's tradition there can very quickly arise a kind of heroism or even fanaticism that destroys people and is counter to the "sober judgment" of which Paul speaks in this context.

In the letter to the Philippians Paul formulates his thought along lines similar to those in Romans. The Old Testament sacrificial terminology echoes even more strongly: "Do all things without murmuring and arguing, so that you may be blameless and innocent, children of God without blemish in the midst of a crooked and perverse generation, in which you shine like stars in the world" (Phil 2:14-15). Two verses later Paul says that his own life will probably soon be "poured out as a libation." When he dictated the letter he was in prison in Ephesus (or Rome?) and had to reckon with the possibility of condemnation and execution. Then his life would be, definitively, a sacrifice. Yet in this context Paul speaks not only of the sacrifice of his own life but at the same time of his joy over the community in Philippi, whose faithful life was a "sacrifice and offering"

(2:17).[124] The idea is the same as that in Rom 12:1. Even if a Christian life does not end with martyrdom it should be from beginning to end a living sacrifice before God. That means, however, that it must belong wholly and entirely and without division to God and God's cause.

In the letters to the Colossians and the Ephesians we again encounter the motifs that we have seen in Romans 12 and Philippians 2. Both letters were written by disciples of Paul. In the letter to the community at Colossae we read:

> And you who were once estranged and hostile in mind, doing evil deeds, [Christ] has now reconciled in his fleshly body through death, so as to present you holy and blameless and irreproachable before him—provided that you continue securely established and steadfast in the faith, without shifting from the hope promised by the gospel that you heard . . . . (Col 1:21-23)

When the Christians at Colossae are told that they were "once estranged and hostile" the phrases are formulated from the point of view of Israel. As Gentiles they were strangers to the people of God and its history; they were even God's enemies. Now, however, they are no longer estranged, but reconciled through Christ, who through his death on the cross has created a space of peace and reconciliation. That space is the *ekklēsia,* and into that space they have been brought.

When it is said that Christ has presented them "holy and blameless and irreproachable before him" there is again an echo of cultic terminology as we encountered it in the letters to the Romans and Philippians. The lives of those who once were Gentiles have been incorporated into the eschatological worship of reconciliation that Christ has founded through his death.[125] Their whole life now participates in this worship and is joined to the sacrifice of Christ. That the former pagans are now "holy and blameless" does not signify a holiness and perfection they have acquired through their own efforts. It is the "whole existence in holiness" that can only be received. It is not a holiness that sticks by magic; it can be lost. Therefore the author of Colossians warns the community at the end of this text to continue "securely established and steadfast" in the salvation received in Christ.

The letter to the Ephesians also emphasizes the "wholeness" and "undividedness" of life before God, but like Colossians it builds it into an

---

[124] For the sentence disposition in Philippians cf. Joachim Gnilka, *Der Philipperbrief.* HThK X/3 (Freiburg: Herder, 1968) 154–55.

[125] Similarly Heb 12:22-24: "But you have come to Mount Zion and to the city of the living God, the heavenly Jerusalem, and to innumerable angels in festal gathering, and to the assembly of the firstborn who are enrolled in heaven . . . to Jesus, the mediator of a new covenant, and to the sprinkled blood . . . ."

image of the *ekklēsia* whose universality now appears in all clarity. In this way the principle of "wholeness" is shown in a new and different dimension. It is necessary, therefore, for us to look at the image of the Church in Ephesians more closely and in detail. This is also called for because Ephesians is, of all the New Testament texts, the one that reflects most fully on the nature of the Church.

In Eph 2:21-22 the Church is called God's "structure," "temple," and "dwelling place." Otherwise, however, the letter uses the image of the "body."[126] Here we see a clear difference from Paul. When he spoke of the "body" of the *ekklēsia* he was always thinking of individual communities such as those in Corinth or Rome. Obviously the Church, for Paul, was more than the local community, and also more than a "sum of individual congregations." It is the eschatological community of salvation, precondition of individual congregations, created by God in Jesus Christ.[127] But this *ekklēsia* of God exists for Paul in the individual local communities. When the believers in the concrete local communities gather they do so as "the church of God" and are at the same time joined to all other local communities.[128]

The situation is no different in Colossians and Ephesians, but there the universal aspect of the Church is in the foreground, as is clearly shown by the use of the concept of the "body." When Ephesians speaks of the *ekklēsia* as the "body of Christ" it never means an individual, local community, but always the whole Church. In addition, the image of the head now appears together with that of the body. Christ is the head of his body, the Church.[129] The Church is thus seen as a cosmic reality; Christ has been raised to heaven and seated at the right hand of God

> far above all rule and authority and power and dominion, and above every name that is named, not only in this age but also in the age to come. And [God] has put all things under his feet and has made him the head over all things for the church, which is his body, the fullness of him who fills all in all. (Eph 1:21-23)[130]

---

[126] Eph 1:23; 2:26; 4:4, 12, 16; 5:23, 30.

[127] Cf. Wolfgang Schrage, *Der erste Brief an die Korinther I (1 Kor 1,16,11)*. EKK VII/1 (Zürich: Benziger, and Neukirchen-Vluyn: Neukirchener Verlag, 1991) 103. Especially important are 1 Cor 10:32 and 12:28.

[128] This is shown in especially impressive fashion by the *adscriptio* in 1 Cor 1:2: "To the church of God that is in Corinth, to those who are sanctified in Christ Jesus, called to be saints, together with all those who in every place call on the name of our Lord Jesus Christ, both their Lord and ours."

[129] Eph 1:22-23; 4:15-16; 5:23.

[130] *NRSV;* cf. the similar translation by Franz Mussner, *Der Brief an die Epheser.* ÖTK 10 (Gütersloh: Gerd Mohn; Würzburg: Echter, 1982) 51. See also idem, *Christus, das All und die Kirche. Studien zur Theologie des Epherserbriefes.* TThSt 5 (2nd ed. Trier: Paulinus, 1968).

The last phrase could also be rendered as "the church . . . the fullness of the one who fills the whole universe." However it is translated, the universal dimension of the whole is clear. No less than six times do we encounter in this short text the word "all" (or "every"). The whole universe is in view. Ephesians is not interested in defining the powers and rulers more exactly; its interest is in showing that there is no longer any power, whatever its name, over which the exalted Christ has not been set as its lord. Probably the author of Ephesians was thinking of demonic powers who rule the world from outside.[131] We would be more likely to speak of the demonic force of evil that gathers within history, hovers "over" society, and repeatedly makes itself apparent as concealment, lying, unfreedom, rivalry, and violence.

Over against these, says Ephesians, is another power in the world that is mightier than all these apparently unconquerable powers and rulers. It is the "power" of the Crucified. Its place is the Church: not because the people in the Church are different, that is, are not in and of themselves inclined to concealment, lying, rivalry, and violence, but because in it, because of Christ, there is a place for reconciliation and peace. The author of Ephesians calls this other thing that is not an achievement of the Church but pure grace "the fullness of Christ." It is the constant and enduring gift of the exalted Christ to his Church. Through this gift it is possible for the body of the Church to be built up in love and to grow toward union with its head.[132]

Christ is, indeed, not only the head of the Church but also the lord of the universe. He not only fills the Church with the fullness of his blessing but with his power he rules the universe and draws it within the realm of his governance; for God has decided from all eternity, as the solemnly formulated thanksgiving at the beginning of the letter says, "as a plan for the fullness of time, to gather up all things in [Christ], things in heaven and things on earth" (Eph 1:10). We may of course ask how this accomplishing of the plan, this gathering of the whole world in Christ, is to take place. Will this dramatic event be something that happens outside the Church, apart from it and independent of it? That is hard to imagine. The author of Ephesians can only have supposed that this bringing together of the world would take place *through the Church and within the Church*. In favor of this idea is another text in which the letter again speaks of the powers and rulers. It interprets from a post-Pauline perspective the humanly unexplainable work of Paul, the apostle to the Gentiles:

---

[131] For more detail see Heinrich Schlier, *Mächte und Gewalten im Neuen Testament*. QD 3 (Freiburg: Herder, 1958). In Ephesians see especially 2:2.

[132] Cf. Eph 2:22-23; 4:15-16.

Although I am the very least of all the saints, this grace was given to me to bring to the Gentiles the news of the boundless riches of Christ, and to make everyone see what is the plan of the mystery hidden for ages in God who created all things; so that through the church the wisdom of God in its rich variety might now be made known to the rulers and authorities in the heavenly places. This was in accordance with the eternal purpose that he has carried out in Christ Jesus our Lord . . . . (Eph 3:8-11)

To understand this text we must keep in mind what the "plan" consists of, this plan that God has made "from eternity," that has been "hidden" in God and constituted the secret design for the universe from the very beginning. It consists of what was already said in the thanksgiving at the beginning of the letter: that it was God's eternal will "to gather up all things in [Christ], things in heaven and things on earth." The Risen One is the archetype and goal of all creation. It moves toward him. In him it will be gathered. In him it will come entirely to itself, that is, in him it will become the pure praise of its creator.

All of this, however, is neither automatic nor programmed. It takes place, rather, in a dramatic story. On the one hand this story, this history has already reached its goal: the Crucified has been elevated to the right hand of God, as lord of the universe and beginning of the new creation.[133] On the other hand what is already reality in the timeless world of God must still be realized in the earthly and historical world.[134] This took place, and still takes place, in the proclamation of the gospel. The triumphant procession of the gospel through the world not only reflects the entry of Christ into rulership but also reveals the previously hidden plan of God to bring together all things in Christ. To the extent that the gospel expands, the powers and rulers that previously dominated the world are deprived of their rule and the historical plan of God is set before their eyes.

---

[133] For the Risen One as beginning of the new creation cf. also Acts 26:23; Rom 8:29; 1 Cor 15:20; Col 1:18; Rev 1:5.

[134] I am here indebted to Rudolf Schnackenburg, *Der Brief an die Epheser.* EKK X (Zürich: Benziger; Neukirchen-Vluyn: Neukirchener Verlag, 1982) 60. See also p. 83: "The boundary between universe and church is not fixed and immovable, but dynamic: the Church is to be continually expanding and taking possession of the universe, not so much extensively as intensively. For its growth consists in internal strengthening, especially in love (4:15), which is the divine principle that works against the powers opposed to God. To the extent that the Church, through the gospel, overcomes the human world that is alienated from God and hitherto subjected to the 'powers' it reveals to the powers opposed to God the manifold wisdom of God (cf. 3:10) and their own dethronement." Cf. also Helmut Merklein in *EDNT* 1:82–83: "Accordingly, the *anakephalaiosis* sets in motion a process that enables the sovereignty of Christ to assert itself through the Church before the nations and the powers . . . and that thus lends a historical dimension to the fulfillment of the universe (1:23; 4:10)."

Those who do not look carefully could feel that all this is very triumphalistic. But we must never forget that the power of the exalted Christ is indeed the power of the helpless crucified Christ, and the victory march of the gospel is nothing other than the building up of communities into the one body that is the Church, which is held together by *agapē*. Only where this *agapē*, which arises from the Crucified's surrender of his life, unites the members of the body does the body grow and draw more and more of the world into the realm of the Risen One's rule.

The theology of the letter to the Ephesians, and previously of the letter to the Colossians, is thus not an overblown cosmological speculation. It reflects very real experience, namely that of the incredible story of the mission begun from the tiny communities in Jerusalem and Antioch and in which Paul, the former persecutor, was given a crucial role by God.

Still another experience grounds this theology: one of the fundamental constants of ancient history was the gulf between Jews and Gentiles. Israel saw the Gentile world as one alienated and distant from God, and the Gentiles as people shut out from God's covenant and promise. The Gentiles in turn saw the Jews as people without religion and accused them of godlessness, lack of culture, and hatred of foreigners.[135]

Against this background the fact that in the communities surrounding the Mediterranean Jews (that is, Jewish Christians) and Gentiles (that is, Gentile Christians) gathered around one table must have been a revolutionary experience for many. The author of Ephesians reminds the Gentile Christian readers that they were once distant from the *politeia* of Israel, its community life, but now in the body of the Church, the eschatological Israel, they have become "citizens with the saints and also members of the household of God."[136] All this has been made possible through Jesus Christ, who through his death has broken down the wall of enmity that separated Jews and Gentiles:[137]

> . . . that he might create in himself one new humanity in place of the two, thus making peace, and might reconcile both groups to God in one body[138] through the cross, thus putting to death that hostility through it. (Eph 2:15-16)

---

[135] Cf. the article "Antisemitismus II" in *TRE* 3:119–22, at 120.

[136] Eph 2:19; cf. 3:6. The "saints" here are probably, as in Eph 1:1; 3:8; 4:12; 6:18, fellow Christians and not the heavenly court of the angels.

[137] The author of Ephesians, as 2:15a shows, regarded the commandments and ordinances of the Torah as the "wall of separation." This author is probably thinking especially of circumcision, as well as the strictures regarding purity and food. Through his death Christ is seen to have annulled these laws. Paul and Matthew would have spoken more cautiously and with greater precision about the validity of the Torah.

[138] There is argument about whether "body" here refers to the crucified body of Christ or the body of the Church. In terms of the language of Ephesians the latter is more likely.

However, the author of Ephesians is no dreamer. He knows that the division between Gentiles and Jews, Gentile Christians and Jews, and even between Gentile Christians and Jewish Christians is still present. Therefore he chooses his words carefully. He says "that he might create . . . and might reconcile." The separation is still there, but in the cross of Christ it is in principle overcome, if only that cross is taken seriously and lived as the reconciliation revealed by God. Then the "one new humanity" would be possible. In the fourth chapter of the letter the image of the "new humanity" is taken up once again:

> The gifts that [the exalted Christ] gave were that some would be apostles, some prophets, some evangelists, some pastors and teachers, to equip the saints for the work of ministry, for building up the body of Christ, until all of us come to the unity of the faith and of the knowledge of the Son of God, to maturity, to the measure of the full stature of Christ. (Eph 4:11-13)

Here again the key word that refers to "perfection" (here translated as "maturity") appears, and with it the principle of "wholeness" that we have repeatedly encountered in the gospels and the letters of Paul. Here it is utterly clear that this is not about *individuals* among the people of God. That was already obvious before: Abraham was addressed as the ancestor of Israel, and therefore the whole people of God in him, and the "you" of the great commandment is addressed not to individuals, but to Israel. But in Ephesians the *communio*-structure of the biblical "whole" is fully illuminated.

"All of us," that is, the *ekklēsia* as such, are to come to "maturity" as human persons so that in the Church the full stature of Christ can develop to its utmost. Everything that equips us as individuals should serve for "building up the body of Christ," and in order that the body may be built up the exalted Christ has given the Church a variety of offices and services. What is at stake in all of this is that the Church should allow itself to be made holy in order that it may stand whole and undivided before Christ, or, as Eph 5:27 says, "so [that he may] present the church to himself in splendor, without a spot or wrinkle or anything of the kind."

Thus Ephesians takes up the long line of tradition regarding the unconditional and undivided surrender to God of those who are called, but applies it consistently to the Church as a whole. However, the letter does not rest with this aspect of "wholeness," but thinks beyond that to the universality of the Church, its world dimension and cosmic extent. This expanded view of "wholeness" in Ephesians may be summarized and further developed as follows:

1. The Church is more than a collection of individual communities. Through the cross of Christ and the fullness of blessing that streams from

the exalted Christ it is a single body. Does Christianity take that seriously? Are not, for example, "free churches" and "free communities" a contradiction to the ecclesiology of Ephesians? They may appeal to the invisible spiritual bond that unites all the churches, but Ephesians speaks of the "body" of the Church, and the nature of a body is certainly to be visibly and tangibly one. Paul and his disciples did not speak of Christ's "bodies," but of the one body for which Christ died.

In terms of the letter to the Ephesians, however, national churches or those bound to a single culture are also absurd. Because the Church is universal it is international. The author of Ephesians presumes that through and in Christ the deepest division that ever existed in human history, that between Jews and Gentiles, has been fundamentally abolished. National churches would certainly be unthinkable for this author. They would, in fact, be an attack on Christ's unifying work of reconciliation. The Church is the first and genuine "International."

2. The *communio* that joins all the local churches into one Church must not, however, be understood only as synchronic, at the level of the contemporary Church of a given time. It is striking how Ephesians speaks of Israel's *politeia,* of the making of the covenants, the promise, the adoption of believers as sons and daughters, and the fullness of time.[139] The Church thus needs not only the *communio* of all current local churches; its need for *communio* with the history of the people of God in its whole diachronic extent is just as great. That, too, is part of its "wholeness." And this *communio* is more than the preservation of individual traditions. It is holding fast to the *whole* tradition. This aspect of the whole tradition and the need to preserve it intact was the subject of further reflection in the Pastoral letters (1 Timothy, 2 Timothy, Titus).[140]

3. The Church's "wholeness" is still more than that. We already saw that in Ephesians Christ is not only the head of the Church but also lord of the universe; nevertheless, his rule over the universe has not yet arrived at its goal. Christ is already set above all the powers and dominions (Eph 1:20-22), but they still rule the world and society. Therefore *through the Church* the exalted Lord draws the world under his rule. The necessary consequence is that the Church itself is worldly. It is not *above* the world or *beyond* the world. We cannot even say that it is *in* the world. No, the

---

[139] For the *politeia* of Israel see Eph 2:12; covenants, 2:12; promise, 2:12; adoption as sons and daughters, 1:5; fullness of time, 1:10.

[140] Cf. especially 1 Tim 6:20; 2 Tim 1:6-14; 3:10-17.

Church itself is world and nothing else.[141] But it is world under the rule of Christ. It is a world in which his fullness is already present. In this sense and only in this sense can we say that through it the whole world and the whole of society are to be drawn into the space of reconciliation that the Risen One creates in the world.

Such a position has consequences. Ephesians itself does not reflect on those consequences, but they are obvious enough. To bring the world together, to draw it to its home, to transform it can certainly not mean standing over against it like know-it-alls and handing it faith from without, but drawing everything there is in the world in the way of reason and enlightenment, goodness and success, into the realm of faith so that it may become the praise of God. The Church's task is to grasp all the spheres of life, to transform all the matter of the world, and to gather into itself all wisdom and beauty so that the new face of the earth can be illuminated and become visible.

The Church must never act like that miserable caliph who ordered the destruction of the unique and magnificent library at Alexandria in which for centuries the books of antiquity had been collected. According to legend he commanded the burning of the library with these words: "Either the books say the same as what is in the Quran, in which case they are superfluous. Or they say something different, in which case they are pernicious." Alas, the Church has also burned books. It was only true to itself when it copied and preserved the wisdom of antiquity, as Islam in many cases also did.

Thus the principle of "wholeness" involves not only the undivided surrender of the people of God, not only its international character, not only taking seriously its full tradition, but also the incorporation of everything that constitutes a world: emotion, reason, education, wisdom, religion, art, play—but equally the world of science, business, the professions, work, leisure. Faith is not something that stands apart from all that or is added to each area as something extra. Faith, instead, brings home everything in the world, including religion, into the redeeming and liberating rule of God.

Obviously that cannot be done without discernment, critical testing, possibly also distancing and rejection. But if the redemption of the world presupposes its transformation the thing to be transformed must first be grasped and accepted. The old principle of christology that nothing can be

---

[141] This does not contradict the statement in Eph 2:6 that believers are already raised with Christ and have their place with him in heaven. That statement does not refer to unworldliness but to the universal redemption of the world that results from sharing in the way of Christ and extends from earth to heaven.

redeemed unless the divine *Logos* assumed it into his human nature[142] is analogously true of the Church: *Quod non est assumptum, non est sanatum*. What is not assumed is not redeemed (and cannot be redeemed).

The Church could not be the space for redemption and liberation opened by Christ if it were unworldly and saw itself simply as an agency for conveying truth. It must not surrender more and more of its tasks to the state so that, in the end, it is reduced to a watered-down separate department of society responsible only for the rites of passage and marginal situations, or acts as guarantor of the hope for life beyond. The Church is about the wholeness of everything there is.

Origen called the Church "the universe of the universe," that is, the ornament and order of the world, the essence of the world, the world fully realized.[143] It is "new creation," and a creation without a world would be a self-contradiction. The Church itself must be world with all the spheres that make up a world: transformed, liberated world under the rule of Christ. In no other way could God at the end be "all in all" (Eph 4:6). To understand redemption in Christ any differently would be to make it pure magic.

This has nothing at all to do with integralism or totalitarianism. It follows from the undivided love with which God gives Godself wholly and entirely to creation. The response of God's creation can only be the same kind of self-giving to God. It happens in the "wholeness" of the Church and its communities.

### 7. The Church's Deepest Wound Is Disunity

Elias Canetti, in the second volume of his autobiography, *Die Fackel im Ohr,* describes the cultural life of Berlin in the 1920s:

> The real tendency of things was centrifugal; they were propelled apart, separating from one other at top speed. Reality was not at the center, where it holds everything together by the reins; instead there were only a multitude of realities and all of them peripheral. They were widely separated from each other; there was nothing to hold them together, and anyone who tried to make an accommodation among them was a falsifier.[144]

What Canetti describes is not only Berlin in 1928 with its books, paintings, and plays, its noise and crowded streets, its animal and intellectual

---

[142] The (oldest?) attestation of the principle is found in the work of John of Damascus (675–749), *De fide orthodoxa* III.6; 12; 20. Cf. Ludwig Weimer, *Die Lust an Gott und seiner Sache. Oder: Lassen sich Gnade und Freiheit, Glaube und Vernunft, Erlösung und Befreiung vereinbaren?* (Freiburg: Herder, 1981) 100.

[143] Origen, *In Ioann.* VI.59.

[144] Elias Canetti, *Die Fackel im Ohr. Lebensgeschichte 1921–1931* (Munich: Carl Hanser, n.d.) 296.

aspects. It is human society as such. It is constantly pulling itself apart if it is not at the moment being driven by the spirit of revolution or war into a questionable unity in which it lumps itself together and is anesthetized by the rush of events. Even ancient society, from the era of Hellenism onward, must have suffered from the falling apart of reality, for in many of its utterances it reveals its longing for unity, for a center of meaning that will hold everything together.

The Stoic worldview imagined the universe as a gigantic body through which water and wind flowed as blood and breath flow through the human body. "We are members of a great body," said Seneca,[145] a body that combines the divine and the human. What in human beings is the soul, God is for the universe. The whole of which we are parts is the One, and this One is divine. "We are God's companions and members."

Another possible way to create a center for the fragmenting world was to unite it through symbol as did the Roman imperial cult. An inscription found in Halicarnassus, in southwestern Asia Minor, of which only a fragment survives reads:

> . . . The eternal and immortal natural power of the universe has given the highest good for the rapturous blessing of humanity by bringing Caesar Augustus [= Octavian] into our happy lives, the father of his fatherland, of the goddess Roma, the Zeus Pater and Savior of the whole race of humanity, whose providence not only fulfilled the prayers of all, but even exceeded them. For land and sea repose in peace. The cities bloom through good laws, harmony and blessing. All good things unfold richly and bear fruits, and the people are full of good hope for the future and good feeling for the present, where with festivals, statues, sacrifices, and songs . . . .[146]

In the original text the rituals for the cult of the divine Augustus were then prescribed. But the fragment breaks off at that point. A number of inscriptions of this type have been found in Asia Minor, and there is good reason why they are there. In Italy it would not have been at all advisable for Augustus to allow himself to be placed on a level with Zeus/Jupiter, but he permitted such statements in the East.

Despite the fact that texts like that from Halicarnassus are diplomatic flatteries of the sort that have been customary in the Orient for two

---

[145] Seneca, *Ep.* 92,30: *Totum hoc, quo continemur, et unum et deus: et socii sumus eius et membra.* Seneca, *Ep.* 95,52: *Membra sumus corporis magni.* Cf. Eduard Schweizer, *sōma, ktl., TDNT* 7:1024–44, at 1038.

[146] CAGI IV/1, no. 894. The author's translation draws on Hans Lietzmann's version in Martin P. Nilsson, *Geschichte der griechischen Religion 2: Die Hellenistische und Römische Zeit* (4th ed. Munich: Beck, 1941–1950) 389. Cf. also Hans-Josef Klauck, *Die religiöse Umwelt des Urchristentums II. Herrscher- und Kaiserkult, Philosophie, Gnosis.* Kohlhammer Studienbücher Theologie 9/2 (Stuttgart: Kohlhammer, 1996) 50.

thousand years, and no matter how many real advantages they produced for the city that offered them, they also witness to the longing for an *oikoumenē* in which peace would reign and in which there would be a center that would tie together all the centrifugal forces in society.

The theology of the letter to the Ephesians stands in sharp contrast to all that. It is not expressed directly, but it is tangibly there: It is not the whole world that is an ensouled body, but only the Church. And what ensouls the Church is not a numinous divinity that belongs to it by nature, but the Holy Spirit who is given to it; that Spirit is clearly defined as the Spirit of God the Father and of Jesus Christ.[147] The Spirit unites the Church and builds it up.

The Lord of the world is not the Roman emperor, but the Crucified, to whom have been subjected all powers and dominions, not by the boots of marching legions but by his defenseless love, which causes the body of the Church to grow ceaselessly toward him and into the world. In this sense the Church is the true place in the world where peace exists and unity is created.

Although it is the same great words that are employed—body, members, cosmos, universe, god, father, savior, superabundance, peace, unanimity—the basis on which Ephesians stands is not ancient philosophy and not Roman state propaganda but the Old Testament promises and the experience of early Christian communities. In actuality the idea of the gathering of the universe through the Church, as outlined in Ephesians, is a transformation of the biblical complex of depictions of the pilgrimage of the nations. What the book of Revelation will describe a few years later,[148] also for Asia Minor, as the worldwide city descending from heaven, its center the Lamb, through whose open gates the peoples of the world enter with their treasures—this the letter to the Ephesians depicts as a body whose head is Christ who through the Church gathers together and fills the whole universe. In fact, at a crucial point the image of the body in Ephesians can also move to the image of God's building, with Jesus Christ as its cornerstone, out of which the whole structure of the Church grows up into a holy temple for God (2:20-22).

---

[147] Ephesians has a clear theology of the Spirit. The Holy Spirit as Spirit of the Father: 1:3, 17; 3:16; 4:30; as the Spirit of Jesus Christ: 4:7-12 (the gifts listed represent the sending of the Spirit from heaven by the ascended Christ); as the Spirit who ensouls the Church, unites it and builds it up: 2:18, 22; 4:3, 4. Cf. also 1:13-14; 3:5; 5:18-19; 6:17-38.

[148] The Revelation of John was probably written between the years 90 and 95 C.E., for it reflects the universal propagation of the imperial cult and thus the total claim of the Roman state in the last years of Domitian's reign. Cf. Jürgen Roloff, *The Revelation of John*. Translated by John E. Alsup (Minneapolis: Fortress, 1993) 8–12. Ephesians already looks back to Paul's activities and fits within the years 80–90 C.E.

That the theology of Ephesians has its true roots in the biblical history of revelation is not without importance. In this way the whole dynamic and the endless superabundance of promise that guide this history enter the equation, so that it is clear that the promise is already fulfilled but its complete realization is yet to come, because that realization surpasses all imagination. The body of Christ is already in the midst of the world, but it has yet to fill the world. The eschatological peace has already been granted in Christ's surrender of his life, but it must be acquired step by step. Unity is already given in Jesus Christ, in his body and in his Spirit, but it is so endangered that the communities must be told:

> . . . lead a life worthy of the calling to which you have been called, with all humility and gentleness, with patience, bearing with one another in love, making every effort to maintain the unity of the Spirit in the bond of peace. There is one body and one Spirit, just as you were called to the one hope of your calling, one Lord, one faith, one baptism, one God and Father of all, who is above all and through all and in all. (Eph 4:1-6)

Further developments have shown how imperiled the unity that Ephesians conjures in this paraenesis has been from the very beginning. The history of the Church has been and is today not only a history of growth in love but also a history of divisions.

This began very early. The first and fundamental division was that between Jews and Christians; we may well call this the primeval division. It endures till today and is perhaps the deeply hidden cause of all other divisions.

Jesus himself was only able to reach a part of Israel although he desired to gather the whole nation. Certainly his tiny group of disciples had in their midst an enormous promise: the Twelve as sign and beginning of the eschatological people of the twelve tribes, installed by Jesus and thus embedded in the people of God as an indelible characteristic.

Beginning at Pentecost the young community in Jerusalem turned again to Israel. That community grew not only in the capital city; daughter communities arose also in Judea and Samaria. When the mission in the Jewish Diaspora began the Jews and Gentiles associated with Judaism constituted the foundation of the new missionary communities. Table fellowship between Jewish and Gentile Christians was a reality. For a short time it looked as though the *ekklēsia* would always be a "church of the circumcision" and a "church of the Gentiles." Out of this experience the author of Ephesians could write that Christ, through his death, had torn down the wall between Israel and the nations, and that was true—irrevocably so.

But in the external history of the Church the weight gradually shifted. The relationship between Jewish and Gentile Christians was never without tensions. In Jerusalem, and not only there, existed a Judaizing movement that required Gentile males to be circumcised and all converts to follow the Law in the Jewish sense. This movement was unable to dominate in all communities, but it was never completely silenced. On the other hand there were more and more Gentile Christian communities that had scarcely any sympathy for the problems of Jewish Christians. Gradually there arose a Gentile Christian self-awareness that was in danger of making a false evaluation of its origins in Israel, if not forgetting them entirely. Paul must already have seen the danger, for in the chapters of his letter to the Romans that are devoted to Israel he warns the Gentile Christians against arrogance toward Israel. Probably the author of Ephesians had similar dangers in mind.

Even before Ephesians was written the Jewish War against Rome (66–74 C.E.) had broken out and had ended in catastrophe for Judaism: Jerusalem was conquered, the Temple burned, a great many inhabitants of the city killed or sent into slavery. The Jewish Christians in Jerusalem did not take part in the war. They fled, probably in October 66 when the first Roman troops appeared before the city. Many of them settled in Pella, east of the Jordan.[149]

We have very little further information about the later development of Jewish Christianity. Much must be inferred indirectly. The church historian Eusebius provides a list of bishops according to which there were fifteen Jewish Christian bishops in Jerusalem from James, the brother of the Lord, until the year 135, the end of the Bar-Kochba revolt.[150] From then on Jews were prohibited on pain of death from entering Jerusalem, now called Aelia Capitolina. However, there must still have been Jewish Christian communities east of the Jordan, in Syria, Asia Minor, and Mesopotamia.[151] In part they were heretical, or regarded as such. Jewish Christianity receded more and more toward the periphery of the Church.

Of course many questions arise at this point: Why did the encounter between Israel and Jesus not turn out differently? Why did it so quickly become a sharp confrontation? Why was even the post-Easter gathering movement scarcely able to alter this sharp opposition? And especially: Why was there not a more open space for Jewish Christians in the Gentile Christian Church and greater understanding for their traditions? Why was Jewish Christianity so swiftly marginalized?

We can attempt a number of answers to these questions. We can reflect long over the problem of where Israel's fault lay and where that of the

---

[149] For the Pella tradition see Eusebius, *Hist. eccl.* III.5.3, and Epiphanius, *Haer.* XXIX.7.7-8; XXX.2.7; *De mensuris* 14-15. Also important is Mark 13:14-23. For the time when the first Roman troops appeared before Jerusalem cf. Josephus, *Bell.* II.19.4 (§§527–32).

[150] Eusebius, *Hist. eccl.* IV.5.3.

[151] Cf. Georg Strecker, "Judenchristentum," *TRE* 17:310–25.

Church, how much was the fault of Jewish Christians and how much the fault of Gentile Christians. It is certainly necessary that theology should repeatedly attack this set of problems. But at some point, as with all other divisions, it will reach a point at which it can go no farther. There was fault on the side of Israel and on the side of the Church; but there was more. There were also struggles over truth, namely the question whether one must not remain faithful to the God of the ancestors, or whether God had acted anew and in a way that surpassed all that had gone before and precisely in doing so had fulfilled the promises made to the ancestors. Had Jesus attempted to lead God's people astray, or was he the final and definitive response of God to the long road trod by Israel? Ultimately, in the face of such questions, the people of God divided.

The Church, as much as Judaism, lost greatly by that division. It is true that it was founded, through the creation of the Twelve, as the *eschatological Israel*. The New Testament communities never understood themselves in any other way.[152] And yet it hesitated to take the honored name of "Israel" for itself directly.[153] Its hesitation was justified and must be taken seriously in our theology, for the Church as it developed after Easter is not yet the whole Israel that Jesus desired. The real Church from this point of view, despite all that has been given to it, is not yet complete. It must remain in expectation of its being as Israel-the-whole.

The Church should be aware of this deficiency in itself. Its difficulty consists not only in the fact that since it became free it has repeatedly persecuted Israel and brought immeasurable suffering upon it. Its trouble is also that through its arrogance toward Judaism it has lost infinitely much: the union of faith and life, the continual blessing of daily life, the compact size of its communities where each can be kept in view, the skepticism toward all kinds of hasty spiritualization, a realistic concept of redemption.

There is a point in history where the losses that occurred as a result of the division between Israel and the Church are immediately and tangibly visible: the rise of Islam and the immense weight that it has brought to play, from then until now, against the expansion of Christianity and therefore also against the history of the world's freedom. It would by no means do justice to Islam to see its origin as an event independent of Judaism and the Church, intended only to give the Arab tribes a religion appropriate for them. Islam is the third monotheistic religion and lays claim to being

---

[152] Cf. Gerhard Lohfink, "Jesus und die Kirche," 50–72.

[153] One exception may be Gal 6:16, where "the Israel of God" may refer to the Church made up of Jews and Gentiles. Thus, e.g., Wolfgang Kraus, *Das Volk Gottes. Zur Grundlegung der Ekklesiologie bei Paulus*. WUNT 85 (Tübingen: Mohr, 1996) 247–52. Or does Paul here mean the Israel that has not yet come to believe? Thus Franz Müssner, *Der Galaterbrief*. HThK IX (Freiburg: Herder, 1974) 417.

Abraham's true heir. Could it have arisen if Judaism and Christianity had been united and given living witness to the one, supranational people of God?

Islam sees in the Quran the continuation of the Torah and the gospel in the sense of the restoration of the original revelation to Adam; Abraham had already wanted to renew that primeval revelation in view of the decline of humanity into polytheism. When Mohammed purified the sanctuary in Mecca from the nature religions that were resident there he adopted Jewish and Christian ideas. But his reforming zeal lacked genuine knowledge of Israel and the Church. He had no experience of Christianity in the form of living communities. As a caravan guide he knew only individual Christians, most of them hermits, who represented a no-longer-orthodox monophysite Christianity. At any rate Mohammed came to think that the Trinity consisted of God, Jesus, and Mary, and that the Holy Spirit was the angel Gabriel.

In order to set himself apart from Jews and Christians he proposed the interpretation that not Isaac but Ishmael, Abraham's other son, was the bearer of the true promise. Thus he came to the following line of descent: Adam with the primeval revelation, Abraham with Ishmael as the restorers of the primeval revelation, Moses as prophet, Jesus as later prophet, and Mohammed as the last and greatest of all prophets. Thus the Arabs, the descendants of Ishmael, were given precedence over the Jews, and Mohammed's prophecy stands at the pinnacle of revelation—and at the same time is the oldest. Crucial in all this was that Mohammed did not think much of what he could find of Judaism and Christianity. He regarded both of them as semi-pagan. This means, however, that his stumbling was caused by the divided people of God.

The Catholic Church in turn failed to meet the challenge posed by Islam. Contrary to the Sermon on the Mount it sought to overthrow it with crusades that ended by cementing the separation between Rome and Constantinople and incited new hatred of the Jews besides. Every major twelfth-century crusade was preceded by a persecution of Jews somewhere in Europe. The crusaders wanted to punish the Muslims for their seizure of "Christ's inheritance" and to avenge Christ's crucifixion on the Jews. The only appropriate way for the Church to encounter Islam, however, would have been in the spirit of Jesus and through familial love between Israel and the Church.

Thus the division of the one people of God into Jews and Christians had consequences for world history. After the Church had gotten used to that first division and come to regard it as natural, further divisions followed. They need not all be listed here; at any rate there has not been a century without divisions, and very few of them have been healed. There were not only the great schisms, such as those between Rome and the Byzantine Church (1054) or between Rome and the churches of the Reformation (beginning in 1517). There were a multitude of other separations from the first century until now. The textbooks of church history would be half as thick if one could eliminate the history of dogmatic conflicts, excommunications, and schisms.

Moreover, there have not only been divisions in the strict sense of the word. Besides these, and almost more frightening, there has been in Europe a falling away of whole groups and classes from the Church. We may recall only the departure of the educated since the European Enlightenment, the socialist movement in the nineteenth century and the loss of the workers, and finally the silent exit of the masses in the last decades. In all these cases we are not talking simply about disappearances. The currently popular image of the gradual evaporation of Christian faith is not the whole truth, for people who have thus been lost to the Church have sought a substitute. Most of them let themselves be gathered somewhere else. From one part of the socialist movement emerged the dialectical materialism of the Soviet Union, with all the signs of a pseudo-church, and many of those who today are leaving the major churches join questionable sects or adopt esoteric religious practices. No one can live for long without a highest good and a hope of some kind. If they do not base themselves in the Christian church and believe in the true God they believe in themselves and in cheap gospels of self-redemption, the market for which is continually expanding.

What I have just said is meant only to indicate that the concept of church division cannot be defined too narrowly. There are not only divisions into newer and newer splinter churches, there is also an exodus from the churches that leads to pseudo-churches.

But let us return to our starting point, the divisions within the Church! It is certainly true of them, as was said of the very first division within the people of God, that what was and is at issue was not only lack of faith, though unbelief is part of the picture on both sides of every division. First of all it was always a question of the truth of faith and of taking seriously, without conditions, the reality of the gospel and the nature of the Church.

However, if the first issue in all divisions is the truth of faith, the fact of the division of the people of God may not be regarded as a matter of course. There are theologians who make a virtue of the painful fact of division and assert that the many churches and confessions reflect, like a thousand facets, the richness of the Christian reality. There is certainly an element of truth in that: all the churches that have gone their separate ways have brought to light elements of faith that were affirmed onesidedly, obscured, or covered over in the Catholic Church. Even all the serious sects have reminded the Church unmercifully that faith demands apostolic life, the genuine community of the faithful. Perhaps in a Church that had hardened itself and become incapable of reform its own tradition could only be brought before its eyes by this means.

And yet the thesis that all separations can simply be explained and even transfigured as the "richness of variety" not only contains a highly dangerous element; it is also unbiblical. The condition of Christianity at the present time is nothing like a colorful field in which wheat is growing and poppies and cornflowers are blooming; it is rather like a broken mirror that distorts the image of Christ.[154] In light of the New Testament the splintering of the people of God cannot be regarded in any other way. There the question of divisions within the communities and within the Church as a whole was already present, and the answer given by New Testament theology is unequivocal.

We have already seen the decisive text from Ephesians: "[make] every effort to maintain the unity of the Spirit" (4:3). We may by no means understand this imperative as putting value only on the "spiritual bond" that invisibly joins all Christians. What is meant, rather, is the Holy Spirit who flows throughout the one body of the Church. Therefore the body of the Church is mentioned even before the Holy Spirit. Both belong together, unmixed and unseparated: "one body and one Spirit" (4:4).

In the Fourth Gospel Jesus prays, concluding his whole discourse at the Last Supper, immediately before his arrest and as part of a solemn farewell prayer, explicitly for the unity of his disciples: "Holy Father, protect them in your name that you have given me, so that they may be one, as we are one" (John 17:11). A little later this prayer is expanded to include all future believers:

> "I ask not only on behalf of these, but also on behalf of those who will believe in me through their word, that they may all be one. As you, Father, are in me and I am in you, may they also be in us, so that the world may believe that you have sent me." (John 17:20-21)

Three things in this prayer for the unity of the disciples and the post-Easter Church are noteworthy: (1) Unity is not something that is natural to the Church. It is God's gift and must be asked for. (2) The unity of the Church reflects the unity between the Father and the Son. As Christ is entirely in the Father and the Father in him, so the Church must be entirely in Christ: only then will it be united. (3) The world's recognition of the mission and thus of the nature of Christ depends on the unity of the Church. No one has ever seen God, and Christ, God's image and reflec-

---

[154] This reflects the words of the Augsburg Synod of 1990 (see n. 83 above) 475–76.

tion, is no longer in the world. What can be seen is only the Church. If it is no longer one, but divided, the world can only indistinctly behold the mystery of Christ. The mirror is shattered. The division of the people of God makes it almost impossible for the world to believe.

All that is so unequivocal that it would be superfluous to adduce other New Testament texts on the question of church unity. Ephesians and the Fourth Gospel are sufficient to show that those who do not see the division of the people of God into churches and confessions, free churches and free communities as an unbearable state of affairs that endangers belief in Christ, those who even legitimate this state of things in hindsight by confusing it with the richness of Christian faith—these have Scripture against them.

However, we must look at the New Testament under another aspect in this connection. It does not consist of twenty-seven individual works set arbitrarily alongside one another like a small library; it is, according to the will of the Church, which created the canon of Sacred Scripture, *a single book* together with the Old Testament. The four gospels are the basis of the New Testament; the two books of the Lukan history are separated; the collection of Pauline letters is equally balanced by the collection of seven so-called "Catholic Letters" with writings of the three "pillars of the first community," namely James, Peter, and John. The compositional intent underlying the New Testament is unmistakable.

If we look more closely at the theological positions of the individual New Testament writings and compare them with one another we can only be astonished at the degree to which they attest the Church's one faith. It has, of course, been customary for a long time to emphasize the differences, divergences, tensions, and contradictions among the various "theologies" in the New Testament writings. There is certainly no question that it contains divergent accentuations and the greatest variety of forms of discourse, word plays, and thought systems. But if we take into account this disparity in forms of speech and thought, it is difficult to locate contradictions in the confession itself. The variety of the New Testament by no means requires the multitude of Christian confessions.

On the contrary: the growth of New Testament traditions within the canon shows a shocking unity in spite of all the variety, a unity that is contrary to all the ordinary experiences in our society. Elias Canetti was right: the true tendency of things is *centrifugal;* they rush apart, separating from each other at top speed. We must also take into account the difficulties of communication in antiquity: messengers traveling for weeks at a time to exchange information among the communities; letters in which no one could explain everything and all too easily could miss the mark in addressing the other. In light of this miserable starting point the fact that a unified faith arose in the many communities surrounding the Mediterranean is one of the great miracles, only to be understood as the working of the historical and meta-historical power of the person of Jesus Christ.

But let us suppose that there were contradictions among the individual New Testament writings at the level of the faith itself. Then more than ever we would have to be serious about the fact that the Sacred Scriptures do not consist of a bundle of assorted documents that can be played off against one another, but rather make up a single book. The historical-critical method in recent decades has, by employing newer exegetical techniques derived from literary theory (synchronic analysis), approached ever more closely to this insight. It has recognized with increasing assurance that the thing to be interpreted is ultimately the canonical "final text" of the Bible, and not only certain parts or preliminary stages.

If, however, it was the authorial will of the Church that created the final text of the Bible, the canon, it can only have understood its own book in such a way that all the divergent threads in it, representing the faith of different communities or regions of the Church, come together in unity. Exegesis must certainly trace the variety of traditions and layers in the Bible in a *historical-critical* manner. That is unavoidable for the sake of interpretation itself. But as soon as it begins to interpret the Bible *theologically*—which is its primary function—it must interpret the final text, and interpret it in terms of its unity.

Those who do so are by no means "falsifiers" in Canetti's sense, people who by force create a harmonious compromise out of disparity. Instead, they take the canon *as canon* seriously. From this point of view as well it is impossible that the canon itself could serve as a basis for the differences among the confessions. It has very deliberately bound together the gospels and the letters, the Petrine and the Pauline, the official and the charismatic, into a united whole.[155]

Obviously a Church that has been restored to unity cannot be rendered uniform. Its unity would have to be rich and varied, with a great deal of color, many forms and languages and individual traditions, but it would have to be *one* Church, and its unity must not be in some sort of invisible realm.

---

[155] Investigations of the authorial intent behind the creation of the canon and the structure that resulted are just beginning. For the New Testament see especially David Trobisch, *Die Endredaktion des Neuen Testaments. Eine Untersuchung zur Entstehung der christlichen Bibel.* NTOA 31. Fribourg: Universitätsverlag, and Göttingen: Vandenhoeck & Ruprecht, 1996.

To this point such unity does not exist. The contrarieties are deeply rooted. The wounds of history are still open. At the same time the churches are becoming more and more a-historical. How can Christianity get beyond this? Shall it say that the unity of the Church belongs to the eschaton, the end of the world, and will only be given when Christ returns? Shall separation remain until then as a sign of the not-yet? That, too, would be contrary to the New Testament, for the eschaton already began at Easter, and in the Fourth Gospel Christ prays not for the unity of his disciples at a time shortly before the end of the world but that they should be one *now,* because otherwise the world cannot believe. Therefore the divisions in the Church must be overcome within history, and as quickly as possible. But how?

This will most certainly not come to pass through the independent action of individual groups or congregations that undertake to create a community around the Lord's Supper according to their own judgment, as it pleases them. That would not be thinking "ecclesially," but "privatistically," contrary to the unanimity of genuine *communio,* contrary to the principle of "wholeness." It would not only fail to take history seriously but would disregard the freedom of those who do not yet consider a community in the Lord's Supper to be possible. Disobedience and arbitrariness will never bring about a genuine unity, but only contribute to new divisions.

Then what can overcome these divisions? The much-lauded practice of dialogue? Obviously discussions between the churches and confessions are of the greatest importance. In particular the historical and theological uncovering of the grounds for division, the misunderstandings and hardenings, the real interests and desires on both sides, as well as becoming thoroughly acquainted with the other's traditions—all this can help to prepare for union. Yet it will not happen solely through dialogues at conference tables and statements of agreement.

Unanimity within a community assembly only happens when those assembled finally cease looking at themselves. As long as they only have themselves in mind they will constantly discover new things that the other has not yet understood, finding new offenses and injuries, new problems that have not yet been resolved. The self-reflection and psychologizing of each and of all will never come to an end. The miracle of unanimity is only possible when the assembly turns away from itself and its own interests and asks about God's interests. What does God will?

The recognition of God's will through looking away from the self happens, however, not only in the head. It presupposes the conversion of the whole person and the conversion of the whole group, and like every conversion it is not only a joyful but also a painful process. What is true of the assembly of a single community is certainly true of the gathering of the Church into unity: there will be no union of the churches without their conversion, and that obviously does not mean only the conversion of the officeholders.

To whom and wherein shall the separated churches convert? To God and God's will, that is, to the historical plan God has for the world. This plan of God is revealed to us nowhere more clearly than in the Old and New Testaments. It is the will of God to have a people in the world so that one can clearly see, by looking at that people, how God proposes that human society should be, so that the world can see the unanimity and peace that is possible in such a people and thus come to peace for itself. It is the will of God to lead the whole world to liberation and redemption through the redemption and liberation that happens in one people.

Formulating things in this way already means taking the Old Testament seriously, and radically so, and Judaism as well. This whole book has been an attempt (helpless, no doubt, at times) to make clear in a number of new facets the basic theme of the Old Testament and Judaism, that God needs a people in the world that lives according to God's will because otherwise the world cannot be redeemed in freedom. Let us have no illusions: this, God's solution, is anything but obvious. It has largely been forgotten.

The conversion that alone can heal the wounds of division would thus first of all be a re-rooting of the Church in the Old Testament and in Jewish reality.[156] It would involve a common return to the sources, to the place where all the divisions began. In this common return to their roots, to Abraham, the churches could learn not only that God desires to have a people in the world that will be a blessing to all other peoples but also— and this is equally important—that God acts in God's people, unceasingly, in ever new ways,[157] and that faith is not in the first place the maintaining of dead statements but daring to believe in God's promises.

---

[156] The Katholische Integrierte Gemeinde, in a series of publications with the series title Heute. Pro ecclesia viva, entitled the first volume *Vom Wiedereinwurzeln im Jüdischen als einer Bedingung für das Einholen des Katholischen* (2nd ed. Bad Tölz: Verlag Urfeld, Schulgraben 2, 83646 Bad Tölz, 1995).

[157] The statement that God's deeds are continuing does not deny that the resurrection of Jesus is the great, unsurpassable, definitive action of God. But it was not simply an act of rescue for Jesus himself. It is not fully attested and by no means realized in its full scope if it does not take form in the Church. In the existence and growth of the Church as a new society the eschatological power of the resurrection of Jesus is demonstrated. To that extent God's actions ended with Jesus, and yet they go on. They go on insofar as the power of Jesus' resurrection must make its way in the Church and through the Church in the whole world. Cf. Gerhard Lohfink, *The Work of God Goes On* 23–27.

The conversion that alone can heal the wounds of division would then require taking the New Testament seriously, and not only the gospels, not only the genuine letters of Paul, but the *whole* New Testament. We have already said that it is the will of the Church, which created the canon, that the New Testament should be read together with the Old Testament as a single book. The process of New Testament canon-building was one of selection. There were many more gospels, revelatory writings, letters, and "acts of the apostles" in the ancient Church than were actually incorporated into the canon. The criterion of selection was "apostolicity," that is, the original, unfalsified tradition that goes back to the apostles.

There was a very solid reason why this criterion was so important and why a canon of authoritative "apostolic" writings was created in accordance with it: false teachings were spreading, divisions were increasing, and there was danger that continuity with the apostolic era might be broken. The choice of the New Testament writings and their compilation was thus already intended to serve the unity of the Church. Precisely in this connection we should make another observation: it is especially the "later writings" in the New Testament that most intensively develop the theme of Church tradition and Church office. This is especially obvious in Ephesians, the Pastorals, the Lukan historical work, and in John 21, the coda to the Fourth Gospel.

Continuity with the apostolic era and service to the unity of the Church therefore mean for the New Testament as a complete composition, among other things, an emphasis on offices in the Church. This is especially evident in Eph 4:8-12, as we already saw in connection with the question of "wholeness." The text speaks first of all of Jesus' ascension and then, with reference to the gifts of the Spirit given to the Church by the exalted Christ, it alludes directly to ecclesiastical office:

> The gifts [the exalted Christ] gave were that some would be apostles, some prophets, some evangelists, some pastors and teachers, to equip the saints for the work of ministry, for building up the body of Christ, until all of us come to the unity of the faith and of the knowledge of the Son of God, to maturity, to the measure of the full stature of Christ. (Eph 4:11-13)

These offices are thus given by Christ to the Church so that the body of Christ may be built up in unity. The connection between offices and unity in the Church is equally important in the theology of the Lukan historical work. For Luke the Twelve secure continuity between the time of Jesus and that of the Church. Like every living organism the people of God also needs its own "genetic information." The Twelve are the enduring memory, so to speak, of what Jesus did and taught. They stand for the integrity of the Jesus tradition. Luke expressly emphasizes that they were present during the whole period when Jesus came and went among his own (Acts 1:21-22). In the great missionary speeches in Acts Luke shows us what the apostles taught. Afterward, Paul becomes the agent of continuity. When he has to leave his missionary territory in the East he gives a farewell address to the elders of the community in Ephesus that is intended, in turn, to reflect continuity with the time to come. It is the only speech in Acts that is addressed exclusively to Church officeholders. For Luke it is Paul's last will and testament to the later Church. There we read:

> "Keep watch over yourselves and over all the flock, of which the Holy Spirit has made you overseers, to shepherd the church of God that he obtained with the blood of his own Son. I know that after I have gone, savage wolves will come in among you, not sparing the flock. Some even from your own group will come distorting the truth in order to entice the disciples to follow them. Therefore be alert, remembering that for three years I did not cease night or day to warn everyone with tears. And now I commend you to God and to the message of his grace, a message that is able to build you up and to give you the inheritance among all who are sanctified." (Acts 20:28-32)

Luke's formulation here clearly reflects his own church's critical situation. There are already false teachers and divisions, and those teachers have arisen in the midst of the communities. In light of this situation in the Church there are two things above all that offer security: the *gospel,* here called "the message of grace," which has the power to build up the Church, and *ecclesiastical office.* Those who exercise office are referred to here as "overseers," in Greek *episkopoi.* Luke is writing from the perspective of his own time, when the Jewish-Christian office of "elders" *(presbyteroi)* had been joined with the Gentile-Christian *episkopoi* to become the crucial ecclesiastical office for the leadership of the communities.

In our context it is important to note that this office of *episkopoi* was already being regarded in terms of service to the unity of the one *ekklēsia.* The officeholders are to *keep watch over* the Church of God, that is, as shepherds they are to continually gather their flocks so that they will not be scattered or decimated by false teachers. Luke thus sees ecclesiastical office and holding fast to the gospel as the guarantees of Church unity. Something similar can be read in the Pastorals.

It is wrong to dismiss all these texts, which make up a significant portion of the New Testament, as late, "early Catholic," or contrary to the charismatic structure of Pauline communities, and to construct a "canon within the canon" out of the purified remnant. If the New Testament is to be interpreted as a single book, and if it was created precisely for the purpose of maintaining the unity of the Church and preserving the apostolic teaching, selective criteria of that sort are inappropriate—quite apart from the fact that Paul had already confronted his communities as an apostle whose duty it was to order, judge, and lead. He was certainly aware of his apostolic responsibility.[158]

The remarkable thing is that within the New Testament tradition there is unmistakably a steady increase in reflection on apostolic office, and within that on ecclesiastical office. Today, in contrast, office is seen by many as an obstacle to the reunion of the separated churches. In particular the office of the Pope in Rome is regarded as the greatest barrier to church unity. We therefore cannot avoid, in conclusion, a brief glance at this question.

The Roman Catholic Church grounds the primacy of the Bishop of Rome in the Petrine succession. For Peter's office and that of his successors it refers primarily to three New Testament texts. Most frequently cited is the promise given by Jesus to Peter in Matthew's gospel:

> "And I tell you, you are Peter, and on this rock I will build my church, and the gates of Hades [= the power of death] will not prevail against it. I will give you the keys of the kingdom of heaven [= the reign of God], and whatever you bind on earth will be bound in heaven [= before God], and whatever you loose on earth will be loosed in heaven." (Matt 16:18-19)

Equally important is a dialogue between the Risen One and Peter in the "coda" to the Fourth Gospel. This final chapter is not part of the oldest form of that gospel, but it is certainly part of the canon.

> When they had finished breakfast, Jesus said to Simon Peter, "Simon son of John, do you love me more than these?" He said to him, "Yes, Lord; you know that I love you." Jesus said to him, "Feed my lambs." A second time he said to him, "Simon son of John, do you love me?" He said to him, "Yes, Lord; you know that I love you." Jesus said to him, "Tend my sheep." He said to him the third time, "Simon son of John, do you love me?" Peter felt hurt because he said to him the third time, "Do you love me?" And he said to him; "Lord, you know everything; you know that I love you." Jesus said to him, "Feed my sheep." (John 21:15-17)

The threefold question reflects Peter's threefold denial. The guilt of his betrayal is thus forgiven. At the same time he is entrusted with the office of shepherding the whole flock, the same office exercised by Christ himself (John 10:14). Obviously the sheep here do not represent a single congregation. They are an image for the whole Church.

A third text important for Petrine primacy is in Luke's gospel, in the context of the Last Supper. Jesus foretells Peter's betrayal: "Simon, Simon,

---

[158] On this subject see further detail in Gerhard Lohfink, *Jesus and Community* 117–22.

listen! Satan has demanded to sift all of you like wheat, but I have prayed for you that your own faith may not fail; and you, when once you have turned back, strengthen your brothers" (Luke 22:31-32). Thus after his repentance Peter is to take responsibility for the Twelve, and beyond them for the Church that will gather around them.

We should note, however, that these three texts are by no means isolated instances within the whole complex of the gospels and Acts.[159] They are embedded in a broad spectrum of passages that show Peter as the spokesman and representative of the other disciples. There is no dissent among biblical scholars at the present time about the prominent position of Peter in the gospels and the post-Easter office that, according to the gospels, was entrusted to him by Christ.

Recent work that focuses its primary attention on the statement of the final text is also agreed that Peter is deliberately portrayed in the gospels, especially Matthew's, as the "type of the true disciple." This means that Peter is the prototype and model of a disciple as such. In him the Church can discern, even in later periods, how a disciple confesses Jesus as Messiah and Son of God, joins with him, and can remain his disciple in spite of his or her own failure.[160]

This insight has major consequences, for it shows that the evangelists did not think one-dimensionally. They not only wanted to show the things that had happened uniquely and once-for-all in and because of Jesus' coming. Beyond that, they wanted to make the events of those days transparent for their own Church's present time. As Peter believed with his whole passionate self, so should every disciple believe. As he repented and thereafter stood undividedly at Jesus' disposal, so should every disciple continually repent and devote his or her life to Jesus' cause.

However, Peter in the gospels is not only the prototype of the disciple. He is also, and to a still greater degree, the prototype of the apostle and thus of officeholders in the Church. This is more than a typology of disciples. In Matthew's gospel, for example, he is the "fundamental figure of the apostle"[161] who comes first in the list of apostles (Matt 10:2) and is installed as the foundation of the future Church (Matt 16:18).

What does it mean that Peter is depicted as the "prototype" of a Church officeholder? We must reflect for a moment on what a "type" or

---

[159] For what follows cf. the essay by Rudolf Pesch, "'Was an Petrus sichtbar war, ist in den Primat eingegangen.' Ergebnisse einer exegetischen Untersuchung bezüglich der Grundlage des Primats und seiner Weitergabe." Not yet published.

[160] For example, Jürgen Roloff depicts Peter as the "prototype of the true disciple." (*Die Kirche im Neuen Testament* [Göttingen: Vandenhoeck & Ruprecht, 1993] 163–65.

[161] This formulation is from Ulrich Luz, *Das Evangelium nach Matthäus 2*. EKK 1/2 (Zürich: Benziger, and Neukirchen-Vluyn: Neukirchener Verlag, 1990) 469.

"prototype" or *"figura"* is.[162] It belongs to the nature of a prototype that it can be duplicated and imitated. A *typos* in Greek is first of all the "stamp," the "pressing," the "copy," but besides this the word also refers to the mold itself, and thus the "model," the "sample," the "prototype" according to which the copy is made. Our concept of a "type" feeds on this second set of meanings. Every type exists in order to shape, to give form, to serve as the prototype for a later reality.

In theological terms we can illustrate this very clearly in terms of the Exodus narratives in the Old Testament (cf. II, 3 above). They became a type, and in their form as written narratives they were conceived from the outset as a type.[163] The narrative of the unique event is transparent for later events in Israel's history. In the Exodus texts the later Israel not only finds itself reflected, which would be saying too little; it forms later experiences into new Exodus narratives along the lines of this model. The Exodus texts are thus typological to the extent that they are open to later realizations of Exodus, and indeed demand them.

Applying this to the primacy-text in Matthew we can say that "if the figure of Peter as sketched in the gospel of Matthew is understood first of all as a type it necessarily follows that in the intention of the evangelist himself it is to be a model, a figure for imitation in the future Church,"[164] and not only a model of the disciple, but also of the officeholder. From this point of view it is clear that the Protestant position according to which the rock foundation of the Church represented by Peter was something historically unique and unrepeatable must be called into question. The sense of Matt 16:18 is not fully exhausted by this position.

Of course the thesis of the *uniqueness* of the "office of the rock" is rooted in the fact that after the death of Peter there was, at first, no Petrine office in the strict sense of the word. Matthew, in any case, had no idea of such an office for the whole Church, and it was a relatively long time before it developed in Rome, where Peter had died a martyr and where his tomb was venerated.

This, however, only establishes that the type proposed in the image of Peter in Matthew required some time for development. That is generally the case with any type: it is only in a subsequent period that it reveals its historical power. Consider the Exodus narratives! "That Matthew himself did not yet see how the office of Peter-the-rock would be concretely realized

---

[162] What follows is indebted to Rudolf Pesch, "'Was an Petrus sichtbar war,'" ms. pp. 9–10.

[163] Cf. Norbert Lohfink, *The Christian Meaning of the Old Testament* (Milwaukee: Bruce, 1968) 67–86.

[164] Rudolf Pesch, "'Was an Petrus sichtbar war'" ms. p. 9.

and developed in the Church does not change the fact that it could show itself to be indispensable and essential for the Church. And the evangelist placed it at a climactic point in his gospel. If Peter is the 'prototype,' so is his function as the foundational rock, and that, too, must therefore be incarnated in the Church."[165]

Something similar may be said of Luke and of the author of John 21. Neither is yet defining a later Petrine office. They are simply presenting images: an officeholder who strengthens his brothers in the apostolic office, a shepherd who tends the whole Church. The Church itself had to attempt to give these images a concrete form, with all the conditional features that are part of any historical realization. The form of the Petrine office only appeared through a process of development, unfolding, and slow testing, stimulated above all by the Church's needs. Can we not also say that it was stimulated by the Holy Spirit, who is to lead the Church "into all the truth" (John 16:13)?

Because the fully realized form of the people of God presupposes a long process of seeking, and because the Church had to discover all its offices, even though they were given to it as an endowment, we may also presume that the office of the papacy is still subject to shaping and unfolding. In terms of the New Testament such a process must be understood above all as a service to the unity of the Church. The one who succeeds to Peter's office is to strengthen his brothers, never forgetting that he is only first among the Twelve. This very thing is sharply emphasized in Matthew's gospel.[166]

*

Here we must break off our discussion. Much more could be said about the Roman primacy. It is a good deal more biblical than it often appears. But equally important is the fact that the slow formation of this office in the Church, and its transformation through the centuries, especially in the twentieth century, show that the Church is something infinitely vital. According to the Bible it is not only a building and a temple but the people of God, the plantation of God, God's own bride, the body of Christ—and even the building is made up of living stones.

The Church did not come into the world as a finished product. Although everything has already been given to it, it must still grow and develop. Because it is the people of God it must go on its journey. Cardinal Jean-Marie Lustiger of Paris said a few years ago, in a speech in Augs-

---

[165] Ibid., ms. p. 10.

[166] The saying about binding and loosing in Matt 16:19 is addressed to all the disciples in 18:18.

burg: "Christianity is just beginning. It is just getting out of its toddler shoes. It is only at an initial stage. It has not yet had a chance to develop." Is that pure rhetoric? Has the people of God not had more than three thousand years to develop, and the Church almost two thousand? Have not many people already buried their hopes for the Church for this very reason, that in spite of all that time it continually fails? The Augsburg Synod of 1990 wrote against such hopeless attitudes:

> We can certainly not ignore the Church's guilt and its deep wounds. Nevertheless we see, in spite of all this misery, the beloved bride of whom it is said that she is more beautiful than the dawn. Its mystery has shone forth in every century: in the words of its Sacred Scripture, in the signs of its sacraments, in the beauty of its church buildings, in the seriousness of its reform movements, in the endless choir of its saints, in its steadfast faith that all the promises of God that have not yet come to pass may be fulfilled today.

That "today" is what is so crucial. We can see with our own eyes more, in some sense, than earlier generations of Christians could see. It is not that we are holier or more faithful than our ancestors! But history has moved forward. No previous century had the opportunity to see as clearly as we do the way followed by the people of God before us: the way of Israel, the way of the early Church of small communities, the way of the imperial Church after Constantine! Modern historical and literary scholarship is a priceless aid to the Church's theology. For the first time we sense what its union with the state has cost the Church. For the first time we can assess the reasons why there have been repeated divisions of the Church. For the first time we understand—standing speechless in face of the Holocaust— what has happened between the Church and Israel.

The Church stands face to face with a new "today." Jean-Marie Lustiger is right when he says that it is taking off its toddler shoes. Today is only the beginning.

# The Church and I

In the course of my life I have experienced the Church in three different ways. As I look through my diaries I see that my lifetime divides naturally into three periods. The first extends from 1934 to 1964, from my
earliest childhood to the end of my work as a parish priest. Those were
thirty years of unchallenged life in the Church. The second segment extends to 1986, during which time, at the commission of my bishop at the
time, Wilhelm Kempf, I continued my studies and became Professor of
New Testament in the Catholic faculty of theology at the university in
Tübingen. Those twenty-two years were also spent in the Church, but
there was a new undercurrent: a critique directed constantly at the Church,
especially what we used to call the "institutional Church." From 1986 onward I have learned to look at the Church with new eyes.

In the course of time it became clear to me, through many encounters,
that these three periods have a common thread that extends throughout my
life. Others had similar experiences and are trying to interpret them. For
that reason alone I am taking the liberty of speaking about them. At the
same time I must admit that what I am about to say cannot be generalized
in every respect. I grew up in Germany. In other parts of the worldwide
Church people had very different experiences during the same years. Not
even for Germany is what I am now describing universally representative.

For one thing, I lived almost entirely in Frankfurt am Main except for
some interruptions caused by the war. In Frankfurt there was an active
Church life, with respect and openness to other confessions and a theologically well-educated clergy. My family belonged to St. Gall, a work-
ing-class parish in the western part of the city with a kind and believing
pastor, a pastoral priest to his fingertips who long before the Council had
gathered a whole group of assistants and coworkers in ministry. This was

311

a very special kind of church situation in a major city. Elsewhere in Germany it may have been quite different. I can only report in a few brief paragraphs how *I* fared with the Church.

\*

In the years before the Second World War there were about 12,000 Catholics in St. Gall. The war brought a serious interruption but in the postwar years the numbers climbed again to about 8,000. Most of these people were already alienated from the Church. Nevertheless there was a varied and colorful life in the Neo-Romanesque church and its surroundings. On Sundays the three Masses were filled to the last pew. Even on weekdays many people went to Mass. Besides the pastor there were two young assistants and two communities of sisters with a clinic for ambulant patients, a retirement home, a home for "fallen girls" (as we used to say), a kindergarten, a large church choir, and various church clubs as well as many youth groups (these last, as everywhere in Germany, forbidden by the Nazis or restricted to the church confines).

Although in this big-city parish those who oriented their lives to the Church were a minority there nevertheless existed something like a Church "milieu." It was evident, for example, in the great Corpus Christi processions, the solemn opening of the May devotions, or when the beloved and respected pastor was killed in a traffic accident. The news of his death spread like lightning: in the blink of an eye the church was filled with people praying.

I can still taste the atmosphere of some of those services: the colors of the church windows fading in the dusk, the flowers, the incense, the crowd of Mass servers, the power of the congregation's singing, the assurance of being secure in God's house. Is all that only the transfigured recollection of a happy childhood? It must be more than that. For me the parish, and with it the universal Church that we always heard about, was something essential. As a child I understood that for my parents the faith was the most important thing of all. Therefore the Church was, above all, my home, and for that very reason it was beautiful.

Of course Christian community life was not confined to our own parish. Our family lived in a housing development for railway workers, separated from the principal part of the parish by a gigantic freight- and switching-yard. For that reason the Church members in that development had a Sunday Mass of their own in the gymnasium of a public school. Before it could take place a good many pieces of athletic equipment had to be pushed into another room, a wooden altar erected, and many chairs set up. During that time the women began decorating the gym with flowers and hanging pieces of cloth in the colors appropriate to the liturgical season. The whole thing was a temporary and provisional arrangement, but for that very reason it gathered the believers in that housing development around the altar—for many years, and long before the Council. Every Saturday quite a few adults and young people heard the call: "Come on, we're going to set up!" That was only meant to refer to setting up the gym, but the careful external preparations for divine worship also served to build up the community.[1]

The wartime night bombing burned down our part of the city, and with it the row house we lived in. When the war ended in 1945 we found a new apartment close to the old parish church, which had also been bombed out and a temporary church set up within its ruins. In the next few years I encountered one last remnant of the Catholic youth movement that had developed an extraordinary influence in Germany between the wars. At that time it had brought young Christians to a more vital faith and especially through the liturgy had bound them more closely to the Church. On the basis of his experiences with that youthful explosion in the Church Romano Guardini had written in 1920:

> A religious process of unimaginable importance has begun: The Church is awakening in people's souls.
>
> Let me be clear: it was always present, and it has always been crucial for the believer who accepted its teaching, followed its direction; its powerful reality was [the believer's] support and assurance. But when the individualistic development since the late Middle Ages had reached a certain height the Church was no longer felt to be at the center of one's true religious life. A believer certainly lived in the Church and was led by it, but lived *the Church* less and less . . .
>
> The individual lived for him- or herself. "I and my Creator" was the only formula for many. Community was not the origin, but something secondary. It was not there from the outset, but was planned, desired, created. Someone went to others, took them in or joined with them, but was not originally part of them, not united to them in a living unity. This was not community, but organization: as everywhere else, so also in the religious sphere. How little did believers at worship consider themselves a community! How loose were the internal ties! How little was the individual conscious of the parish! How individualistically was "communion," the sacrament of community, understood![2]

---

[1] Translator's note: the author's German word, *"aufbauen,"* means literally "build up," but the parallelism does not translate in English, where the corresponding term for arranging a room as described here is "set up."

[2] Romano Guardini, "Das Erwachen der Kirche in der Seele," *Hochland* 19 (1922) 257–67, at 257, 259.

Guardini then describes how "where the fountains of the new age are, in the youth movement . . . the colossal fact of 'church' is once again a living thing." Finally he says:

> But all that must have its effect not only in books and speeches, but where the Church primarily exists for individuals: in the parish. If this process of "church movement" advances it must lead to a renewal of community consciousness. That is the normal way for Church to be experienced. That an individual should live with it, feel responsible for it together with others, work for it: this is the measure of true, not merely purported churchliness.[3]

Has Guardini's prophecy been fulfilled? As early as 1947 Ida Friederike Görres wrote:

> There is an "awakening of the Church in souls." There is also a "dying of the Church in souls." We see it all around us, among us, seldom as a sudden collapse before the lightning bolt of a catastrophe . . . but as a slow, creeping, imperceptible dying through freezing and impoverishment, spiritual undernourishment and hardening. That continues until the Church appears to them nothing more than an external and foreign body, pressing, demanding, provoking, nothing but an organization, a force, a power structure.[4]

That was also prophetic. It is true that the youth movement was being revived in 1945. There were community Masses, devotional celebrations, trips, camps, plays for the laity, home evenings, leadership groups, a weekly evening prayer for youth in one of the side chapels of the cathedral. Hundreds of young people gathered for the monthly youth preaching in one of the large churches in the center of Frankfurt.

However, that did not last long. It is remarkable how quickly all that "youth movement" dissipated in the Sixties. When I now read the songs and worship texts from those days I am not surprised. Here was a highly stylized language, vague at crucial points. It spoke of a "kingdom" and meant the kingdom of Christ, but in some strange way Germany and the German people were always mixed up in that kingdom. They spoke of "building" the kingdom of Christ. But where and how could that take place? Each was to witness to Christ in school or at work. But the more secularized society became, the more difficult it was. That the youth movement so rapidly broke up is a sign that it had no solid ground on which its great words like "new age," "covenant," "kingdom," "self-

---

[3] Ibid., 263, 265.

[4] Ida F. Görres, *Die leibhaftige Kirche. Gespräch unter Laien* (Einsiedeln: Johannes, 1994 [1st ed. Frankfurt: J. Knecht, 1950] 7). At this point she is quoting from an earlier essay of hers written in 1947.

development," "formation of life in Christ" could be lived, beyond youth-ful enthusiasm, in genuine social community.

As I look back, however, I question not only the youth movement but the church milieu I experienced as a child and youth. There was certainly much there that was good. There was even something like an "awakening of the Church in souls." And yet that Church suffered from shocking de-ficiencies. It can scarcely be blamed for them, but they are obvious to us today.

The Church did not prevent the two world wars, and could not prevent them. They simply broke over it. But what is disturbing today is some-thing beyond the mere fact of the two wars: the Church is the body of Christ, beyond all boundaries, the people of God among the nations. That in 1914 Christians went enthusiastically to war against Christians, bap-tized against baptized, was not seen in any way as a destruction of what the Church is in and of its very nature, a destruction that cried out to heaven. That was the real catastrophe. And that Hitler's war was a crimi-nal act that Christians in Germany should have resisted from the outset was again not a question that disturbed the consciences of very many.

I am not concerned with the question of whether such resistance was even possible, or what its cost might have been. What concerns me is that participation in the two world wars was not even seen by most baptized people in Germany as a problem for Christian consciences. Something similar can be said of the Church's paralysis while the synagogues burned and Christians in Germany should have arisen on behalf of their Jewish sisters and brothers. When I was a child I saw men and women who were forced to sew a yellow star of David on their garments; then one day I didn't see them any more.

Certainly the churches in Germany resisted Hitler. One of our assistant priests from St. Gall was imprisoned by the state secret police (the Gestapo) because of his preaching. But that resistance was brought on by the increasing restrictions on Church life, the confiscation of Church prop-erty, or the elimination of the mentally ill. The questions of war and the persecution of the Jews struck a spark in very few.

All this shows that in the first half of the twentieth century in Germany the blooming Catholic Church did not stand altogether on solid ground, even with its great wealth of priestly and religious vocations, its many clubs and institutions, its liturgical movement, its good numbers of mass-goers, and the Christian milieu that still existed or was building itself anew. There were some very thin places, some undermined stretches that could collapse at any moment. It was not simply empty traditions that caused faith to vanish from many Christian families in the second half of the twentieth century. The same thing happened even where Church life was vigorous or newly awakened. That is exactly why I have spoken about it.

\*

In 1968 students in the United States and in western Europe began to pose radical questions to their society. Since that time those questions have been posed in the Church as well. I still remember very well how this critical questioning overtook me as I was writing my dissertation. It was not that I had previously known nothing about the Church's sin and the crises in its history, but that was more or less filed in my head under the topic of apologetics, the defense of Christianity. Now, however, there arose in many, and also in me, a deep current of enduring dissatisfaction with the concrete appearance of the Church. Everything should be different, from the Vatican to the smallest parish.

We wanted an end to ecclesiastical pomp, to unintelligible rites, to worn-out hymns, to curial bureaucracy, to clerical dress. We wanted human language in worship, new songs, prayers about our real lives, priests who talked like normal people and fostered communication. We longed for bishops who no longer lived in palaces, but in rented quarters somewhere, and for Christians who lived in a way that was believable for everyone in society. "In the midst of the world," at first unnoticed and then truly noticeable: that was our secret ideal.

For me and many others in Germany Vatican II was not a particularly moving event. Of course we rejoiced over the pictures we saw on television, the commentary by the Jesuit Mario von Galli, and the initiative of the cardinals who gave the Council a new direction from the very beginning. But theologically what the conciliar documents said had long been familiar to me, or so I thought. It was quite a long time before I realized what the Council meant when seen against the background of the whole sweep of Church history, and what riches it had formulated.

In the Sixties I subscribed to an American weekly paper, *The National Catholic Reporter.* I liked it because there was nothing comparable among the Church papers in Germany. Social wrongs in South America were denounced, North American bishops were openly criticized, social trends were carefully observed. In those days criticism of the Church was lodged in every corner of our consciousness.

Unfortunately this critique was associated with a naïve scapegoat ideology: it was the fault of the bishops and the Roman curia that the Church was increasingly rejected by the public, because they were obstacles to every sensible reform. If the Church had more reform-friendly bishops it would again be young and attractive. This latent dissatisfaction broke into the open when Pope Paul VI published his encyclical *Humanae vitae* in 1968. At that time I preached against the encyclical for three Sundays in a row in a little church in the town where I was studying and where I said Sunday Mass on a regular basis, and I wrote an angry letter to Cardinal Döpfner in Munich.

In Tübingen, then, my perspective gradually shifted, at first without expression. It was still the case that the critical barbs in my lectures and publications were directed primarily against the apprehensive traditionalists within the Church and almost never against the follies of the other side. But little by little I began to have doubts about the list of changes that was advanced first by a few spokespersons and then by more and more Catholics in Germany: abolition of the law of celibacy, ordination of women, permission for divorce within the Church, democratic election of bishops, intercommunion, up-to-date credal formulas, and so on.

Would the Church be renewed if all that was accomplished? I believed it less and less. Renewal would presuppose conversion, and this relentlessly promoted list had very little to do with conversion. There were other churches that had experimented with all these things for centuries or decades. Faith had not grown greater there or the congregations more active. The colossal collapse of faith in Germany—beginning for educated people with the Enlightenment and for the general population in the middle of the twentieth century—had to have other reasons. Ultimately the God-question was at the heart of the matter.

This is clear from a good many personal testimonies written in the twentieth century. Noteworthy among them is the autobiography of Vilma Sturm, *Barfuß auf Asphalt.* It was important to me because it reflected much of what I observed in my own surroundings. Vilma Sturm, a journalist, was representative of many phases of German Catholicism. She grew up in the Catholic Rhineland, was influenced in her youth by Thomas à Kempis's *Imitation of Christ,* experienced something of the youth movement in Burg Rothenfels, later took part enthusiastically in so-called "left-wing Catholicism" and carried on the "Political Night Prayer" together with Dorothee Sölle and others for three years in the church of St. Anthony in Cologne. In old age she lost her faith. The description of this process makes up the impressive conclusion to her autobiography.[5] In later years she lived in Cologne and for some time attended the church of St. Agnes.

> I was at home in St. Agnes, satisfied enough for a while. Then that came to an end. After that I drifted away, like a boat without sail or rudder, driven

---

[5] Vilma Sturm, *Barfuß auf Asphalt. Ein unordentlicher Lebenslauf* (Cologne: Kiepenheuer und Witsch, 1981) 327–28.

only by the current. The current was those around me who were dear to me: my daughter, not married at the altar, my unbaptized grandchildren—she, her husband, and his mother, converted to Catholicism twenty years before, formally left the Church. Many of my friends as well were just not interested any more, not even my brother and his family. Often it was pure hatred, still more often indifference and satiety. . . .

It was certainly not because of this or that failure on the part of the Church; with the exception of Pope John it had long been for us more or less a matter of indifference or an institution to be resisted. But why did we, in the course of time, turn away from the congregation and from Mass, and from the Bible and prayer, finally from any kind of openly-expressed piety at all? I don't know. I find myself in the midst of a process of dissolution that is happening in me without my willing it. I drift farther and farther away into emptiness, where there is no one else, not even an echo, when I try to call out. The shores from which I came are scarcely visible any longer, and the words, the names I once had for the Holy have dissolved in the mist.

The words in the church are not my words any longer; I know no words at all with which I could worship together with other people. . . . Even the first words of the Our Father or the Credo paralyze my tongue. Shall I call it "Father," this ghastly mystery behind the course of the world? Never and nowhere to be discovered (because it is beyond time and space), and certainly not "above"—for where is above, where below, when we stand on a rotating globe? He has withdrawn beyond every concept, every word, every address. At the utmost I can say: I hope that he is; nothing more.

I hope that he is, that he will be there at the hour of my death and allow me to be with him in the never and nowhere in which he dwells. At the same time I shudder at the idea that it may be different, that nothing remains for me but coffin and grave and corruption. But I only shudder in the darkness, at night when I cannot sleep. In the daytime I am like all those who live as if there were no death.

This account is entirely representative of what has happened in the last several decades in Germany and other European countries: in many families the faith does not extend to the next generation. Not everyone can formulate her or his situation as precisely as Vilma Sturm. For many it is more superficial and less noticed. But it happens. It is like an unstoppable erosion.

The crucial statement in Sturm's memoir is that God is "never and nowhere to be discovered." The Bible says that God dwells "in unapproachable light" (1 Tim 6:16), which seems to be the same thing. However, the Bible's fundamental statement is that this hidden God has opened the inmost heart of God's divine self, binding that self irrevocably to the world in God's people and in Jesus Christ. The fundamental movement of salvation history is precisely this, that God becomes accessible to the world, that God finds a place in the world where the divine will can be known and the divine name can be called upon. In some way Vilma Sturm knew all that, but the place has faded away, and therefore her God has vanished.

That the Church as the place of God's physical presence had become less and less recognizable, even repellent for many, had occupied my thoughts again and again during my further studies. At first I thought that the primary task would be to translate the ancient statements of faith more clearly into today's reality and to find the right language for twentieth-century Christians. Thus besides my scholarly work I moved about quite a bit, preaching and giving lectures, talking about the image of God in the Bible, the Easter narratives in the gospels, everything that comes "after death," and "what I find fascinating about Jesus," about Jesus' parables and miracles, and about the forms and genres in the Bible. I could scarcely keep up with the constant demands.

But was there any sense in it all? What good is translation if there is no shore on which the ferry can make fast? What good is it to transform old words into new ones if the word has no ground on which it can be sown? Even the most conscientious lectures and presentations fall on deaf ears if there is no place where the great words of theology are really lived and where a life lived together in faith sustains theology. There has never been, in the whole history of the Church, so much religious education for children and such a well-organized system of adult education as there now is in Germany. And yet the dislocation of Christianity is increasing.

I wrote my doctoral dissertation on "The Ascension of Jesus in the Lukan Corpus." The question of the correct "translation" was the utmost focus of my concern. But then I began searching, more and more seriously, to discover what the Church is. It was no accident that I wrote my *Habilitationsschrift* on "The Gathering of Israel" as a dominant thread in Lukan ecclesiology. Later the subject of the Church in the New Testament occupied my attention more and more, and not only theoretically.

Others had similar experiences. We longed for a Church in which the community of faith could be concretely experienced. That had been a fundamental idea in the Catholic youth movement. Now it reasserted itself, though in another shape. From the Seventies onward Christians had gathered in many places in Germany to try to live their faith together. Often they called themselves something like "family circle" or, if there was more sociological thinking behind them, "base communities." The longing for more vital worship in which all participated played a major role in this, as did concern for the faith of children in a more and more faithless environment.

Most of these groups wanted to get away from privatistic faith, from worship services at which one neither knew the next person in the pew nor wanted to have anything to do with him or her. They also wanted to get away from the kind of ecclesiastical life that was too much oriented to institutional forms. I recall how in such a group in Rottenburg that I joined with great expectations we found ourselves forced for at least *one* year at a time to choose two people to be responsible for the group: there had at least to be someone who would call the others together. But otherwise everything was supposed to be spontaneous and grow out of the group itself.

At that time I wrote my book, *Wie hat Jesus Gemeinde gewollt?* My goal was to show on the basis of the New Testament that faith requires community, and in fact a community whose features clearly distinguish it from the rest of society. My interest was in the message of the text, the social form of Christian faith, but the book has to be understood as the description of a sequence: from community *(Gemeinschaft)* to ecclesial community *(Gemeinde),* in a kind of *direttissima* quickly achievable by every group that would come together, and legitimated by Jesus himself.

Only later did it come to me, after I had entered a new horizon of experience, that there is no such way to achieve "ecclesial community." Jesus had to die so that his disciples could become church. Without his death the Twelve would have understood nothing and would have gone on arguing among themselves. According to Luke they were still doing it at the Last Supper. It is certainly part of all this that the Church from ancient times has desired to have the relics of martyrs or saints with it wherever it has gathered as community. No matter how much the cult of relics was corrupted, in all centuries it has reflected the Church's knowledge that community is impossible without some people who have given their whole lives.

To that extent community is something dangerous. Where it exists it lives out of the death and resurrection of Jesus or not at all. Where it exists it has a share in the great history through which God leads God's people. Therefore it cannot be "made," but is created by God alone. Hence also the many disappointed people who came together to make something new for themselves, usually to meet their own needs, only to see the new thing slip through their fingers.

I might have been one of those disappointed people if I had not encountered the Integrierte Gemeinde in 1982, through my acquaintance with the New Testament scholar Rudolf Pesch and the accounts given me by my brother Norbert. It was the answer to many of the questions about the renewal of the Church that had occupied me for such a long time. After a period of getting acquainted, in 1986 I resigned my professorship in Tübingen and, with the consent of my bishop, and taking my aged parents with me, I moved to Munich.

*

I wanted to speak about how things have been between the Church and me. In the end I found the thing that so many biblical texts speak about, the thing I had so long desired. At this point I must describe it, and tell something about life in the Integrierte Gemeinde. But I don't know how to go about it. Colors are hard to describe. And how can anyone explain a rose in words alone? It has to be seen.

In the first chapter of the Fourth Gospel (1:35-51) there is a remarkable scene. Jesus passes by John the Baptizer and two of John's disciples. John points to Jesus and says: "Look, here is the Lamb of God!" The two disciples then follow Jesus. He turns and asks them: "What are you looking for?" They do not say: "We would like to know who you really are, what you are about, how you understand yourself and what your concerns are." They do not ask any of that; instead, they inquire: "Rabbi, where are you staying?" And Jesus answers them: "Come and see."

That is: when God is at work in God's people it is impossible just to talk about it. One must put one's feet in motion. The two disciples did so: "They came and saw where he was staying, and they remained with him that day." What they really saw when they were with Jesus is left out of the narrative. It is not described. And yet it changed their lives, for on the next day one of them, Andrew, said to his brother Simon: "We have found the Messiah."

A few verses later this "come and see" is repeated, but this time not by Jesus. It is Philip who says it to Nathanael. He had told Nathanael with great joy: "We have found him about whom Moses in the law and also the prophets wrote, Jesus son of Joseph from Nazareth." To Nathanael's skeptical question, "Can anything good come out of Nazareth?" Philip responds: "Come and see."

This means that it is not the privilege of the Messiah to speak in such a way. The call to "come and see" can continue in the Church; indeed, it must continue. The Second Vatican Council calls the Church the "messianic people."[6] The signs of the Messiah therefore are not restricted to Jesus; they continue in the Church, repeatedly coming to the fore—in order to be looked upon. It is not a question of theologians' talking about this, or of past theologians' having spoken of it, or of God's having spoken at one time. Therefore I can only say at this point:

Since I have joined the Integrierte Gemeinde and its Association of Priests, without deserving it, as one who came late, I have been permitted to experience the beauty of the Church anew: the wealth and healing power of its sacraments, the precious value of its traditions, the appropriate and therefore humanly fitting structural plan of its communities, its international character, its origins in the discerning power of Israel, its social structure, its world-embeddedness.

---

[6] *Lumen gentium* 2.9.

I have learned that there can be, even today, that Christian "milieu"[7] that in my childhood rescued my faith and gave me a home—now certainly in a different form, much more worldly, much more exposed and enlightened, and by that very fact much stronger and more sustaining. Finally, I have learned that God can do God's work even with weak and sinful people whose strength is never adequate to the tasks that constantly confront them. And for that I give God praise.

---

[7] "Milieu" is here understood as a social form, a world of life that requires faith in order to be lived at all. This social form, of course, is not something secondary added to faith, for example because society as a whole is pagan or secularized; rather, faith by its very nature is *communio* whose purpose is to be incarnated as a way of life. "Milieu" here by no means describes a "city of refuge" or a "sealed-off space."

# Church, What Do You Have to Say for Yourself?

*Arnold Stötzel*

I came late to the world, when everything was already in place. To say I came from the wilderness would be imprecise. To say I come from nothing would be closer to the truth. He found me. That's all. My dwelling was the pursuit of a trace, a scent that was foreign to me.

When they built the tower in Babel I thought to myself: power has bedded with human beings for a very long time. Standing before the pyramids I said: religion they have, too. In the Roman forum I thought: an empire like this one? At the feet of Plato I mused: a wisdom not at home here? Is there any need for me? My sole equipment was this question. It made me a vagabond among the peoples and the ages.

As I sought to be who I am, my education began. I slipped into the robe of religion, and it fell to tatters on my body. Should I not found a religion? I made an alliance with power and the state, dreamed of an empire of my own, acted like them. This dream shattered. Should I inaugurate a different kind of realm? I saw the nations come and go, living according to their own laws. Should I be a people that lives differently? And all the wisdom I encountered in the schools of the world spurred me to form myself after that which I perceived, and from the restlessness of my questioning existence.

I am the bringer and the sufferer of God's enlightening wisdom about the heavens and the earth, the unique mediator of salvation for this planet. For my sake it bears the honored name, "star of redemption," for I bear in me the measure of God; God's view of our world is engraved in my form and my history. Look at me: I am sinful and have sinful children, but I was made holy for my service—not for my own sake, but for the sake of the world. I am immaculate as a bride, beautiful to look upon because I have been purified.

He found no other. That is the reason for my humility, my pride, and my misery. The song of my "happy fault" is the hymn of salvation for the world.

# A Word of Thanks

In the process of this book's coming to be, many people have contributed their suggestions and friendly criticism. I am deeply grateful to them all. But if I were simply to write out the usual list of thanks, beginning with my brother Norbert and including Willibald Heilmann, Marius Reiser, Ludwig Weimer, and Rudolf Pesch, and all the way to Hans Pachner, who tirelessly sought out bibliographic references, I would be saying far too little. So here at the conclusion I will call yet another biblical text to my aid.

In the second book of his two-volume opus Luke describes how Barnabas brought Paul to Antioch, where he found prophets and teachers in the community. Luke mentions Simeon Niger, Lucius of Cyrene, and Manaen, a youthful comrade of Herod the Tetrarch. It was much the same with me. I am certainly no Paul, but I too, when I came to the Integrierte Gemeinde in Munich, found theologians with whom I have worked ever since: the patrologist Arnold Stötzel, from among whose beautiful texts I have chosen the closing pages for this book; the systematic theologian Ludwig Weimer; the canon lawyer Titus Lenherr; from a younger generation Bernhard Koch and later the Hungarian Tamás Czopf, both systematic theologians with great gifts for languages and for music. Before me the New Testament scholar Rudolf Pesch had exchanged his professorship in Freiburg for learning and teaching in the Integrierte Gemeinde. Others, including Maria Jaklitsch, Mechthild Wallbrecher, Bruno Alber, and Peter Zitta should be mentioned in the category of "prophets." From them I learned, though I was often slow to comprehend, to see people and things with the eyes of faith.

This was a common life and exchange such as I had never experienced before. Sometimes we ask ourselves whether it is even imaginable that people of such different backgrounds, and often with such different view-points, should live in unanimity and seek to formulate theology for today out of their common experience of the Church. And yet we have learned from experience that this is not only imaginable, it is possible. We ourselves know it as a miracle, and we tremble in the hope that it may remain so.

Where would we have been without the charism of Traudl and Herbert Wallbrecher, who began in 1947 to seek for theologians who would join them in their search for the buried treasure of the people of God? Since 1967 Ludwig Weimer has been with them, asking unceasingly: How can God speak in the world? How can God be all-powerful and still pour out God's very self to the point of powerlessness? What is God's will for the world and how can that will be known? What does that help that we call redemption look like? He began as a biblical theologian and then pressed his inquiry into Church dogma in order to translate the faith of the Bible and the catechism into the situation after the European Enlightenment. All that, too, has gone into this book. It owes a great deal to Ludwig Weimer.

But if the thing is described in this way it still remains false, somehow. Theological talk, even the unanimity of theologians is always secondary. Before it come those who provoke and sustain theology. If I were to list the names here I would not know where to stop. The miracle is that there were people who, after the Holocaust, did the one needful thing: set out to seek God's first love, the people from whom all the world shall receive blessing.

# Index of Scripture

*Genesis*

| | |
|---|---|
| 1:1–2:4 | 7–10, 14, 161 |
| 1:1-10 | 21 |
| 1:31 | 15 |
| 2:2-3 | 140 |
| 2:4b–4:26 | 15–18 |
| 2:9 | 24 |
| 3:8-10 | 25 |
| 3:17-19 | 22 |
| 4:6-7 | 19 |
| 5:1-32 | 9 |
| 6:11-12 | 15 |
| 9:7 | 10 |
| 10 | 14 |
| 11:1-9 | 22 |
| 11:10-12 | 10 |
| 12 | 28–31 |
| 12:1 | 61 |
| 12:3 | 197 |
| 12:4 | 36 |
| 14:19 | 4 |
| 17:1 | 274 |
| 17:17 | 61 |
| 18:14 | 61 |
| 18:17-19 | 31 |
| 21:1 | 61 |
| 22:1-19 | 61 |
| 22:16 | 62 |
| 25:27-34 | 63 |
| 35:23 | 63 |
| 48 | 63 |

*Exodus*

| | |
|---|---|
| 1:7 | 11, 227 |
| 1:11 | 69 |
| 1:15-21 | 70 |
| 2:11-14 | 71 |
| 5:1-4 | 71 |
| 12:38 | 58 |
| 13:2, 11-16 | 64 |
| 14:11-12 | 90 |
| 15:1-18 | 68 |
| 16:7-8 | 91 |
| 18 | 147 |
| 19:5-6 | 38 |
| 19:6 | 114, 192 |
| 20:2 | 75 |
| 20:3-5 | 78 |
| 20:22–23:33 | 78 |
| 21:24-25 | 84 |
| 23:4-5 | 85 |
| 24:4-11 | 192 |
| 24:7 | 36 |
| 32:7-14 | 97 |
| 34:11-26 | 78, 81 |
| 34:18-22 | 81 |
| 40:36-38 | 106 |

*Leviticus*

| | |
|---|---|
| 17:10-14 | 230 |
| 19:18 | 76–77, 85, 277 |
| 19:33-34 | 77 |

*Numbers*

| | |
|---|---|
| 3:11-13 | 64 |
| 11:4-6 | 91 |
| 13:1–14:4 | 65 |
| 13:27-28 | 91 |
| 13:32-33 | 92 |
| 14:2-4 | 92 |
| 14:7-9 | 92 |
| 14:20-35 | 92 |
| 14:22-23 | 65 |
| 14:31 | 65 |

*Deuteronomy*

| | |
|---|---|
| 5:2-3 | 239 |
| 6:4-7 | 272 |
| 6:4-5 | 121, 275, 277 |
| 6:5 | 76 |
| 6:20-25 | 75–76 |
| 6:20-23 | 272 |
| 7:6-8 | 37 |
| 15:1-6 | 84 |
| 15:7-11 | 83 |
| 15:12-18 | 84 |
| 15:12-15, 17 | 82–83 |
| 16:1-17 | 82 |
| 18:13 | 274 |
| 21:22-23 | 203–04 |
| 23:13-14 | 80 |
| 24:5 | 77 |
| 24:12-15 | 83 |
| 26:5-10 | 34, 67 |
| 30:1-6 | 51 |
| 33:2 | 36 |

*Joshua*

| | |
|---|---|
| 24:14-15 | 275 |
| 24:15 | 57 |

*Judges*

| | |
|---|---|
| 1:18-36 | 55 |
| 5:15-17 | 108 |
| 9:8-15 | 110 |
| 19–21 | 109 |
| 19:14-15 | 110 |

*1 Samuel*

| | |
|---|---|
| 8:5-8 | 111 |
| 8:19-20 | 110 |

*2 Samuel*

| | |
|---|---|
| 7:16 | 112 |
| 8:1-2 | 109 |
| 13:12 | 57 |

*1 Kings*

| | |
|---|---|
| 12:16 | 111 |
| 18:21 | 100 |
| 19:10 | 101 |
| 19:18 | 101 |
| 19:19-21 | 101 |
| 19:21 | 29 |

*2 Chronicles*

| | |
|---|---|
| 36:23 | 125 |

*Tobit*

| | |
|---|---|
| 13:10-18 | 22 |

*2 Maccabees*

| | |
|---|---|
| 7:28 | 5, 7 |

*Psalms*

| | |
|---|---|
| 2 | 225 |
| 96:5 | 5 |
| 104 | 14 |
| 104:24 | 15–16 |
| 111:4 | 252 |

*Wisdom*

| | |
|---|---|
| 13:1-9 | 2–3, 7 |

*Isaiah*

| | |
|---|---|
| 11:12-13 | 53 |
| 24:21-22 | 144 |
| 25:6-8 | 144 |
| 30:26 | 156 |
| 33:24 | 156 |
| 42:1 | 127–28 |
| 43:3-4 | 37, 149 |
| 45:21 | 231 |
| 52 | 129–30 |
| 52:7-12 | 134 |
| 52:13–53:12 | 193 |
| 53:1 | 190 |
| 54:6-8 | 99 |
| 56:7 | 188 |
| 56:8 | 54 |
| 57:18 | 156 |
| 60 | 22 |

| | |
|---|---|
| 60:1-11 | 23 |
| 61:1-2 | 135 |

*Jeremiah*

| | |
|---|---|
| 7:11 | 188 |
| 23:7-8 | 53 |
| 31:27 | 44 |
| 31:31-34 | 250 |

*Ezekiel*

| | |
|---|---|
| 5:5 | 33 |
| 18:2 | 123 |
| 18:20 | 123 |
| 20 | 92 |
| 21:7 | 185 |
| 31:3-8 | 41–42 |
| 37:1-14 | 206 |
| 37:21-22 | 53 |
| 47:7, 12 | 24 |
| 48:30-35 | 25 |

*Daniel*

| | |
|---|---|
| 3:28-30 | 92 |
| 7 | 178–79, 181 |

*Hosea*

| | |
|---|---|
| 2:1-3, 23-25 | 45 |
| 4:1-3 | 97 |
| 6:6 | 123 |
| 11:1-3 | 98 |
| 11:1 | 37 |
| 11:8-9 | 98 |
| 13:4 | 5 |

*Joel*

| | |
|---|---|
| 2:13 | 123 |

*Micah*

| | |
|---|---|
| 4:1-5 | 23 |

*Zechariah*

| | |
|---|---|
| 14:20-21 | 87, 188 |

*Malachi*

| | |
|---|---|
| 4:5-6 | 124 |

*Matthew*

| | |
|---|---|
| 3:9 | 65–66 |
| 4:10-11 | 128 |
| 4:25 | 85 |
| 5:1 | 85 |

| | |
|---|---|
| 5:17-20 | 160 |
| 5:17-18 | 76 |
| 5:20 | 86 |
| 5:21-22 | 277 |
| 5:22 | 170 |
| 5:27-28 | 170, 277 |
| 5:31-32 | 170 |
| 5:37 | 170 |
| 5:42 | 170 |
| 5:43-47 | 276 |
| 5:45 | 276 |
| 5:48 | 275–77 |
| 6:1-18 | 276 |
| 6:10 | 135 |
| 6:11 | 160 |
| 6:24 | 276 |
| 6:25-34 | 276 |
| 7:3-5 | 276 |
| 7:21-23 | 276 |
| 8:11 | 250 |
| 10:2 | 306 |
| 10:3 | 174 |
| 10:42 | 172 |
| 12:30 | 46, 54 |
| 13:32 | 41 |
| 13:44-46 | 46–47, 139 |
| 13:44 | 142 |
| 13:45-46 | 142 |
| 16:18-19 | 305 |
| 16:18 | 306–07 |
| 18:21-22 | 235 |
| 18:22 | 160 |
| 18:23-35 | 142–43 |
| 19:21 | 171 |
| 19:28 | 183–84 |
| 20:1-16 | 143, 148, 150 |
| 20:15 | 152 |
| 20:20 | 181 |
| 21:10-11 | 248 |
| 21:15 | 247 |
| 21:23–22:46 | 247 |
| 21:43 | 246 |
| 22:21 | 249 |
| 23:37-38 | 195 |
| 25 | 30 |
| 26:28 | 250 |
| 26:73 | 213 |

| 27:25 | 246, 248 |
| 27:55-56 | 247 |

| Mark | |
| 1:10-11 | 127 |
| 1:13 | 128 |
| 1:15 | 129, 130, 134, 165 |
| 1:16-20 | 160 |
| 1:21-39 | 140 |
| 1:27 | 133 |
| 1:39 | 160 |
| 1:41 | 155 |
| 2:5 | 155 |
| 2:7 | 155 |
| 2:11 | 155 |
| 2:13-17 | 166 |
| 2:15 | 161 |
| 2:17 | 155 |
| 2:19 | 173 |
| 2:21-22 | 161 |
| 3:6 | 185–86 |
| 3:13-19 | 161 |
| 3:14-15 | 131 |
| 3:14 | 169, 174–75 |
| 3:20-35 | 158 |
| 3:33 | 159 |
| 3:34-35 | 159 |
| 4:1-9 | 142 |
| 4:3-8 | 43–44 |
| 4:11 | 160 |
| 4:13-20 | 44 |
| 4:30-32 | 40, 142 |
| 5:18 | 169 |
| 5:19-20 | 169 |
| 5:34 | 155 |
| 5:41 | 155 |
| 6:5-6 | 157 |
| 6:6-13 | 162 |
| 6:7 | 175 |
| 6:14-29 | 162–63 |
| 6:30-44 | 143–47 |
| 6:30 | 175 |
| 7:1-23 | 122 |
| 7:15, 21-23 | 86 |
| 7:34 | 155 |
| 8:27-33 | 175–80 |
| 8:28-30 | 176 |

| 8:31 | 178 |
| 9:25 | 155 |
| 9:32 | 180 |
| 9:34-35 | 180 |
| 10:18 | 152 |
| 10:21-22 | 171 |
| 10:29-30 | 132 |
| 10:30 | 150 |
| 10:32-34 | 181 |
| 10:42-44 | 160 |
| 10:42-45 | 181, 182 |
| 10:45 | 179 |
| 10:52 | 166 |
| 11:15 | 187–88 |
| 11:17 | 188 |
| 11:22-24 | 226 |
| 11:28 | 189 |
| 12:17 | 181 |
| 12:30 | 277 |
| 12:41-44 | 171–72, 277–79 |
| 14:3-9 | 143, 166 |
| 14:17-25 | 190–93 |
| 14:22 | 155 |
| 14:25 | 194 |
| 15:38 | 194 |

| Luke | |
| 3:9 | 29 |
| 3:16-17 | 173 |
| 4:16-30 | 135–36 |
| 5:1-11 | 143 |
| 6:12-20 | 168 |
| 6:15 | 174 |
| 6:21 | 145 |
| 6:38 | 148 |
| 7:1 | 168 |
| 8:1-3 | 222 |
| 8:19-21 | 222 |
| 9:51-52 | 184–85 |
| 9:51-56 | 166 |
| 9:57-58 | 165 |
| 9:60 | 170 |
| 9:61-62 | 29 |
| 9:62 | 170 |
| 10:3-11 | 167 |
| 10:23 | 173 |
| 10:23-24 | 137 |

| | |
|---|---|
| 11:20 | 137 |
| 12:32 | 132 |
| 13:19 | 41 |
| 13:20-21 | 41 |
| 13:32-33 | 185 |
| 14:7-10 | 183 |
| 14:15-24 | 138–39 |
| 15:11-32 | 142, 148 |
| 16:16-17 | 186 |
| 19:1-10 | 166 |
| 19:5 | 13 |
| 22:24-27 | 182 |
| 22:24 | 184 |
| 22:28 | 184 |
| 22:31-32 | 306 |
| 24:33 | 206 |
| 24:39 | 207 |

*John*
| | |
|---|---|
| 1:16 | 142 |
| 1:35-40 | 174 |
| 1:46 | 273 |
| 2:1-12 | 140–42 |
| 3:1-2 | 166 |
| 10:10 | 149 |
| 10:14 | 305 |
| 10:30 | 138 |
| 11:43 | 155 |
| 12:37-38 | 190 |
| 13:7 | 184 |
| 14:9 | 138 |
| 15:15 | 182 |
| 16:13 | 308 |
| 17:11 | 298 |
| 17:20-21 | 298 |
| 19:25-27 | 200 |
| 19:38 | 166 |
| 21:15-17 | 305 |

*Acts*
| | |
|---|---|
| 1:8 | 266 |
| 1:12-14 | 220 |
| 1:13 | 214 |
| 1:14 | 221, 223, 224 |
| 1:15-26 | 221 |
| 1:21-22 | 221, 232, 304 |
| 1:23-26 | 227 |
| 2:1 | 221 |

| | |
|---|---|
| 2:41 | 265 |
| 2:43-47 | 223 |
| 2:44, 47 | 221 |
| 2:46 | 148 |
| 4:23-31 | 224–226 |
| 4:32–5:42 | 228 |
| 4:32-34 | 207 |
| 4:34 | 148 |
| 4:36-37 | 132, 214 |
| 5:30-32 | 205 |
| 6:1-7 | 226–27, 230 |
| 6:1-2 | 164 |
| 6:5 | 161 |
| 8:12-13 | 266 |
| 8:38 | 265 |
| 9:18 | 265 |
| 10:48 | 265 |
| 12:12 | 213–14 |
| 13:1-3 | 228–29 |
| 14:26-27 | 229 |
| 14:27 | 232 |
| 15:1-35 | 229–32 |
| 16:15 | 265 |
| 16:30-34 | 265 |
| 17:27 | 19 |
| 18:1-5 | 215 |
| 18:8 | 266 |
| 18:18-19 | 215 |
| 18:24-28 | 215 |
| 19:5-6 | 266 |
| 20:28-32 | 304 |

*Romans*
| | |
|---|---|
| 3:31 | 76 |
| 6:3-4 | 208–09 |
| 6:6 | 209 |
| 6:13 | 210 |
| 8:4 | 76 |
| 8:22 | 210 |
| 9:2-5 | 241 |
| 9:6-8 | 64 |
| 11:1-29 | 241–44 |
| 11:17-24 | 246 |
| 11:29 | 245 |
| 12:1-6 | 280–81 |
| 12:1 | 282 |
| 16:3-5 | 215 |

*1 Corinthians*
10:1-6, 10      96
10:1-13         213
10:16-17        257
11:18           256, 257
11:20-22        256
11:21           255
11:22           257
11:23-25        255
11:27           257
11:30           257
12:8-11, 28     260
12:12-13        258
12:24-27        259
15:3-5          208
15:9            218
16:19           215

*2 Corinthians*
5:17            156
6:2             135

*Galatians*
1:13            218
2:14            264
2:19-20         259
3:26-29         211
6:1-2           234

*Ephesians*
1:10            284
1:20-22         288
1:21-23         283
2:5-6           210
2:15-16         286
2:20-22         292
2:21-22         283

3:8-11          284–85
4:1-6           293
4:3             298
4:4             298
4:6             290
4:8-13          303
4:11-13         287
5:27            287

*Philippians*
2:1-5           236
2:1-3           260
2:6-11          236, 260
2:12            122
2:14-15         281
2:17            281–82
3:6             267

*Colossians*
1:21-23         282
4:16-17         233

*1 Thessalonians*
5:14            234

*Hebrews*
11:1-7          28

*1 Peter*
1:1-2           38
2:9             38

*1 John*
1:1             155
3:14            223

*Revelation*
21:1–22:5       21–26

# Subject Index

Abraham, 28–30, 61–63, 197, 211, 274

action of God, 134, 156–57

actions of Jesus, 163, 190

adherents of Jesus, 166–67, 169–70

*agapē*
  as bond of community, 261
  community life as, 212, 213
  and death of Jesus, 200
  fulfillment of Torah, 85
  greatest charism, 258
  and sin, 199–200

anti-Judaism, Christian, 77, 251

apostles. *See* the Twelve

apostolic life, 175, 176

apostolic office, 174–75

assembly, the. *See also* Church;
  community; *ekklēsia*
  archetype of, 232
  center of, 223
  and Church's memory, 251–52
  conflict in, 227, 229–30
  eucharistic, 252
  as locus of Church, 220
  of Pentecost, 220–22
  prayer in, 224–26
  praxis of, 233–35
  and reconciliation, 235
  and unanimity, 226, 227, 230–31,
    235, 301

atonement, 198–200. *See also* Jesus,
  death of

baptism
  catechumenate as beginning of, 269
  and death of Jesus, 208
  of Diaspora Jews, 266–68
  entry into a way of life, 269, 271
  as exodus, 76, 212–13
  of infants, 269
  and inviolability of the child,
    271–72
  and John the Baptizer, 66
  and mystery religions, 208–09
  in New Testament, 208–11
  in New Testament Church, 265–68
  and physical death, 223
  and resurrection, 210
  social consequences of, 211–12

*basileia. See* reign of God

blessing of fruitfulness, 10–11

body of Christ, 259–64, 286, 292

broken bread of the Passover meal,
  the, 190–91, 193

catechumenate, 212, 264–65, 268–69,
  272–73

charisms, 258, 260, 281

Christ, 34, 283–85. *See also* body of
  Christ; Jesus

Church. *See also* assembly; community;
  *ekklēsia*

and accommodation to society, 72
archetype of, 220, 223
and attainment of insight, 228–29
and baptism, 211
bodiliness of, 207
collective memory of, 241
complicity of, in Holocaust, 48–49
and conflict, 230
consequences of Jesus' resurrection
  in, 207
and conversion, 301–02
as cosmic reality, 283
denial of gospel by, 136
and division of reality, 145, 146
as ensouled body, 292
as eschatological Israel, 163
as eschatological people of God,
  147–48
and exodus, 216–18
false division in, 172–73
and false memory, 251
and false theology of Israel's loss
  of election, 246–50
and "final text" of Bible, 300
fundamental expression of, 222–23
Gentile, and relationship with Israel,
  241–44
and history of division, 293
imperial, 216
incomplete, 163, 295
as Israel, 242
and Jewish content of Christianity,
  245–46
and lordship of Christ, 284–85
loss of community in, 216–18, 233
and loss of Jewish Christians,
  294–96
and loss of whole groups and
  classes, 297
memory of, 241, 252
and multiplications of the loaves,
  145
and necessity of Petrine office,
  307–08
as new creation, 290
and persecution of the Jews,
  244–45, 251

and powers and rulers, 284
as physical presence of Christ, 259
renewal of, 136
and re-rooting in the Old Testament,
  302
and rise of Islam, 295–96
role of, in faith, 271
as single body of Christ, 287–88
as a society, 106–07
as state religion, 118
structure of, 168–69
and surrender, 287
and synagogal communities, 118
and Torah, 76–77, 88
and the Twelve, 163
and unity of New Testament, 303
and "wall of division," 293–94
as world, 288–90
city of God. *See* New Jerusalem
common meal, 173–74, 232
*communio. See* unity
community, the. *See also* assembly;
  Church; *ekklēsia*
as apostolic, 207, 298
as body of Christ, 258–59
as a catechumenate, 273
and charisms, 258
and the common table, 182
crucial element of, 264
and cultural memory, 238
of disciples, 205
and diversity, 260–61
and exodus, 214–18
and faith, 262
foundational event of, 260
fundamental principle of, 259
loss of, 216–18
and multiplication of the loaves,
  144, 278–79
New Testament, and parishes,
  216–17
New Testament, place of house
  churches in, 262–64
as part of Church, 287–88
role of, in faith, 271
and sacramental individualism,
  256–58

size of, 221–22, 233, 261
and surrender of Christ, 286
and union with eucharistic body of
    Christ, 257
as victory of Christ, 286
and widows and orphans, 278
correction, communal, 234–35, 264
creation
    divine praise of, 18
    and God's omnipotence, 39–40
    in Greek philosophy, 3–4, 14
    and history, 9–13
    indirect, 8–9
    and the *logos*, 6
    multiplicity of, 14–15
    in Near Eastern religions, 4
    and new society, 8
    not separate from history, 10, 11
    in Old Testament, and Near Eastern
        accounts, 7–8
    questions concerning, 18
    and salvation history, 20–21
    and sin (corruption), 15–18. *See also*
        the Fall; sin
    and wholeness, 290
crucifixion, 203–04
cup of blessing, 191–93

Day of Atonement, 187
deuteronomic Law, 58, 83–84
deuteronomistic history, 104–05,
    111–12, 118
Diaspora, 113, 115, 117, 123
discernment
    and Israel's faith, 5–6, 33–34
    and assembly, 234, 251
    in Church today, 228–29
    and wholeness, 289–90
disciples. *See also* discipleship
    calling of, 131–32, 134, 169
    danger in life of, 167–68
    and death of Jesus, 204
    and family, 159–60
    as gathering of eschatological Israel,
        131, 142
    limited number called, 165–66, 167
    and multiplication of the loaves,
        145–47
    and promise to Abraham, 30
    as used in New Testament, 164–65
discipleship, 102, 165, 169–70, 216.
    *See also* disciples
disunity, 290–91. *See also* division
divine election, 63, 65
    of Israel, 37–38, 244, 246–50
    of people of God, 21, 38
division. *See also* disunity
    and arrogance toward Israel, 294
    and conversion, 301–02
    in *ekklēsia*, 304
    historical consequences of, 296–97
    between Jews and Gentiles, 293–96
    and New Testament theology,
        298–99
    overcoming of, 301
    and reality of gospel, 297
    and rise of Islam, 295–96
    and truth of faith, 297

Easter vigil, 73, 212–13, 252–53
ecclesiastical office, 303–04. *See also*
    office in the Church; Petrine office
Egypt, symbolism of, 68–70
*ekklēsia. See also* assembly; Church;
    community
    as assembly of the whole, 219
    baptism in, 265–68
    conflict in, 226–27
    as continual assembly, 221, 223, 232
    division in, 304
    as eschatological Israel, 241
    and family, 222
    and founding of communities, 229
    founding of, as Jewish history,
        240–41
    and gathering of people of God, 59
    house churches in, 262–64
    and Jerusalem community, 229
    of Pentecost, 220–223
    and prayer for the Holy Spirit, 222
    and reconciliation, 282, 284
    and Sanhedrin, 224–25
    and Sinai, 219
    unity of, 221

universality of, 283–84
and wholeness, 287
and women, 222
El (God), 56–57
end time, 124–25, 176, 205, 224, 301
eschatological feast, 138–39
eschatological Israel, 161–63, 205–06,
227, 295. *See also* eschatological
people of God
eschatological people of God. *See also*
eschatological Israel
and baptism, 73
and call to perfection, 170–72
and community, 172–73
as dining communities, 147
radical ethos of, 170–71
and restoration of Israel, 231
and salvation, 200
structure of, 168–69, 172
and unanimity, 180
eschatological Temple, 188, 292
eschatology, present, 138–39
*eschaton. See* end time
Eucharist, 184, 233, 250, 252, 255–57
Exodus, 70-75
as archetype, 220–221
and baptism, 212–13
and collective memory of Israel,
238, 240
as critique of royal period, 69
and gathering of Israel, 51–52
many-layered, 68–70
and pilgrimage feasts, 82
as prototype, 307
purpose of, 73, 214

faith (revelation)
and action of God, 157
and apostolic life, 298
and baptism, 76
Christian, 262–63
in Church today, 261–62
Church's role in, 271–72
community's role in, 271
and conflict with Jesus, 189–90
and "final text" of Bible, 300
and God's promises, 302

integrating tendency of, 262–63
not automatic, 102
not otherworldly, 122–23
parent's role in, 62, 270–71
and religion, difference between,
6–7, 95–97
and representation, 197
and sacraments, 156
social dimension of, 106
and tangible reality, 154–55
and transformation of world, 87
and wholeness, 289
and will of God, 87
Fall, the, 17–18. *See also* creation, and
sin; sin
family, 158–60, 222, 262–63
freedom, of creation, 19
freedom, of God, 19
freedom, human, 16–20
and body of Christ, 261
and God's call, 101–02
and God's omnipotence, 39–40
and revolution, 26–27
and structure of people of God, 172
and transformation of society, 119
and wholeness, 279

gathering
of eschatological Israel, 227
as fundamental feature of Church,
218
of Israel, 51, 58–60
of people of God, 138–39
of universe, 292
Gentiles, 35–36, 229–30, 286
God of Israel, 2, 5. *See also* El; YHWH
god-fearers, 266–68
gods of the nations, 2, 5, 78–79
God's omnipotence, 39–40, 48
gospel (good news), 130, 134, 136,
285, 304
Gospels, 126
guilt. *See* sin

*halakah*, 187
history, 5–6, 226, 232. *See also* creation
and history
Holocaust, 48, 239, 240

Holy Spirit, 205, 222, 292
Horeb. *See* Sinai
house churches, 262–64

Islam, 295–96
Israel. *See also* people of God
  collective memory of, 236–40
  conquest of, 55–56
  egalitarian, 58, 108–09, 111
  as eschatological people of God, 156
  faith of, 1–2, 33–34
  and firstborn, 63–64
  and freedom of belief, 239
  and Gentile Church, 244
  and Gentiles, 286
  indigenous groups of, 55–56, 69
  infidelity of, 65, 90–96, 97–100. *See
    also* YHWH, exclusive worship of
  and Jesus' death, 192–93
  and John the Baptizer, 65–66
  and kingship, 107–108
  a "late people," 34
  and Levites, 64–65
  location of, 32–33
  Moses group of, 57, 68–70, 72–73
  and natural descent, 60–61, 63–65
  and New Jerusalem, 25–26
  origins of, 54–58
  and Paul, 64, 241–44
  as people of YHWH, 108
  resistance of, to God's will, 93–95
  role of parents in faith of, 272
  royal (national) period of, 109–11
  and rule of God, 106
  as Servant of God, 127–28
  and sign-actions of Jesus, 155–56
  Sinai as foundation of, 219
  and slandering the land, 65
  and statehood, 118
  as synagogal confederation,
    114–19
  as Temple community, 112–14
  as tribal society, 56–58, 107–08
  and view of history, 105

Jesus. *See also* Christ
  actions of, 153–55
  baptism of, 126–28, 133
  center of Israel, 173
  and cleansing of Temple, 187–89
  as definitive interpretation of Torah,
    86
  definitive presence of God, 138
  as eschatological Shepherd, 147
  and establishment of eschatological
    Israel, 161–63
  and existing social order, 158
  and family, 158–59
  and gathering of Israel, 54, 59
  glory of, 140–42
  and healing, 154
  hostility toward, 185–90
  and institutions, 157–58, 160
  and journey to Jerusalem, 184–85
  and judgment of Israel, 195
  as messenger of gospel, 130
  as Messiah, 176–78, 205
  opposition to, 158–59
  as representative of Israel, 127–28
  resurrection of, 205
  revolution of, 177
  as Servant of God, 196
  and sinners, 152–53
  and old society, 181
  as Son of Man, 177–79
  temptation of, 128
  story of, as Jewish history, 240–41
  and Torah, 128, 186–87
  and will of God, 159
  words of, 153, 155
Jesus, death of
  as *agapē*, 200
  as atonement, 193–96, 249–50
  and baptism, 208
  cause of, 189–90
  coalition responsible for, 225
  and consequences for Israel, 248–50
  as covenant, 196
  and divine profligacy, 149
  purpose of, 192–93
  and reign of God, 196
  and representation, 194–96
  and Temple worship, 187–89
  and "wall of separation," 286–87
  and wholeness, 279–80

and will of God, 179–80
Jewish Christianity, 294–95
Jewish War, 249, 294
Jews. *See* Israel
John the Baptizer, 65–66, 125–26,
    173, 194–95, 266
jubilee year. *See* rhythm of sevens
Judaism, 115, 302

*laos. See* adherents of Jesus
Last Supper. *See* Passover meal; table
    serving
liturgy, 252
Lord's Supper. *See* Eucharist
love. *See agapē*
love of God, 98–100

memory, 238–41, 251
Messiah, 119–20. *See also* Christ;
    Jesus
mountain of God. *See* Sinai
mystery religions, 208–09

new creation, 21–22, 140, 156. *See
    also* eschatological people of God,
    reign of God
new family, 184, 190, 200. *See also*
    people of God; reign of God
new Jerusalem, 22–26, 292. *See also*
    new creation; reign of God
new society, 150–53. *See also* eschato-
    logical people of God; people of
    God; reign of God
    behavior in, 160
    and creation, 8, 22, 25
    and Exodus, 72
    founded by God alone, 73
    and gathering of Israel, 59–60
    and table serving, 181–84
New Testament. *See also* Old Testament
    baptismal theology of, 208–11
    centrality of love in, 122
    and Church's faith, 299
    commonalities with Old Testament,
        121–25
    and division, 298–99
    exodus in, 213–16
    newness of, 125, 133

and murmuring (grumbling), 96–97
    ordering of, 126
    purposes of creation of, 304–05
    as single book, 304
    as single book with Old Testament,
        299, 300, 303
    theological perspective of, 128
    and Torah, 85–87
    unity in, 299–300

office in the Church, 174–75. *See also*
    ecclesiastical office; Petrine office
Old Testament. *See also* New Testa-
    ment; Torah
    and atonement, 198
    basic theme of, 302
    decisive characteristic of, 124–25,
        133
    Eastern religious ideas, 4
    generations in, 8–10, 60–61, 63
    and Greek philosophy, 2–4
    and history, 5–6
    history of resistance to YHWH, 90
    and imperial Church, 217
    and origins of people of Israel, 58
    and reign of God, 136–37
    and sacrificial terminology in New
        Testament, 280, 281–82
    and wholeness, 273–75

Paradise, 16–18, 22–26, 128
passion predictions, structure of,
    180–81
Passover, 67–68. *See also* pilgrimage
    feasts
Passover meal, 238–39
    of Jesus, 190–91, 195, 200
patriarchal narratives, 27–28, 60–65, 67
Paul, 64, 76, 96–97, 304
Pentateuch. *See* Torah
Pentecost, 219, 223
people, the. *See* adherents of Jesus
people of God. *See also* Israel, new
    society, reign of God
    as body of Christ, 261
    and creation, 11
    and divine election, 1
    and freedom, 5–6

God's need for, 1
and the individual, 123–24
and murmuring (grumbling), 96–97
and new society, 151–52
not a natural entity, 63–65
and old society, 151
and poor of world, 30
proper form of, 119
and representation, 197–98
resurrection of, 206
and the state, 70–72
and synagogal communities, 118
and ten commandments, 75–76
and twelve tribes of Israel, 26
persecution
of Christians, 212
of Jews, 136, 239
of Jews by Christians, 244–45, 251,
296
of *ekklēsia*, 227–28
Peter. *See* Petrine office
Petrine office, 305–08. *See also* ecclesiastical office; office in the Church
Pharaoh, symbolism of, 68–69
pilgrimage feasts, 82, 158. *See also*
Passover
pilgrimage of the nations, 23, 188,
231, 243, 292
plan of God. *See* will of God
powers and rulers, 210, 284, 285, 288
prayer, 224–26
profligacy of God, 149–50
prophecy. *See* discernment

redemption. *See* salvation
reign of God, 41–47, 134–37. *See also*
eschatological Israel; eschatological people of God; new creation; new family; new society
and action of God, 157
and assembly, 235
and baptism, 208
central to Jesus' preaching, 208
concrete, 130–31
and death of Jesus, 200–01, 208
and family, 132–33, 159–60
growth of, 160–61

as festive banquet, 144–45, 147
hour of, 194–95
and justice, 152
locus of, 184
as realized, 135–36
resistance to, 138–39
and restoration of Israel, 128–30
and the Temple, 188–89
religion, 6–7, 95–97, 198
representation, 194–98, 270. *See also*
atonement
revelation. *See* faith
revolution, God's, 27–29, 39, 152. *See
also* reign of God
revolution, violent, 26–27, 29, 177
rhythm of sevens, 81, 82–83

Sabbath, 140. *See also* rhythm of sevens
sacrifice. *See* surrender
sacrifice of Isaac, 61–62
sacramental structure of Jesus' actions
objections to, 156–58
at Passover meal, 190
sacraments, 140, 156
salvation. *See also* Abraham; reign of
God; revolution, God's; salvation
history
and confluence, 31–36
and death of Jesus, 193
and divine election, 36–39
in Eleusinian mysteries, 253–54
as festive banquet, 143–44, 224
as gathering of Israel, 52, 53
and God's choice of Abraham, 31,
35, 128
and God's choice of Israel, 31
as incorporation into Church as
social body, 255
and individualism, 254–55
and Israel's choice of God, 36
Israel's resistance to, 92–95
and physical death, 223–24
and resurrection of Jesus, 205
and sacraments, 156
slowness of, 34–35
superabundance of, 140–44, 293
universality of, 21–22

and visions of judgment in Revelation, 25
and God's wrath, 98–99
salvation history, 100–105. *See also* salvation
and Church's memory, 252
and creation, 20–21, 154–55
fundamental law of, 148–49
and Gentile Church, 242–44
Sanhedrin, 189–90, 203–04, 225, 226
Saul. *See* Paul
Seven, the, 227
sign-actions of Jesus, 153–55, 159
and cleansing of the Temple, 187–89
at Passover meal, 190–91
sin (corruption), 39–40, 48–49. *See also* creation, and sin; the Fall
in New Testament baptismal theology, 209–10
social dimension of, 199–200
Sinai, 219, 223
and cultural memory of Israel, 238
and forgiveness of sin, 250
and Jesus' death as atonement, 196
and nation-state, 114
as symbol of new society, 73
Son of Man, 177–79, 181
surrender. *See also* atonement
of Abraham, 62, 274
and "in Christ," 260
and Church, 287
Jesus', and lordship of Christ, 286
reasonable, 280–81
to work of God, 142
synagogal community, 114–19, 217

table serving, 181–84
Temple, 25, 112–14, 187–89, 194
Torah
and *agapē*, 85, 121–22
and Church, 76–77
core of, 78
and creation, 79–80
centrality of love in, 121–22
and contemporaneity of generations, 38–39

creates community, 84
and death of Jesus, 196
egalitarian, 58
and gathering of Israel, 51–52
as God's social order, 106, 113–14
and Jesus, 85–86, 128, 186–87
and new society, 73, 75, 160
and patriarchal narratives, 64
purity laws of, 87–88
and Quran, 296
and reconciliation, 84
and rest of Old Testament, 126
and righteous society, 83–84, 87–88
and royal period, 114
and Sabbath, 82
and Sermon on the Mount, 176, 275
and synagogal communities, 115, 117
and time, 80–83
and will of Yhwh, 94
Twelve, the
as agents of continuity, 303–04
conversion of, 175–76
and death of Jesus, 200
diversity of, 174
and eschatological Israel, 295
and establishment of eschatological Israel, 161, 163
and gathering of Israel, 131
and Jerusalem community, 205, 213
as institution, 161
mission of, 206
and mission, 174–75
and office of judging, 183–84
and Pentecost *ekklēsia*, 221
and power of Jesus, 162–63
as restored Israel, 161
and rivalry, 180
and table serving 182–89
as sign-action, 162
as symbol, 169
and unanimity, 180–81, 184
and unanimity of *ekklēsia*, 227

unanimity, 226–27, 230–31, 235–36
and Holy Spirit, 223
and prayer, 226

and will of God, 301–02
characteristics of, 298–99
desire for, 291–92
as diachronic, 288
and ecclesiastical office, 303
and "final text" of Bible, 300
gospel as guarantee of, 304
and Holy Spirit, 292
in New Testament traditions,
 299–300
and Petrine office, 308
and uniformity, 300

wholeness
 and creation, 290
 and Christian life, 282
 and death of Jesus, 279–80
 and the *ekklēsia*, 287
 and Eucharist, 301
 and the great commandment,
  277–79
 in Old Testament, 273–75

in Sermon on the Mount, 275–77
as surrender, 280–81
and tradition, 288
widows and orphans as symbols of,
 278
and the world, 288–89
will of God
 and assembly, 235
 and conversion, 301–02
 and death of Jesus, 179–80
 and gospel, 285
 Israel's resistance to, 93–95
 and lordship of Christ, 285
 and reign of God, 40–41
 and surrender, 281
wrath of God, 97–99

YHWH, 56–57, 68, 98–100, 106, 110,
 122
 exclusive worship of, 78–79, 84,
  274–76. *See also* Israel, infidelity of